J. Warren Holleran, THE SYNOPTIC GETHSEMANE

To my beloved parents
with gratitude and
affection —

Your loving son,

Warren

Analecta Gregoriana

Cura Pontificiae Universitatis Gregorianae edita
Vol. 191. Series Facultatis Theologicae: Sectio B, n. 61

J. WARREN HOLLERAN

THE SYNOPTIC GETHSEMANE

A CRITICAL STUDY

Università Gregoriana Editrice

ROMA 1973

J. WARREN HOLLERAN

THE SYNOPTIC GETHSEMANE

A CRITICAL STUDY

Università Gregoriana Editrice

ROMA 1973

Quest'opera di J. Warren Holleran, THE SYNOPTIC GETHSEMANE, è stata pubblicata con l'approvazione ecclesiastica (Vicariato di Roma, 24 marzo 1972) dalla Università Gregoriana Editrice, Roma 1973, e stampata dalla Tipografia della Pontificia Università Gregoriana.

TABLE OF CONTENTS

PART TWO: REDACTION

ABBREVIATIONS

B.-A.-G.	—	William F. Arndt and F. Wilbur Gingrich. *A Greek-English Lexicon of the New Testament and Other Early Christian Literature*. A translation and adaptation of Walter Bauer's *Griechisch-Deutsches Wörterbuch*, 4th rev. Ger. ed. Chicago and Cambridge, 1959.
B.-D.-F.	—	F. Blass and A. Debrunner. *A Greek Grammar of the New Testament and Other Early Christian Literature*, tr. Robert W. Funk from the 9th-10th Ger. ed. Chicago, 1961.
B	—	*Biblica.*
BG	—	Martin Dibelius. *Botschaft und Geschichte.* 2 vols. Tübingen, 1953-56.
BJRL	—	*Bulletin of the John Rylands Library.*
BK	—	*Bibel und Kirche.*
BQR	—	*Baptist Quarterly Review.*
BR	—	*Biblical Research.*
BS	—	*Bibliotheca Sacra.*
BVC	—	*Bible et vie chrétienne.*
BW	—	*Biblical World.*
CB	—	*Cultura bíblica.*
CBQ	—	*Catholic Biblical Quarterly.*
CQ	—	*The Crozer Quarterly.*
CQR	—	*Church Quarterly Review.*
CT	—	*La Ciencia Tomista.*
DB	—	*Dictionnaire de la Bible.*
DBS	—	*Dictionnaire de la Bible: Supplément.*
DTC	—	*Dictionnaire de théologie catholique.*
DTT	—	*Dansk teologisk tidsskrift.*
EE	—	*Estudios eclesiásticos.*
EQ	—	*The Evangelical Quarterly.*
ET	—	*Expository Times.*
ETL	—	*Ephemerides theologicae Lovanienses.*
EvT	—	*Evangelische theologie.*
Exp	—	*The Expositor.*
G	—	*Gregorianum.*
GTT	—	*Gereformeerd theologisch tijdschrift.*
J	—	*Judaica.*
JBL	—	*Journal of Biblical Literature.*
JR	—	*Journal of Religion.*
JTS	—	*Journal of Theological Studies.*
LQ	—	*The Lutheran Quarterly.*
LumV	—	*Lumière et vie.*

LV   —   *Lumen Vitae.*
MNEKR   —   *Mitteilungen und Nachrichten für die evangelische Kirche in Russland* (Riga).
MTZ   —   *Münchener theologische Zeitschrift.*
NKZ   —   *Neue kirchliche Zeitschrift.*
NRT   —   *Nouvelle revue théologique.*
NT   —   *Novum Testamentum.*
NTS   —   *New Testament Studies.*
RA   —   *Revue apologétique.*
RB   —   *Revue biblique.*
RE   —   *[Baptist] Review and Expositor.*
RHPR   —   *Revue d'histoire et de philosophie religieuses.*
RSPT   —   *Revue des sciences philosophiques et théologiques.*
RSR   —   *Recherches de science religieuse.*
RTh   —   *Revue thomiste.*
RTP   —   *Revue de théologie et de philosophie.*
SAB   —   *Sitzungsberichte der Königlich Preussischen Akademie der Wissenschaften zu Berlin.*
S.-B.   —   H. Strack and P. Billerbeck. *Kommentar zum Neuen Testament aus Talmud und Midrasch*, 4th ed. 6 vols. Munich, 1965.
SJT   —   *Scottish Journal of Theology.*
SO   —   *Symbolae Osloenses.*
ST   —   *Studia theologica.*
STK   —   *Svensk teologisk kvartalskrift.*
TDNT   —   *Theological Dictionary of the New Testament*, ed. Gerhard Kittel and Gerhard Friedrich, tr. and ed. Geoffrey W. Bromiley. Grand Rapids, 1964 —.
Th   —   *Theology.*
ThSt   —   *Theological Studies.*
TLZ   —   *Theologische Literaturzeitung.*
TS   —   *Theologische Studien.*
TSK   —   *Theologische Studien und Kritiken.*
TWNT   —   *Theologisches Wörterbuch zum Neuen Testament.* Stuttgart, 1933-.
TZ   —   *Theologische Zeitschrift.*
USQR   —   *Union Seminary Quarterly Review.*
VD   —   *Verbum Domini.*
VS   —   *La vie spirituelle.*
ZKT   —   *Zeitschrift für katholische Theologie.*
ZNW   —   *Zeitschrift für die neutestamentliche Wissenschaft.*
ZTK   —   *Zeitschrift für Theologie und Kirche.*
ZWT   —   *Zeitschrift für wissenschaftliche Theologie.*

BIBLIOGRAPHY

LIST OF WORKS CONSULTED

I. TEXTS AND REFERENCE WORKS

ALAND, K. *Synopsis Quattuor Evangeliorum*, 2nd ed. Stuttgart, 1965.
———; BLACK, M.; METZGER, B. M.; and WIKGREN, A. *The Greek New Testament*. Stuttgart, 1967.
ARNDT, W. F., and GINGRICH, F. W. *A Greek-English Lexicon of the New Testament and Other Early Christian Literature*, translated and adapted from the 4th rev. Ger. ed. of Walter Bauer's *Griechisch-Deutsches Wörterbuch zu den Schriften des Neuen Testaments und der übrigen urchristlichen Literatur*. Chicago and Cambridge, 1959.
BAUER, J. B. *Sacramentum Verbi. An Encyclopedia of Biblical Theology*, tr. Joseph Blenkinsopp, David J. Bourke, N. D. Smith, and Walter P. van Stigt from the 3rd Ger. ed. 3 vols. New York, 1970.
BEYER, K. *Semitische Syntax im Neuen Testament*, Vol. I Satzlehre Teil 1, 2nd ed. Göttingen, 1962.
BLASS, F., and DEBRUNNER, A. *A Greek Grammar of the New Testament and Other Early Christian Literature*, tr. Robert W. Funk from the 9th-10th Ger. ed. Chicago, 1961.
DE SOLAGES, B. *Synopse grecque des évangiles. Méthode nouvelle pour résoudre le problème synoptique.* Leiden, 1959.
HATCH, E., and REDPATH, H. A. *A Concordance to the Septuagint and the Other Greek Versions of the Old Testament.* 2 vols. and supplement. Graz, 1954.
The Holy Bible. Revised Standard Version 1952.
KITTEL, G., and FRIEDRICH, G., eds. *Theologisches Wörterbuch zum Neuen Testament*. Stuttgart, 1933-. English translation: *Theological Dictionary of the New Testament*, tr. and ed. Geoffrey W. Bromiley. Grand Rapids, 1964-.
LIDDELL, H. G., and SCOTT, R. *A Greek-English Lexicon*, ed. Henry Stuart Jones, 9th ed. Oxford, 1966.
MOULTON, J. H.; HOWARD, W. F.; and TURNER, N. *A Grammar of New Testament Greek.* 3 vols. Edinburgh, 1957-63.
———, and MILLIGAN, G. *The Vocabulary of the Greek Testament.* Grand Rapids, 1960.
MOULTON, W. F., and GEDEN, A. S. *A Concordance to the Greek Testament*, 4th ed. Edinburgh, 1963.
RAHLFS, A., ed. *Septuaginta*, 7th ed. 2 vols. Stuttgart, 1962.
STRACK, H. L., and BILLERBECK, P. *Kommentar zum Neuen Testament aus Talmud und Midrasch*, 4th ed. 6 vols. Munich, 1965.

WESTCOTT, B. F., and HORT, FENTON J. A. *The New Testament in the Original Greek*, 2nd ed. 2 vols. London and New York, 1896-98.
ZORELL, F. *Lexicon Graecum Novi Testamenti*, 3rd ed. Paris, 1961.

II. COMMENTARIES

A. *Bible*

BLACK, M., and ROWLEY, H. H., eds. *Peake's Commentary on the Bible.* London, 1967.
BROWN, R. E; FITZMYER, J. A.; and MURPHY, R. E., eds. *The Jerome Biblical Commentary.* 2 vols. Englewood Cliffs, N. J., 1968.
BUTTRICK, G. A., *et al.*, eds. *The Interpreter's Bible.* 12 vols. New York and Nashville, 1951-57.
FULLER, R. C.; JOHNSTON, L.; and KEARNS, C., eds. *A New Catholic Commentary on Holy Scripture.* London, 1969.

B. *Synoptics*

HOLTZMANN, H. J. *Die Synoptiker*, 3rd ed. Tübingen and Leipzig, 1901.
INNITZER, T. Kardinal. *Kommentar zur Leidens- und Verklärungsgeschichte Jesu Christi*, 4th ed. Vienna, 1948.
KLOSTERMANN, E., and GRESSMANN, H. *Handbuch zum Neuen Testament.* Vol. II: *Die Evangelien*, ed. Hans Lietzmann. Tübingen, 1919.
LOISY, A. *Les Évangiles synoptiques.* 2 vols. Ceffonds, 1907-08.
MAJOR, H. D. A.; MANSON, T. W.; and WRIGHT, C. J. *The Mission and Message of Jesus: an Exposition of the Gospels in the Light of Modern Research.* London, 1940.
MONTEFIORE, C. G. *The Synoptic Gospels.* 2 vols. London, 1927.
STAAB, K. *Das Evangelium nach Markus und Lukas.* Würzburg, 1956.
WEISS, B. *Die Evangelien des Markus und Lukas.* Göttingen, 1901.
WEISS, J. *Die Schriften des Neuen Testaments.* Vol. I. Göttingen, 1907.

C. *Mark*

BRANSCOMB, B. H. *The Gospel of Mark*, 5th ed. London, 1948.
CARRINGTON, P. *According to Mark: A Running Commentary on the Oldest Gospel.* Cambridge, 1960.
CRANFIELD, C. E.B. *The Gospel according to St. Mark.* Cambridge, 1959.
GOGUEL, M. *L'Évangile de Marc.* Paris, 1909.
GOULD, E. P. *A Critical and Exegetical Commentary on the Gospel according to St. Mark.* Edinburgh, 1907.
GRUNDMANN, W. *Das Evangelium des Markus.* Berlin, 1959.
HAENCHEN, E. *Der Weg Jesu, Eine Erklärung des Markus-Evangeliums und der kanonischen Parallelen*, 2nd ed. Berlin, 1968.
HAUCK, F. *Das Evangelium des Markus.* Leipzig, 1931.
HUNTER, A. M. *The Gospel according to Saint Mark*, 7th ed. London, 1962.
JOHNSON, S. E. *A Commentary on the Gospel according to St. Mark.* London, 1960.
KLOSTERMANN, E. *Das Markusevangelium.* Tübingen, 1950.
LAGRANGE, M.-J. *Évangile selon Saint Marc.* Paris, 1929.

LOHMEYER, E. *Das Evangelium des Markus*, 16th. ed. Göttingen, 1963.
LOISY, A. *L'Évangile selon Marc.* Paris, 1912.
MENZIES, A. *The Earliest Gospel: a Historical Study of the Gospel according to Mark.* London, 1901.
MINEAR, P. S. *Saint Mark.* London, 1963.
NINEHAM, D. E. *The Gospel of St Mark.* Baltimore, 1963.
PLUMMER, A. *The Gospel according to St. Mark.* Cambridge, 1914.
RAWLINSON, A. E. J. *The Gospel according to St. Mark,* 7th ed. London, 1949.
SCHANZ, P. *Commentar über das Evangelium des heiligen Marcus.* Freiburg, 1881.
SCHMID, J. *Das Evangelium nach Markus,* 5th ed. Regensburg, 1963.
SCHNIEWIND, J. *Das Evangelium nach Markus.* Göttingen, 1952.
SCHWEIZER, E. *Das Evangelium nach Markus.* Göttingen, 1967.
SWETE, H. B. *The Gospel according to St. Mark,* 2nd ed. London, 1902.
TAYLOR, V. *The Gospel according to St. Mark,* 2nd ed. London, 1966.
URICCHIO, F. M., and STANO, G. M. *Vangelo secondo San Marco.* Turin, 1966.
WEISS, B. *Das Marcusevangelium und seine synoptischen Parallelen.* Berlin, 1872.
WELLHAUSEN, J. *Das Evangelium Marci.* Berlin, 1903.

D. Matthew

ALLEN, W. C. *A Critical and Exegetical Commentary on the Gospel according to S. Matthew,* 3rd ed. Edinburgh, 1957.
BONNARD, P. *L'Évangile selon Saint Matthieu.* Neuchatel, 1963.
COX, G. E. P. *The Gospel according to Saint Matthew,* 3rd ed. London, 1958.
FENTON, J. *The Gospel of St Matthew.* Baltimore, 1963.
FILSON, F. V. *A Commentary on the Gospel according to St. Matthew.* London, 1960.
GAECHTER, P. *Das Matthäus Evangelium.* Innsbruck, 1963.
GRUNDMANN, W. *Das Evangelium nach Matthäus.* Berlin, 1971.
KEIL, C. F. *Commentar über das Evangelium des Matthäus.* Leipzig, 1877.
KLOSTERMANN, E. *Das Matthäus-Evangelium.* Tübingen, 1938.
LAGRANGE, M.-J. *Évangile selon Saint Matthieu,* 3rd ed. Paris, 1927.
LOHMEYER, E. *Das Evangelium des Matthäus,* ed. Werner Schmauch, 3rd ed. Göttingen, 1962.
MCNEILE, A. H. *The Gospel according to St. Matthew.* London, 1915.
MEYER, H. A. W. *Critical and Exegetical Handbook to the Gospel of Matthew,* tr. Peter Christie from 6th Ger. ed., rev. and ed. William Stewart. 2 vols. Edinburgh, 1879.
PLUMMER, A. *An Exegetical Commentary on the Gospel according to St. Matthew.* London, 1910.
SCHANZ, P. *Commentar über das Evangelium des heiligen Matthäus.* Freiburg, 1879.
SCHLATTER, A. *Der Evangelist Matthäus,* 6th ed. Stuttgart, 1963.
SCHMID, J. *Das Evangelium nach Matthäus,* 4th ed. Regensburg, 1959.
SCHNIEWIND, J. D. *Das Evangelium nach Matthäus.* Göttingen, 1964.
STAAB, K. *Das Evangelium nach Matthäus.* Würzburg, 1963.
WEISS, B. *Das Matthäusevangelium und seine Lucas-Parallelen.* Halle, 1876.
———. *Das Matthäus-Evangelium.* Göttingen, 1898.

ZAHN, T. *Das Evangelium des Matthäus*, 4th ed. Leipzig and Erlangen, 1922.

E. *Luke*

BROWNING, W. R. F. *The Gospel according to Saint Luke.* London, 1960.
CAIRD, G. B. *The Gospel of St Luke.* Baltimore, 1963.
CREED, J. M. *The Gospel according to St. Luke.* London, 1930.
ELLIS, E. E. *The Gospel of Luke.* London, 1966.
GRUNDMANN, W. *Das Evangelium nach Lukas.* Berlin, 1961.
HAHN, G. L. *Das Evangelium des Lucas erklärt.* 2 vols. Breslau, 1892-94.
HAUCK, F. *Das Evangelium des Lukas.* Leipzig, 1934.
LAGRANGE, M. J. *Évangile selon Saint Luc*, 8th ed. Paris, 1948.
LEANEY, A. R. C. *A Commentary on the Gospel according to St. Luke*, 2nd ed. London, 1966.
LOISY, A. *L'évangile selon Luc.* Paris, 1924.
LAGRANGE, M.-J. *Évangile selon Saint Luc*, 8th ed. Paris, 1948.
MILLER, D. G. *Saint Luke*, 2nd ed. London, 1963.
PLUMMER, A. *A Critical and Exegetical Commentary on the Gospel according to S. Luke*, 5th ed. Edinburgh, 1960.
RENGSTORF, K. H. *Das Evangelium nach Lukas*, 8th ed. Göttingen, 1958.
SCHANZ, P. *Commentar über das Evangelium des heiligen Lucas.* Tübingen, 1883.
SCHLATTER, A. *Das Evangelium des Lukas.* Stuttgart, 1931.
SCHMID, J. *Das Evangelium nach Lukas*, 4th ed. Regensburg, 1960.
TINSLEY, E. J. *The Gospel according to Luke.* Cambridge, 1965.
WEISS, J., and BOUSSET, W. *Das Lukas-Evangelium*, in *Die Schriften des Neuen Testaments*, Vol. I, 3rd ed. Göttingen, 1917.
WELLHAUSEN, J. *Das Evangelium Lucae.* Berlin, 1904.
ZAHN, T. *Das Evangelium des Lucas*, 3rd and 4th ed. Leipzig, 1920.

F. *John*

BARRETT, C. K. *The Gospel according to St John.* London, 1962.
BERNARD, J. H. *The Gospel according to St. John.* Edinburgh, 1963.
BROWN, R. E. *The Gospel according to John.* 2 vols. New York, 1966-70.
BULTMANN, R. *Das Evangelium des Johannes*, 18th ed. Göttingen, 1964. Eng. tr. *The Gospel of John. A Commentary*, tr. G. R. Beasley-Murray. Oxford, 1971.
HOSKYNS, E. C. *The Fourth Gospel*, ed. Francis Noel Davey, 2nd ed. London, 1961.
STRATHMANN, H. *Das Evangelium nach Johannes.* Göttingen, 1954.
WESTCOTT, B. F. *The Gospel according to Saint John.* London, 1958.

III. SPECIAL STUDIES

A. *The Synoptic Gethsemane*

AARS, J. "Zu Matth. 26,45 und Marc. 14,41," *ZWT*, 38 (1895), 378-383.
ALEXANDER, W. M.; CUNNINGHAM, J. G.; WATT, D. G.; and MILNE, G. "The Meaning of Christ's Prayer in Gethsemane," *ET*, 7 (1895-96), 34-38.

ARMBRUSTER, C. J. "The Messianic Significance of the Agony in the Garden,"
    Scripture, 16 (1964), 111-119.
ARTHUS, M., and CHANSON, V. "Les sueurs de sang," *RTh*, 6 (1898), 673-696.
ASCHERMANN, H. "Zum Agoniegebet Jesu, Luk. 23, 43-44," *Theologia Viato-
    rum*, 5 (1953-54), 143-149.
BALDWIN, E. St. G. "Gethsemane: the fulfilment of a prophecy," *BS*,
    77 (1920), 429-436.
BARBOUR, R. S. "Gethsemane in the Tradition of the Passion," *NTS*, 16
    (1970), 231-251.
BERNARD, J. H. "St. Mark xiv. 41, 42," *ET*, 3 (1891-92), 451-453.
BIRDSALL, J. N. "*Egrêgoreô*," *JTS*, 14 (1963), 390-391.
BLACK, M. "The Cup Metaphor in Mark 14:36," *ET*, 59 (1947-48), 195.
BOMAN, T. "Der Gebetskampf Jesu," *NTS*, 10 (1964), 261-273; also in *Die
    Jesus-Überlieferung im Lichte der neueren Volkskunde*. Göttingen,
    1967.
BONNETAIN, P. "La cause de l'agonie de Jésus," *RA*, 50 (1930), 681-690.
———. "La crainte de la mort en Jésus agonisant," *RA*, 53 (1931), 276-295.
BOOBYER, G. H. "*APECHEI* in Mark 14, 41," *NTS*, 2 (1955-56), 44-48.
BRUN, L. "Engel und Blutschweiss Lc 22:43-44," *ZNW*, 32 (1933), 265-276.
CANTINAT, J. "L'agonie de Jésus," *VS*, 88, no. 382 (1953), 272-281.
CHASE, T. "*To loipon*, Matt. xxvi. 45," *JBL*, 6 (1886, part I), 131-135.
CRANFIELD, C. E.B. "The Cup Metaphor in Mark 14:36 and Parallels," *ET*,
    59 (1947-48), 137-138.
DE ZWANN, J. "The Text and Exegesis of Mark xiv. 41, and the Papyri,"
    Exp, 6th ser., 12 (1905), 459-472.
DIBELIUS, M. "Gethsemane," *CQ*, 12 (1935), 254-265; also in German in
    Botschaft und Geschichte, Vol. I (Tübingen, 1953), 258-271.
DURAND, A.; VACANT, A.; and Dr. BARABAN. "Agonie du Christ," *DTC*, I (Paris,
    1930), col. 615-624.
FEDERKIEWICZ, P. "Agonia Chrystusa Pana w Ogrojcu (Uwagi egzegetyczne
    do Łk 22, 43 n.)," *Ruch Biblijny i Liturgiczny*, 13 (1960), 119-126.
FIEBIG, P. "Jesu Gebet in Gethsemane," *Der Geisteskampf der Gegenwart*,
    66 (1930), 121-125.
FONCK, L. "Passio SS. Cordis in horto Gethsemani," *VD*, 8 (1928), 161-170,
    193-204.
GAMBA, G. G."Agonia di Gesù," *Revista Biblica*, 16 (1968), 159-166.
GILBERT, J. "The Agony in the Garden," *Exp*, 3rd ser., 5 (1887), 180-193.
GLORIEUX, P. "Le mystère de l'agonie," *VS*, 19 (1928-29), 601-641.
HARNACK, A. "Probleme im Texte der Leidensgeschichte Jesu," *SAB* (Berlin,
    1901), pp. 251-266.
HEITMÜLLER, F. "Gethsemane," *Jesu Dienst*, 17 (1938), 314-318.
HÉRING, J. "Simples remarques sur la prière à Gethsémané. Mattieu
    26:36-46; Marc 14:32-42; Luc 22:40-46," *RHPR*, 39 (1959), 97-102.
———. "Zwei exegetische Probleme in der Perikope von Jesus in Gethse-
    mane," *Neotestamentica et Patristica* (Leiden, 1962), pp. 64-69.
HOLZMEISTER, U. "Spricht Epiphanius (Ancoratus 31, 4) vom Blutschweiss
    des Herrn oder von seinen Tränen?", *ZKT*, 47 (1923), 309-314.
———. "Exempla sudoris sanguinei (Lc. 22, 44)," *VD*, 18 (1938), 73-81.
HÖRSEHELMANN, F. "Seelenkampf des Herrn Jesu in Gethsemane," *MNEKR*,
    23 (1890), 453-463.
HUDSON, J. T. "Irony in Gethsemane?", *ET*, 46 (1934-35), 382.

INDEMANS, J. H. H. A. "Das Lukasevangelium XXII, 45,"*SO*, 32 (1956), 81-83.
JOHNSON, S.L., Jr. "The Agony of Christ," *BS*, 124, (1967), 303-313.
KEEN, W. W. "The Bloody Sweat of our Lord," *BQR*, 14 (1892), 169-175.
————. "Further Studies on the Bloody Sweat of our Lord," *BS*, 54 (1897), 469-483.
KENNY, A. "The Transfiguration and the Agony in the Garden," *CBQ*, 19 (1957), 444-452.
KUHN, K. G. "Jesus in Gethsemane," *EvT*, 12 (1952-53), 260-285.
KURRIKOFF, A. "Christus in Gethsemane," *MNEKR*, 24 (1891), 23-34.
LEBRETON, J. "L'Agonie de Notre-Seigneur," *RA*, 33 (1921-22), 705-725; 34 (1922), 9-22.
LESCOW, T. "Jesus in Gethsemane," *EvT*, 26 (1966), 141-159.
————. "Jesus in Gethsemane bei Lukas und im Hebräerbrief," *ZNW*, 58 (1967), 215-239.
LESÊTRE, H. "Sueur de Sang," *DB*, V (Paris, 1928), col. 1878.
LIGHTFOOT, R. H. "A Consideration of Three Passages in St. Mark's Gospel," in *In Memoriam Ernst Lohmeyer* (Stuttgart, 1951), pp. 110-115.
LINNEMANN, E. "Gethsemane Mk. 14,32-42 / Mt. 26,36-46 / Lk. 22,40-46. Entstehung, Überlieferung und Bearbeitung der Perikope," in *Studien zur Passionsgeschichte* (Göttingen, 1970), pp. 11-40, 178f.
MALAN, C. "La crainte que ressent le seigneur Jésus à l'approche de la mort," *RTP*, 31 (1898), 439-452.
MARTIN, G. "Agonie de Notre-Seigneur," *DB*, I (Paris, 1926), col. 273-275.
McCASLAND, S.V. "Abba, Father," *JBL*, 72 (1953), 79-91.
M'MICHAEL, E. F.; ROSS, J.; and WALLIS, R. E. "Our Lord's Prayer in Gethsemane," *ET*, 7 (1895-96), 502-505.
PELCÉ, F. "Jésus à Gethsémani. Remarques comparatives sur les trois récits évangéliques," *Foi et Vie*, 65, No. 4 (1966), 89-99.
PETAVEL, E. "The House of Gethsemane," *Exp*, 4th ser., 3 (1891), 220-232.
PETITOT, H. "L'agonie de Jésus," *VS*, 22 (1930), 238-256; 23 (1930), 24-40.
RABEAU, G. "Agonie du Christ," *Catholicisme*, I (Paris, 1948), col. 226-228.
ROBINSON, B. P. "Gethsemane: the Synoptic and the Johannine Viewpoints," *CQR*, 167 (1966), 4-11.
ROBSON, J. "The Meaning of Christ's Prayer in Gethsemane," *ET*, 6 (1894-95), 522-523.
SCHRAGE, W. "Bibelarbeit über Markus 14, 32-42," in *Bibelarbeiten, gehalten auf der rheinischen Landessynode 1967 in Bad Godesberg* (n. p., n. d.), pp. 21-39.
SCHÜRMANN, H. "Lk. 22, 42a das älteste Zeugnis für Lk 22, 20?", *MTZ*, 3 1952, 185-188.
SCHWARTZ, J. W. "Jesus in Gethsemane," *LQ*, 22 (1892), 267-271.
SKARD, E. "Kleine Beiträge zum Corpus Hellenisticum Novi Testamenti," *SO*, 30 (1953), 100-103.
SMISSON, E. A. "Mark xiv. 41: *apechei*," *ET*, 40 (1928-29), 528.
SMITH, H. "Acts xx. 8 and Luke xxii. 43," *ET*, 16 (1904-05), 478.
STARKIE, W. J. M. "Gospel according to St. Matthew xxvi. 45 and xxviii. 2," *Hermathena*, 19 (1922), 141-143.
STOOKE-VAUGHAN, F. S. "Sit Ye Here," *ET*, 6 (1894-95), 94-95.
THOMAS, W. H. G. "The Agony in Gethsemane," *ET*, 6 (1894-95), 522.
THOMSON, A. E. "The Gethsemane Agony," *BS*, 67 (1910), 598-610.
————. "Our Lord's Prayer in the Garden," *BS*, 97 (1940), 110-116.
TOM, W. "De bede van Christus in Gethsemané," *GTT*, 57 (1957), 213-219.

Trémel, Y.-B. "L'agonie de Jésus," *LumV*, 13, no. 68 (1964), 79-103.

Vail, A. L. "Gethsemane," *RE*, 20 (1923), 188-200.

van Unnik, W. C. " 'Alles ist dir möglich' (Mk 14, 36)," in *Verborum Veritas. Festschrift für Gustav Stählin*, ed. O. Böcher and K. Haacker. Wuppertal, 1970.

Voltolini, R. "Über den blutigen Schweiss Christi," *Allgemeine Evangelisch-Lutherische Kirchenzeitung*, 18 (1885), 269-271, 295-297.

Weijden, A. *De Doodsangst van Jezus in Gethsemani*. Amsterdam, 1947.

West, T.; Whyte, J.; Reith, J.; Little, J. A. S.; and Grant, Mrs. I. "The Meaning of Christ's Prayer in Gethsemane," *ET*, 7 (1895-96), 118-121.

Wilson, W. E. "Our Lord's Agony in the Garden," *ET*, 32 (1920-21), 549-551.

Wulf, F. " 'Der Geist ist willig, das Fleisch schwach' (Mk 14, 38)," *Geist und Leben*, 37 (1964), 241-243.

Zeydner, H. "*Apechei*, Mark XIV: 41," *TS*, 23 (1905), 439-442.

B. John and Hebrews

Andriessen, P., and Lenglet, A. "Quelques passages difficiles de l'Épître aux Hébreux (5, 7-11; 10, 20; 12, 2)," *B*, 51 (1970), 207-220.

Brandenburger, E. "Text und Vorlagen von Hebr. V 7-10. Ein Beitrag (1969), zur Christologie des Hebräerbriefs," *NT*, 11 (1969), 190-224.

Braumann, G. "Hebr 5:7-10," *ZNW*, 51 (1960), 278-280.

Brown, R.E. "Incidents that Are Units in the Synoptic Gospels but Dispersed in St. John." *CBQ*, 23 (1961), 143-160; also in *New Testament Essays* (London and Dublin, 1965), pp. 192-213.

Cerfaux, L. "Le sacre du Grand-Prêtre (selon Hébr. 5:5-10)," *BVC*, 21 (1958), 54-58.

Coste, J. "Notion grecque et notion biblique de la 'souffrance éducatrice' (à propos d'Hébreux V, 8)," *RSR*, 43 (1955), 481-523.

Friedrich, G. "Das Lied vom Hohenpriester im Zusammenhang von Hebr. 4, 14-5, 10," *TZ*, 18 (1962), 95-115.

Gibson, J.M., "The Gethsemane of the Fourth Gospel," *ET*, 30 (1918-19), 76-79.

Harnack, A. von. "Zwei alte dogmatische Korrekturen im Hebräerbrief," *SAB* (Berlin, 1929), pp. 62-73.

Jeremias, J. "Hbr 5:7-10," *ZNW*, 44 (1953), 107-111.

Linton, O. "Hebreerbrevet och 'Den historiske Jesus': en Studie till Hebr. 5:7," *STK*, 26 (1950), 335-345.

Omark, R. E. "The Saving of the Savior. Exegesis and Christology in Hebrews 5:7-10," *Interpretation*, 12 (1958), 39-51.

Rasco, E. "Christus, granum frumenti, Io. 12,24," *VD*, 37 (1959), 12-25, 65-77.

————. "La oración sacerdotal de Cristo en la tierra según Hebr. 5, 7," *G*, 43 (1962), 723-755.

Rissi, M. "Die Menschlichkeit Jesu nach Hebr. 5, 7-8," *TZ*, 11 (1955), 28-45.

Strobel, A. "Die Psalmengrundlage der Gethsemane-Parallele Hbr. 5:7ff.," *ZNW*, 45 (1954), 252-266.

Vitti, A. M. "Didicit ... obedientiam," *VD*, 12 (1932), 264-272.

————. "Exauditus est pro sua reverentia," *VD*, 14 (1934), 86-92, 108-114.

IV. General Studies

Aland, K. "Neue Neutestamentliche Papyri," *NTS*, 3 (1956-57), 261-286; 9 (1962-63), 303-316; 10 (1963-64), 62-79; 11 (1964-65), 1-21; 12 (1965-66), 193-210.

——. *Studien zur Überlieferung des Neuen Testaments und seines Textes.* Berlin, 1967.

Albertz, M. *Die Botschaft des Neuen Testaments.* 4 vols. Zürich, 1947-57.

Allen, W. C. "The Original Language of the Gospel according to Mark," *Exp*, 6th Ser., 1 (1900), 436-443.

——. "The Aramaic Element in St. Mark," *ET*, 13 (1901-02), 328-330.

Andrews, M. E. "Peirasmos, A Study in Form-Criticism," *Anglican Theological Review*, 24 (1942), 229-244.

Anonymous. "Erklärung einiger dunkeln Stellen des N. T.," *TSK*, 16 (1843), 103-140.

Bailey, J. A. *The Traditions Common to the Gospels of Luke and John.* Leiden, 1963.

Banks, J. S. "Professor Deissmann on Jesus at Prayer," *ET*, 11 (1899-1900), 270-273.

Barclay, W. *Flesh and Spirit: An Examination of Galatians 5.19-23.* Nashville, 1962.

Barr, A. "The Use and Disposal of the Marcan Source in Luke's Passion Narrative," *ET*, 55 (1943-44), 227-231.

Barth, K. *Church Dogmatics.* Vol. IV: *The Doctrine of Reconciliation,* Part I, tr. G. W. Bromiley. Edinburgh, 1961.

Bartsch, H.-W. "Die Passions- und Ostergeschichten bei Matthäus. Ein Beitrag zur Redaktionsgeschichte des Evangeliums," in *Basileia* (Stuttgart, 1959), pp. 27-41.

Baumann, R. "Abba, lieber Vater. Zum biblischen Gottesbild," *BK*, 22 (1967), 73-78.

Beare, F. W. *The Earliest Records of Jesus.* Oxford, 1962.

Beasley-Murray, G. R. *A Commentary on Mark Thirteen.* London, 1957.

——. *Baptism in the New Testament.* London, 1963.

Beauchamp, P. "Prière," *Vocabulaire de théologie biblique* (Paris, 1962), col. 850-858.

Benoit, P. *Exégèse et théologie.* 2 vols. Paris, 1961.

——. "Les outrages à Jésus Prophète (Mc xiv 65 par.)," *Neotestamentica et Patristica* (Leiden, 1962), pp. 92-110.

——. *Passion et Résurrection du Seigneur.* Paris, 1966.

Bentzen, A. *King and Messiah.* London, 1955; tr. from the German *Messias, Moses redivivus, Menschensohn. Skizzen zum Thema Weissagung und Erfüllung.* Zürich, 1948.

Bernard, J. H. "A Study of St. Mark x 38, 39," *JTS*, 28 (1927), 262-270.

Bertram, G. *Die Leidensgeschichte Jesu und der Christuskult.* Göttingen, 1922.

——. "Thambos, ktl.," *TDNT*, III (Grand Rapids, 1965), 4-7.

Best, E. *The Temptation and the Passion: the Markan Soteriology.* Cambridge, 1965.

Betz, O. "Jesu Heiliger Krieg," *NT*, 2 (1958), 116-137.

Bieder, W. "Skythrôpos," *TWNT*, VII (Stuttgart, [1964], 451-452.

Birdsall, J. N. "Who Is This Son of Man?" *EQ*, 42 (1970), 7-17.

BLACK, M. *An Aramaic Approach to the Gospels and Acts*, 3rd ed. Oxford, 1967.

——. "The 'Son of Man' Passion Saying in the Gospel Tradition," *ZNW*, 60 (1969), 1-8.

——. "The Son of Man Problem in Recent Research and Debate," *BJRL*, 45 (1962-63), 305-318.

——. "Servant of the Lord and Son of Man," *SJT*, 6 (1953), 1-11.

BLIGH, J. "Matching Passages, 2: St Matthew's Passion Narrative," *Way*, 9 (1969), 59-73.

BLINZLER, J. *Die neutestamentlichen Berichte über die Verklärung Jesu.* Münster, 1937.

——. "Passionsgeschehen und Passionsbericht des Lukasevangeliums," *BK*, 24 (1969), 1-4.

BOOBYER, G. H. *St. Mark and the Transfiguration Story.* Edinburgh, 1942.

BONSIRVEN, J. *Saint Paul, Épître aux Hébreux.* Paris, 1943

BORGEN, P. "John and the Synoptics in the Passion Narrative," *NTS*, 5 (1958-59), 246-259.

BORNHÄUSER, K. *Studien zum Sondergut des Lukas.* Gütersloh, 1934.

——. *Die Leidens- und Auferstehungsgeschichte Jesu.* Gütersloh, 1947.

BORNKAMM, G. *Jesus of Nazareth*, tr. Irene and Fraser McLuskey with James M. Robinson from 3rd Ger. ed. New York, 1960.

——; BARTH, G.; and HELD, H. J. *Tradition and Interpretation in Matthew*, tr. Percy Scott. Philadelphia, 1963.

BORSCH, F. H. *The Christian and Gnostic Son of Man.* Studies in Biblical Theology, Second Series, 14. London, 1970.

——. *The Son of Man in Myth and History.* Philadelphia, 1967.

BOUSSET, W. *Kyrios Christos*, tr. John E. Steely. Nashville and New York, 1970.

BOWMAN, J. *The Gospel of Mark. The New Christian Jewish Passover Haggadah.* Leiden, 1965.

BRATCHER, R. G., and NIDA, E. A. *A Translator's Handbook on the Gospel of Mark.* Leiden, 1961.

BRAUMANN, G. "Leidenskelch und Todestaufe (Mc 10:38f.)," *ZNW*, 56 (1965), 178-183.

BROWN, R. E. "The Pater Noster as an Eschatological Prayer," *ThSt*, 22 (1961), 175-208; also in *New Testament Essays* (London and Dublin, 1965), pp. 217-253.

BROWN, S. *Apostasy and Perseverance in the Theology of Luke.* Analecta Biblica No. 36. Rome, 1969.

BRUCE, F. F. *Commentary on the Epistle to the Hebrews.* London, 1964.

——. *The New Testament Development of Old Testament Themes.* Grand Rapids, 1968.

BÜCHSEL, F. "Die Blutgerichtsbarkeit des Synedrions," *ZNW*, 30 (1931), 202-210.

——. *"Didômi, ktl.,"* *TDNT*, II (Grand Rapids, 1964), 166-173.

——. *"Thymos, ktl.,"* *TDNT*, III (Grand Rapids, 1965), 167-172.

BULTMANN, R. *The History of the Synoptic Tradition*, tr. John Marsh. New York and Evanston, 1963.

——. *Theology of the New Testament*, tr. Kendrick Grobel. 2 vols. London, 1959-65.

——. *"Lypê, ktl.,"* *TDNT*, IV (Grand Rapids, 1967), 313-324.

———, and Kundsin, Karl. *Form Criticism: Two Essays on New Testament Research*. New York, 1966.

BUNDY, W. E. *Jesus and the First Three Gospels*. Cambridge, U. S .A., 1955.

BURKILL, T. A. *Mysterious Revelation. An Examination of the Philosophy of St. Mark's Gospel*. Ithaca, 1963.

BURNEY, C. F. *The Aramaic Origin of the Fourth Gospel*. Oxford, 1922.

BURTON, E. DE WITT. *Spirit, Soul, and Flesh. The Usage of* Pneuma, Psychê *and* Sarx *in Greek Writings and Translated Works from the Earliest Period to 180 A. D.; and of their Equivalents* Rûaḥ, Nephesh *and* Bâsâr *in the Hebrew Old Testament*. Chicago, 1918.

BUSE, I. "St.John and the Marcan Passion Narrative," *NTS*, 4 (1957-58), 215-219.

BUSSMANN, W. *Synoptische Studien*. 3 vols. Halle, 1925-31.

BUTLER, B. C. *The Originality of St Matthew. A Critique of the Two-Document Hypothesis*. Cambridge, 1951.

CADBURY, H. J. *The Style and Literary Method of Luke*. 2 vols. Cambridge, U.S.A., 1919-20.

———. *The Making of Luke-Acts*, 2nd ed. London, 1961.

CADOUX, A. T. *The Sources of the Second Gospel*. London, 1935.

CADOUX, C. J. *The Historic Mission of Jesus*. London, 1941.

———. "The Imperatival Use of *hina* in the New Testament," *JTS*, 42 (1941), 165-173.

CARMIGNAC, J. "Fais que nous n'entrions pas dans la tentation," *RB*, 72 (1965), 218-226.

CAVALLIN, A. "*(to) loipon*. Eine bedeutungsgeschichtliche Untersuchung," *Eranos*, 39 (1941), 121-144.

CAZELLES, H. "L'Esprit de Dieu dans l'Ancien Testament," in *Le Mystère de l'Esprit-Saint* (Paris, 1968), pp. 15-43.

CERFAUX, L. and CAMBIEN, J. "Luc (Évangile Selon Saint," *DBS*, V (Paris, 1957), col. 545-594.

CHASE, F. H. *The Lord's Prayer in the Early Church*. Cambridge, 1891.

CHORDAT, J.-L. *Jésus devant sa mort dans l'évangile de Marc*. Paris, 1970.

COLON, J.-B. "Marc (Évangile selon Saint)," *DBS*, V (Paris, 1957), col. 835-862.

COLPE, C. "*Ho huios tou anthrôpou*," *TWNT*, VIII (Stuttgart, 1969), 403-481.

COLWELL, E. C. *Studies in Methodology in Textual Criticism of the New Testament*. Leiden, 1969.

CONZELMANN, H. *The Theology of St Luke*, tr. Geoffrey Buswell. London, 1964.

———. "Historie und Theologie in den synoptischen Passionsberichten," in *Zur Bedeutung des Todes Jesu. Exegetische Beiträge* (Gütersloh, 1967), pp. 35-53; Eng. tr. "History and Theology in the Passion Narratives of the Synoptic Gospels," *Interpretation*, 24 (1970), 178-197.

———. *An Outline of the Theology of the New Testament*, tr. John Bowden from the 2nd Ger. ed. of 1968. New York and Evanston, 1969.

COPPENS, J. and DEQUEKER, L. *Le Fils de l'homme et les Saints du Très-Haut en Daniel VII, dans les Apocryphes et dans le Nouveau Testament*, 2nd ed. Bruges, 1961.

CREED, J. M. "Some Outstanding New Testament Problems. II. 'L' and the Structure of the Lucan Gospel: A Study of the Proto-Luke Hypothesis," *ET*, 46 (1934-35), 101-107.

———. "The Supposed 'Proto-Lucan' Narrative of the Trial before Pilate: A Rejoinder," *ET*, 46 (1934-35), 378-379.

CULLMANN, O. *Dieu et César.* Neuchatel, 1956; also in *Études de théologie biblique,* Neuchatel, 1968), pp. 75-131.
———. *Immortalité de l'âme ou Résurrection des Morts.* Neuchatel, 1956.
———. *The Christology of the New Testament,* tr. Shirley C. Guthrie and Charles A. M. Hall, 2nd ed. London, 1963.
CURTIS, J. B. "An Investigation of the Mount of Olives in the Judaeo-Christian Tradition," *Hebrew Union College Annual,* 28 (1957), 137-180.
DAHL, N. A. "Die Passionsgeschichte bei Matthäus," *NTS,* 2 (1955-56), 17-32.
DALMAN, G. *Die Worte Jesu,* 2nd ed., Vol. I. Leipzig, 1930.
———. *Sacred Sites and Ways. Studies in the Topography of the Gospels,* tr. Paul Levertoff. London, 1935.
DAUBE, D. "The Gospels and the Rabbis," *Listener,* 56 (1956), 342-346.
———. "The Sleeping Companions," in *The New Testament and Rabbinic Judaism* (London, 1956), pp. 332-335.
———. "A Prayer Pattern in Judaism," in *Studia Evangelica,* I (Berlin, 1959), 539-545.
———. "Death as a Release in the Bible," *NT,* 5 (1962), 82-104.
DAVIES, W. D. "Paul and the Dead Sea Scrolls: Flesh and Spirit," in *The Scrolls and the New Testament,* ed. Krister Stendahl (New York, 1957), pp. 157-182.
———. *Paul and Rabbinic Judaism: Some Rabbinic Elements in Pauline Theology,* 2nd ed. London, 1962.
DEISSMANN, A. *Light from the Ancient East. The New Testament Illustrated by Recently Discovered Texts of the Graeco-Roman World,* tr. Lionel R. M. Strachan from the 4th Ger. ed. New York and London, [1927].
DELLING, G. "*Baptisma, Baptisthênai,*" *NT,* 2 (1957-58), 92-115.
DEWAR, F. "Chapter 13 and the Passion Narrative in St Mark," *Th,* 64, no. 489 (1961), 99-107.
DHANIS, E. "De Filio hominis in Vetere Testamento et in judaismo," *G,* 45 (1964), 5-59.
DIBELIUS, M. *From Tradition to Gospel,* tr. B. L. Woolf from 2nd rev. ed. London, 1934.
———. "Das historische Problem der Leidensgeschichte," *ZNW,* 30 (1931), 193-201. And also in *Botschaft und Geschichte,* Vol. I (Tübingen, 1953), 248-257.
———. "La signification religieuse des récits évangéliques de la Passion," *RHPR,* 13 (1933), 30-45.
———. *Gospel Criticism and Christology.* London, 1935. And also in *Botschaft und Geschichte,* Vol. I (Tübingen, 1953), 293-358.
———. *Jesus.* Berlin, 1939.
———. *Botschaft und Geschichte.* 2 vols. Tübingen, 1953-56.
DODD, C. H. *History and the Gospel.* London, 1938.
———. *According to the Scriptures.* London, 1965.
———. *The Parables of the Kingdom.* London, 1963.
———. *The Interpretation of the Fourth Gospel.* Cambridge, 1963.
———. *Historical Tradition in the Fourth Gospel.* Cambridge, 1963.
DUPONT, J. *Les Béatitudes,* Vol. II: *La Bonne Nouvelle.* Paris, 1969.
EBELING, H. J. *Das Messiasgeheimnis und die Botschaft des Marcus-Evangelisten.* Berlin, 1939.
EDWARDS, R. A. "The Eschatological Correlative as a *Gattung* in the New Testament," *ZNW,* 60 (1969), 9-20.

ELLIS, E.E. and WILCOX, M., eds. *Neotestamentica et Semitica: Studies in Honour of Matthew Black.* Edinburgh, 1969.

FARMER, W.R. *The Synoptic Problem: A Critical Analysis.* New York and London, 1964.

FARRER, A. *A Study in St. Mark.* Oxford, 1952.

——. *St. Matthew and St. Mark.* London, 1954.

FASCHER, E. *Die Formgeschichtliche Methode.* Giessen, 1924.

——. *Jesus und der Satan.* Halle, 1949.

FEIGEL, F.K. *Der Einfluss des Weissagungsbeweises und anderer Motive auf die Leidensgeschichte.* Tübingen, 1910.

FEINE, P. *Eine vorkanonische Überlieferung des Lukas.* Gotha, 1891.

FENTON, J.C. "Inclusio and Chiasmus in Matthew," in *Studia Evangelica,* I (Berlin, 1959), 174-179.

FEUILLET, A. "Le logion sur la rançon," *RSPT,* 51 (1967), 365-402.

——. "La coupe et le baptême de la passion (Mc, x, 35-40; cf. Mt, xx, 20-23; Lc, xii, 50)," *RB,* 74 (1967), 356-391.

——. "Les trois grandes prophéties de la Passion et de la Résurrection des évangiles synoptiques," *RTh,* 67 (1967), 533-560; 68 (1968), 41-74.

FIELD, F. *Notes on the Translation of the New Testament.* Cambridge, 1899.

FINEGAN, J. *Die Überlieferung der Leidens- und Auferstehungsgeschichte Jesu.* ZNW, Beiheft 15. Giessen, 1934.

FITZMYER, J.A. Review of Matthew Black, *An Aramaic Approach to the Gospels and Acts,* 3rd ed., *CBQ,* 30 (1968), 417-428.

FLENDER, H. *St Luke: Theologian of Redemptive History,* tr. Reginald H. and Ilse Fuller. London, 1967.

FLESSEMAN-VAN LEER, E. "Die Interpretation der Passionsgeschichte vom Alten Testament aus," in *Zur Bedeutung des Todes Jesu. Exegetische Beiträge* (Gütersloh, 1967), pp. 79-96.

FLORIT, E. *Il metodo della "storia delle forme" e sua applicazione al racconto della Passione.* Rome, 1935.

FLUSSER, D. "The Dead Sea Sect and Pre-Pauline Christianity," in *Scripta Hierosolymitana.* IV: *Aspects of the Dead Sea Scrolls,* ed. Chaim Rabin and Yigael Yadin, 2nd ed. (Jerusalem, 1965), pp. 215-266.

——. *Jesus,* tr. Ronald Walls. New York, 1969.

FOAKES-JACKSON, F.J., and LAKE, K., eds. *The Beginnings of Christianity.* 5 vols. London, 1920-33.

FORMESYN, R.E.C. "Was there a Pronominal Connection for the 'Bar Nasha' Selfdesignation?" *NT,* 8 (1966), 1-35.

FORREST, D.W. "Did Jesus Pray with his Disciples?", *ET,* 11 (1899-1900), 352-357.

FULLER, R.H. *The Mission and Achievement of Jesus: An Examination of the Presuppositions of New Testament Theology.* London, 1963.

——. *The Foundations of New Testament Christology.* New York, 1965.

GARDNER-SMITH, P. *St. John and the Synoptic Gospels.* Cambridge, 1938.

GEORGE, A.R. "The Imperative Use of *hina* in the New Testament," *JTS,* 45 (1944), 56-60.

GEORGE, A. "Jésus et les psaumes," in *A la rencontre de Dieu. Mémorial Albert Gelin* (Le Puy, 1961), pp. 297-308.

——. "Tradition et rédaction chez Luc. La construction du troisième évangile," *ETL,* 43 (1967), 100-129.

——. "Comment Jésus a-t-il perçu sa propre mort?," *LumV*, 20, No. 101 (1971), 34-59.

GERHARDSSON, B. *Memory and Manuscript. Oral Tradition and Written Transmission in Rabbinic Judaism and Early Christianity*, tr. Eric J. Sharpe. Uppsala, 1961.

——. "Jésus livré et abandonné d'après la Passion selon Saint Matthieu," (1969), *RB*, 76 (1969), 206-227.

GLAUE, P. *Die Vorlesung heiliger Schriften im Gottesdienste. I. Bis zur Entstehung der altkatholischen Kirche*. Berlin, 1907.

GOGUEL, M. "A propos du procès de Jésus," *ZNW*, 31 (1932), 289-301.

——. *Jésus*. Paris, 1950.

——. *Jesus and the Origins of Christianity*. 2 vols. New York, 1960.

GOPPELT, L. "*Pinô ... potêrion, ktl.*," *TDNT*, VI (Grand Rapids, 1968), 135-160.

GRANT, F. C. *The Gospels. Their Origin and their Growth*. London, 1957.

——. *The Earliest Gospel*. New York, 1943.

GREEVEN, H. *Gebet und Eschatologie im Neuen Testament*. Gütersloh, 1931.

GRUNDMANN, W. *Die Geschichte Jesu Christi*, 2nd ed. Berlin, 1959.

——. "*Ischyô*," *TDNT*, III (Grand Rapids, 1965), 397-402.

GUILLET, J. *Jésus devant sa vie et sa mort*. Paris, 1971.

GUNDRY, R. H. *The Use of the Old Testament in St. Matthew's Gospel with Special Reference to the Messianic Hope*. Leiden, 1967.

GUY, H. A. *The Origin of the Gospel of Mark*. London, 1954.

HAENCHEN, E. "Historie und Geschichte in den johanneischen Passions-berichten," in *Zur Bedeutung des Todes Jesu. Exegetische Beiträge* (Gütersloh, 1967), pp. 55-78; Eng. tr. "History and Interpretation in the Johannine Passion Narrative," *Interpretation*, 24 (1970), 198-219.

HAHN, F. *Christologische Hoheitstitel. Ihre Geschichte im frühen Christentum*, 3rd ed. Göttingen, 1966; Eng. tr. *The Titles of Jesus in Christology. Their History in Early Christianity*, tr. Harold Knight and George Ogg. New York and Cleveland, 1969.

HAMMAN, A. *La Prière. I. Le Nouveau Testament*. Tournai, 1958.

——. "Lignes maîtresses de la prière johannique," in *Studia Evangelica*, I (Berlin, 1959), 309-320.

——. "The Prayer of Jesus," *The Way*, 3 (1963), 174-183.

HANSEN, M. B. "Den historiske Jesus og den himmelske ypperstepraest i Hebraeerbrevet," *DTT*, 26 (1963), 1-22.

HANSON, A. T. *The Wrath of the Lamb*. London, 1957.

HARNACK, A. VON. *Sprüche und Reden Jesu. Die zweite Quelle des Matthäus und Lukas*. Leipzig, 1907.

HATCH, W. N. PAINE. *The 'Western' Text of the Gospels*. Evanston, 1937.

HAUFE, G. "Das Menschensohn-Problem in der gegenwärtigen wissenschaftlichen Diskussion," *EvT*, 26 (1966), 130-141.

HAWKINS, J. C. *Horae Synopticae. Contributions to the Study of the Synoptic Problem*, 2nd ed. Oxford, 1909.

HEILER, F. *Das Gebet*. München, 1923.

HELMBOLD, H. *Vorsynoptische Evangelien*. Stuttgart, 1953.

HENGEL, M. *Nachfolge und Charisma. Eine exegetisch-religionsgeschlichtliche Studie zu Mt 8, 21f. und Jesu Ruf in die Nachfolge*. Berlin, 1968.

HÉRING, J. *L'épître aux Hébreux*. Neuchatel and Paris, 1954.

HIGGINS, A.J. B. *Jesus and the Son of Man*. London, 1964.

————. "Son of Man-*Forschung* since 'The Teaching of Jesus'," in *New Testament Essays,* ed. A. J. B. Higgins (Manchester, 1959), pp. 119-135.

————. "Is the Son of Man Problem Insoluble?" in *Neotestamentica et Semitica: Studies in Honour of Matthew Black,* ed. E. Earle Ellis and Max Wilcox (Edinburgh, 1969), pp. 70-87.

HILL, D. *Greek Words and Hebrew Meanings: Studies in the Semantics of Soteriological Terms.* Cambridge, 1967.

HILLMANN, W. *Aufbau und Deutung der synoptischen Leidensberichte. Ein Beitrag zur Kompositionstechnik und Sinndeutung der drei älteren Evangelien.* Freiburg, 1941.

HIRSCH, E. *Die Frühgeschichte des Evangeliums.* I. *Das Werden des Markus-Evangeliums,* 2nd ed. Tübingen, 1951. II. *Die Vorlagen des Lukas und das Sondergut des Matthaeus.* Tübingen, 1941.

HOBART, W. K. *The Medical Language of St. Luke.* Dublin, 1882.

HÖLLER, J. *Die Verklärung Jesu.* Freiburg, 1937.

HOOKER, M. D. *Jesus and the Servant.* London, 1959.

————. *The Son of Man in Mark.* London, 1967.

HOSKYNS, E. C., and DAVEY, N. *The Riddle of the New Testament.* London, 1947.

HUNKIN, J. W. " 'Pleonastic' *archomai* in the New Testament," *JTS,* 25 (1923-24), 390-402.

HUPPENBAUER, H. "*Bâsâr* 'Fleisch' in den Texten von Qumran (Höhle I)," *TZ,* 13 (1957), 298-300.

HUTTON, W. R. "The Kingdom of God has Come," *ET,* 64 (1952-53), 89-91.

HYATT, J. P. "The View of Man in the Qumran 'Hodayot'," *NTS,* 2 (1955-56), 276-284.

IBER, G. *Überlieferungsgeschichtliche Untersuchungen zum Begriff des Menschensohnes im Neuen Testament.* Heidelberg, 1953.

JACQUEMIN, M. E. "La portée de la troisième demande du 'Pater'," *ETL,* 25 (1949), 61-76.

JANNARIS, A. N. "Misreadings and Misrenderings in the New Testament," *Exp,* 5th Series, 8 (1898), 422-432.

JEREMIAS, J. "Das Gebetsleben Jesu," *ZNW,* 25 (1926), 123-140.

————. "Der Lösegeld für Viele (Mk 10, 45)," *J,* 3 (1948), 249-264.

————. "Perikopen-Umstellungen bei Lukas?", *NTS,* 4 (1957-58), 115-119.

————. *The Central Message of the New Testament.* London, 1965.

————. *The Eucharistic Words of Jesus,* tr. Norman Perrin from 3rd Ger. ed. with author's rev. to July 1964. London, 1966.

————. *The Prayers of Jesus.* London, 1967.

————. *The Problem of the Historical Jesus,* tr. Norman Perrin. Philadelphia, 1967.

————. "Die älteste Schicht der Menschensohn-Logien," *ZNW,* 58 (1967), 159-172.

————. "*Polloi,*" *TDNT,* VI (Grand Rapids, 1968), 536-545.

————. *New Testament Theology. Part One: The Proclamation of Jesus,* tr. John Bowden. London, 1971.

JOÜON, P. "Les verbes *boulomai* et *thelô* dans le Nouveau Testament," *RSR,* 30 (1940), 227-238.

JUNCKER, A. *Jesu Stellung in der Geschichte des Gebets.* Berlin, 1922.

KIDDLE, M. "The Passion Narrative in St. Luke's Gospel," *JTS,* 36 (1935), 267-280.

KILPATRICK, G. D. *The Origins of the Gospel according to St. Matthew.* Oxford, 1946.

――――. "Some Notes on Marcan Usage," *The Bible Translator*, 7 (1956), 51-56.

KISTEMAKER, S. *The Psalm Citations in the Epistle to the Hebrews.* Amsterdam, 1961.

KITTEL, G. *Die Religionsgeschichte und das Urchristentum.* Gütersloh, 1932.

――――. "Abba," *TDNT*, I (Grand Rapids, 1964), 5-6.

――――. "Akoloutheô, ktl.," *TDNT*, I (Grand Rapids, 1964), 210-216.

KLAMETH, G. *Die neutestamentlichen Lokaltraditionen Palästinas in der zeit vor den Kreuzzügen.* II. *Die Ölbergüberlieferungen.* Neutestamentliche Abhandlungen 10 (Münster, 1923), Heft 2.

KLAUSNER, J. *Jesus of Nazareth: his Life, Times and Teaching*, tr. Herbert Danby. London, 1925.

KLEINKNECHT, H.; RAD, G. VON; KUHN, K. G.; and SCHMIDT, K. L. "Basileus, basileia, ktl.," *TDNT*, I (Grand Rapids, 1964), 564-593.

――――; GRETHER, O.; PROCKSCH, O.; FICHTNER, J.; SJÖBERG, E.; and STÄHLIN, G. "Orgê, ktl.," *TDNT*, V (Grand Rapids, 1967), 382-447.

――――; BAUMGÄRTEL, F.; BIEDER, W.; SJÖBERG, E.; and SCHWEIZER, E. "Pneuma, ktl.," *TDNT*, VI (Grand Rapids, 1968), 332-455.

KNOX, W. L. *Some Hellenistic Elements in Primitive Christianity.* London, 1944.

――――. *The Sources of the Synoptic Gospels.* 2 vols. Cambridge, 1953-57.

KORN, H. *PEIRASMOS. Die Versuchung des Gläubigen in der griechischen Bibel.* Stuttgart, 1937.

KOSMALA, H. *Hebräer-Essener-Christen.* Leiden, 1959.

KRUSE, H. " 'Pater Noster' et Passio Christi," *VD*, 46 (1968), 3-29.

KUHN, K. G. "*Peirasmos-hamartia-sarx* im Neuen Testament und die damit zusammenhängenden Vorstellungen," *ZTK*, 49 (1952), 200-222; Eng. tr. with some rev. "New Light on Temptation, Sin and Flesh in the New Testament," in *The Scrolls and the New Testament*, ed. Krister Stendahl (New York, 1957), pp. 94-113.

KÜMMEL, W. G. *Promise and Fulfilment. The Eschatological Message of Jesus*, tr. Dorothea M. Barton, 2nd ed. London, 1961.

KUSS, O. *Der Brief an die Hebräer.* Regensburg, 1966.

LAGRANGE, M.-J. *The Gospel of Jesus Christ.* 2 vols. New York, 1938.

LARCHER, C. *L'actualité chrétienne de l'Ancien Testament, d'après le Nouveau Testament.* Paris, 1962.

LEANEY, A. R.C. *The Rule of Qumran and Its Meaning.* London, 1966.

LEBRETON, J. *Vie et enseignement de Jésus-Christ.* Paris, 1935.

――――. *The Spiritual Teaching of the New Testament.* Westminster, 1960.

LEDÉAUT, R. *La nuit pascale.* Analecta Biblica No. 22. Rome, 1963.

――――. "Le substrat araméen des évangiles: scolies en marge de l'*Aramaic Approach* de Matthew Black," *B*, 49 (1968), 388-399.

LEE, E. K. "St. Mark and the Fourth Gospel," *NTS*, 3 (1956-57), 50-58.

LÉON-DUFOUR, X. "Matthieu et Marc dans le récit de la Passion," *B*, 40 (1959), 684-696.

――――. "Passion (Récits de la)," *DBS*, VI (Paris, 1960), col. 1419-1492.

――――. *Les Évangiles et l'histoire de Jésus.* Paris, 1963.

LESÊTRE, H. "Gethsémani," *DB*, III (Paris, 1926), col. 229-234.

――――. "Prière," *DB*, V (Paris, 1922), col. 663-676.

LICHT, J. "An Analysis of the Treatise on the Two Spirits in DSD," in *Scripta Hierosolymitana*. IV: *Aspects of the Dead Sea Scrolls*, ed. Chaim Rabin and Yigael Yadin, 2nd ed. (Jerusalem, 1965), pp. 88-100.

LIEBERMANN, S. *Hellenism in Jewish Palestine*. *Studies in the Literary Transmission, Beliefs, and Manners of Palestine in the I Century B. C. E. - IV Century C. E.* New York, 1950.

LIETZMANN, H. *Einführung in die Textgeschichte der Paulusbriefe an die Römer*, 2nd ed. Tübingen, 1928.

————. "Der Prozess Jesu," *SAB* (Berlin, 1931), pp. 313-322.

————. "Bemerkungen zum Prozess Jesu," *ZNW*, 30 (1931), 211-215; 31 (1932), 78-84.

LIGHTFOOT, J. B. *St. Paul's Epistle to the Galatians*, 3rd ed. London and Cambridge, 1869.

LIGHTFOOT, R. H. *History and Interpretation in the Gospels*. Bampton Lectures 1934. New York, n. d.

————. *The Gospel Message of St. Mark*. Oxford, 1950.

LINDARS, B. *New Testament Apologetic*. *The Doctrinal Significance of the Old Testament Quotations*. Philadelphia, 1961.

LOHMEYER, E. *Galiläa und Jerusalem*. Göttingen, 1936.

————. *Gottesknecht und Davidssohn*. Göttingen, 1953.

LOHSE, E. "Die Bedeutung des Pfingstberichtes im Rahmen des lukanischen Geschichtswerkes," *EvT*, 13 (1953), 422-436.

————. "Lukas als Theologe der Heilsgeschichte," *EvT*, 14 (1954), 256-275.

————. *Märtyrer und Gottesknecht*. *Untersuchungen zur urchristlichen Verkündigung vom Sühntod Jesu Christi*. Göttingen, 1955.

————. *Die Geschichte des Leidens und Sterbens Jesu Christ*. Gütersloh, 1964; Eng. tr. *History of the Suffering and Death of Jesus Christ*, tr. Martin O. Dietrich. Philadelphia, 1967.

LOISY, A. *Les livres du Nouveau Testament*. Paris, 1922.

LOTZ, W. "Das Sinnbild des Bechers," *NKZ*, 28 (1917), 396-407.

LÖVESTAM, E. *Spiritual Wakefulness in the New Testament*, tr. W. F. Salisbury. Lund, 1963.

LYS, D. *L'homme dans l'Ancien Testament*. Montpellier, 1959.

————. *Nèphèsh*. *Histoire de l'âme dans la révélation d'Israël au sein des religions proche-orientales*. Paris, 1959.

————. *Rûach*. *Le souffle dans l'Ancien Testament*. *Enquéte anthropologique à travers l'histoire théologique d'Israël*. Paris, 1962.

————. *La chair dans l'Ancien Testament: "Bâsâr."* Paris, 1967.

MACHEN, J. G. *The Origin of Paul's Religion*. New York, 1936.

MANSON, T. W. *The Servant-Messiah*. *A study of the Public Ministry of Jesus*. Cambridge, 1953.

————. *The Teaching of Jesus*, 2nd ed. Cambridge, 1955.

————. "The Lord's Prayer," *BJRL*, 38 (1955-56), 99-113, 436-448.

MANSON, W. *Jesus the Messiah*. London, 1944.

MARCHEL, W. "Abba Pater! Oratio Christi et christianorum (Mc. 14.36)," *VD*, 39 (1961), 240-247.

————. *Abba, Père! La prière du Christ et des chrétiens*. Analecta Biblica No. 19. Rome, 1963.

————. *Dieu Père dans le Nouveau Testament*, tr. from the German by Madeleine Cé. Paris, 1966.

MARLOW, R. "The *Son of Man* in Recent Journal Literature," *CBQ*, 28 (1966), 20-30.

MARSHALL, I. H. "The Synoptic Son of Man Sayings in Recent Discussion," *NTS*, 12 (1965-66), 327-351.

———. "The Son of Man in Contemporary Debate," *EQ*, 42 (1970), 67-87.

MARXSEN, W. *Der Evangelist Markus. Studien zur Redaktionsgeschichte des Evangeliums*, 2nd ed. Göttingen, 1959.

———. *The Beginnings of Christology: A Study in Its Problems*, tr. Paul J. Achtemeier from the 2nd Ger. ed. of 1964. Philadelphia, 1969.

MASSON, C. "Le reniement de Pierre. Quelques aspects de la formation d'une tradition," *RHPR*, 37 (1957), 24-35.

MAURER, C. "Knecht Gottes und Sohn Gottes im Passionsbericht des Markusevangeliums," *ZTK*, 50 (1953), 1-38.

MAUSER, U. W. *Christ in the Wilderness*. Naperville, 1963.

McCOWN, C. C. "Jesus, Son of Man. A Survey of Recent Discussion," *JR*, 28 (1948), 1-12.

MEECHAM, H. G. "The Meaning of (*to*) *loipon* in the New Testament," *ET*, 48 (1936-37), 331-332.

———. "The Imperatival Use of *hina* in the New Testament," *JTS*, 43 (1942), 179-180.

MEISTERMANN, B. *Gethsémani, Notices historiques et descriptives*. Paris, 1920.

MERX, A. *Markus und Lukas*. Berlin, 1905.

METZGER, B. M. *The Text of the New Testament. Its Transmission, Corruption, and Restoration*. Oxford, 1964.

MEYER, E. *Ursprung und Anfänge des Christentums*. 3 vols. Stuttgart, 1921-23.

MICHAELIS, W. "*Piptô, ktl.*," *TDNT*, VI (Grand Rapids, 1968), 161-173.

MICHEL, O. *Der Brief an die Hebräer*, 11th ed. Göttingen, 1960.

MINETTE DE TILLESSE, G. *Le secret messianique dans l'Évangile de Marc*. Paris, 1968.

MONTEFIORE, H. *A Commentary on the Epistle to the Hebrews*. London, 1964.

MORGENTHALER, R. *Die lukanische Geschichtsschreibung als Zeugnis. Gestalt und Gehalt der Kunst des Lukas*. 2 vols. Zürich, 1949.

MOULE, C. F. D. *An Idiom Book of New Testament Greek*, 2nd ed. Cambridge, 1960.

MOWINCKEL, S. *He That Cometh*, tr. G. W. Anderson. Oxford, 1959.

MURPHY, R. E. "*Bśr* in the Qumrân Literature and *Sarks* in the Epistle to the Romans," in *Sacra Pagina*, ed. J. Coppens, A. Descamps and É. Massaux (Paris and Gembloux, 1959), II, 60-75.

NEILL, S. *The Interpretation of the New Testament, 1861-1961*. London, 1964.

NICOLARDOT, F. *Les procédés de rédaction des trois premiers Évangélistes*. Paris, 1908.

NIELEN, J. M. *Gebet und Gottesdienst im Neuen Testament*. New York and Freiburg, 1963. English translation: *The Earliest Christian Liturgy*. St. Louis, 1941.

OEPKE, A. "*Egeirô... grêgoreô*," *TDNT*, II (Grand Rapids, 1964), 333-339.

———. "*Katheudô*," *TDNT*, III (Grand Rapids, 1965), 431-437.

OSTY, E. "Les points de contact entre le récit de la passion dans Saint Luc et Saint Jean," in *Melanges Jules Lebreton*, Vol. I (Paris, 1951-52), 146-154.

OTT, W. *Gebet und Heil. Die Bedeutung der Gebetsparänese in der lukanischen Theologie.* Munich, 1965.

OTTO, R. *The Idea of the Holy*, tr. John W. Harvey. London, New York and Toronto, 1943.

———. *The Kingdom of God and the Son of Man*, tr. F. V. Filson and B. Lee-Woolf. London, 1951.

PALLIS, A. *A. Few Notes on the Gospels according to St. Mark and St. Matthew.* Liverpool, 1903.

PEDERSEN, J. *Israel: Its Life and Culture*, I-II. London and Copenhagen, 1959.

PERRIN, N. "The Son of Man in Ancient Judaism and Primitive Christianity: A Suggestion," *BR*, 11 (1966), 17-28.

———. *Rediscovering the Teaching of Jesus.* New York and Evanston, 1967.

———. "The Creative Use of the Son of Man Tradition by Mark," *USQR*, 23 (1967-68), 357-365.

———. "The Son of Man in the Synoptic Tradition," *BR*, 13 (1968), 3-25.

PERRY, A. M. *The Sources of Luke's Passion-Narrative.* Chicago, 1920.

———. "Some Outstanding New Testament Problems. V. Luke's Disputed Passion-Source," *ET*, 46 (1934-35), 256-260.

POELMAN, R. "The Prayer of Jesus," *LV*, 19 (1964), 9-44.

POPKES, W. *Christus Traditus. Eine Untersuchung zum Begriff der Dahingabe im Neuen Testament.* Zürich, 1967.

POWER, E. "Gethsémani," *DBS*, III (Paris, 1938), col. 632-659.

PREISS, T. *Le Fils de l'homme. Fragments d'un cours sur la Christologie du Nouveau Testament.* Études Theologiques et Religieuses, 26, 3 (Montpellier, 1951), and 28, 1 (Montpellier, 1953).

PROCKSCH, O. *Petrus und Johannes bei Marcus und Matthäus.* Gütersloh, 1920.

———, and BÜCHSEL, F. "*Lyô, ktl.*," *TDNT*, IV (Grand Rapids, 1967), 328-356.

RADERMAKERS, J. "The Prayer of Jesus in the Synoptic Gospels," *LV*, 24 (1969), 561-578.

RAMSEY, A. M. *The Glory of God and the Transfiguration of Christ.* London, 1967.

———. "The Narratives of the Passion," in *Contemporary Studies in Theology*, I (London, 1962); also in *Studia Evangelica*, II (Berlin, 1964), 122-134.

REHKOPF, F. *Die lukanische Sonderquelle. Ihr Umfang und Sprachgebrauch.* Tübingen, 1959.

RENGSTORF, K. H. "*Hamartôlos, anamartêtos*," *TDNT*, I (Grand Rapids, 1964), 317-335.

———. "*Manthanô, ktl.*," *TDNT*, IV (Grand Rapids, 1967), 390-461.

REYMANN, G. "Gethsemane," *Palästinajahrbuch des Deutschen evangelischen Instituts für Altertumswissenschaft des heiligen Landes zu Jerusalem*, 5 (1909), 87-96.

RIESENFELD, H. *Jésus Transfiguré: l'arrière-plan du récit évangélique de la transfiguration de Notre-Seigneur.* Copenhagen, 1947.

———. "Tradition und Redaktion im Markusevangelium," *ZNW*, Beiheft 21 (Giessen, 1954), pp. 157-167.

———. *The Gospel Tradition and its Beginnings. A Study in the Limits of 'Formgeschichte.'* London, 1961; also in *Studia Evangelica*, I (Berlin, 1959), 43-65.

――――. *"Hyper," TWNT*, VII (Stuttgart, 1969), 510-518.

RIGGENBACH, E. *Der Brief an die Hebräer.* Leipzig, 1913.

ROBINSON, H. W. *The Christian Doctrine of Man.* Edinburgh, 1911.

ROBINSON, J. M. *The Problem of History in Mark.* London, 1962.

ROBINSON, J. A. T. *The Body. A Study in Pauline Theology.* London, 1963.

ROBINSON, T. H. *The Epistle to the Hebrews.* London, 1933.

ROCHE, J. "Que ta volonté soit faite," *VS*, 93 (1955), 249-268.

ROHDE, J. *Rediscovering the Teaching of the Evangelists*, tr. Dorothea M. Barton. Philadelphia, 1968.

SABBE, M. "De transfiguratie van Jezus," *Collationes Brugenses et Gandavenses*, 4 (1958), 467-503.

――――. "La rédaction du récit de la Transfiguration," *Recherches bibliques*, 6 (n. p., 1962), 65-100.

SABOURIN, L. *Rédemption sacrificielle. Une enquête exégétique.* Bruges, 1961.

――――. *The Names and Titles of Jesus*, tr. Maurice Carroll. New York, 1967.

SALOM, A. P. "The Imperatival Use of *hina* in the New Testament," *Australian Biblical Review*, 6 (1958), 123-141.

SAND, A. *Der Begriff "Fleisch" in der paulinischen Hauptbriefen.* Biblische Untersuchungen, 2. Regensburg, 1967.

SANDAY, W. *The Life of Christ in Recent Research.* New York, 1908.

――――, and HEADLAM, A. C. *A Critical and Exegetical Commentary on the Epistle to the Romans*, 14th ed. New York, 1913.

SANDERS, E. P. *The Tendencies of the Synoptic Tradition.* Cambridge, 1969.

SCHEIFLER, J. R. "El hijo del hombre en Daniel," *EE*, 34 (1960), 789-804.

SCHELKLE, K. H. *Die Passion Jesu in der Verkündigung des Neuen Testaments. Ein Beitrage zur Formgeschichte und zur Theologie des Neuen Testaments.* Heidelberg, 1949.

SCHICK, E. *Formgeschichte und Synoptikerexegese. Eine critische Untersuchung über die Möglichkeit und die Grenzen der formgeschichtlichen Methode.* Neutestamentliche Abhandlungen, 28, 2-3 (Münster, 1940).

SCHILLE, G. "Das Leiden des Herrn," *ZTK*, 52 (1955), 161-205.

――――. "Erwägungen zur Hohepriesterlehre des Hebräerbriefes," *ZNW*, 46 (1955), 81-109.

――――. "Bemerkungen zur Formgeschichte des Evangeliums. Rahmen und Aufbau des Markus-Evangeliums," *NTS*, 4 (1957), 1-24.

SCHLATTER, A. *Markus, der Evangelist für die Griechen.* Stuttgart, 1935.

SCHLIER, H. *"Thlibô, thlipsis," TDNT*, III (Grand Rapids, 1966), 139-148.

SCHMAUCH, W. "Der Ölberg," *TLZ*, 77 (1952), 391-396.

――――. *... zu achten aufs Wort: Ausgewählte Arbeiten.* Göttingen, 1967.

SCHMID, J. *Matthäus und Lukas.* Freiburg, 1930.

SCHMIDT, K. L. *Der Rahmen der Geschichte Jesu.* Berlin, 1919.

SCHNACKENBURG, R. "Der Sinn der Versuchung Jesu bei den Synoptikern," *Theologische Quartalschrift*, 132 (1952), 297-326.

――――. "Der Menschensohn im Johannesevangelium," *NTS*, 11 (1965), 123-137.

SCHNEIDER, C. *"Kathêmai, kathizô, kathezomai," TDNT*, III (Grand Rapids, 1966), 440-444.

SCHNEIDER, G. *Verleugnung, Verspottung und Verhör Jesu nach Lukas, 22, 54-71. Studien zur lukanischen Darstellung der Passion.* Munich, 1969.

――――. "Gab es eine vorsynoptische Szene 'Jesus vor dem Synedrium'?", *NT*, 12 (1970), 22-39.

SCHNEIDER, J. *"Erchomai, ktl.,"* *TDNT*, II (Grand Rapids, 1964), 666-684.

SCHNIEWIND, J. *Die Parallelperikopen bei Lukas und Johannes*, 2nd ed. Hildesheim, 1958.

SCHÖTTGEN, Ch. *Horae Hebraicae et Talmudicae in universum Novum Testamentum.* Dresden and Leipzig, 1733.

SCHREIBER, J. *Theologie des Vertrauens. Eine redaktionsgeschichtliche Untersuchung des Markusevangeliums.* Hamburg, 1967.

——. *Die Markuspassion. Wege zur Erforschung der Leidensgeschichte Jesu.* Hamburg, 1969.

SCHRENK, G. *"Boulomai, boulê, boulêma,"* *TDNT*, I (Grand Rapids, 1964), 629-637.

——. *"Thelô, thelêma, thelêsis,"* *TDNT*, III (Grand Rapids, 1967), 44-62.

——, and QUELL, G. *"Patêr, ktl.,"* *TDNT*, V (Grand Rapids, 1968), 945-1022.

SCHULTHESS, F., and LITTMANN, E. *Grammatik des christlichpalästinischen Aramäisch.* Tübingen, 1924.

SCHULZ, A. *Nachfolgen und Nachahmen. Studien über das Verhältnis der neutestamentlichen Jüngerschaft zur urchristlichen Vorbildethik.* Munich, 1962.

——. *Suivre et imiter le Christ d'après le nouveau testament*, tr. Jean-Louis Klein. Paris, 1966.

SCHULZ, S. *Untersuchungen zur Menschensohnchristologie im Johannesevangelium.* Göttingen, 1957.

SCHÜRMANN, H. *Quellenkritische Untersuchung des lukanischen Abendmahlsberichtes Lk. xxii, 7-38.* Neutestamentliche Abhandlungen, 19,5; 20,4-5 (Münster, 1953-57).

SCHWEITZER, A. *The Mystery of the Kingdom of God: the Secret of Jesus' Messiahship and Passion*, tr. W. Lowrie. London, 1925.

——. *The Quest of the Historical Jesus*, 3rd ed. London, 1963.

——. *Geschichte der Leben-Jesu-Forschung*, 6th ed. Tübingen, 1951.

SCHWEIZER, E. "Röm. 1, 3f. und der Gegensatz von Fleisch und Geist vor und bei Paulus," *EvT*, 15 (1955), 563-571.

——. *Erniedrigung und Erhöhung bei Jesus und seinen Nachfolgern.* Zürich, 1955: Eng. tr. with rev. and abridgments *Lordship and Discipleship.* London, 1960.

——. "Die hellenistische Komponente im neutestamentlichen *sarx*-Begriff," *ZNW*, 48 (1957), 237-253.

——. "Der Menschensohn (Zur eschatologischen Erwartung Jesu)," *ZNW*, 50 (1959), 185-209.

——. "The Son of Man," *JBL*, 79 (1960), 119-129.

——. "The Son of Man Again," *NTS*, 9 (1962-63), 256-261.

——. "Zur Frage des Messianisgeheimnisses bei Markus," *ZNW*, 56 (1965), 1-8.

——; BAUMGÄRTEL, F.; and MEYER, R. *"Sarx, ktl.,"* *TWNT*, VII (Stuttgart, 1964), 98-151.

SEESEMANN, H. *"Peira... peirasmos, ktl.,"* *TDNT*, VI (Grand Rapids, 1968), 23-36.

SIGGE, T. *Das Johannesevangelium und die Synoptiker.* Münster, 1935.

SIMPSON, M. A. "The Kingdom of God has Come," *ET*, 64 (1952-53), 188.

SJÖBERG, E. *Der verborgene Menschensohn in den Evangelien.* Lund. 1955.

SMALLEY, S. S. "The Johannine Son of Man Sayings," *NTS*, 15 (1969), 278-301.

SPICQ, C. *L'Épître aux Hébreux.* 2 vols. Paris, 1953.

———. *Dieu et l'homme selon le Nouveau Testament.* Paris, 1961.

SPITTA, F. *Die synoptische Grundschrift in ihrer Überlieferung durch das Lukasevangelium.* Leipzig, 1912.

STACEY, W. D. *The Pauline View of Man: In Relation to its Judaic and Hellenistic Background.* London, 1956.

STAPLES, P. "The Kingdom of God has Come," *ET*, 71 (1959-60), 87-88.

STAUFFER, E. *"Agôn, ktl.," TDNT*, I (Grand Rapids, 1964), 134-140.

STENDAHL, K., ed. *The Scrolls and the New Testament.* New York, 1957.

STEWART, A. "Did Jesus Pray with his Disciples?," *ET*, 11 (1899-1900), 477-478.

STÖGER, A. "Eigenart und Botschaft der lukanischen Passionsgeschichte," *BK*, 24 (1969), 4-8.

STRAUSS, D.F. *The Life of Jesus Critically Examined,* tr. George Eliot from 4th Ger. ed. London, 1892.

———. *The Life of Jesus for the People,* authorized tr., 2nd ed. 2 vols. London, 1879.

STRECKER, G. "Die Leidens- und Auferstehungsvoraussagen im Markusevangelium," *ZTK*, 64 (1967), 16-39.

STREETER, B.H. *The Four Gospels: A Study of Origins.* London, 1927.

SUHL, A. *Die Funktion der alttestamentlichen Zitate und Anspielungen im Markusevangelium.* Gütersloh, 1965.

SUNDWALL, J. *Die Zusammensetzung des Markusevangelium.* Åbo, 1934.

SURKAU, H.-W. *Martyrien in jüdischer und frühchristlicher Zeit.* Göttingen, 1938.

TASKER, R. V. G. *The Biblical Doctrine of the Wrath of God.* London, 1951.

TAYLOR, V. *Behind the Third Gospel: A Study of the Proto-Luke Hypothesis.* Oxford, 1926.

———. *The Formation of the Gospel Tradition.* London, 1933.

———. "Professor J.M. Creed and the Proto-Luke Hypothesis," *ET*, 46 (1934-35), 236-238.

———. *Jesus and his Sacrifice: A Study of the Passion Sayings in the Gospels.* London, 1955.

———. *The Names of Jesus.* London, 1959.

———. "The Origin of the Marcan Passion-Sayings," *NTS*, 1 (1954-55), 159-167.

———. *The Life and Ministry of Jesus.* New York, 1955.

———. "Modern Issues in Biblical Studies. Methods of Gospel Criticism," *ET*, 71 (1959-60), 68-72.

———. *New Testament Essays.* London, 1970.

———, and WINTER, P. "Sources of the Lucan Passion Narrative," *ET*, 68 (1956-57), 95.

TEEPLE, H. M. "The Origin of the Son of Man Christology," *JBL*, 84 (1965), 213-250.

TEMPLE, S. "The Two Traditions of the Last Supper, Betrayal, and Arrest," *NTS*, 7 (1960-61), 77-85.

THACKERAY, H. St. John. *The Septuagint and Jewish Worship: A Study in Origins,* 2nd ed. London, 1923.

THIEL, R. *Drei Markus-Evangelien.* Berlin, 1938.

THRALL, M. E. *Greek Particles in the New Testament. Linguistic and Exegetical Studies.* Leiden, 1962.

TÖDT, H. E. *The Son of Man in the Synoptic Tradition,* tr. Dorothea M. Barton from 2nd. Ger. ed. London, 1965.

TRILLING, W. *Das Wahre Israel.* Leipzig, 1959.

TURNER, C. H. "Marcan Usage: Notes, Critical and Exegetical on the Second Gospel," *JTS*, 25 (1924), 377-386; 26 (1925), 12-20, 145-156, 225-240, 337-346; 27 (1926), 58-62; 28 (1927), 9-30, 349-362; 29 (1928), 275-289, 346-361.

VAGANAY, L. "Matthieu (Évangile selon Saint)," *DBS*, V (Paris, 1957), col. 940-956.

VAN DEN BUSSCHE, H. "Si le grain de blé ne tombe en terre," *BVC*, 2, No. 5 1954), 53-67.

VAN DODEWAARD, J. "Die sprachliche Übereinstimmung zwischen Markus-Paulus und Markus-Petrus," *B*, 30 (1949), 91-108.

VANHOYE, A. "De 'aspectu' oblationis Christi secundum Epistolam ad Hebraeos," *VD*, 37 (1959), 32-38.

———. "Structure et théologie des récits de la Passion dans les évangiles synoptiques," *NRT*, 89 (1967), 135-163. English translation: *Structure and Theology of the Accounts of the Passion in the Synoptic Gospels*, tr. C. H. Giblin. Collegeville, 1967.

VERMES, G. "The Use of *bar nâsh/bar nâshâ* in Jewish Aramaic," in Matthew Black, *An Aramaic Approach to the Gospels and Acts*, 3rd ed. (Oxford, 1967), Appendix E, pp. 310-328.

VIELHAUER, P. "Gottesreich und Menschensohn in der Verkündigung Jesu," in *Festschrift für Günther Dehn*, ed. W. Schneemelcher (Neukirchen, 1957), pp. 51-79.

———. "Jesus und der Menschensohn. Zur Diskussion mit Heinz Eduard Tödt und Eduard Schweizer," *ZTK*, 60 (1963), 133-177.

VON CAMPENHAUSEN, H. F. *Die Idee des Martyriums in der alten Kirche.* Göttingen, 1936.

VOSTÉ, J. M. *De Passione et morte Jesu Christi.* Rome, 1937.

WEIDEL, K. "Studien über den Einfluss des Weissagungsbeweises auf die evangelische Geschichte," *TSK*, 23 (1910), 83-109, 163-195; 25 (1912), 167-286.

WEISS, B. *Die Quellen des Lukasevangeliums.* Stuttgart and Berlin, 1907.

WEISS, J. *Das älteste Evangelium.* Göttingen, 1903.

WELLHAUSEN, J. *Einleitung in die drei ersten Evangelien*, 2nd ed. Berlin 1911.

WENDLING, E. *Die Entstehung des Marcus-Evangeliums.* Tübingen, 1908.

WERNLE, P. *Die synoptische Frage.* Freiburg, Leipzig and Tübingen, 1899.

WILLIAMS, C. S. C. *Alterations to the Text of the Synoptic Gospels and Acts.* Oxford, 1951.

WINDISCH, H. *Der Hebräerbrief*, in *Handbuch zum Neuen Testament*, IV, 3 (Tübingen, 1913).

———. "Angelophanien um den Menschensohn auf Erden," *ZNW*, 30 (1931), 215-233.

———. "Joh 1, 51 und die Auferstehung Jesu," *ZNW*, 31 (1932), 199-204.

WINTER, P. "The Treatment of His Sources by the Third Evangelist in Luke XXI-XXIV," *ST*, 8 (1954), 138-172.

———. "On Luke and Lucan Sources," *ZNW*, 47 (1956), 217-242.

WOLFF, H. W. *Jesaja 53 im Urchristentum*, 3rd ed. Berlin, 1952.

WREDE, W. *Das Messiasgeheimnis in den Evangelien.* Göttingen, 1901.

ZERWICK, M. *Untersuchungen zum Markus-Sitl. Ein Beitrag zur stilistischen Durcharbeitung des Neuen Testaments.* Rome, 1937.

ZIMMERLI, W., and JEREMIAS, J. "Pais theou," *TDNT*, V (Grand Rapids, 1968), 654-717.

———. *The Servant of God.* London, 1957.

INTRODUCTION

The scope of this work is a methodical investigation of the account of Jesus' prayer between the Supper and the Arrest, as it is reported in the three synoptic gospels. In this respect it is an exegetical study.

Its purpose is to determine as closely as possible the specific meaning which the authors of these accounts intended them to bear in the context of their own gospels. In this respect it is a study in biblical theology.

The plan of the work is simple. Part One is a detailed consideration of the empirical data of our problem in each of the synoptic accounts, dealing with the questions of textual criticism, exegesis, and literary analysis.

Part Two is a theory of sources and redactions, which offers three explanatory hypotheses to answer the genetic questions raised by the data analyzed in Part One.

Part Three is a theological synthesis of the meaning of the synoptic accounts and their sources, based on the findings of Parts One and Two.

It has been our hope in writing this work on the synoptic Gethsemane that it may prove a contribution to the more detailed study of individual elements in the gospel passion tradition.

I wish to make grateful acknowledgment here to all those who have helped me in one way or another to bring this work to completion. I offer my sincerest thanks to Most Rev. Joseph T. McGucken, Archbishop of San Francisco, and to the Rector, staff and students of the North American College and the Graduate House in Rome, where I was living and working for the major portion of this research and writing. To my professors both at the Biblical Institute and the Gregorian University I am permanently indebted, particularly to Very Rev. Francis J. McCool, S. J., at the former, and most especially to my director at the latter, Rev. Donatien Mollat, S. J., whose painstaking and conscientious guidance was to me a model of how generous a truly great scholar can be in sharing the fruits of his own maturity and wisdom with an eager disciple. And finally to my family and friends, whose encouragement has always sustained me, I express once more my enduring gratitude.

PART ONE

ANALYSIS

CHAPTER ONE

LITERARY ANALYSIS OF MARK 14:32-42

Verse 32: *Kai erchontai eis chôrion hou to onoma Gethsemani, kai legei tois mathêtais autou: kathisate hôde heôs proseuxômai.*

Characteristic of Mark's style in his gospel is the simple linking in succession of sentences and sections by the use of paratactic *kai*.[1] This usage is so recurrent with him as to have been termed excessive, monotonous, and even vulgar.[2] In comparison with Matthew and Luke, Mark shows a clear preference not only for *kai* over *de* or *tote*, but more particularly for coordinate constructions generally over the use of participles or subordinating conjunctions.[3] There are twenty occurrences of paratactic *kai* in the eleven verses of his Gethsemane account, sixteen of them introducing clauses in the narrative. Zerwick defends the use of *kai* over *de* here as natural to the movement of the passage.[4] Yet in the parallels only ten of Matthew's clauses and

---

[1] John C. Hawkins, *Horae Synopticae. Contributions to the Study of the Synoptic Problem*, 2nd ed. (Oxford, 1909), pp. 14, 150-151; Rudolf Bultmann, *The History of the Synoptic Tradition*, tr. John Marsh (New York, 1963), p. 339.

[2] B.-D.-F., 442, 458; James Hope Moulton and Nigel Turner, *A Grammar of New Testament Greek*, III (Edinburg, 1963), 334.

[3] James Hope Moulton and Wilbert Francis Howard, *A Grammar of New Testament Greek*, II (Edinburgh, 1957), 420; Vincent Taylor, *The Gospel according to St. Mark*, 2nd ed. (London, 1966), pp. 48-49; and Max Zerwick, *Untersuchungen zum Markus-Stil* (Rome, 1937), p. 2, counts 591 *kai* to 113 *de* used as sentence-connectives in the narrative portions of Mark, considering each new finite verb a sentence. He rightly rejects Wohleb's attempt to differentiate Markan sources by the criterion of which particle predominates. For a comparison of the texts of Matthew and Luke with Mark on this point, see the lists provided in Paul Wernle, *Die synoptische Frage* (Freiburg, Leipzig and Tübingen, 1899), pp. 21-23, 150f.

[4] *Op. cit.*, pp. 4f. Mistakenly he has counted here only 15 *kai*-connectives instead of 16. Zerwick's "psychological" theory about Mark's use of *kai*

seven of Luke's are introduced by *kai,* and both employ more participles.

The question raised by this stylistic idiosyncrasy of Mark's is whether it is evidence simply of his own rudimentary Greek or else of Aramaic influence behind his text. For while parataxis is certainly more common in Aramaic than in literate Greek, Deissmann has shown from the Greek papyri that it is not really less common in popular Greek.[5] So the evidence leaves the question to be answered either way. Moulton points out that of itself the phenomenon demonstrates at most "elementary culture, and not the hampering presence of a foreign idiom that is being perpetually translated into its most literal equivalent."[6] Yet he maintains against Deissmann at least for Johannine parataxis that it must have been influenced by the LXX usage of *kai* for the Hebrew *waw*.[7] Taylor cautions against claiming Aramaic influence where there are not additional, less ambiguous indications of Aramaic usage in a passage.[8] But the general conformity of Markan parataxis to Semitic narrative style is recognized,[9] and Black, arguing particularly from the almost total absence of the hypotactic aorist participle construction in Mark, concludes that "Aramaic influence must have been a contributory factor."[10]

The verb *erchontai* introduces another notable feature of Mark's style, viz., his constant employment of the historical present tense, which is used in the brief compass of his gospel a proportionately higher number of times than in any other book of the LXX or the New Testament. Only the translator of I Samuel (151 instances) in the former and John (162 instances) in

---

and *de* is contested on linguistic grounds by Margaret E. Thrall, *Greek Particles in the New Testament. Linguistic and Exegetical Studies* (Leiden, 1962), pp. 50-63.

[5] Adolf Deissmann, *Light from the Ancient East,* tr. Lionel R. M. Strachan from the 4th German ed. (New York and London, [1927]), pp. 131-136.

[6] James Hope Moulton, *A Grammar of New Testament Greek,* 3rd ed., I (Edinburgh, 1957), 12.

[7] James Hope Moulton and George Milligan, *The Vocabulary of the Greek Testament* (Grand Rapids, 1960), p. 314; see also C. F. Burney, *The Aramaic Origin of the Fourth Gospel* (Oxford, 1922), p. 6.

[8] Taylor, *op. cit.,* p. 57.

[9] B.-D.-F., 458; Moulton and Turner, *op. cit.,* III, 334-335.

[10] Matthew Black, *An Aramaic Approach to the Gospels and Acts,* 3rd ed. (Oxford, 1967), pp. 61-69; quotation on p. 69. But to the contrary see E. P. Sanders, *The Tendencies of the Synoptic Tradition* (Cambridge, 1969), pp. 249-251.

the latter even approach Mark in frequency.[11] in Matthew the usage is much rarer, and in Luke almost nonoccurrent. Accordingly, it is worth remarking that, while Matthew's usage throughout his gospel coincides with Mark's in only twenty-one cases altogether, in the Gethsemane account alone he matches eight of Mark's nine verbs in the historical present.[12] Elsewhere he tends more frequently to substitute the aorist for Mark's historical present and imperfect tenses, although he does regularly employ *legei* and *legousin*.[13] Luke, despite classical precedents, consistently avoids Mark's historical present tenses (with the sole exception of Lk 8:49 / Mk 5:35), apparently regarding them as a vulgarism.[14] It has been suggested that the common use of the historical present in the New Testament developed as an equivalent to the participial sentence construction in Aramaic.[15] But the tense is found everywhere in classical and modern Greek, whether in cultured or common speech, in the papyri, the LXX or Josephus,[16] and so there is nothing particularly Semitic about it or even about its frequency in Mark and John.[17] It is little more than a vivid stylistic mannerism favored by some and avoided by others.[18] There is, moreover, a recognizable tendency in post-classical Greek to use it increasingly with verbs of speaking, seeing, coming, going, bringing, sending, and the like.[19] And this is reflected in the fact that nearly half of the occurrences in Mark, about three-fourths of those in Matthew, and two-thirds of those in Luke involve verbs of speaking.[20] After a careful study of the uses of the historical present in I Samuel, Thackeray comes to the following conclusion, which he also applies to Mark: "The main function is thus, I maintain, to introduce a date, a new

---

[11] Hawkins, *op. cit.*, pp. 143-144, 213-214.

[12] *Ibid.*, pp. 144-149, where in comparison with the 151 instances listed for Mark (none in the parables), 93 are listed for Matthew (15 of them in parables), and only 9 with certainty for Luke (5 of them in parables). Hawkins' statistics are based on the text of Westcott and Hort.

[13] Willoughby C. Allen, *A Critical and Exegetical Commentary on the Gospel according to S. Matthew*, 3rd ed. (Edinburgh, 1957), p. xx.

[14] Moulton, *op. cit.*, I, 121; B.-D.-F., 321.

[15] Willoughby C. Allen, "The Original Language of the Gospel according to Mark," *Exp*, 6th Ser., I (1900), 436-443; idem, "The Aramaic Element in St. Mark," *ET*, 13 (1901-02), 329; C. F. Burney, op. cit., pp. 87f.

[16] Moulton and Turner, *op. cit.*, III, 60-61.

[17] Black, *op. cit.*, p. 130.

[18] Moulton, *loc. cit.*; Saners, op. cit., pp. 253f.

[19] Moulton and Howard, *op. cit.*, II, 456-457; Moulton and Turner, *loc. cit.*

[20] See Hawkins, *loc. cit.*, and p. 148, n. 1.

scene, a new character, occasionally a new speaker; in other
words a fresh paragraph in the narrative." [21]   In a more detailed
study of Mark's own text Zerwick arrives at similar results. Noting the alternation between the historical present, aorist and
imperfect tenses within the individual narratives throughout the
gospel, he concludes that the prevailing pattern in Mark's use of
tenses is to adopt the present for his introduction and the past
for his continuation or conclusion. Thus verbs of coming, bringing, leading, gathering and the like at the beginning of a pericope
are generally in the present. When they are not, it is usually
because they are transitional or preparatory to a verb which
Mark regards as more properly initiating the action. Of particular interest is Zerwick's observation that in a few cases the
pattern is repeated, so that one gets the impression of two or
three fresh starts within a single pericope. The Gethsemane
narrative is a striking example with the three historical presents
of *erchesthai* in vv. 32, 37 and 41 (cf. 5: 35-43; 10: 23-31; 14: 26-31).[22]

Another peculiarity of *erchontai* here has been noted by C. H.
Turner. It is one of a number of third-person "impersonal"
plurals in Mark, followed by a singular verb (*legei*) and standing
possibly for the first-person plural of an original eyewitness account.[23] Taylor [24] and Cranfield [25] also recognize this possibility
without fully endorsing it. Black rejects it, preferring to see the
repetition of verbs in the third person which refer to subjects
already mentioned as characteristic of simple Semitic narrative.
Consequently, for him the construction proves no more than a
helpful criterion in some instances for determining the primitive
text of Mark.[26] It is a construction frequent in Mark but generally
avoided by Matthew and Luke, both of whom here have the
singular with Jesus as subject (Mt 26: 36; Lk 22: 39).

Mark's characterization of the place where this scene after
the supper occurs is *chôrion hou to onoma Gethsemani. Chôrion*

---

[21] Henry St. John Thackeray, *The Septuagint and Jewish Worship*, 2nd
ed. (London, 1923), pp. 20-22; quotation on p. 21; also quoted in Moulton and
Turner, *op. cit.*, III, 61-62.

[22] Zerwick, *op. cit.*, pp. 49-57. Moulton, *loc. cit.*, has observed in the
papyri an alternation between tenses within a single narrative similar to
that in Mark.

[23] C. H. Turner, "Marcan Usage: Notes, Critical and Exegetical, on the
Second Gospel," *JTS*, 26 (1924-25), 231.

[24] Taylor, *op. cit.*, pp. 47-48, 551.

[25] C. E. B. Cranfield, *The Gospel according to Mark* (Cambridge, 1959),
p. 430.

[26] Black, *op. cit.*, pp. 127-128.

means "a piece of land," "a field," and the meagerness of descriptive detail suggests what may have been "a (former) farmstead or country estate planted with olive trees."[27] For the name Gethsemane (Hebrew: *gat sh^emanim*) means "press of oils,"[28] and it is most natural to think of an olive-grove in this connection.[29] Likely enough it was now one of the private gardens on the outskirts of Jerusalem,[30] with perhaps an abandoned farm-building that could serve as a suitable refuge for Jesus and his disciples.[31] Grundmann conjectures that it may have belonged to the man in whose house Jesus had just eaten supper with his disciples.[32] Neither Luke nor John give the name Gethsemane. Both speak of it as a "place" (*topos*: Lk 22:40; Jn 18:2), which Luke (v. 39) identifies as in the vicinity of the Mount of Olives, a location agreeing with Mk 14:26, although, if 14:32-42 was an originally independent story, there is not necessarily any connection between vv. 26 and 32.[33] John (18:1) speaks of the place further as a "garden" (*kêpos*) located across the wady Kedron. Both he and Luke indicate that Jesus frequently went there with his disciples. Wellhausen observes that on this occasion Jesus' intention in leaving the house was more than simply prayer, since his disciples would not have had to accompany him for that.[34] And Montefiore suggests that perhaps he meant to avoid arrest, which he feared.[35] The latter supposition is reconcilable with the text of Mark or Matthew, but seems to be expressly excluded by the mention in Lk 22:39 of Jesus' custom, which Jn 18:2 treats as the basis for Judas' knowledge of his whereabouts.[36]

---

[27] Taylor, *loc. cit.*

[28] But see Joseph Klausner, *Jesus of Nazareth: his Life, Times and Teaching* (London, 1925), p. 330, n. 5, for another derivation.

[29] B. H. Branscomb, *The Gospel of Mark*, 5th ed. (London, 1948), p. 267.

[30] Henry Barclay Swete, *The Gospel according to St. Mark*, 2nd ed. (London, 1902), p. 341.

[31] Ernst Haenchen, *Der Weg Jesu. Eine Erklärung des Markus-Evangeliums und der kanonischen Parallelen*, 2nd ed. (Berlin, 1968), p. 489, n. 1.

[32] W. Grundmann, *Das Evangelium des Markus* (Berlin, 1959), p. 291.

[33] Dennis Eric Nineham, *The Gospel of St Mark* (Baltimore, 1963), p. 391. And see below Chapter 4.

[34] J. Wellhausen, *Das Evangelium Marci* (Berlin, 1903), p. 127.

[35] C. G. Montefiore, *The Synoptic Gospels* (London, 1927), I, 343.

[36] The close affinities of Luke and John in their passion narratives and elsewhere have led scholars to postulate a tradition of some sort shared by them in common, just as the affinities of Mark and Matthew have led to a similar supposition for them. See, for example, Xavier Léon-Dufour, "Passion (Récits de la)," *DBS*, VI (Paris, 1960), col. 1439-44, 1448, 1454, 1473; and also Julius Schniewind, *Die Parallelperikopen bei Lukas und Joannes*,

Today the exact location of Gethsemane itself can only be conjectured. The site usually pointed out has been traditional only since 326 A.D., when the Empress Helena visited Jerusalem. But long before that all traces of a grove or garden would have been destroyed when, according to Josephus' account in *Bellum Judaicum* VI.I.1, Titus cut down all the trees on that side of the city and when no Christians remained in Jerusalem to preserve a reliable tradition of the site.[37]

The disciples to whom Jesus addresses the words *kathisate hôde heôs proseuxômai* must, according to v. 33, be the eight from whom Jesus separates himself along with the trusted three.[38] Though invited to stay where he leaves them, they play no further role until the arrest.[39] Jesus seeks neither their company nor their support, but turns instead to solitary prayer.[40] *Heôs proseuxômai*[41] may mean either "while I pray"[42] or "until I have prayed."[43] But the difference in meaning is not significant. Jesus seems accustomed elsewhere in Mark's gospel to withdrawing from his disciples to pray alone, e.g., in 1:33 and 6:46. So there is reason enough for him do so here.[44]

2nd ed. (Hildesheim, 1958); John Amedee Bailey, *The Traditions Common to the Gospels of Luke and John* (Leiden, 1963); E. Osty, "Les points de contact entre le récit de la passion dans Saint Luc et Saint Jean," in *Mélanges Jules Lebreton*, I (Paris, 1951-52), 146-154; Peder Borgen, "John and the Synoptics in the Passion Narrative," *NTS*, 5 (1958-59), 246-259.

[37] A. Plummer, *The Gospel according to St. Mark* (Cambridge, 1914), p. 326. For background and description of the presently recognized site, see Francesco M. Uricchio and Gaetano M. Stano, *Vangelo secondo San Marco* (Turin, 1966), pp. 583f.

[38] So Swete, Plummer, *loc. cit.*, and Erich Klostermann, *Das Markusevangelium* (Tübingen, 1950), p. 150.

[39] Haenchen, *op. cit.*, p. 490, n. 2.

[40] F. Hauck, *Das Evangelium des Markus* (Leipzig, 1931), p. 173.

[41] The indicative is read by D Γ Θ Ψ 13. 108. 209. 700 *al.* But for *heôs* with the subjunctive and without *an* see B.-D.-F., 383 (2).

[42] So Lagrange and Taylor *ad loc.*

[43] So Plummer and Klostermann *ad loc.*

[44] See Swete, *loc. cit.*; Allan Menzies, *The Earliest Gospel: a Historical Study of the Gospel according to Mark* (London, 1901), p. 257; Ernst Lohmeyer, *Das Evangelium des Markus* (Göttingen, 1963), p. 314; Joachim Jeremias, "Das Gebetsleben Jesu," *ZNW*, 25 (1926), 130-131; *idem, The Prayers of Jesus* (London, 1967), pp. 73, 75.

Verse 33: *Kai paralambanei ton Petron kai ton Iakôbon kai ton Iôannên met' autou, kai êrxato ekthambeisthai kai adêmonein.*

As Loisy and Bultmann have remarked, v. 33 seems a doublet of v. 32.[45] In any case, the three disciples are specially singled out here, as in 1:29, 5:37, 9:2, and 13:33. Luke and John omit the names of the disciples, just as they omit the name of the place.[46] If we read the definite article before each name,[47] then the observation of Swete[48] has some force that Mark thereby "sets each individuality before the mind separately," while Mt 26:37 gives the prominence to Peter. Montefiore[49] follows Loisy[50] here in regarding the separation of the three disciples as historically doubtful as in the transfiguration episode and considering a special Petrine source for the particulars as improbable. If that is so, we have all the more reason to ask why in Mark's account Jesus should separate the three from the rest only to leave them immediately afterwards. Plummer[51] suggests that he took them for sympathy and understanding; Cranfield[52] for company in his anguish and loneliness and to witness his temptation and obedience; and for Hauck[53] they are to witness his most intimate emotions, though not to help or console him in any way. Haenchen[54] objects to this line of explanation in Cranfield as taking too much for granted by presupposing the historicity of the account, a psychologizing interest on the part of Mark, and a complete foreknowledge on the part of Jesus of his temptation and victory. Lohmeyer[55] and Grundmann[56] suggest,

---

[45] Klostermann, p. 150. The significance of this fact will become clear below in Chapter 4.

[46] Julius Schniewind, *Das Evangelium nach Markus* (Göttingen, 1952), p. 186.

[47] There is strong evidence for both possible readings. The definite article is repeated before the names of James and John in B A W Ψ Fam. 13 *al*; it is omitted by ℵ C ⅁ D Γ Θ Φ 0112. 0116 *pm*.

[48] *Op. cit.*, p. 342.

[49] *Op. cit.*, p. 343.

[50] Alfred Loisy, *Les Évangiles synoptiques* (Ceffonds, 1907-08), II, 560.

[51] *Op. cit.*, p. 326.

[52] *Op. cit.*, pp. 430f.

[53] *Op. cit.*, p. 173.

[54] *Loc. cit.*

[55] *Op. cit.*, p. 314.

[56] *Op. cit.*, p. 291.

after the analogies in 5:35-43 and 9:2-10, that the three who up to now had shared in the greatest and most secret revelations again accompany him to receive a revelation hidden from the community. Yet, as Nineham [57] points out, Jesus' prayer is hardly a revelation and the sleeping disciples may not even have heard it. And so on this supposition we are driven to ask if perhaps their lack of faith and understanding has not *prevented* some revelation. More than Jesus' need for human companionship seems to be at stake, but in the end we may be able to do no more than admit with Taylor that why Jesus took the three is simply not indicated further than that they are bidden to watch (v. 34) and pray (v. 38).[58]

But if the disciples receive no revelation of Jesus' divine glory, they certainly learn something of the secret of his humanity. For at that point he "began to be greatly distressed and troubled" (RSV). The verb *êrxa(n)to* is often used by Mark with the infinitive in an auxiliary sense, but here it seems to preserve its strong sense of "began." [59] Indeed what followed was altogether "a new experience in emotional suffering — mingled amazement and terror." [60] Swete's description cannot be bettered: "The Lord was overwhelmed with sorrow (see next verse), but his first feeling was one of terrified surprise. Long as he had foreseen the Passion, when it came clearly into view its terrors exceeded his anticipations. His human soul received a new experience — *emathen aph' hôn epathen*, and the last lesson of obedience began with a sensation of inconceivable awe. With this there came another, that of overpowering mental distress — *êrxato ... adêmonein. ... Adêmonein* forms a natural sequel to *ekthambeisthai*, representing the distress which follows a great shock, 'the confused, restless, half-distracted state' (Lightfoot) which may be worse than the sharp pain of a fully realized sorrow." [61]

The two infinitives, then, express the strongest possible emotion.[62] *Ekthambeisthai* "denotes being in the grip of a shudder-

---

[57] *Op. cit.*, p. 391.

[58] *Op. cit.*, p. 552. But cf. Hans Jürgen Ebeling, *Das Messiasgeheimnis und die Botschaft des Marcus-Evangelisten* (Berlin, 1939), pp. 174-176.

[59] M.-J. Lagrange, *Évangile selon Saint Marc* (Paris, 1929), p. xciii; J. W. Hunkin, " 'Pleonastic' *archomai* in the New Testament," *JTS*, 25 (1923-24), 394; Taylor, *Mark*, p. 48.

[60] Plummer, *op. cit.*, p. 327.

[61] *Op. cit.*, p. 342.

[62] S. E. Johnson, *A Commentary on the Gospel according to St. Mark* (London, 1960), p. 235: "The words ... are so strong that it is difficult to

ing horror in the face of the dreadful prospect before him." [63]
And *adêmonein* 'to be in anguish,' which occurs in the N. T. only
here, in the Mt parallel, and in Phil 2:26, if it derives after Bultmann's suggestion from the root *a-dêm* 'apart from people,' emphasizes the loneliness of Jesus culminating in the final loneliness
of his death.[64] We are not to see in the depth and intensity of
this emotion any sign of mental illness.[65] Rather we should
recognize that Mark is unafraid to depict Jesus with such overpowering emotions, does not see them as a fault, and, if anything,
seems to be relying upon the most personal recollections of the
event on the part of someone who was there.[66] The very boldness
of the description is its best claim to authenticity. Matthew
weakens it and Luke omits it altogether. Taylor's estimate is
compelling: "With every desire to avoid unwarranted psychological interpretations, it is impossible to do any kind of justice to
Mark's words without seeing in them something of the astonish-
ment of the Son of Man who knows He is also the Suffering
Servant of Isa. liii. It is too little observed that the description
and the saying which follows belong to the brief interval before
Jesus leaves His three disciples. The intensity of the anguish
drives Him from them to seek peace before the face of His
Father." [67] Jesus' anguish and horror are depicted not like the
stories of Jewish or Christian martyrs but in accordance with
the gospel passion predictions. Not stoically, but biblically Jesus
enters into the suffering he shares with men as willed by God.[68]

---

express them in English." - Johannes Weiss, *Die Schriften des Neuen Testaments,* I (Göttingen, 1907), p. 209: "Markus wohl sagen: Jesus war wie
betäubt von Schmerz." - Lagrange, *Marc,* p. 387: "La pensée de la passion
se présente avec une telle force, que Jésus en est surpris et terrifié. Au
lieu de réagir fortemente, il est comme désemparé." - Lohmeyer, *Markus,*
p. 314: "Die griechischen Wörter malen den aüssersten Grad eines grenzen-
losen Entsetzens und Leidens."
  [63] Cranfield, *op. cit.,* p. 431.
  [64] Grundmann, *op. cit.,* pp. 291f.
  [65] Klostermann, *op. cit.,* p. 150.
  [66] Hauck, *loc. cit.*
  [67] *Op. cit.,* p. 552.
  [68] Eduard Schweizer, *Das Evangelium nach Markus* (Göttingen, 1967),
p. 179.

Verse 34: *Kai legei autois: perilypos estin hê psychê mou heôs thanatou; meinate hôde kai grêgoreite.*

In this lament of Jesus are clearly recognizable echoes of the O. T., particularly of the Psalms (Ps 42:5, 6, 11; 43:5; 116:3), which the singing of the Hallel shortly before (Mk 14:26) may have spontaneously suggested.[69] Jesus finds himself in the same situation as the Psalmist, although he speaks these words to his disciples, not to God.[70] They express the strongest contrast between the distress of Jesus here and the joyful courage of the Jewish and Christian martyrs.[71]

Heôs thanatou is usually taken as a reference to Jon 4: 3-9, but E. Klostermann cites also Judg 16:16; 3 Kings 19:4; Sir 37:2; and Hauck adds Sir 51:6. The expression has been understood in a variety of ways.[72] The most obvious and at the same time the most trivial interpretation is a temporal sense, like the Vulgate translation *usque ad mortem* 'until death.'[73] A second interpretation gives a sense more of degree than of time, rendered by an expression like "sad to death" in English and meaning a sorrow as great as it can be only at the moment of death.[74] But

---

[69] Robert Horton Gundry, *The Use of the Old Testament in St. Matthew's Gospel with Special Reference to the Messianic Hope* (Leiden, 1967), p. 59. He remarks further that dependence on the LXX here seems clear both from the rarity of *perilypos* there and from the fact that the Hebrew verb means "to be bowed (or cast) down" (*loc. cit.*). Augustin George, "Jésus et les psaumes," in *A la rencontre de Dieu. Mémorial Albert Gelin* (Le Puy, 1961), pp. 297-308, studying the manner in which Jesus cites the Psalms, suggests that here "la brièveté et la liberté de la référence sont des indices favorables à son attribution à Jésus" (p. 305).

[70] Lohmeyer, *op. cit.*, p. 314.

[71] Cranfield, *op. cit.*, p. 431.

[72] Jean Héring has considered a good number of translations and interpretations in two articles: "Simples remarques sur la prière à Gethsémané," *RHPR*, 39 (1959), 97-102; and "Zwei exegetische Probleme in der Perikope von Jesus in Gethsemane," *Neotestamentica et Patristica* (Leiden, 1962), pp. 64-69. The second article is a revision of the first with some additional materials. For convenience we adopt his designations.

[73] So, for example, A. Schlatter, *Der Evangelist Matthäus*, 6th ed. (Stuttgart, 1963), p. 751.

[74] So Theodor Kardinal Innitzer, *Kommentar zur Leidens- und Verklärungsgeschichte Jesu Christi* (Vienna, 1948), p. 123; and perhaps Hauck, *Markus*, p. 173: "Er so traurig ist wie einer, der sich dem Tode nahe weiss." See also A. H. McNeile, *The Gospel according to St. Matthew* (London, 1915), p. 390.

the majority of exegetes find themselves choosing between a third and fourth interpretation, which Héring calls a consecutive and a final sense respectively. The consecutive sense is given in English by "so sad I could die," and means a sorrow that can bring on death. Thus Swete speaks of "a sorrow that well-nigh kills,"[75] and Taylor of "a sorrow which threatens life itself."[76] J. Weiss thinks this is to be preferred to the final sense, because Jesus would not have shuddered before death if he desired to die.[77] Montefiore[78] and Nineham[79] think either a consecutive or final sense likely. The final sense may be rendered in English by "so sad I want to die," and means a sorrow that brings with it the desire for death. Wellhausen, E. Klostermann, Lohmeyer, Grundmann, E. Schweizer, and Bultmann all prefer this last interpretation.[80] Héring prefers it too, because it is clearly the meaning of the expression *lelypêmai heôs thanatou* in the context of Jon 4:3-9, the passage lying behind Mk 14:34. But he contends that no one up to now has successfully met the objection that

---

[75] *Op. cit.*, p. 342.   So also Ezra P. Gould, *A Critical and Exegetical Commentary on the Gospel according to St. Mark* (Edinburgh, 1907), p. 269: "*My sorrow is killing me*, is the thought; *it is crushing the life out of me.*"

[76] *Op. cit.*, p. 553.

[77] J. Weiss, *Die Schriften des N. T.*, p. 209.   See also H. A. W. Meyer, *Critical and Exegetical Handbook to the Gospel of Matthew* (Edinburgh, 1879), II, 219; Paul Schanz, *Commentar über das Evangelium des heiligen Matthäus* (Freiburg, 1879), p. 520; Paul Gaechter, *Das Matthäus Evangelium* (Innsbruck, 1963), p. 864; A. E. J. Rawlinson, *The Gospel according to St. Mark*, 7th ed. (London, 1949), p. 211; Josef Schmid, *Das Evangelium nach Markus*, 5th ed. (Regensburg, 1963), p. 275; and Uricchio and Stano, *op. cit.*, p. 585.

[78] *Op. cit.*, p. 343.

[79] *Op. cit.*, p. 391.

[80] Wellhausen, p. 127: "*Heôs thanatou* (1 Reg. 19,4 Jon. 4,9) = so dass ich tot sein möchte.   Der Tod selber ist nicht das Schreckliche, sonder was vorausgeht und dazu führt." - E. Klostermann, p. 150: "Das *heôs thanatou* ist nicht = 'als ob der Tod mir nahte,' sondern nach Jud 16,16 III Regn 19,4 Sir 37,2 = 'so dass ich lieber tot sein möchte'." - Lohmeyer, p. 314: "Was kann das anderes sagen, als dass der Tod hier der ersehnte Freund ist, der 'Seine Seele' von der Last dieser unsäglichen Trauer befreit?" - Grundmann, p. 292: "Der Grund seiner Trauer und seiner Angst ist nicht der Tod allein, da er sich den Tod als Erlösung aus Trauer und Angst wünscht."   He echoes Klostermann against J. Weiss and Cullmann. - E. Schweizer, p. 179: " 'Bis zum Tod' ... bedeutet: 'so, dass ich lieber schon tot wäre'." - Rudolf Bultmann, *TDNT*, IV (Grand Rapids, 1967), 323, n. 1: "The meaning is obvious: 'to be so full of sorrow that I would rather be dead,' not 'of sorrow which leads to death,' or 'which lasts until death,' or even 'as if death were approaching'."

such a meaning is contradicted by the following verses in which Jesus prays to be delivered from death. The incompatibility is resolved, he suggests, if the fear of death in vv. 35-36 is taken as Jesus' horror at the prospect of crucifixion and the desire for death in v. 34 is taken with his prayer as a petition for deliverance *here and now* through a peaceful death in Gethsemane before his arrest. In this supposition fear and desire are mutually reconcilable, and *heôs thanatou* can bear the same meaning it does in the context of Jon 4. And thus the final temptation, which Jesus overcame in prayer to his Father, was the wish for peaceful and premature deliverance from his fate.[81]

Daube offers some support for this position by tracing the picture of Jesus presented here by Mark back to the O. T. tradition of the "weary prophet," of which Moses, Elijah, Jeremiah and Jonah are the principal examples in lamenting their life and praying for the deliverance of death.[82] "The words spoken by Jesus," he writes, "are in a tradition; and they express such deep despair that we must not deny a trace of the idea of death being a desirable release from life in this condition, cornered by the enemy, about to be abandoned by the most cherished friends."[83]

The combination of aorist and present imperatives in the phrase *meinate hôde kai grêgoreite* is odd but explicable. The first is a completed linear action regarded as a whole, expressed through a complexive aorist,[84] and having a meaning like "don't go away." The second is an action hanging in the balance, expressed through a present imperative with durative force,[85] and having a meaning like "be on guard constantly." According to Taylor,[86] the senses distinguish a definite act from an abiding attitude. "They were at once to cease from accompanying him, and were to continue to be watchful," writes Plummer;[87] and Lagrange[88] expresses the meaning similarly.

In contrast with the eight other disciples, who were only told to stay where he left them, Jesus tells the three to "watch."

---

[81] Héring (see above p. 14, n. 72), *RHPR*, pp. 99-101; *Neotestamentica et Patristica*, pp. 65-69.

[82] Cf. Num 11:14-15; I Kings 19:4; Jer 15:10; 20:14-18; Jon 4:3-9.

[83] David Daube, "Death as Release in the Bible," *NT*, 5 (1962), 94-98; quotation on p. 98.

[84] B.-D.-F., 332 (1).

[85] *Idem*, 336 (1).

[86] *Op. cit.*, p. 553.

[87] *Op. cit.*, p. 327.

[88] *Op. cit.*, p. 387.

Clearly the command to watch is in opposition to the disciples' later sleep. But the precise reason for this command has been variously explained. Menzies [89] and E. Klostermann [90] claim that he asked them to watch only so that he might have their companionship as sympathetic friends. Montefiore [91] and Johnson [92] see them as companions who were also to warn him of the approach of intruders. But Lohmeyer objects that if that were the reason, Jesus would have given the command to the eight, not just the three; and he concludes, like Swete,[93] that he wanted them to be witnesses of the prayer which followed.[94] Swete and E. Schweizer [95] are surely right in pointing out that the command to watch must be allowed more than its literal meaning of "stay awake." It denotes as well a readiness of spirit in the face of crisis and temptation, even though this sense derives from the later community (cf. Mk 13:34-37). But Cranfield [96] is right, too, in criticizing C. K. Barrett for holding that *grêgoreite* means "not that they were not to go to sleep, but that they were to look out for the *parousia*." [97] This is stretching for meanings too far outside the context. When the context itself is examined more closely however, a further meaning does appear: the meaning of the Passover night watch. And it gives us perhaps the most satisfactory explanation of Jesus' exhortation to the disciples to watch and his disappointment at their failure. Understanding the Last Supper as a Passover meal,[98] we must recognize that Mark has meant to join the Gethsemane scene with it by means of the singing of the Hallel on the way to the Mount of Olives (14:26). According to Ex 12:42, the Passover night "was a night of watching by the Lord." And Mark, by joining the two scenes, is calling attention to the fact that they form part of the same celebration.[99] On their arrival at Gethsemane, then, Jesus

---

[89] *Op. cit.*, p. 257.

[90] *Op. cit.*, p. 150.

[91] *Op. cit.*, p. 344.

[92] *Op. cit.*, p. 235.

[93] *Op. cit.*, p. 343.

[94] *Op. cit.*, p. 314.

[95] *Op. cit.*, p. 180.

[96] *Op. cit.*, p. 432.

[97] C. K. Barrett, "Important Hypotheses Reconsidered - The Holy Spirit and the Gospel Tradition," *ET*, 67 (1955-56), 144.

[98] See Joachim Jeremias, *The Eucharistic Words of Jesus*, tr. Norman Perrin, 3rd ed. with the author's rev. to July 1964 (London, 1966), pp. 15-84.

[99] P. S. Minear, *Saint Mark* (London, 1963), p. 123.

and his disciples still formed a company united for the celebration of the Passover, a *ḥabhura*, which according to Rabbinic rules could remain intact even if some of them dozed, but not if they fell into deep sleep.[100] Jesus' command to watch, then, has in this context a very specific meaning. It is an exhortation to his disciples to maintain the Passover union: "they should not let the *ḥabhura* come to an early close." [101] The prayer of Jesus which follows shows what was meant by this "night of watching by the Lord." The sleep of the disciples shows what faithless servants they are (Mk 13:33-37), unready for deliverance.[102]

Verse 35: *Kai proelthôn mikron epipten epi tês gês, kai proseucheto hina ei dynaton estin parelthê ap' autou hê hôra.*

The meaning of the expression *proelthôn mikron*[103] here is that Jesus separated himself from his disciples, but only by a short distance — not "for a short time" — to begin his prayer. Menzies,[104] Plummer[105] and Lagrange[106] all see this as proof that the disciples could see and hear Jesus at prayer. J. Weiss[107] argues to the contrary that the sleepy or sleeping disciples could not have heard him; or if they had, they could not have slept. But it can be doubted whether the phrase was ever intended to resolve such a question. Lohmeyer points instead to the O. T. parallels: Abraham, who directs his attendants to stay where they are while he draws apart with Isaac to pray (Gen 22:5); Moses, who leaves the elders behind while he climbs Mount Sinai

---

[100] S.-B., I (Munich, 1965), 969-970 (on Mt 25:5).

[101] David Daube, *The New Testament and Rabbinic Judaism* (London, 1956), pp. 332-335; quotation on p. 334. Roger Le Déaut, *La nuit pascale*, Analecta Biblica 22 (Rome, 1963), p. 286, n. 70, quotes J. van Goudoever, *Biblical Calendars*, p. 160: "The Synoptic Gospels tell of the night-watch which Jesus held with his disciples in Gethsemane on the Mount of Olives. This night-watch is in fact the Passover night." See also John Bowman, *The Gospel of Mark. The New Christian Jewish Passover Haggadah* (Leiden, 1965), pp. 277f.

[102] Minear, *op. cit.*, p. 124.

[103] The reading *proselthôn* is also well attested, but makes no sense here.

[104] *Op. cit.*, pp. 257f.

[105] *Op. cit.*, p. 327.

[106] *Op. cit.*, p. 387.

[107] *Op. cit.*, p. 209.

alone to pray (Ex 24:2, 14); and the High Priest, who leaves his attendants before the veil of the Temple while he alone climbs the steps to the Holy of Holies (Lev 16:17). In each of these cases, as in the case of Jesus at Gethsemane, Lohmeyer sees the hour of a God-given task to be performed or revelation to be received.[108] But there is no demonstrable correlation between these O. T. examples and Mark's Gethsemane scene. For one thing, the absence of *proerchomai* from any of these texts leaves us with no strict verbal correspondence.[109] And for another, where *proerchomai* does occur in the Scriptures, it is not employed to set the stage for any special task or revelation.[110] So Lohmeyer's opinion is without linguistic foundation in respect to Mark. In Matthew's text, on the other hand, there are firmer philological grounds for recognizing a parallel.[111]

Menzies [112] takes the imperfect tenses *epipten* [113] and *proseucheto* of duration. But they are better understood of repeated action: Jesus fell to the earth again and again, praying his prayer over and over.[114] The very vividness of the image thus evoked may have been what suggested the further use of the imperfect to Swete: [115] namely, the imperfect used to describe a scene as taking place under the eyes of the narrator. Lagrange [116] follows Swete in adopting this sense; but Taylor [117] hesitates, although

---

[108] *Op. cit.*, p. 315.

[109] The comparable verbs in Gen 22 are *poreuomai* (vv. 3, 6, 8) and *dierchomai* (v. 5); in Ex 24 *anabainô* (vv. 1, 9, 12, 13, 15, 18) and *eiserchomai* (v. 18); and in Lev 16 *eisporeuomai* (vv. 2, 17, 23) and *eiserchomai* (v. 3).

[110] Cf. for the LXX Gen 33:3, 14; Jdt 2:19; 12:15; 15:13; Est 1:1e; Pr 8:24; Sir 32(35):10; 2 Macc 4:34; 14:21; 3 Macc 2:26; 4 Macc 4:6; and for the N. T. Mt 26:39 (= Mk 14:35); Mk 6:33; Lk 1:17; 22:47; Acts 12:10, 13; 20:5, 13; 2 Cor 9:5.

[111] See below Chapter 2 on Mt 26:36. And cf. the remark of Uricchio and Stano, *op. cit.*, p. 583, to the effect that Lohmeyer's references here show more erudition than relevance.

[112] *Loc. cit.*

[113] The aorist *epesen*, or still more obviously *epesen epi prosôpon*, is an inferior reading suggested by Mt par.

[114] So Paul Schanz, *Commentar über das Evangelium des heiligen Marcus* (Freiburg im Breisgau, 1881), p. 390; Bernahrd Weiss, *Das Marcusevangelium und seine synoptischen Parallelen* (Berlin, 1872), p. 459; Loisy, *Évangiles synoptiques*, II, p. 563, n. 2; Plummer, *Mark*, p. 327. For the linking of *piptô* with attitudes of worship and prayer elsewhere in the N. T., see Wilhelm Michaelis, "*Piptô, ktl.*," *TDNT*, VI (Grand Rapids, 1968), 163.

[115] *Op. cit.*, p. 343.

[116] *Op. cit.*, p. 387.

[117] *Op. cit.*, p. 553.

he admits that it finds support in the Greek grammars of Winer-Moulton and Robertson. Jesus' attitude of prostration in prayer suggests the most humble and intense supplication (cf. Gen 17:3, 17; Lk 5:8,12; 17:16), and all the more so as it was a repeated gesture.[118]

V. 35b and v. 36 are doublets of the prayer of Jesus, content.[119] Wellhausen's remark [120] that the direct adds nothing the former reporting indirectly and the latter directly its to the indirect form proves injustified in the exegesis. And the notion shared by Lohmeyer, Taylor and Cranfield that v. 35 is some kind of preparation for the words of Christ quoted in v. 36 is singularly weak and unenlightening. In any case, the doublet does not recur in the synoptic parallels. Haenchen [121] notes the sharp contrast between the words of the prayer and the cool precision of the Passion predictions. Jesus must believe that it is possible for God to save him from the hour that lies ahead. And so the condition *ei dynaton estin* is not a doubt

---

[118] The picture of repeated prostrations implied in the verb form *epipten* is not without parallel in the Rabbinic literature. Rabbi J^ehuda (ca. 150) said of Rabbi Aqiba (d. ca. 135): "Wenn er aber für sich allein betete, konnte man ihn auf dieser Seite liegend verlassen, u. wenn man wiederkam, fand man ihn auf der andern Seite wegen der verschiedenen Arten des Niederkniens u. des Sichniederwerfens..., die er auszufüren pflegte." See S.-B., II, 260.

[119] For the significance of these and other doublets discernible in Mark's Gethsemane account see below Chapter 4. Rudolf Bultmann, *The History of the Synoptic Tradition* (New York, 1963), p. 312f., points out a tendency in the development of the gospel narrative material toward transposing indirect reports into direct speech. Without denying the tendency E. P. Sanders, *op. cit.*, (see above p. 6, n. 10), pp. 256-262, has shown that Bultmann's evidence is incomplete and one-sided. There are seven instances where Matthew has indirect for Mark's direct speech, and fifteen where he has direct for Mark's indirect speech. And the case is just the opposite for Luke, who has eleven instances of indirect for Mark's direct speech, and only six instances of direct for Mark's indirect speech. Within the gospel of Mark itself Bultmann mentions two examples besides the present case where an indirect report has a parallel in direct discourse: cf. Mk 6:34/8:2; 15:37/15:34. We might note as well Mk 8:31 as compared to 9:31 and 10:33f. But none of these verses is in immediate sequence like Mk 14:35f., and perhaps the only genuine analogy to the Gethsemane prayer is in Mk 6:8-11, where the first two verses give an indirect report and the last two (introduced like 14:36 by the formula *kai elegen*) give a direct quotation of Jesus' mission charge to the disciples.

[120] *Op. cit.*, pp. 127f.

[121] *Op. cit.*, p. 491.

of God's power, but an expression of his willing subordination to the divine plan.[122]   Schniewind [123] remarks perceptively how this condition has slipped unintentionally, as it were, into direct discourse.   And Matthew, when he rewrites v. 36, takes it over in preference to the *panta dynata soi* he found there.   Branscomb [124] cannot see insisting too much on the verbal accuracy of the prayer, since for him v. 35 merely sums up the recollections of the disciples.   For Wellhausen the prayer is no more than a surmise on the part of the disciples, to whom Jesus had revealed his despondency but who did not hear the prayer at all.   And for J. Weiss, followed by Montefiore,[125] the words of the prayer belong to neither Jesus nor the disciples, but are the result of Mark's successful attempt to express the demands of the situation: "Die natürlichste Annahme is doch wohl, dass Jesus wortlos gebetet habe." [126]

The "hour" here probably came into common speech from the language of astrology (= "the hour of fate"), as Wellhausen [127] and E. Klostermann [128] suggest.   But it had passed through a long development in Jewish apocalyptic-eschatological traditions before Jesus took it on his lips in prayer, and through a still further development in Christian tradition before Mark used it with the resonance it possesses in his context.   "Hour" as an eschatological term occurs more frequently in Daniel than in any other O. T. book, usually in the form *hôra (tês) synteleias* (8:17, 19; 11:35, 40, 45), signifying the apocalyptic hour of catastrophe and fulfilment.   Jesus uses it as suitable to express the time for the fulfilment of his Messianic destiny.[129]   In Christian usage the "hour" becomes an almost technical term for the time of salvation,[130] so much so that Nineham [131] feels the occurrence of the expression in a prayer of Jesus raises a question.   But this question is resolved if Jesus took the term over from Jewish apocalyptic tradition, even though Mark's account cannot but Chris-

---

[122] So Lagrange, p. 387; Klostermann, p. 150; Grundmann, p. 292.
[123] *Op. cit.*, p. 186.
[124] *Op. cit.*, p. 268.
[125] *Op. cit.*, p. 344.
[126] *Op. cit.*, p. 209.
[127] *Op. cit.*, p. 128.
[128] *Op. cit.*, p. 150.
[129] *Taylor*, p. 553; Cranfield, p. 432; Grundmann, p. 292.
[130] Rawlinson, p. 212.   See Mk 1:15; 13:32; Lk 22:14, 53; and especially Jn 2:4; 7:30; 8:20; 12:23, 27; 13:1; 16:21; 17:1.
[131] *Op. cit.*, p. 392.

tianize the meaning. Even within the brief compass of the account, however, Mark's use of the term is not univocal: the technical meaning in vv. 35 and 41 must be distinguished from the literal use of *hôra* 'an hour's time' in v. 37. But if the "hour" of v. 35 is the hour of eschatological fulfilment, how can Jesus pray that it should pass him by? Lohmeyer [132] suggests that this question is answered only at v. 41, where it become clear that the eschatological hour is also the hour of the Son of Man's betrayal into the hands of sinners. Jesus prays, then, not simply to be spared the sufferings of the approaching hour,[133] but to be delivered according to the Father's will from the hands of those to whom he is betrayed.

> Verse 36:   *Kai elegen: Abba ho patêr, panta dynata soi; parenengke to potêrion touto ap' emou; all' ou ti egô thelô alla ti sy.*

Once again the imperfect tense *elegen* shows that the prayer of Jesus is repeated over and over again. Possibly too, according to Swete's previous suggestion, Mark continues to echo the vivid eyewitness account of his source. B. Weiss [134] holds that, although the prayer which follows may not contain all that Jesus said on his first withdrawal, yet it does contain this one saying heard by the disciples and used by the evangelist to fill out the content of repeated prayers (e.g., v. 39).

The Aramaic-Greek expression *abba ho patêr* occurs in the N. T. only here and in Rom 8:15 and Gal 4:6. In all three places it is obviously meant as a prayer formula, though only here is it reported as the direct address of Jesus to his Father. The exact genesis of *abba* even as a profane form of address is disputed. Most commonly it has been taken as the Aramaic emphatic state, a determinative form (= "the father") serving as a vocative or vocative possessive in the place of *abbi* (vocative possessive with first person singular pronominal suffix), which had

---

[132] *Op. cit.*, p. 315.

[133] So B. Weiss, p. 459; Swete, p. 343; Lagrange, pp. 387f.; and R. S. Barbour, "Gethsemane in the Tradition of the Passion," *NTS*, 16 (1970), 233, who suggests the prayer "might also imply that God should use other means altogether, through which he, Jesus, would be not so much vindicated as simply put to one side."

[134] *Loc. cit.*

fallen out of use.[135]   But Joachim Jeremias claims that the process
was just the reverse of that.   First of all, he argues, the emphatic
state in Aramaic is not *abba*, but *abha*.[136]   Secondly, *abba* is not
a determinative but an exclamatory form, without suffix or
inflection,[137] deriving ultimately from the language of children.
Even before N. T. times it had replaced both the form *abhi*, in
its vocative and non-vocative (i.e., with first person singular suffix) uses, and the emphatic state *abha*.   Thus by Jesus' time
abba had become the common family address of the father, not
only among the small children but even among the adults.[138]   The
significance of the word in Jesus' prayer derives from the fact
that i̇ nall the literature of Palestinian Judaism not a single example can be found of this use of *abba*, without suffix or qualification of any kind, as an *address* to God in prayer.   And in the
Targums the term occurs only rarely and with reserve even as
an assertion of God's Fatherhood.   And the reason for that is
not far to seek: the word is simply too familiar for a Jew to
employ without fear of disrespect in addressing God.   Yet Jesus
uses the word here in Gethsemane, and the Gospel evidence shows
that, with the sole exception of Mk 15:34, which is a simple
citation of Ps 22:2, he used it every time he addressed his Father.
It is the revelation of a profound and entirely new relationship
with God, and Jeremias concludes that "the address itself is
without question an incontestable characteristic of the *ipsissima
vox Jesu.*" [139]

---

[135] So B.-A.-G., s. v. *abba*; G. Dalman, *Die Worte Jesu*, 2nd ed. (Leipzig,
1930), I, 157; S.-B., II, 49f.; and Gerhard Kittel, "Abba," *TDNT*, I (Grand
Rapids, 1964), 5 f.   With regard to Kittel it should be noted that this article
is a translation from the first volume of the German *TWNT* (1933).   He had
already changed his view before it appeared in print.   See his *Die Religionsgeschichte und das Urchristentum* (Gütersloh, 1932), pp. 92-94 and 146, n. 214.

[136] His reference here is to E. Littmann, *Orientalia*, 21 (1952), 389.

[137] See T. Nöldeke, in the supplement to F. Schulthess and E. Littmann,
Grammatik des christlich-palästinischen Aramäisch (Tübingen, 1924), p. 156.

[138] Joachim Jeremias, *The Prayers of Jesus*, Studies in Biblical Theology,
2nd Ser., 6 (London, 1967), pp. 58-60.

[139] *Ibid.*, p. 112.   For the background of the argument developed in this
paragraph, see Jeremias, *op. cit.*, pp. 11-65, 108-112; Witold Marchel, *Abba,
Père! La prière du Christ et des chrétiens*, Analecta Biblica 19 (Rome, 1963),
pp. 103-120, 129-145; Gerhard Kittel, *art. cit.*   For the most recent discussion
of Jesus' unique employment of the term *abba*, cf. David Flusser, *Jesus*,
tr. Ronald Walls (New York, 1969), pp. 94f. and n. 159, and Jacques Guillet,
Jésus devant sa vie et sa mort (Paris, 1971), pp. 236f. and n. 26, with Joachim
Jeremias, *New Testament Theology. Part One: The Proclamation of Jesus*,
tr. John Bowden (London, 1971), pp. 61-68, 189, 197.

Granted that *abba* is the habitual address of Jesus to his Father in prayer, the question must now be asked whether it is possible or likely that he used the whole bilingual expression *abba ho patêr* just as it stands in Mark. In other words, does this expression take its origin from Jesus himself, from community traditions, or simply from Mark? Some of the most distinguished exegetes have seen no impossibility in the whole phrase having been spoken by Jesus in his prayer. Both Swete [140] and Taylor [141] grant the possibility; and Plummer, after Sanday and Headlam,[142] considers it much more probable than that *ho patêr* is an explanatory interpolation of Mark's: "Translation injected into such a prayer would be unnatural." [143] The assumption underlying this point of view is that Jesus, like his contemporaries in Palestine, spoke both languages and therefore would have found it natural enough to pray in both.[144] Repetition in prayer is to be expected, particularly under the influence of strong emotion. And Schöttgen's examples of the bilingual duplication of similar short formulas have been widely quoted: e.g., *nai, amên* (Apoc 1:7), or the Jewish woman who addressed the judge *mry kyry*, where *kyry* stands for the Galilean pronunciation of the Greek *kyrie* and translates *mry* 'Lord.' [145] In spite of all this, however, it is thoroughly improbable that Jesus addressed his Father in both languages at the beginning of his prayer. Since he normally spoke Aramaic, it would not have been the least bit natural for him at this moment of deep crisis and communion with the Father to be switching from one language to another. Moreover, he would have had to create the whole expression himself, since we have already seen that what was original about his prayer in contrast with his contemporaries was that he should address God as *abba* at all. *Ho patêr* is not just a repetition, then, it is a literal translation deriving from the mistaken supposition that the vocative *abba* is the emphatic form *abha*.[146]

------

[140] *Op. cit.,* p. 344.

[141] *Op. cit.,* p. 553.

[142] William Sanday and Arthur C. Headlam, *A Critical and Exegetical Commentary on the Epistle to the Romans,* The International Critical Commentary, 14th ed. (New York, 1913), p. 203, commenting on Rom 8:15.

[143] *Op. cit.,* p. 328.

[144] J. B. Lightfoot, *St. Paul's Epistle to the Galatians,* 3rd ed. (London and Cambridge, 1869), pp. 167-169; M.-J. Lagrange, *Epître aux Galates* (Paris, 1950), p. 105; *idem, Marc,* p. 388.

[145] Ch. Schöttgen, *Horae Hebraicae et Talmudicae in universum Novum Testamentum* (Dresden and Leipzig, 1733), p. 252.

[146] Jeremias, *The Prayers of Jesus,* p. 59 and n. 35; Marchel, *op. cit.,* p. 125.

But if the expression did not originate with Jesus, neither did it originate with Mark. The possibility allowed by Swete [147] that *ho patêr* is an interpretive note of Mark's equivalent to *ho estin patêr* is appealing but too simple. It is appealing because Mark regularly interprets Aramaic words and phrases with parenthetical Greek equivalents (e.g., 3:17; 5:41; 7:11, 34; 10:46; 15:22, 34). But it is too simple because in every other case there is an expression to indicate that interpretation is taking place and there is no likelihood of mistaking the interpretations for the words of Jesus. More importantly, this view faces the formidable difficulty that the expression *abba ho patêr* is a stereotype existing prior to the Gospel of Mark in Gal 4:6 (49-50 A. D.) and Rom 8:15 (55 A. D.). In spite of that, Turner,[148] followed by Montefiore,[149] still adopts the view that *ho patêr* is one more of Mark's explanatory parentheses, only differing from the rest in that it came to him ready-made from familiar usage, possibly in the Lord's Prayer.

Granted that Jesus did not use the phrase and Mark did not invent it, only one possibility remains: it had its origins somewhere in the early Christian communities, as its presence in Galatians and Romans attests. Further than that, I do not think it possible to determine with precision whether it originated in the bilingual Palestinian community as a kind of liturgical formula,[150] or in the gentile communities as a kind of explanatory catechetical or liturgical stereotype for those who knew no Aramaic.[151] F.H. Chase suggested that by Mark's time *abba ho patêr* was the current equivalent of the opening of the Lord's

---

[147] *Loc. cit.*

[148] Turner, *JTS*, 26 (1924-25), 154f.

[149] *Op. cit.*, pp. 344f.

[150] So Schöttgen, J. B. Lightfoot, Swete, Lohmeyer, Taylor, *loc. cit.*; Marchel, pp. 126f.; Gottlob Schrenk, "*Pater, ktl.*," *TDNT*, V (Grand Rapids, 1968), 984, n. 247.

[151] So B. Weiss, p. 459; Menzies, p. 258; Loisy, *Évangiles synoptiques*, II, 564; *idem*, *Marc*, p. 412; Rawlinson, p. 212; Turner and Montefiore, *loc. cit.*; Lagrange, *Marc*, p. 388; *Grundmann*, p. 293; and see also S. Vernon Mc Casland, "Abba, Father," *JBL*, 72 (1953), 79-91, who considers that *abba* has passed as a loan word from Semitic into Greek and stands as a simple metonym for "God." Hans Lietzmann, *Einführung in die Textgeschichte der Paulusbriefe and die Römer*, 2nd ed. (Tübingen, 1928), p. 83f., sees at work here the typical liturgical custom of employing foreign words at the more solemn points of the service; and similarly, J. Van Dodewaard, "Die sprachliche Übereinstimmung zwischen Markus-Paulus und Markus-Petrus," *B*, 30 (1949), 105; and Uricchio and Stano, *op. cit.*, p. 586.

Prayer in its shorter Lucan form.[152]   If that is so, then we can
accept the judgment of B. Weiss [153] that the common form of
Christian address at prayer has here been put into the mouth
of Jesus by anticipation, so long as we remember that it was from
him that Christians learned to call God "Father" in the first
place. *Abba* was Jesus' prayer, *ho patêr* an addition of the
community, and the whole phrase became so set a formula that
Mark or his source did not hesitate to attribute it as it stood to
Jesus.

    Panta dynata soi parallels *ei dynaton estin* in the indirect
form of the prayer in v. 35.   Schanz,[154] following A. Klostermann,
is of the opinion that Mark meant it as a corrective for his gentile
readers, who might have been led by the conditional to think
of God as somehow subject to fate.   But it is better to see the
phrase as having its origins in Markan soteriology and going
back to the context of 10:27: *panta gar dynata para tô theô*.
There as here, and for example in Job 42:2, it is not so much
a question of physical omnipotence on God's part, but of His
power, in contrast with the impotence of man, to achieve His
purposes by no matter what means.[155]   The faith that Jesus had
there taught his disciples he here expresses in his own prayer,
believing that nothing is per se impossible for the Father and
that "even now it is possible to defeat Judas and the Sanhedrin,
to resist Pilate and the power of Rome, even to defy death." [156]

    As he had prayed for the passing of "the hour" in v. 35, so
now Jesus prays that the Father will remove "this cup," by caus-
ing it to pass him by.[157]   With this juxtaposition Mark shows

---

[152] F. H. Chase, *The Lord's Prayer in the Early Church* (Cambridge,
1891), p. 24 (cited by Swete, p. 344). And see Lietzmann, *op. cit.*, p. 83.

[153] *Op. cit.*, p. 459; so also Gould, *The Gospel according to St. Mark*, p. 270.

[154] *Op. cit.*, p. 391.

[155] B. Weiss, *loc. cit.*; cf. Gen 18:14 [LXX], and see Robert Horton Gundry,
op. cit. (see above p. 14, n. 69), pp. 38f.

[156] Swete, *loc. cit.*

[157] Here as in the preceding verse *apo* denotes separation or alienation.
See B.-D.-F., 211.   Again, as with v. 35, there arises the question of how
Jesus can petition the removal of the cup, especially after he has just
offered his disciples the cup of the New Covenant at the supper. Jeremias,
New Testament Theology, I, 138, suggests with C. K. Barrett that "the petition
has an eschatological reference: it considers the possibility that God might
bring in his reign even without suffering to precede it." Augustin George,
"Comment Jésus a-t-il perçu sa propre mort?", *LumV*, 20, No. 101 (1971),
46, prefers to think that Jesus saw his death as the failure of his mission
and the loss of his people, and that he was here petitioning a delay of
death and a prolongation of his mission in the effort to save his people.

that he understands the two expressions as somehow equivalent. Lohmeyer suggests that he meant the cup as a clarifying image from the O. T. for the obscure and unspecific hour.[158] But the precise figurative significance of the cup has itself proven difficult to determine. Apart from the literal occurrences of the term in the N. T.,[159] it is used figuratively by the three synoptics only here (cf. the parallel in Jn 18:11) and by Mark and Matthew in the scene of the Zebedees' request. The rest of the figurative occurrences in the N. T. are confined to the Apocalypse, where it is the cup of God's avenging wrath (Apoc 14:10; 16:19; 18:6) or the cup of Babylon's abominations (17:4), two concepts which doubtless belong together as 18:3-6 shows.[160] The Apocalypse is reflecting in this way the dominant O. T. usage of the term, as developed principally by the prophets.[161] The majority of O. T. occurrences of *potêrion* are figurative rather than literal,[162] and in nearly all instances the figure stands, as in the Apocalypse, for the anger or punishment of God.[163] So, on the one hand, the notion that *potêrion* is simply "an expression for destiny in both good and bad senses" [164] is too broad for the O. T. texts; and on

---

In any case Jesus was not simply cowering before the prospect of suffering and death.

[158] *Op. cit.*, p. 315.

[159] Mt 10:42; 23:25f.; 26:27; Mk 7:4, 9:41; 14:23, Lk 11:39; 2217, 20; 1 Cor 10:16, 21; 11:25-28.

[160] Friedrich Büchsel, "*Thymos, ktl.*," TDNT, III (Grand Rapids, 1965), 168; Gustav Stählin, "*Orgê, ktl.*," TDNT, V (Grand Rapids, 1967), 437; Leonhard Goppelt, "*Pino ... potêrion, ktl.*", TDNT, VI (Grand Rapids, 1968), 149, 151f.; and for a full treatment of the concept of "wrath" as employed in the Apocalypse, see A. T. Hanson, *The Wrath of the Lamb* (London, 1957), Ch. 7, pp. 159-180.

[161] For the probable origins in North Semitic mythology and the development in Hebrew literature of the image of the "cup of wrath," see Hanson, *op. cit.*, pp. 27-40.

[162] Literal use of the word *potêrion* is confined in the LXX to Gen 40:11, 13, 21; 2 Sam 12:3; 1 Kg 7:26; 2 Chr 4:5; Est 1:7; Pr 23:31; Jer 35:5.

[163] Thus Ps 75:8; Hab 2:16; Is 51:17, 22; Jer 25:15, 17, 28; 49:12; 51:7; Lam 2:13; 4:21; Ez 23:31-33. For the passages bearing other meanings — Ps 11:6; Ps 16:5; Ps 23:5; Ps 116:13; Jer 16:7 — see Goppelt, art. cit., p. 150, n. 23; A. Feuillet, "La coupe et le baptême de la passion," RB, 74 (1967), 371f.; and also Rudolf Otto, *The Kingdom of God and the Son of Man* (London, 1938), pp. 280-283.

[164] B.-A.-G., s. v. *potêrion*, 2. This appears to be an attenuation of the O. T. concept of God's judgment against Israel introduced by later Rabbinical tradition. See S.-B., I, 836-838; Goppelt, *art. cit.*, p. 152, n. 39; Gerhard Delling, "BAPTISMA, BAPTISTHÊNAI," NT, 2 (1957-58), 94; Feuillet, art. cit., pp. 374, 376.

the other hand, the restriction of the figure to the notion of suffering and death [165] is too narrow.[166]

The question, then, is whether we are to take the cup of which Jesus speaks in Mk 10:38f. par. and 14:36 par. in the same sense as we must take it in the figurative usage of the O.T. and the Apocalypse or whether we can assign it some special meaning of its own. The difficulty with adopting the first alternative is that in the O.T. it is the guilty, not the innocent, who are made to drink the cup of God's wrath, and in the synoptic texts there is no reference to wrath, as there is in the Apocalypse.[167] The prophetic imagery of drunkeness, debauchery and ruin associated with drinking the cup [168] would alone seem to preclude the application of this O.T. meaning to the cup drunk by Jesus. Yet, despite these difficulties, the first alternative seems preferable if only because no other context of meaning can be satisfactorily determined. The cup of Jesus certainly includes his suffering and death, but it means much more than that.[169] For first of all, it is a cup of suffering that has been sent by God; [170] secondly, it is a cup not simply of destiny but of judgment; [171] and finally, it is a cup of wrathful punishment undergone in the place of the guilty.[172] To accept Jesus as "himself the object of

---

[165] So Loisy, Plummer, Lagrange, Lohmeyer, *ad loc.*; M. Black "The Cup Metaphor in Mark 14:36," *ET*, 59 (1947-48), 195; Stählin, art. cit., p. 437, n. 386.

[166] Ernest Best, *The Temptation and the Passion: the Markan Soteriology* (Cambridge, 1965), p. 153.

[167] Hanson, *op. cit.*, pp. 126f.

[168] For details see Wilhelm Lotz, "Das Sinnbild des Bechers," *NKZ*, 28 (1917), 400; Delling, *loc. cit.*; Feuillet, art. cit., p. 373.

[160] Goppelt, art. cit., pp. 152f.

[170] J. H. Bernard, "A Study of St. Mark x 38, 39," *JTS*, 28 (1927), 265; Goppelt, art. cit., p. 144; Feuillet, art. cit., pp. 372-375f.

[171] Goppelt, art. cit., pp. 139, 150, 153; Delling, art. cit., p. 95. For the O.T. linking of cup and sword as twin images of judgment, see Lotz, art. cit., p. 401. And for the linking with similar meaning of cup and baptism in Mk 10:38f., see G. R. Beasley-Murray, *Baptism in the New Testament* (London, 1963), pp. 72-77; Best, *op. cit.*, pp. 153f; Delling, art. cit., pp. 92-115; Stählin, art. cit., pp. 436f. Feuillet, art. cit., pp. 377-383, prefers to see the baptism image as deriving from the penitential rite already familiar to Jesus' disciples and so linking his death rather with sin than with judgment.

[172] C. E. B. Cranfield, "The Cup Metaphor in Mark 14:36 and Parallels," *ET*, 59 (1947-48), 137f.: Grundmann, *op. cit.*, p. 293; Schmid, *op. cit.*, p. 276: Taylor, *op. cit.*, p. 554; *idem, Jesus and his Sacrifice: A Study of the Passion Sayings in the Gospels* (London, 1955), pp. 152, 261-263; Delling, art. cit., p. 95; Feuillet, art. cit., p. 376; Stählin, art. cit., pp. 445f. Martin Albertz,

the wrath of God" [173] is difficult only if we limit our understanding of the sense in which the O. T. uses the concept of wrath to the subjective animus of God,[174] rather than recognize that it also embraces the objective historical calamities consequent upon the sins of men.[175] If there can be no question of Jesus having suffered from the former, the gospels leave little doubt that he was a victim of the latter (cf. Mk 14:41).[176] And his prayer for the removal of such a cup is perfectly comprehensible.

Still Jesus is portrayed not merely as a passive victim of men's malice, but rather as the vicarious agent of their redemption.[177] And this portrayal raises the further question of how, given the uniqueness of Jesus' sacrifice, he can invite his disciples to share his cup, as he appears to do in Mk 10:38f. Feuillet suggests that the question in v. 38, like the one in 2:19, actually anticipates a negative answer, and thus expresses not a condition for the disciples' association with Jesus' glory but the strict impossibility of it.[178] Nevertheless, as v. 39 intimates, the disciples too will share somehow in what is about to overtake their Master, at least through a moral, perhaps even through a sacramental, participation in the cup he drains.[179] The saying is not

---

Die Botschaft des Neuen Testaments, I, 1 (Zürich, 1947), 100; II, 1 (Zürich, 1954), 86f., 105, 110, 112, 114; II, 2 (Zürich, 1957), 31, 126, maintains that in his death Jesus as the Jewish Messiah vicariously drains the cup of wrath offered by God through the prophets to the gentiles, and thereby brings salvation to those who stand outside the Passover salvation community.

[173] Best, *op. cit.*, p. 153.

[174] Even the N. T., though certainly more theological and less psychological than the O. T. in its conception of God's wrath, never does away completely with the notion that it is an actual attitude in God. See Stählin, art. cit., pp. 407, 424 f.; and R. V. G. Tasker, *The Biblical Doctrine of the Wrath of God* (London, 1951), p. 16.

[175] See Hanson, *op. cit.*, pp. 125f.

[176] See Tasker, *op. cit.*, p. 35.

[177] Cf. especially Mark's use of *lytron anti pollôn* in 10:45 and *hyper pollôn* in 14:24; and see Taylor, *Jesus and his Sacrifice*, pp. 74, 99-105, 125-139, 257-263; Joachim Jeremias, *The Eucharistic Words of Jesus*, tr. Norman Perrin (London, 1966), pp. 166-168, 179-182, 225-231; idem, "Der Lösegeld für Viele (Mk 10,45)," *J*, 3 (1948), 249-264; idem, "Polloi," *TDNT*, VI (Grand Rapids, 1968), 536-565; Friedrich Büschel, "*Lytron*," s. v. "*Lyô, ktl.*," *TDNT*, IV (Grand Rapids, 1967), 340-349; Harald Riesenfeld, "*Hyper*," *TWNT*, VIII (Stuttgart, 1969), 510-518.

[178] Feuillet, art. cit., pp. 356, 363f.

[179] Taylor, *op. cit.*, p. 99; Best, *op. cit.*, pp. 154-157; Feuillet, art. cit., pp. 364f., 371, 383-388. The thesis of Georg Braumann, "Ieidenskelch und Todestaufe (Mc 10:38f.)," *ZNW*, 56 (1965), 178-183, that the cup and baptism

a prophecy of the martyrdom of James and John.[180] But it was
inevitable that among persecuted Christians the cup should early
become a symbol for martyrdom.[181] And Surkau has aptly remarked of the prayer in Mk 14:36: "Die Gemeinde, die den bet-
enden Herrn dies Wort in den Mund legt, zeigt dadurch, dass
sie ihn in die Reihe der Märtyrer stellt." [182]

Just as the faith with which Jesus addresses his Father receives stronger expression through the *panta dynata soi* of v. 36,
so does the condition (*ei*, v. 35) under which he prays in the
phrase that follows: *all' ou ti egô thelô alla ti sy*.[183] The prayer,
says Lagrange, "is modified or rather completed with a reserva-
tion: surrender to the will of the Father." [184] But the phrase as it
stands is grammatically incomplete, lacking a principal verb.
Menzies [185] contends that the phrase expresses Jesus' recognition
that the divine will is fixed, and he suggests the addition of a
simple future tense to complete the sentence. But few exegetes
would agree with his interpretation or require that anything be
supplied or understood, least of all a form like *genêthêtô* (Mt
26:42) or *ginesthô* (Lk 22:42), which would demand *mê* rather
than *ou* as the form of negation. It is clear that Matthew and
Luke have attempted here to bring Jesus' prayer into closer
alignment with the third petition of the Our Father and that
Mark is more original. Swete's paraphrase ("However, the ques·
tion is not what is my will, etc.") has won many important adher-
ents,[186] although B. Weiss [187] and Schanz [188] both found something
strangely cold and modern about completing the phrase as a
question. There is even in Mark undoubtedly an echo of the Our
Father in its Matthean form. But E. Klostermann insists: "Diese

---

sayings originated in a context of early Christian sacramental disputes
lacks external support and offers no reason why the two saying should
have been joined in the tradition or applied jointly by Mark to the passion
and death of Jesus.

[180] Bernard, art. cit., pp. 262f.; Feuillet, art. cit., pp. 359-363.

[181] Hans-Werner Surkau, *Martyrien in jüdischer und frühchristlicher
Zeit* (Göttingen, 1938), p. 85, n. 12; Goppelt, art. cit., p. 153.

[182] *Loc. cit.*, n. 14.

[183] For the use of the interrogative *ti* here in place of the relative *ho ti*,
see B.-D.-F., 298 (4).

[184] *Op. cit.*, p. 388.

[185] *Op. cit.*, p. 258.

[186] Swete, p. 344, is followed by Plummer, Lagrange, Lohmeyer, Taylor,
Cranfield, *ad loc.*

[187] *Op. cit.*, p. 459.

[188] *Op. cit.*, p. 391.

Ergebung drückt etwas ganz anderes aus, als die dritte Bitte des Vaterunsers." [189] And Lohmeyer goes on to elaborate how he sees the difference: "Es scheint, als solle hier nicht menschliche Willkür dem göttlichen Willen entgegengesetzt werden, sondern als spräche einer, der auch Gott gegenüber das besondere Recht hat, von 'Seinem Willen' zu sprechen und gerade deswegen Sich dem höheren Willen Gottes beugt." [190] Schniewind [191] sees the parallelism to the Our Father in Matthew on a somewhat larger scale: not only in the address and in the third petition, but also in the final petition for deliverance from temptation (cf. Mk 14:38). And because of this parallelism, the absence of close witnesses, and the obviously model character of the prayer, Nineham [192] is led to conclude with Branscomb [193] that the whole of v. 36 is a reverent conjecture of the early Church, elaborating the details of a tradition too scanty for its own religious use.[194]

Daube has come to a different conclusion about the origins of Jesus' prayer in a study where he compares its structure as reported in the Synoptics, not with the Lord's Prayer, but with parallels in Jewish prayer. He discovers underlying it a traditional threefold pattern: namely, acknowledgment ("Father, all things are possible to thee") — wish ("remove this cup from me") — surrender ("yet not what I will, but what thou wilt"). Even in the Jewish prayer-book of today there is a similar threefold prayer of commendation on one's deathbed, and the structure can be traced through a long history in Judaism right back into the O. T., at least in the twofold wish-surrender antithesis. He considers that the threefold structure, such as we find in Jesus' prayer, belongs to a stage in the development more formalized than the O. T. examples and common in later Rabbinic literature, a stage at which a pious Jew preparing for death made use of a solemn ritual confession. And he suggests that Mark has reported Jesus' prayer at his final hour in this traditional

---

[189] *Op. cit.*, p. 151.
[190] *Op. cit.*, p. 316.
[191] *Op. cit.*, p. 187.
[192] *Op. cit.*, p. 392.
[193] *Op. cit.*, p. 268.
[194] The opinion has also been put forward that the influence ran in the opposite direction, viz., that the Gethsemane scene was the original *Sitz im Leben* of the third petition of the Lord's Prayer. See Heinz Kruse, " 'Pater Noster' et Passio Christi," *VD*, 46 (1968), 8; Gerhard Schneider, *Verleugnung, Verspottung und Verhör Jesu nach Lukas 22, 54-71* (Munich, 1969), p. 186, n. 116.

Jewish pattern of a declaration accepting death in love. Thus
Daube hopes to resolve the question of how at least the structure of Jesus' prayer at Gethsemane could easily have been
known, although its only witnesses were disciples dozing or
asleep some distance away.[195]

> Verse 37: *Kai erchetai kai heuriskei autous ka-*
> *theudontas, kai legei tô Petrô: Simôn, katheudeis?*
> *ouk ischysas mian hôran grêgorêsai?*

The only answer Jesus receives when he returns from prayer
is to find his trusted three disciples, whom he had asked to watch,
asleep.[196] No reason is given for their sleep, but it is clear that
they have failed him. And in their failure the silence of God
speaks to Jesus his answer: "The hour has come; the Son of
Man is betrayed into the hands of sinners" (v. 41). Their sleep,
then, is more than casual drowsiness. It is a sign to Jesus and
a warning to the community, as the admonition of Jesus in the
next verse shows.[197] Loisy is of the opinion that the Gethsemane
tradition centered originally around Jesus' supreme trial and
that Mark was the first to introduce the apostles, particularly
Peter, in this unfavorable light.[198] Hauck [199] notes that it is only
Mark who preserves the detail that Jesus on his first return addressed his rebuke to Peter in the singular. In Matthew Peter
is addressed in the plural from the start, and Mark's awkward
transition from the singular to the plural between v. 37 and v. 38
is thus eliminated. In Luke the three have disappeared altogether and the disciples in general are addressed, Jesus comes only
once to find them sleeping, their sleep is excused as *apo tês lypês*,
and his reproof is modified to the single question *ti katheudete*.
In this way questions raised by Mark's or Matthew's text no
longer occur, e.g., why did Jesus take the three apart in the first
place? to whom was the admonition addressed? when did they
rejoin the rest? But more importantly, these modifications

---

[195] David Daube, "A Prayer Pattern in Judaism," *Studia Evangelica,*
I (Berlin, 1959), 539-545.
[196] For the historical present here, see above p. 8.
[197] See Lohmeyer, pp. 316f.; Grundmann, p. 293; Cranfield, *Mark,*
p. 434.
[198] *Evangiles synoptiques,* II, 566.
[199] *Op. cit.,* p. 173.

provide clear evidence of the tendencies at work in the development of the tradition. Matthew has almost imperceptibly softened the rebuke to Peter by having Jesus address him in the plural, as if he were the representative of the rest of the disciples.[200] And Luke has done all he could to minimize the apostles' failure and to generalize the admonition of Jesus. Bultmann has noted the strong tendency in the tradition to individualize by naming.[201] Here the development has taken place in the opposite direction, and obviously for apologetic motives. It is unthinkable that the first generation of Christians could have invented a story so manifestly derogatory of Peter and the other apostles that the evangelists themselves felt the immediate need to tone it down. It is far more likely that the story has strong historical roots and even goes back to Peter himself. Branscomb,[202] who is generally skeptical about the historical character of the account, nevertheless believes that the details of the disciples' sleep and their arousal by Jesus must go back to their own testimony. Schanz,[203] B. Weiss,[204] and Menzies [205] all remark that the sharp reproach addressed to Peter alone could only go back to him. And J. Weiss, who is certainly more critical than his father about the historical elements here, can write: "Dass Petrus dies beschämende Erlebnis (Markus erzählt es in dreifachsteigernder Wiederholung) später weiter erzählt hat, dass er so ungeschminkt sagt, wie er der Grösse dieser Stunde nicht gewachsen war, ist ein Zeichen der Ehrlichkeit der Überlieferung, die auch sonst hervortritt." [206] If Mark does not spare Peter here, notes Lagrange,[207] he is only preserving the echo of Peter, who

---

[200] E. Schweizer, *Markus*, p. 180, illustrates this representative function of Peter elsewhere in a number of passages where one evangelist attributes to Peter what another attributes to all the disciples. Cf. Mk 11:21/Mt 21:20; Mt 15:15/Mk 7:17; Mk 13:3/Mt 24:3; Mt 18:21/Lk 17:4; Lk 12:41f./Mt 24:45.

[201] Rudolf Bultmann, *The History of the Synoptic Tradition*, p. 310. But he also thinks that "those sections of the tradition which use the names of individual disciples come from an earlier time when the idea of the Twelve as Jesus' constant companions had not yet been formed or successfully carried through" (p. 345). Among these sections he does not include the Gethsemane account, which he regards as legendary (p. 267). But see Sanders, *op. cit.*, (see above p. 6, n. 10), pp. 88f.

[202] *Op. cit.*, p. 268.

[203] *Op. cit.*, p. 391.

[204] *Op. cit.*, p. 460.

[205] *Op. cit.*, pp. 258f.

[206] *Op. cit.*, p. 210.

[207] *Op. cit.*, p. 389.

does not spare himself. And even the presence, as Taylor observes, of "the obvious paranetic *motif* in no way compromises the tradition; on the contrary, it was only because the fact were known that the example could be cited." [208]

E. Meyer [209] sees a small but all the more significant sign of authenticity in Jesus' use of the name "Simon" here, the only time it occurs in Mark outside of 3:16. Swete makes much of this reversion to Peter's earlier name: "For the time he is 'Peter' no more; the new character which he owed to Jesus is in abeyance. He who was ready to die with the Master (v. 31) has been proved not to possess the strength of will (*ouk ischysas*) requisite for resisting sleep during the third part of a single watch (*mian hôran*)." [210] But Loisy [211] may be closer to the truth in not wishing to exaggerate the importance of the usage. He thinks that "Simon" was probably in common use until after the resurrection, when it was eclipsed by "Peter" and Christian tradition came to see him more as the "rock" of the Church. Nevertheless, "c'est bien le pêcheur Simon et non l'apôtre Pierre, qui apparait en cette circonstance." [212]

The particular pain and poignancy of Jesus' reproach to Peter derives from the reference back to v. 34 and the command to watch. If we understand that command as the exhortation to share the Paschal night watch in an unbroken *habhura*, the reason for Jesus' disappointment and the sharpness of his reproach becomes clear. His own watch has been a prayer of anguish to accept the cup of suffering which will inaugurate the New Covenant, to give himself over to the hour willed by his Father for his deliverance into the hands of sinners. The disciples' sleep has been the acting out of the parable of the servants bidden to watch, visited by their master three times in the night, and found sleeping (Mk 13:34-36).[213] It is proof of their utter unreadiness to share in the Paschal deliverance which is at hand.

---

[208] *Op. cit.*, p. 554.

[209] E. Meyer, *Ursprung und Anfänge des Christentums* (Stuttgart, 1921-23), I, 150. See also Grundmann, p. 293.

[210] *Op. cit.*, p. 345. He is followed here by Plummer, E. Klostermann, Taylor, and Nineham, *ad loc.*

[211] *Évangiles synoptiques*, II, 566. So also Rawlinson and Lagrange, *ad loc.*

[212] *Idem, Marc*, p. 413.

[213] Minear, *Saint Mark*, p. 124.

Verse 38: *Grêgoreite kai proseuchesthe, hina mê elthête eis peirasmon; to men pneuma prothymon, hê de sarx asthenês.*

Without any indication that there is a different audience, the address changes abruptly from the singular in v. 37 to the plural here. Wellhausen [214] considers this and the suddenly metaphorical meaning of "watch" as out of tune with the rest of the passage and an indication that the saying may have been spoken by Jesus on another occasion. For Bultmann [215] the whole verse had a later origin in the language of Christian edification. Montefiore [216] considers either of these conclusions possible. But Lohmeyer [217] objects to the notion of interpolation on any grounds, since he feels that the context itself demands a clarification of what is meant by "waking" and "sleeping" here. Neither, according to him, can we quibble about Jesus addressing sleeping disciples, since on those grounds we should have to eliminate v. 37 and v. 40b as well. Nevertheless, it is clear that with the plural address and the general character of the saying Mark has in mind more than the three disciples at Gethsemane, just as in 13:32-37 he had in mind more than the four who were directly addressed, an intention which 13:37 makes quite explicit.[218] That the exhortation to watch has a figurative as well as a literal meaning here should not be seriously contested, since that is the case throughout the N. T. Yet not too much should be made of this point either, for the literal sense is what is primarily meant and it fits the context very well. In any case, the figurative sense was an early development in the Christian community and would not have been lost on Mark or his readers. Wakefulness in both senses is often combined with prayer elsewhere in the N. T. (e.g., Lk 21:36; Eph 6:18; Col 4:2; I Pet 4:7), since it is understood not only as a physical condition for prayer, but also as a spiritual resistance to the powers of evil which dominate in night and darkness, and hence as a condition for overcoming temptation (e.g., Rom 13:11-12; I Cor 16:13; Eph 6:10-18; I Thess 5:8; I Pet 5:8-9).[219]

---

[214] *Op. cit.*, p. 128.
[215] *Op. cit.*, p. 268.
[216] *Op. cit.*, p. 345.
[217] *Op. cit.*, p. 317.
[218] See Hauck, p. 173; E. Klostermann, p. 151; Grundmann, p. 293; E. Schweizer, p. 180f.
[219] See Evald Lövestam, *Spiritual Wakefulness in the New Testament,*

What is new in the exhortation of v. 38, as compared with that of v. 34, is that the disciples are asked to pray as well as to watch. And Plummer [220] notes that the present imperative yields a sense of continuous prayer. The question immediately occurs as to whether the *hina*-clause that follows expresses purpose, content, or command. Cadoux [221] has opted for the imperatival use; but this forms a strange parallel with the two previous imperatives in the sentence, and it is considered less likely by Taylor [222] who prefers the opinion of Meecham [223] that the clause is expressing the content of the prayer, as in 13:18 and 14:35.[224] The clear echo of the sixth petition of the Lord's Prayer only reinforces this opinion.[225] Moreover, it is clear that this is the meaning of the expression as it occurs in Luke. There the disciples are bidden only to pray, not to watch, and the content of their prayer is given in two forms: first, by an infinitive clause (22:40) and secondly, by a *hina*-clause (22:46). But the case is different for Mark. If we give equal value to the combined imperatives to watch and to pray, and especially if we see the combination as already strongly traditional, then we can interpret the *hina*-clause only as final, expressing the purpose of this twofold activity.[226]

J. Carmignac,[227] from a study of the pattern of negation before a causative verb in Semitic examples from the O. T. and Qumran,

---

tr. W. F. Salisbury (Lund, 1963), pp. 65-67, 70, 91, 138 and n. 2, 139; and also Albrecht Oepke, "*Egeirô . . . grêgoreô (agrypneô),*" *TDNT*, II (Grand Rapids, 1964, 338f.

[220] *Op. cit.,* p. 329.

[221] C. J. Cadoux, "The Imperatival Use of *hina* in the New Testament," *JTS*, 42 (1941), 165-173.

[222] *Op. cit.,* p. 554.

[223] H. G. Meecham, "The Imperatival Use of *hina* in the New Testament," *JTS*, 43 (1942), 179-180. See also the further articles of the same title by A. R. George, *JTS*, 45 (1944), 56-60, and by A.P. Salom, *Australian Biblical Review*, 6 (1958), 123-141.

[224] So also Plummer, Hauck, E. Klostermann, Cranfield, *ad loc.,* and A. H. McNeile, *The Gospel according to St. Matthew* (London, 1915), p. 391.

[225] Swete, p. 346, following Chase, *op. cit.,* p. 61f., notes that the Syriac versions use the same verb to translate *eispherein* (Mt 6:13; Lk 11:4) and *erchesthai* (Mk 14:38), merely changing th conjugations, and that in all likelihood the Hebrew or Aramaic originals of the passages also used but one root for both verbs.

[226] So H. A. W. Meyer, *Critical and Exegetical Handbook of the Gospel of Matthew* (Edinburgh, 1879), II, 220; B. Weiss, p. 460; Lagrange, p. 390; Karl Georg Kuhn, "Jesus in Gethsemane," *EvT*, 12 (1952-53), 285, n. 41.

[227] J. Carmignac, "Fais que nous n'entrions pas dans la tentation," *RB*, 72 (1965), 218-226. So also Héring, *RHPR*, 39 (1959), 98, n. 6, for *eiselthein*

concludes that *elthête* here means "enter into the object of" or "succumb to," not simply "fall into," temptation. What the temptation is, is not so easily determined. It has been interpreted in at least three ways: in the general senses of solicitation to evil or proof by affliction or in the specific sense of some particular danger. Swete[228] believes that in the present context, as in the Lord's Prayer, the predominant meaning of temptation is solicitation to evil. But he has few followers. Loisy argues that temptation here has the sense of proof by affliction and that it referred originally not to any trial of the apostles but to the supreme trial Jesus was facing in his death. According to him, the whole preoccupation of the Gethsemane tradition, like the tradition preserved in the previous temptation account or in Heb 4:15 and 5:7, centered in Jesus' hour and cup and trial, and Mark only confused the issue by speaking also of a trial of the apostles. What he must have found in his source, and in fact what Jesus must have said, was something more like: "Pray that *I* enter not into temptation." Lk 22:46 is obviously dependent on Mark, but in 22:40 Luke has remained more faithful to the tradition by placing Jesus' words at the beginning of the scene where they belong, and by preserving the formula *proseuchesthe mê eiselthein [me] eis peirasmon*, which may well have occurred with the bracketed word in his source.[229] All of this is more ingenious than convincing. And Plummer makes the point that there is not a single instance in the Gospels where Jesus asks the prayers of his disciples for himself: *he* prays for *them*, not they for him.[230] In spite of that, and in spite of the lack of any textual support, Héring has recently resurrected Loisy's opinion and judges that Mark himself corrected the tradition "parce que l'idée d'une prière d'intercession des disciples pour leur maître, dont 'la chair' aurait été 'faible,' a dû, sans doute, lui sembler intolérable."[231] And he believes that this hypothesis provides better grounds for the extreme disappointment of Jesus over the disciples' sleep. But we have already seen still better grounds for the latter. And the conjecture should be abandoned, since the verse really raises no

---

in Matthew and Luke. And see Kruse, art. cit. (see above p. 31, n. 194), pp. 10-13; and Jeremias, *New Testament Theology*, I, 202.

[228] *Op. cit.*, p. 346.

[229] Loisy, *Évangiles synoptiques*, II, 561f., 567f.; *idem*, Marc, pp. 414-416.

[230] Plummer, *op. cit.*, p. 329; and M.-J. Lagrange, *Évangile selon Saint Luc*, 8th. ed. (Paris, 1948), p. 559, makes a similar point: "Jamais Jésus ne se montre dépendant de ses apôtres pour ses rapports avec son Père."

[231] Art. cit., p. 98.

problem that cannot be solved without it. Moreover, the argument from Lk 22:40, based on the insertion of a subject for the infinitive different from the subject of the principal verb, does violence to the grammar of the phrase.[232]

We are left, then, with the third meaning of temptation in the specific sense of a particular danger. And the question reduces to whether this danger is immanent, eschatological, or something of both. Albert Schweitzer[233] and Martin Dibelius,[234] as well as the commentaries of Lohmeyer, Taylor, Grundmann, Schniewind, and Nineham, ad loc., take an eschatological view of the temptation, connecting it with the last days spoken of in Mk 13. The vocabulary "watch," "hour," "temptation," certainly belongs to the end-time of Judaeo-Christian expectation (cf. Mk 13:32-37; Jn 5:25-29; Rom 13:11; I Thess 5:6; Apoc 3:2 f., 10; etc.), and the context makes clear that Jesus and his disciples are engaged in a death-struggle with the powers of Satan. Seesemann notes that while "it should not be forgotten, of course, that every affliction, and therewith every peirasmos, is an eschatological tribulation or temptation according to the total understanding of the preaching of Jesus," the specific reason given here for watching and praying is the weakness and susceptibility of man under trial, not the imminence of the last events.[235] And C. H. Dodd,[236] followed by Beasley-Murray,[237] granting the "eschatological" character of all the events of Jesus' ministry, judges that both the admonition in Mk 14:38 and the parable in 13:33-37 refer to more immediate events: namely, those about to engulf Jesus and his disciples in the passion, which Jesus saw as the beginning of the great tribulation connected with the coming of the kingdom. It is an immediate crisis, not a far-off advent, that he has in view.[238] K. G.

---

[232] Lagrange, loc. cit.

[233] Albert Schweitzer, Das Messianitäts- und Leidensgeheimnis Jesu (Leipzig and Tübingen, 1901), p. 92; idem, The Quest of the Historical Jesus, tr. W. Montgomery, 3rd ed. (London, 1963), p. 390.

[234] Martin Dibelius, "Gethsemane," CQ, 12 (1935), 258f.; BG, I (Tübingen, 1953), 263f.

[235] Heinrich Seesemann, "Peira... peirasmos, ktl.," TDNT, VI (Grand Rapids ,1968, 31f.; quotation on p. 31; and see Heirich Schlier, "Thlibô, thlipsis" TDNT, III (Grand Rapids, 1966), 144-146.

[236] C. H. Dodd, The Parables of the Kingdom, rev. ed. (London, 1963), pp. 120-124, and p. 123, n. 17.

[237] G. R. Beasley-Murray, A Commentary on Mark Thirteen (London, 1957), p. 111.

[238] Similarly Menzies, p. 259; Hauck, p. 173; Haenchen, Der Weg Jesu, p. 491, n. 5.

Kuhn has succeeded in tracing the roots of this notion of temptation as at once eschatological and immanent back to the pre-Christian Palestinian context represented by the sectarian literature discovered at Qumran. There the world is conceived of as a battleground between the forces of good and evil, light and darkness, God and Satan. And the life of man is a continual struggle between those who belong to God and those who belong to Satan, the Sons of Light and the Sons of Darkness. Watch-fulness and prayer are indispensable aids in this life-struggle of the Sons of Light. When the final judgment comes, God will utterly destroy the forces of evil. But even now He is with His own, and their present victory over Satan and Sin is His work and already a continual anticipation of definitive victory at the end. N. T. thought on the victory of God's kingdom over Satan's through Christ's coming is conceptually, but not structurally, dif-ferent from that of the Qumran community. Just as God's king-dom is through Christ's coming both an immanent as well as an eschatological reality, so is the situation of those who belong to this kingdom a constant *peirasmos* and every victory of theirs in Christ a present anticipation of his ultimate end-time victory. In Gethsemane it was Christ's willingness to watch and pray and the disciples' unwillingness that accounted for his victory in temptation and their defeat.[239]

The question posed by Mark's contrast of *pneuma* and *sarx* in the second half of v. 38 is from what context he derives this opposition and therefore what he means by it. Does it stem from O. T., Pauline, Hellenistic, or Qumran circles of thought?

In the LXX *pneuma*, which is the usual equivalent of the Hebrew *rûaḥ*, in impersonal reference can mean simply wind or breath; in reference to man, it can designate the principle of his bodily life, or the seat of his feeling, thought and will, or the spirit divinely effected in him; in reference to God, it may signify his effective power, specifically his creative power, his inner nature,

---

[239] Karl Georg Kuhn, "*Peirasmos - hamartia - sarx* im Neuen Testament und die damit zusammenhängenden Vorstellungen," *ZTK*, 49 (1952), 200-222; Eng. tr., with some rev., "New Light on Temptation, Sin and Flesh in the New Testament," in *The Scrolls and the New Testament*, ed. Krister Stendahl (New York, 1957), pp. 94-113; *idem, EvT*, 12 (1952-53), 274-285; A. R. C. Leaney, *The Rule of Qumran and Its Meaning* (London, 1966), p. 126. Recently R. S. Barbour, art. cit., (see above p. 22, n. 133), pp. 244-248, has suggested that the gospel conception of Jesus' struggle in Gethsemane goes further than Kuhn's view of it as temptation by Satan and implies the additional aspect of testing by God.

or his personal being.[240] *Sarx*, which is the most frequent LXX
rendering of the Hebrew *bâsâr*, is used in the O. T. literally for the
flesh of men or animals, for the body, or for mankind or the whole
animal kingdom, and more broadly as an expression for blood-
relationship, a euphemism for the genital organs, a designation of
man's whole external existence or even his whole internal attitude,
or finally as an equivalent of man's creaturely frailty and mor-
tality in comparison with God.[241]

Thus *pneuma* is used both of God and man, but *sarx* only of
man, never of God. For *pneuma*, which stands for the power of
God, can be communicated to man; but *sarx*, which stands for
human nature in all its weakness and dependence, can never
characterize God. For the O. T. to say that man is flesh is not
simply to say that man is not God, but rather to say that man
depends wholly on God. And the obverse could clearly never be
the case.[242] If there is a dualism envisioned by this O. T. contrast
of flesh and spirit, it is not anthropological but cosmic, not within
man himself but between God or God's world and man or man's
world. The Greek antithesis of body and soul is utterly foreign to
Hebrew thought. For the O. T. the flesh of man is the whole of
man, as much as his soul or spirit is.[243] Consequently, the O. T.
does not look upon flesh as the material principle of man's sinfulness, nor does it see the contrast between man and God as that
between what is inherently sinful and what is inherently holy.
If man sins, it is not because he has a lower nature which is evil,
but because in his creaturely weakness (= "flesh") before God
his whole self sometimes seeks an existence independent of God.[244]
Of itself "flesh" in the O. T. "directly connotes weakness and is
hardly associated with sin." [245] At least by the time of Is 31:3;

---

[240] Friedrich Baumgärtel, "*Pneuma, ktl.*," *TDNT*, VI (Grand Rapids,
1968), 359-364.

[241] *Idem*, "*Sarx, ktl.*," *TWNT*, VII (Stuttgart, 1964), 105-107.

[242] Daniel Lys, *La chair dans l'Ancien Testament: "Bâsâr"* (Paris, 1967),
pp. 141f.

[243] See Johannes Pedersen, *Israel: Its Life and Culture*, I-II (London
and Copenhagen, 1959), 176-178; John A. T. Robinson, *The Body. A Study in
Pauline Theology* (London, 1963), pp. 11-15; Eduard Schweizer, *et al.*, "*Sarx,
ktl.*," *TWNT*, VII (Stuttgart, 1964), 123; Lys, *op. cit.*, pp. 139, 143.

[244] Lys, *op. cit.*, pp. 135-139.

[245] Roland E. Murphy, "*Bśr* in the Qumrân Literature and *Sarks* in the
Epistle to the Romans," in *Sacra Pagina* (Paris, 1959), II, 62; and similarly
E. De Witt Burton, *Spirit, Soul, and Flesh. The Usage of* Pneuma, Psychê
and Sarx *in Greek Writings and Translated Works from the Earliest Period
to 180 A. D.; and of their Equivalents* Rûaḥ, Nephesh *and* Bâsâr *in the*

40:6-8; Ps 56:5 *sarx* had come to characterize the world of man just as *pneuma* did the world of God, a division of the cosmos into spheres reflected also in the LXX translation of Num 16:22 and 27:16 not as "God of the spirits of all flesh," but as "God of spirits and of all flesh." [246]

A number of commentators have maintained that these O. T. conceptions are at the origin of Mark's spirit-flesh opposition.[247] In particular, Eduard Schweizer claims that the expression "willing spirit" in Mark derives from Ps 51:12 (MT v. 14: *rûaḥ nedîbâh*), where this spirit is identified not simply with the spirit that God puts within man in v. 10 (MT v. 12) but with God's holy Spirit in v. 11 (MT v. 13). For him Mk 14:38b, like Ps 51, conceives of God's Spirit as given to man in such a way that he can somehow recognize it as his own and experience its power over all his human weakness, and thus represents a nuance somewhere between the cosmic dualism of Hebrew thought generally and Greek anthropological dualism.[248] The difficulty with Schweizer's position is threefold. First, the contrast in Ps 51 is not between spirit and flesh but wholly between God's Spirit and man's spirit, between man's spirit as precarious and sinful when acting independently of God and man's spirit as renewed by the gift of God's Spirit, once he is open again to depend on God for his life. So Ps 51 still mirrors the cosmic dualism of O. T. thought. Secondly, while it is surely preferable to understand "holy spirit" (literally "spirit of holiness") in v. 11b (MT v. 13b) as God's Spirit because of the parallelism with "thy presence" in the first half of the verse, the identification of *rûaḥ nedîbâh* with God in the following verse is open to serious question.[249] Thirdly, what is absent from

---

Hebrew Old Testament (Chicago, 1918), p. 73: "Of any corrupting power of either body or flesh to drag down the soul there is no trace in the Old Testament. The *bâsâr* is sometimes spoken of as weak, but never as a power for evil."

[246] Eduard Schweizer, "*Pneuma, ktl.,*" *TDNT*, VI, 393 and n. 353; *idem*, "*Sarx, ktl.,*" *TWNT*, VII, 108f.

[247] See Taylor, p. 555; Haenchen, p. 492; Lohmeyer, pp. 317f.; Schweizer, *Markus*, p. 181; Cranfield, p. 434; Uricchio and Stano, p. 588. And see H. Wheeler Robinson, *The Christian Doctrine of Man* (Edinburgh, 1911), pp. 95f., and p. 81: "The flesh is not the spirit's enemy, but the spirit's weakness, the gate through which the peril may easily come."

[248] Cf. Eduard Schweizer, "Röm. 1, 3f. und der Gegensatz von Fleisch und Geist vor und bei Paulus," *EvT*, 15 (1955), 570f.; *TDNT*, VI, 396f.; *TWNT*, VII, 123 f.; and *Markus*, p. 181; also Robert Horton Gundry, *op. cit.* (see above p. 14, n. 69), pp. 59f.

[249] See Daniel Lys, *Rûach. Le souffle dans l'Ancien Testament* (Paris,

the Psalm text, as indeed from the O. T. generally, is precisely what Lohmeyer calls the "almost ascetical" character of the saying we find in the gospel text. Mk 14:38 is speaking of the willingness of man's spirit, not of God's, and of man's struggle to overcome thereby the weakness of his flesh, e. g., specifically through the ascetical disciplines of vigilance and prayer.[250] Accordingly, we must look elsewhere than in the O. T. for the origins of Mark's conception.

Does Pauline thought provide the context? This has been affirmed.[251] But most commentators would answer in the negative.[252] For a time many scholars thought that Paul himself had taken over his spirit-flesh opposition from Hellenism,[253] but today this opinion has been largely replaced by a recognition of Paul's dependence on the O. T. and Judaism.[254] The half-dozen or so distinguishable senses in which Paul uses *pneuma* — mostly for God or his divine influence, but also for the Christian *pneuma* created by God in believers, or even as an equivalent for man's natural spirit (= *psyché*), and occasionally for seducing spirits or their evil influence — so closely correspond to the categories of O. T. and inter-testamental usage that Paul's work has come to be regarded as a development or variation on themes derived from Jewish tradition.[255] The same assertion holds true when we examine Paul's use of *sarx* — for bodily substance, for man indi-

---

1962), pp. 282-284, 293-295; David Hill, *Greek Words and Hebrew Meanings: Studies in the Semantics of Soteriological Terms* (Cambridge, 1967), p. 242; and the exchange between Robert G. Bratcher and Eduard Schweizer in *Interpretation*, 16 (1962), 490-492; 17 (1963), 122f.

[250] Lohmeyer, *op. cit.*, p. 317; Kuhn, art. cit., *EvT*, 12 (1952-53), 276-278; and see Hill and Bratcher, *loc. cit.*

[251] So, for example, Swete, pp. 346f., and Hauck, p. 173; and see Wilfred L. Knox, *Some Hellenistic Elements in Primitive Christianity* (London, 1944), p. 3.

[252] See Menzies, p. 259; Wellhausen, p. 128; Loisy, *Évangiles synoptiques*, II, 567, n. 3; *idem, Marc*, p. 414; Rawlinson, p. 212; Lagrange, p. 390; Lohmeyer, p. 317; Taylor, p. 555; Schmid, p. 276.

[253] So, for example, H. Lüdemann, O. Pfleiderer, K. Holsten, H. J. Holtzmann, W. Bousset, K. Lake, C. G. Montefiore, W. Morgan. For this and the following note, see W. David Stacey, *The Pauline View of Man: In Relation to its Judaic and Hellenistic Background* (London, 1956), pp. 41-54.

[254] So, for example, A. Schweitzer, H. St. J. Thackeray, H. W. Robinson, H. A. A. Kennedy, E. De Witt Burton, W. D. Davies, J. A. T. Robinson, W. D. Stacey.

[255] Stacey, *op. cit.*, pp. 128-138; for classification of Paul's usage, cf. s. v. *"pneuma"* B.-A.-G. and Zorell, *Lexicon Graecum Novi Testamenti*, 3rd ed. (Paris, 1961).

vidually or generically, for the solidarities of relationship or descent, for the world or sphere in which man dwells, for man in his weakness before God, or for man as enslaved by sin. Here again Paul is but employing or developing meanings already anticipated in Hebrew thought.[256] Even Paul's *sarx-pneuma* opposition, which is a contrast between man and the superhuman, between creaturely weakness and God-given power, not between the weakness and strength of man himself, must be seen as a development of basically O. T. anthropology.[257] And if that is so, then the Markan opposition of flesh and spirit fits no better into the context of Pauline thought than it does into that of the O. T. itself.

Does it follow that Mk 14:38 is simply the product of Hellenistic Christian reflection, as the implied dualism, the parenetic content, the obviously rhetorical Greek style, balance and rhythm of the verse, and the contrast of *men* and *de* so rarely found in Mark would seem to suggest?[258] Despite its Greek terminology and style, the antithesis in Mark "does not have the same sense as in Hellenistic psychology; what stands opposed to (sinful) flesh is not a better part of man but the divine election."[259] Mark's thought is no more dualistic in the Greek sense than that of late Judaism represented, for example, in the Qumran writings.[260] Yet the dichotomy between flesh and spirit within man himself seems decidedly more pronounced both in Mark and in the Qumran writings than it is in either Paul or the O. T.[261]

---

[256] Stacey, *op. cit.*, pp. 154-173; Alexander Sand, *Der Begriff "Fleisch" in der paulinischen Hauptbriefen* (Regensburg, 1967), pp. 295-300; and for classification of Paul's usage, cf. Rudolf Bultmann, *Theology of the New Testament*, tr. Kendrick Grobel, I (London, 1959), pp. 232-239; J. A. T. Robinson, *op. cit.* (see above p. 40, n. 243), pp. 17-26; Schweizer, *TWNT*, VII, 124-136; B.-A.-G. and Zorell, *op. cit.*, s. v. "*sarx*."

[257] W. D. Davies, *Paul and Rabbinic Judaism: Some Rabbinic Elements in Pauline Theology*, 2nd ed. (London, 1962), pp. 19f.; J. A. T. Robinson, *op. cit.*, pp. 11f., 20 and n. 1; Stacey, *op. cit.*, pp. 174-180. This statement stands despite Paul's employment on occasion of an "anthropological *pneuma*." See Schweizer, *TDNT*, VI, 415-437, esp. 434ff. And, of course, it is not always the same meanings which are being contrasted by the antithesis of the two terms, as Burton, *op. cit.*, pp. 197f., shows.

[258] Knox, *loc. cit.*; Johnson, *op. cit.*, p. 236; and see further below Chapter 4. The likelihood that the verse is simply a gloss is contested by Schweizer, art. cit., *EvT*, 15 (1955), 570, n. 33.

[259] Schweizer, *TDNT*, VI, 396f.

[260] *Idem, TWNT*, VII, 123f.

[261] Karl Georg Kuhn, art. cit., in *The Scrolls and the New Testament*, p. 105 and n. 33; J.A.T. Robinson, *op. cit.*, p. 20, n. 1.

This is what has led Kuhn to see the anthropology of the Qumran community as the proximate context for the formulation found in Mk 14:38b, without thereby denying the O. T. foundations underlying both.[262] What Kuhn sees as differentiating the Qumran anthropology from that of the O. T. is that "flesh" stands in contrast not only to God, but also to the "spirit of truth" which believers are predestined to receive from God. "Man as 'flesh' is unworthy of God and prone to do evil, or rather, prone to succumb to the Evil One, while the spirit of the pious, as the 'spirit of truth,' places him in the battlefront on God's side against the Evil One. Thus 'flesh' becomes a contrast to the 'spirit' which rules the pious man and determines his good actions, and dwells within him; consequently 'flesh' becomes the area of weakness through the natural inclinations of man; it becomes almost synonymous with evil." [263] Kuhn is overstating the case when he identifies "flesh" as the sphere of ungodly power,[264] for the term is used at Qumran, as it is in the O. T., to designate the whole man as weak and mortal, and its association with sin is secondary and contextual.[265] The basic dualism in the Qumran documents is neither the simple antithesis of man and God in the O. T., nor yet the more developed antithesis of flesh and spirit in Paul, but rather the dualism of two spirits — the spirit of truth and the spirit of evil, both created by God — warring against each other with man as their battlefield and spoil until the end, when God will assure the triumph of the spirit of truth in the predestined.[266]

Even this dualism, which Kuhn ascribes to the influence of Iranian thought,[267] has its O. T. antecedents.[268] Nor does it com-

---

[262] Kuhn, art. cit., *EvT*, 12 (1952-53), 275-282.

[263] Kuhn, art. cit., in *The Scrolls and the New Testament*, p. 101; and see A. R.C. Leaney, *The Rule of Qumran and Its Meaning* (London, 1966), p. 255.

[264] *Ibid.*, pp. 103f.

[265] Hanswalter Huppenbauer, "[Bâsâr] 'Fleisch' in den Texten von Qumran (Höhle I)," *TZ*, 13 (1957), 298-300; Murphy, art. cit., *Sacra Pagina*, II, 61f., 68, 74f.: Rudolf Meyer, "*Sarx, ktl.*," *TWNT*, VII, 109-111; Sand. *op. cit.*, pp. 253-273, 303.

[266] J. Philip Hyatt, "The View of Man in the Qumran 'Hodayot'," *NTS*, 2 (1955-56), 280; W. D. Davies, "Paul and the Dead Sea Scrolls: Flesh and Spirit," in *The Scrolls and the New Testament*, pp. 171-177; Jacob Licht, "An Analysis of the Treatise on the Two Spirits in DSD," in *Scripta Hierosolymitana*, IV: *Aspects of the Dead Sea Scrolls*, ed. Chaim Rabin and Yigael Yadin, 2nd ed. (Jerusalem, 1965), pp. 88-100.

[267] Karl Georg Kuhn, "Die Sektenschrift und die iranische Religion," *ZKT*, 49 (1952), 296-316; and see Schweizer, *TDNT*, VI, 389f.

[268] See Hyatt, art. cit., pp. 283f.; Meyer, *TWNT*, VII, 113.

pletely displace the flesh-spirit dualism of the N. T.   For both the N. T. and at least some of the Scrolls share the view that "there is a contrast between the presence and the absence of the Holy Spirit in man who is of the flesh," and that "the Holy Spirit makes carnal man into spiritual man." [269]   This does not prove N. T. dependence upon the Qumran community, but it does provide a context for comparison with the flesh-spirit contrast in Paul and Mark closer than that of O. T., Greek or Gnostic thought.   Despite similarities, the differences between Paul and the Scrolls here are numerous and notable.[270]   And there is certainly no plausibility about reading into Mark's brief saying on flesh and spirit the whole Qumran framework of predestination, dualism and eschatology in which its own conceptions were elaborated.   But at the same time the conceptual background of Mark's saying is surely closer to Qumran than Paul is.   According to the Scrolls, where "flesh" is simply what man is in his creaturely weakness, and hence the root of his sinfulness, the faithful have received through God's predestination the "spirit of truth," through which they are able to will the good and overcome sin by disciplining and mastering the flesh.   Both this immanent dualism and this functional asceticism are features new to the O. T. opposition of flesh and spirit, but shared in common by Mk 14:38b and the Qumran literature.[271]   Accordingly, the meaning of Mk 14:38 is that God has gifted the elect with a willing spirit, but if this spirit is to prevail over their weakness before God as men of flesh, it must be active, as it is in Jesus, through the discipline of watchfulness and prayer.

Verse 39: *Kai palin apelthôn prosêuxato ton auton logon eipôn.*

B. Weiss [272] calls attention to the fact that the repeated returns to prayer bear out the meaning of the imperfect of repeated action

---

[269] David Flusser, "The Dead Sea Sect and Pre-Pauline Christianity," in *Scripta Hierosolymitana*, IV, esp. pp. 252-263; quotations on p. 257.

[270] See Kuhn, art. cit., in *The Scrolls and the New Testament*, pp. 104-196; Davies, *ibidem*, pp. 160-171, 177-182; Murphy, art. cit., pp. 74-76; Schweizer, *TWNT*, VII, 131 and n. 266.

[271] Kuhn, art. cit., *EvT*, 12 (1952-53), 275-282; Grundmann, *op. cit.*, p. 294. From the origin of both halves of v. 38 in one and the same tradition Kuhn, p. 284, concludes to the unity of the verse as a whole.

[272] *Op. cit.*, p. 461.

encountered in v. 35. But others see in the repetition only a
literary device to bring out the point of the scene.[273] Zerwick
notes that Mark elsewhere (e.g., 1:20; 3:31; 5:33; 11:6; 15:8)
employs indirect discourse to avoid the prolixity of direct
discourse and unwarranted repetition, and he singles out 14:70 as
a particularly striking parallel to the present verse. Both at
Gethsemane and at the Denial of Peter it is on the first and third
occasion that the words of the principal figure are quoted, while
the second occasion is reported indirectly merely as a repetition
of the first.[274] In any case, although no further information is
given about this prayer, the repetition does serve to heighten tension, particularly by setting the lonely figure of the Son of Man
at prayer against that of the sleeping, spiritually blinded disciples.[275]

The phrase *ton auton logon eipôn* is omitted by D it. Taylor [276]
and Cranfield [277] consider it a gloss. Wellhausen [278] follows D here
and adopts the shorter reading without the reference back to
14:36. But if the phrase is retained, then it means "speaking to
the same effect," or "uttering the same petition," rather than
"saying the same word(s)." [279] And since v. 39 is taken over whole
by Matthew (26:44) for his description of the third prayer of
Jesus, the phrase must have belonged to the original text of
Mark.[280]

Verse 40: *Kai palin elthôn heuren autous katheudontas, êsan gar autôn hoi ophthalmoi katabarynomenoi, kai ouk êdeisan ti apokrithôsing autô.*

Like the final phrase in v. 39, *palin* in v. 40 is omitted by D it.
But there is more reason to retain it, notes Taylor, because of
the *to triton* in v. 41.

---

[273] Loisy, *Marc*, p. 416, holds that Mark uses the three prayers to fill
out the three watches of the night. Montefiore, *op. cit.*, p. 345, finds the
triple going and coming of Christ "dramatic, but scarcely historic."
[274] Max Zerwick, *op. cit.* (see above p. 5, n. 3), p. 31.
[275] Cf. Lohmeyer, Nineham, E. Schweizer, *ad loc.*
[276] *Op. cit.*, p. 555.
[277] *Op. cit.*, p. 434.
[278] *Op. cit.*, p. 128.
[279] So Swete, Plummer, Rawlinson, *ad loc.*
[280] Jack Finegan, *Die Überlieferung der Leidens- und Auferstehungsgeschichte Jesu* (Giessen, 1934), p. 18.

There are striking echoes in this verse of the Synoptic Transfiguration accounts: in particular, the sleep of the disciples in Lk 9:32 (*êsan bebarêmenoi hypnô*), and the inability of the disciples to answer in Mk 9:6 (*ou gar êdei [ho Petros] ti apokrithê; ekphoboi gar egenonto*). With regard to the sleep of the disciples, Loisy [281] was of the opinion that tradition had associated the Transfiguration and Gethsemane scenes as the two extremes of Jesus' glory and pain before his death, and that the presence of this detail in both Mk 14:40b and Lk 9:32 is due not to literary dependence, but to this association in the tradition. Yet it is remarkable how many more parallels there are to Gethsemane in Luke's Transfiguration account than in Mark's or Matthew's. Not only are the disciples depicted as asleep, but in both scenes Luke describes the action as taking place on a mount at night, he has the disciples "follow" Jesus there, and he shows Jesus, in contrast to his weak disciples, praying and strengthened by heavenly messengers.[282] This assimilation of details between the two accounts in Luke seems to exhibit a stage in the development and interpretation of the tradition which prepares for the ultimate disappearance in John of the Gethsemane and Transfiguration accounts as individual scenes, and for the emergence in Jn 12:23-30 of a fresh account containing features of both.[283]

With regard to the inability of the disciples to answer, B. Weiss [284] points out that the meaning of the phrase about not knowing what to answer is quite different in the two contexts of Mark where it occurs. In Mk 9:6 the confusion is explained as the result of fear. In 14:40c the phrase bears its proper meaning: the

---

[281] *Évangiles synoptiques*, II, 568f.

[282] M. Sabbe, "La rédaction du récit de la Transfiguration," *Recherches Bibliques*, VI (n.p., 1962), 92-95; Anthony Kenny, "The Transfiguration and the Agony in the Garden," *CBQ*, 19 (1957), 444-452; Hans Conzelmann, *The Theology of St Luke*, tr. Geoffrey Buswell (London, 1964), p. 58.

[283] For the fusion of the Gethsemane and Transfiguration traditions in John, see Edwin Clement Hoskyns, *The Fourth Gospel*, ed. Francis Noel Davey, 2nd ed. (London, 1961), pp. 81f., 423-427; followed by Arthur Michael Ramsey, *The Glory of God and the Transfiguration of Christ* (London, 1967), pp. 123f.; and see Rudolf Bultmann, *Das Evangelium des Johannes* (Göttingen, 1964), p. 327, n. 7; followed by Raymond E. Brown, *The Gospel according to John* (i-xii) (New York, 1966), p. 476. Opposed to this point of view is C. H. Dodd, *Historical Tradition in the Fourth Gospel* (Cambridge, 1963), p. 69 and n. 1, who, while recognized Jn 12:27f. as an equivalent of the Synoptic Gethsemane account, denies that it is a parallel to the Transfiguration.

[284] *Op. cit.*, p. 461.

disciples do not know what excuse to give when Jesus reproaches them for sleeping. Lohmeyer and Taylor,[285] on the other hand, feel that v. 40b is offering an explanation or excuse for the sleep of the disciples, perhaps similar in nature to the *apo tês lypês* of Lk 22:45. But Riesenfeld seems closer to Mark's mind in taking the disciples' inability to answer in both contexts as a sign of their incomprehension before the revelation of essentially messianic motifs: the glory of the Messiah at the Transfiguration and his humiliation at Gethsemane. *Ekphoboi gar egenonto* in Mk 9:6 is not offered as an excuse for their confusion, but as a statement of their obduracy. For the disciples' fear, here as elsewhere in Mark, has a theological meaning: namely, their lack of faith and understanding of the messianic import of Jesus' words and actions. Since in the Gethsemane scene, moreover, Jesus' *ekthambeisthai kai adêmonein* are messianic motifs, Mark there uses sleep rather than fear as the image of the disciples' incomprehension.[286]

While these interpretations of the meaning of the disciples' sleep and confusion in Mark are all possible, it seems preferable to see the whole of v. 40 as illustrating in an unmistakable way the rupture of the Paschal communion of which we spoke above in discussing vv. 34 and 37. Thus Rabbi Jose ben Halaphta (ca. 150 A.D.), who has often preserved much earlier traditions, transmits a rule for the Passover meal which in all likelihood goes back to N.T. times: namely, that the meal may be resumed if some of the members of the company doze, but not if they fall into deep sleep.[287] Daube argues that the rule would certainly have applied to the situation of Jesus and the disciples in Gethsemane, and that it was what gave point to his exhortation to wakefulness. But what was the criterion to distinguish dozing from sleeping? Much later, at the beginning of the fifth century, we find one given by Rabbi Aschi (d. 427) which is strikingly reminiscent of Mark's description of the disciples: a man is dozing "if, when addressed, he replies but does not know how to answer

---

[285] *Ad loc.*

[286] Harald Riesenfeld, *Jésus transfiguré: l'arrière-plan du récit évangélique de la transfiguration de Notre-Seigneur* (Copenhagen, 1947), pp. 281-291. Similarly E. Schweizer, "Zur Frage des Messiasgeheimnisses bei Markus," *ZNW*, 56 (1965), 3, and G. Minette de Tillesse, *Le secret messianique dans l'Évangile de Marc* (Paris, 1968), pp. 275f., who also suggests that this motif corresponds to a condition actually prevailing in Mark's church (p. 442).

[287] S.-B., I, 969f.

sensibly." [288]   Even in N. T. times some such criterion may have
been current. If so, then we have good reason to see in the repeated returns of Jesus to his first dozing (vv. 37, 40) and then
ultimately sleeping disciples (v. 41: *katheudete to loipon kai
anapauesthe*) Mark's graphic description of the gradual dissolu-
tion of the Passover *ḥabhura* and the final loneliness of Jesus
before his hour.[289]

> Verse 41: *Kai erchetai to triton kai legei autois:
> katheudete to loipon kai anapauesthe; apechei;
> êlthen hê hôra, idou paradidotai ho huios tou
> anthrôpou eis tas cheiras tôn hamartôlôn.*

Mark does not explicitly say that Jesus withdrew a third
time to pray. And this was not, as Menzies suggests, because "the
reporter had been too sleepy to notice it" [290]   Rather, it was because this verse is meant to emphasize his third return to the
sleeping disciples.[291]   Matthew shifts the emphasis back equally
to the praying Jesus by filling in the content of his second prayer
(26:42) and by using Mark's description of the second withdrawal
to prayer for his own description of the third (26:44). The effect
of Mark's text is certainly a growing indictment of the disciples
for their failure to respond to Jesus' admonitions and reproaches.
And it is easy to miss the significance of Jesus' threefold prayer.
Rabbinic literature contains a number of examples of the repetition of prayer, especially under trial.[292]   And 2 Cor 12:8 is probably
evidence of a tradition of tripling prayer to overcome temptation.[293]   Luke has either missed this point in his reduction of
Mark, or else he has followed another tradition. Loisy opts for
the latter alternative. He criticizes the tripling in Mark as an
artificial construct, which except for the first prayer lacks sufficient content, and which was probably meant simply to fill
in the hours of the third watch and bring into relief by contrast
the soon to follow threefold denial of Peter and the insensitivity

---

[288] *Ibid.*, p. 970.
[289] D. Daube, *The New Testament and Rabbinic Judaism*, pp. 332-335;
Grundmann, *op. cit.*, p. 294.
[290] *Op. cit.*, p. 260.
[291] For the historical present tense here, see above p. 8.
[292] S.-B., I, 994f.
[293] Lagrange, *op. cit.*. p. 390.

4

of the disciples to Jesus' threefold appeal.[294] Branscomb, too, finds the threefold rhythm artificial — "almost liturgical." [295]

Katheudete to loipon kai anapauesthe is a difficult phrase to interpret. How is it to be taken: as interrogative, imperative, or indicative? Grammatically all three are possible. Nevertheless, B. Weiss considers it impossible to interpret the phrase as a question because *to lopon* cannot mean "still," [296] the meaning it would have to bear if the present tense of the verb has its normal force. If, on the other hand, *to loipon* is understood in its usual sense of "henceforth" or "from here on," then the simple present tense cannot be used to ask whether the disciples will go on sleeping for the rest of the night.[297] Thus, he argues, the phrase must be taken as a command, not a question.[298] Yet both Plummer and Bernard, while referring *to loipon* to the future, regard it as an obstacle to the imperative rather than to the interrogative interpretation of the phrase.[299] Actually the chief difficulty with taking *katheudete* as imperative here is contextual. For it stands in glaring contradiction to the preceding *grêgoreite kai proseuchesthe* of v. 38, and more significantly still with the immediately following *egeiresthe, agômen* of v. 42. Loisy resolves this tension on the supposition that the pre-Markan tradition knew only the saying "Sleep now and take your rest" (a possibility frustrated by the arrival of Judas), and that everything after the obscure, transitional *apechei* (v. 41b) is redactional.[300] Other commentators, in the attempt to reconcile an imperative interpretation of v. 41 with the context, have resorted to considering it ironic.[301] Still others, considering irony out of place, have followed St. Augustine in seeing the command as permissive of a short time

---

[294] *Loisy, Evangiles synoptiques,* II, 571f.; *Marc,* p. 416.

[295] *Op. cit.,* p. 268.

[296] Essentially the meaning is future-oriented: "from now," while "still" is past-oriented: "until now." See Moulton and Turner, *op. cit.,* III, 336.

[297] But see *ibidem*; and B.-A.-G., s. v., 3. a. α.

[298] B. Weiss, pp. 462f. So also Schanz, pp. 391f.; Loisy, *Evangile synoptiques,* II, 570; *Marc,* pp. 417f.; Lagrange, pp. 390-392; Schmid, p. 277; Lidell and Scott, s. v., 3.

[299] Plummer, p. 330; J. H. Bernard, "St. Mark xiv. 41, 42," *ET,* 3 (1891-92), 451-453. He paraphrases: "Are you sleeping and resting *for the time that yet remains?*" (p. 453).

[300] *Loc. cit.* (see above n. 294).

[301] So J. Weiss, Swete, Lagrange, Schmid, *ad loc.* And see also Meyer, *op. cit.* (see above p. 15, n. 77), II, 222f.; McNeile, *op. cit.* (see above p. 14, n. 74), p. 392; Uricchio and Stano, *op. cit.,* p. 589.

of rest, now that the reasons for wakefulness no longer exist.[302] But this latter course leaves the contextual tension unresolved.

The best solution for the problem lies in taking another meaning for *to loipon* and giving a different rendering to *katheudete*. The adverbial use of *(to) loipon* in Hellenistic Greek developed an inferential senso of "so, then, therefore, thus," which eventually came to predominate.[303] In fact, it has been argued that with but few exceptions the expression has become even in the N. T. little more than a transitional particle introducing a logical conclusion or a new departure in the development and essentially equivalent in usage to *oun*.[304] Such an inferential meaning for *to loipon*, probably coupled here with what Cavallin has designated as an interjectional function,[305] fits with any rendering of *katheudete* that has been suggested and leaves the choice open to be determined by the sense of the context rather than the sense of the adverb. The less common, though still possible, meaning of "meanwhile" found in Josephus (*Ant.* 18, 272) could also fit at least with an indicative or an interrogative rendering of the verb.[306] J. Aars, opting for the inferential sense of *to loipon*, felt that the phrase in question translates most naturally in the indicative as a painful or melancholy exclamation: "So you are sleeping and taking your rest!"[307] But the interrogative rendering, favored by Bernard, Pallis,[308] and the commentaries of Well-

---

[302] So Menzies, p. 260; Innitzer, *op. cit.* (see above p. 14, n. 74), p. 130. And see also B. Weiss, *Das Matthäus-Evangelium*, 3rd ed. (Göttingen, 1898), p. 462; Carl Friedrich Keil, *Commentar über das Evangelium des Matthäus* (Leipzig, 1877), p. 551; Theodor Zahn, *Das Evangelium des Matthäus*, 4th ed. (Leipzig and Erlangen, 1922), p. 703; and Pierre Bonnard, *L'Évangile selon Saint Matthieu* (Neuchatel, 1963), p. 384.

[303] See Moulton and Milligan, s. v.; Moulton and Turner, *loc. cit.*; B.-D.-F., 451 (6).

[304] Cf. A. N. Jannaris, "Misreadings and Misrenderings in the New Testament," *Exp*, 5th ser., 8 (1898), 428-431; C. F. D. Moule, *An Idiom Book of New Testament Greek*, 2nd ed. (Cambridge, 1960), p. 161; and Margaret E. Thrall, *Greek Particles in the New Testament* (Leiden, 1962), pp. 25-30.

[305] Anders Cavallin, "*(to) loipon*. Eine bedeutungsgeschichtliche Untersuchung," *Eranos*, 39 (1941), 121-144, esp. 133-142.

[306] See B.-A.-G., *loc. cit.*

[307] J. Aars, "Zu Matth. 26, 45 und Marc. 14, 41," *ZWT*, 38 (1895), 378-383; and similarly Thomas Chase, "*To loipon*, Matt. xxvi. 45," *JBL*, 6 (1886, Part I), 131-135, who takes the phrase as imperative, assigns the same meaning for *to loipon* or alternatively considers it as an accusative of inner content with *katheudete* (= "Sleep the rest of your sleep").

[308] Bernard, art. cit.; A. Pallis, *A Few Notes on the Gospels according to St. Mark and St. Matthew* (Liverpool, 1903), p. 24.

hausen, Plummer, E. Klostermann, Rawlinson, Hauck, Lohmeyer, Taylor, Cranfield, Haenchen, and E. Schweizer, *ad loc.*, does seem the best interpretation on the whole because of the context. Taking v. 41 as a reproachful question eliminates the contradiction which is generated in regard to vv. 38 and 42 by taking it as a command, and fits better with the fact that the previous reproaches, expressed in v. 37 and implied (*apokrithôsin*) in v. 40, were also questions.

Without doubt the single word *apechei* poses the most difficult exegetical question in Mark's account. Any number of meanings have been proposed for it, and none of them is entirely satisfactory. That this has been the case almost from the start is shown by the quantity of textual variants which are obviously attempts to achieve an appropriate sense. *Apechei* is omitted from the text altogether by Ψ 50 892 k and the Bohairic version; but this is little more than the readiest avenue of escape. Among the Latin versions the Vulgate, d and q read *sufficit*, although this meaning is supported by only a few late, uncertain examples from the literature and papyri.[309] A number of Greek MSS. (D W Θ Φ, Fam. 13, 565, 1009, 1071, 1216, 1365), many of the Old Latin versions (a b c d f ff² q r¹), the Armenian, and among the Syriac versions the Sinaitic, the Harclean and the Peshitta contain the addition *to telos* or its equivalent. Taylor[310] thinks that this may well have been the original reading, attested as it is by a small but important group of Western, Caesarean and Eastern authorities, and fitting well with the eschatological vocabulary of the surrounding context. But it may just as well have come into Mark's text later under the influence of the saying in Lk 22:37, *to peri emou telos echei*, in an attempt to make sense out of the solitary and enigmatic *apechei*.[311] And the suspicion that this latter possibility is the case is only confirmed by a study of the differences among the MSS and versions containing the reading *to telos*. The Greek side of Codex Bezae reads *apechei to telos kai hê hôra*, which the Latin side renders *sufficit finis et hora*, whatever that may mean. c is close to d in lacking any equivalent for *êlthen*, which, however, appears in the rest of the

---

[309] Cf. B.-A.-G., s. v. *apechô*; B.-D.-F., 129; A. Pallis, *op. cit.*, pp. 22f.; J. de Zwaan, "The Text and Exegesis of Mark XIV 41, and the Papyri," *Exp*, 6th ser., 12 (1905), 461-464; and Taylor, *op. cit.*, p. 556.

[310] *Op. cit.*, pp. 556f.

[311] So Cranfield, *Mark*, p. 435; but cf. James T. Hudson, "Irony in Gethsemane?" *ET*, 46 (1934-35), 382.

versions. a is alone in interpreting the phrase *consummatus est finis advenit hora.* c f ff² and r¹ instead of *sufficit* read *adest*, which de Zwaan claims must have been translating an alteration of *apechei* to *epechei* in the underlying Greek text; and, in fact, one cursive does show this reading.[312] The Syriac versions, too, seem to attest something like *êngiken* (Taylor) or less probably *epechei* (de Zwaan). The testimony, then, is anything but univocal either for the text or for its meaning. *Pace* Taylor, the evidence is that the textual variants exhibit no consistent trend and are best explained as attempts to clarify the admittedly difficult and obscure original reading *apechei*, which nevertheless possesses much stronger and more universal support among the witnesses.[313]

Those who regard the longer reading as original have been in no more agreement about its meaning than those who follow the shorter. Paul-Louis Couchoud bypasses the difficulty of its meaning in the context by treating it like a marginal note, as in k.[314] James T. Hudson, followed by Taylor,[315] has given *apechei* its normal intransitive meaning and rendered the phrase as an ironical question: "The end is far away?" This requires treating *katheudete* and *anapauesthe* as questions also: "Still asleep? still resting?" And he maintains that failure to see this was what gave rise to the other scribal and translational variants.[316] Matthew Black has resorted to the explanation that the Greek text such as we have in D resulted from the misreading of a Dalath as a Rish in the original Aramaic of the passage. And thus *reheq* 'is far-off' replaced *deheq* 'is pressing,' so that the proper translation should have been: "The end and the hour are pressing," or following other readings than D: "The end is pressing, (and) the hour has come." Furthermore, he is able to adduce an exact parallel to this expression in a proverb from the Babylonian Talmud: "He who tries to press the hour, him the hour presses."[317] Finally, there is also the suspiciously ad hoc suggestion

---

[312] J. de Zwaan, art. cit., p. 464.
[313] ℵ A B C K L X Δ Π 0112 Fam 1 28 700 1010 1079 1195 1230 1241 1242 1253 1344 1546 1646 2148 2174   Letc it^aur, ¹ vg cop^sa, ^bo (^mss) Augustine.
[314] Paul-Louis Couchoud, "Notes de critique verbale sur St. Marc et St. Matthieu," *JTS*, 34 (1933), 113-138.
[315] *Loc. cit.*
[316] Hudson, *loc. cit.* (see above p. 52, n. 311).
[317] Matthew Black, *op. cit.*, (see above p. 6, n.10), pp. 225f.

that the phrase has a plain indicative meaning like "this is the end," [318] or "it is the end [of the matter]." [319]

The shorter reading of the simple *apechei* has exercised the ingenuity of translators and exegetes to an even greater extent than the longer. The majority of them have followed the Vulgate, d and q in adopting the dubiously attested translation "it is enough." Enough of what? B. and J. Weiss and Schanz [320] take it as referring to Jesus' own situation, not to the disciples: "Jesus hat gesiegt und bedarf die Jünger nicht mehr." [321] Swete [322] regards it as a transition from Jesus' momentary play of irony in the imperatives *katheudete* and *anapauesthe* to the resumption of his usual seriousness in what follows. Plummer [323] considers "enough" the correct meaning, but leaves unspecified the reference. Lagrange finds Swete's interpretation overly subtle and, like Loisy,[324] prefers to see *apechei* in relation to what has preceded, viz., the watching and praying of the disciples: "Le v. 41 indique que le moment de veiller en priant est terminé; on est entré dans la phase de l'action." [325] But a greater number of commentators tend to view it as a reference rather to the sleep of the disciples, since the account has been at pains to show precisely that they have not really been watching and praying at all.[326]

Basing themselves on the claim that such an impersonal usage of *apechei* is unexampled and such a meaning rare, another group of interpretations have developed from the attempt to supply a subject for *apechei* from the immediate context and to allow the verb one of its more usual meanings. Thus an unsigned article, which appeared in *Theologische Studien und Kritiken* for 1843, translates: "He [Judas] is far away," taikng *ho paradidous me* of v. 42 as the understood subject of *apechei*.[327]

---

[318] B.-A.-G., s. v.

[319] B.-D.-F., 129.

[320] *Ad loc.*

[321] B. Weiss, *op. cit.*, p. 463.

[322] *Op. cit.*, p. 348.

[323] *Op. cit.*, p. 330.

[324] *Évangile synoptiques*, II, 569f.

[325] *Op. cit.*, p. 392.

[326] So Wellhausen, p. 128, who considers v. 41b secondary because of the Son of Man saying, and connects *apechei* directly with *egeiresthe* in v. 42; E. Klostermann, p. 151, who with Bultmann prefers to regard both vv. 41b and 42 as redactional; and Rawlinson, Hauck, Grundmann, Cranfield, Nineham, *ad loc.*

[327] Anonymous, "Erklärung einiger dunkeln Stellen des Neuen Testaments," *TSK*, 16 (1843), 103-140; see pp. 103-106 for Mk 14:41.

But this interpretation labors under the difficulty that Jesus must contradict immediately what he has just said by affirming the arrival of the betrayer on the scene. To account for the abrupt change, we must imagine that Jesus has suddenly seen or heard the approaching crowd and recognized Judas among them, suppositions that have no foundation in the text.

Adolf Deissmann has documented from the papyri and ostraca a personal use of *apechein* as a technical term in commercial receipts and contracts meaning "to have received." [328] Developing this lead, J. de Zwaan notes further that nowhere in the papyri is *apechein* used impersonally or with the sense "it is enough." And so, turning to Mk 14:41, he appeals to the context (Mk 14:11, 18-20, 42f.) and concludes that Judas must be the subject of *apechei* and so translates v. 41: "*Judas* did receive *the promised money*. The hour is come, the Son of Man is betrayed into the hands of sinners." [329] G. H. Boobyer is carrying this line of interpretation only one step further when he observes that, among the six N. T. occurrences of *apechein* in the meaning of "to have received" or "to receive" — Mt 6:2, 5, 16; Lk 6:24; Phil 4:18; Philem 15 — the last mentioned signifies the receiving of one person by another. He argues that *apechei* in Mk 14:41 is logically connected with the following betrayal and arrest, and that it therefore has the same subject: namely, Judas, who with the help of the crowd that comes with him is about to "take possession" of Jesus. Thus he translates vv. 41-42: "You are still asleep? Still resting? He is taking possession of (me)! The hour has come! Behold, the Son of Man is being delivered into the hands of sinners. Arise! Let us go! Behold, the one who hands me over is near." [330] These last two interpretations offered by de Zwaan and Boobyer may certainly be criticized for reading too much into *apechei*. In addition, de Zwaan, like the author of the first opinion we discussed, has had to make the same gratuitous assumptions about Jesus' sudden recognition of Judas, in order to reconcile his translation of *apechei* with the preceding

---

[328] Adolf Deissmann, *Bible Studies*, tr. Alexander Grieve, 2nd ed. (Edinburgh, 1909), p. 229; *op. cit.* (see above p. 6, n. 5), pp. 110-112; Moulton and Milligan, s. v., add a few further examples to those almost contemporary with the N. T. writings supplied by Deissmann.

[329] J. de Zwaan, art. cit. (see above p. 52, n. 309), pp. 466-471: quotation on p. 470; see also E. A. Smisson, "Mark xiv. 41: *apechei*," *ET*, 40 (1928-29), 528.

[330] G. H. Boobyer, "*APECHEI* in Mark 14, 41," *NTS*, 2 (1955-56), 44-48; quotation on p. 48.

imperatives *katheudete* and *anapauesthe*. Boobyer avoids this
incongruity by translating both verbs as questions, but he cannot
escape the ultimate difficulty facing all three opinions, the difficulty which resides precisely in attempting to provide a meaning for *apechei* from the surrounding context of the passion narrative when originally the Gethsemane account may have been
altogether independent of its present context, as we shall later
try to show.[331]

Perhaps because of the formidable difficulties facing the
personal interpretation of *apechei*, the suggestion has also been
made that it be taken in its technical commercial sense, but impersonally: "it is receipted in full," "the account is closed."[332]
But this makes little sense in the context except on the basis of
the same assumptions that support the personal interpretation,
and so proves no more successful. Bauer (s. v.) offers the further
conjecture by analogy with the expression *ouden apechei* 'nothing hinders' that *apechei* here might be translated "that is a hin-
drance," with reference to the sleep of the disciples at the hour
of crisis. Black rejects the conjecture of Torrey that *apechei*
has resulted from a translator's mistake in giving the Syriac
meaning of "enough" to the original Aramaic *kaddu* 'already.'
For the word usually means "already" in both dialects, and the
translator would have had to go out of his way to choose the
much less common and suitable meaning "enough," and then
to render it by a Greek verb only rarely carrying that meaning.[333]
And Pallis' conjecture that *apechei* evolved through *apestê* from
an original *epestê* is altogether mistaken according to Blass.[334]
After reviewing all the opinions that have been offered, it is not
hard to understand why Baljon[335] should have considered the
reading absurd and rejected it as a gloss, and why even so distinguished an exegete as Ernst Lohmeyer[336] in despair should
have followed in his footsteps.

Elthen hê hôra announces that the hour, over which Jesus
had prayed in v. 35, has not passed him by. Rather, the hour of
God has struck, not simply the hour of betrayal and arrest, but
the hour that brings the climax to Jesus' messianic ministry,

---

[331] See below Chapter 4.
[332] B.-A.-G., s. v.; B.-D.-F., 129.
[333] Black, *op. cit.*, p. 225.
[334] B.-D.-F., 129.
[335] J. M. S. Baljon, *Novum Testamentum Graece ... in usum studioso-
rum* (Groningae, 1898), *ad loc.*
[336] *Op. cit.*, p. 318.

the eschatological hour of fulfilment through his deliverance into the hands of sinners.[337] Zerwick comments that the reversal of word order in the two concluding phrases of v. 41, placing the verbs *êlthen* and *paradidotai* emphatically before their respective subjects, is Mark's subtle way of stressing the present fulfilment of the previous passion announcements in 9:31 and 10:33.[338]

The Son of Man saying which follows here belongs to a complex of sayings that is surely among the most problematic in the whole New Testament. Despite an immense volume of literature, which continues to accumulate on the subject, there is at present little unanimity of scholarly opinion in answer to any number of vexing questions. For example, contemporary scholars cannot agree as to which of the three generally recognized classifications of the saying — sayings about the Son of Man's earthly activity, his passion, or his parousia — are authentic with Jesus, products of community tradition, or secondary formulations of the evangelists. Little wonder that there is even greater divergency of results in determining the origins of individual sayings. Again, the derivation of the term "Son of Man" itself is disputed. And there is no unequivocal answer even to the seemingly simple question of whether Jesus ever actually used it as a self-designation. It is beyond the scope of our treatment to come to grips with the larger issues of the Son of Man problem.[339] The most we can hope for in regard to the saying

---

[337] Lohmeyer, Taylor, *ad loc.* E. Schweizer, *op. cit.*, p. 181, describes it thus: "So wird betont, dass sich in dieser zeitlichen 'Stunde' (v. 37) die 'Stunde' Gottes (schon v. 35 ähnlich), im 'Ausliefern' an die Behörden das von Gott beschlossene 'Ausliefern' vollzieht."

[338] Cf. the order subject-verb (*ho paradidous me êngiken*) in v. 42 immediately following. It is no merely stylistic peculiarity of Mark's. See Zerwick, *op. cit.* (see above p. 5, n. 3), pp. 99-102.

[339] For this we must refer the reader to the literature. Helpful summaries of the debate in recent decades can be found in the following articles: C. C. McCown, "Jesus, Son of Man. A Survey of Recent Discussion," *JR*, 28 (1948), 1-12; A. J. B. Higgins, "Son of Man-*Forschung* since *The Teaching of Jesus*," in *New Testament Essays*, ed. A. J. B. Higgins (Manchester, 1959), pp. 119-135; Matthew Black, "The Son of Man Problem in Recent Research and Debate," *BJRL*, 45 (1962-63), 305-318; G. Haufe, "Das Menschensohn-Problem in der gegenwärtigen wissentschaftlichen Diskussion," *EvT*, 26 (1966), 130-141; Ransom Marlow, "The *Son of Man* in Recent Journal Literature," *CBQ*, 28 (1966), 20-30; I. Howard Marshall, "The Synoptic Son of Man Sayings in Recent Discussion," *NTS*, 12 (1965-66), 327-351; and *idem*, "The Son of Man in Contemporary Debate," *EQ*, 42 (1970), 67-87; J. N. Birdsall, "Who Is This Son of Man?" *EQ*, 42 (1970), 7-17. Among the

before us is to determine something of its prehistory, its use in
Mark's gospel, and its meaning.

---

more important current literature, one should consult the following:
Matthew Black, "Servant of the Lord and Son of Man," *SJT*, 6 (1953), 1-11;
idem, "The 'Son of Man' Passion Sayings in the Gospel Tradition," *ZNW*,
60 (1969), 1-8; Frederick Houk Borsch, *The Son of Man in Myth and
History* (Philadelphia, 1967); *idem, The Christian and Gnostic Son of Man*
(London, 1970); Rudolf Bultmann, *The History of the Synoptic Tradition*,
tr. John Marsh (New York and Evanston, 1963); *idem, Theology of the
New Testament*, tr. Kendrick Grobel, I (London, 1959); Carsten Colpe,
"*Ho huios tou anthrôpou*," *TWNT*, VIII (Stuttgart, 1969), 403-481; Hans
Conzelmann, *An Outline of the Theology of the New Testament*, tr. John
Bowden (New York and Evanston, 1969); Oscar Cullmann, *The Christology
of the New Testament*, tr. Shirley C. Guthrie and Charles A. M. Hall, 2nd ed.
(London, 1963); Richard A. Edwards, "The Eschatological Correlative as a
Gattung in the New Testament," *ZNW*, 60 (1969), 9-20; Reginald H. Fuller,
The Mission and Achievement of Jesus (London, 1963); *idem, The Founda-
tions of New Testament Christology* (New York, 1965); Ferdinand Hahn,
Christologische Hoheitstitel, 3rd ed. (Göttingen, 1966); Eng. tr. *The Titles
of Jesus in Christology*, tr. Harold Knight and George Ogg (New York and
Cleveland, 1969); A. J. B. Higgins, *Jesus and the Son of Man* (London,
1964); *idem*, "Is the Son of Man Problem Insoluble?" in *Neotestamentica
et Semitica: Studies in Honour of Matthew Black*, ed. E. Earle Ellis and
Max Wilcox (Edinburgh, 1969), pp. 70-87; Morna D. Hooker, *The Son of
Man in Mark* (London, 1967); Gerhard Iber, *Überlieferungsgeschichtliche Untersuchungen zum Begriff des Menschensohnes im Neuen Testament*
(Diss. Heidelberg, [1953]); Joachim Jeremias, "Die älteste Schicht der
Menschensohn-Logien," *ZNW*, 58 (1967), 159-172; Willi Farxsen, *The Begin-
ings of Christology: A Study in its Problems*, tr. Paul J. Achtemeier (Philadel-
phia, 1969); Sigmund Mowinckel, *He That Cometh*, tr. G. W. Anderson
(Oxford, 1959); Rudolf Otto, *The Kingdom of God and the Son of Man*,
tr. F. V. Filson and B. Lee-Woolf (London, 1951); Norman Perrin, *Redis-
covering the Teaching of Jesus* (New York and Evanston, 1967); *idem*, "The
Son of Man in Ancient Judaism and Primitive Christianity: A Suggestion,"
BR, 11 (1966), 17-28; *idem*, "The Creative Use of the Son of Man Traditions
by Mark," *USQR*, 23 (1967-68), 357-365; *idem*, "The Son of Man in the
Synoptic Tradition," *BR*, 13 (1968), 3-25; Rudolf Schnackenburg, "Der
Menschensohn im Johannesevangelium," *NTS*, 11 (1965), 123-137; S. Schulz,
Untersuchungen zur Menschensohnchristologie im Johannesevangelium
(Göttingen, 1957); Eduard Schweizer, *Erniedrigung und Erhöhung bei
Jesus und seinen Nachfolgern* (Zürich, 1955); Eng. tr. *Lordship and Disciple-
ship* (London, 1960); *idem*, "Der Menschensohn," *ZNW*, 50 (1959), 185-209;
idem, "The Son of Man," *JBL*, 79 (1960), 119-129; *idem*, "The Son of Man
Again," *NTS*, 9 (1962-63), 256-261; Erik Sjöberg, *Der verborgene Menschen-
sohn in den Evangelien* (Lund, 1955); S. S. Smalley, "The Johannine Son of
Man Sayings," *NTS*, 15 (1969), 278-301; G. Strecker, "Die Leidens- und
Auferstehungsvoraussagen im Markusevangelium," *ZTK*, 64 (1967), 16-39;
Vincent Taylor, *New Testament Essays* (London, 1970); H. M. Teeple, "The
Origin of the Son of Man Christology," *JBL*, 84 (1965), 213-250; Heinz Eduard

Bultmann regarded all of the passion sayings, chiefly because of their total absence from Q, as *vaticinia ex eventu* formulated by the later Hellenistic Church.[340] But linguistic evidence and carefully conducted tradition-historical analysis do not support this conclusion, particularly in the case of the saying we are presently considering and its counterpart in Mk 9:31a. An analysis of the range of terms common to these two sayings will show why. First of all, the absolute use of *paradidômi* without any interpretive phrase cannot simply be due to the influence of Is 53. For such an explicit connection is established only with Rom 4:25; 8:32; 1 Cor 11:23, all of which stem from the pre-Pauline community. Hence synoptic passion sayings like these where the connection does not yet exist, must be of still earlier origin.[341] Secondly, the present tense *paradidotai* very likely represents an underlying Aramaic participle with a future meaning.[342] Thirdly, the expression *eis cheiras* (= *lîdê*) betrays Aramaic influence. Fourthly, the Aramaic play on words (*bar nâshâ/benê nâshâ*) behind Mk 9:31a — and possibly also behind 14:41b if *tôn hamartôlôn* is secondary — points to the same origins.[343] Finally, by adopting Kuhn's form-critical analysis of the Markan Gethsemane pericope as a whole, in preference to that of Bultmann, who comes to regard vv. 41b and 42 as secondary, H. E. Tödt can claim the existence of a pre-Markan account whose point is precisely the hour of the Son of Man's deliverance.[344] Thus the origins of some of the sayings about the

---

Tödt, *The Son of Man in the Synoptic Tradition*, tr. Dorothea M. Barton (London, 1965); Philipp Vielhauer, "Gottesreich und Menschensohn in der Verkündigung Jesu," in *Festschrift f"r Günther dehn*, ed. W. Schneemelscher (Neukirchen, 1957), pp. 51-79; *idem*, "Jesus und der Menschensohn. Zur Diskussion mit Heinz Eduard Tödt und Eduard Schweizer," *ZTK*, 60 (1963), 133-177.

[340] Bultmann, *The History of the Synoptic Tradition*, pp. 152 and n. 1, 268; and *Theology of the New Testament*, I, 28-31.

[341] Tödt, *op. cit.* (see above pp. 57-59, n. 339), pp. 156-161, 168f.

[342] Joachim Jeremias, art. cit. (see above pp. 57-59, n. 339), p. 169 and n. 30. But see B.-D.-F., 323 (1).

[343] Jeremias, *loc. cit.*; Tödt, *op. cit.*, pp. 176-180. See W. Zimmerli and J. Jeremias, *The Servant of God* (London, 1957), p. 102. F. Hahn, *op. cit.* (see above pp. 57-59, n. 339), p. 48, n. 4, is of the opinion that Mk 14:41b, like 9:31a, must originally have read *anthrôpôn* for *hamartôlôn* precisely because of the word play. And E. Lohmeyer, *Das Evangelium des Markus*, p. 301, notes a similar play between "the Son of Man" and "that man" in 14:21.

[344] Tödt, *op. cit.*, pp. 199 and n. 2, 200. For Kuhn's analysis, as opposed to Bultmann's, see below Chapter 4.

suffering Son of Man are pre-Markan and have their roots in the Aramaic-speaking Palestinian community.[345]   Ferdinand Hahn carries this conclusion one step further when he distinguishes among the passion sayings two types on the basis of whether or not there is a reference to the Scriptures, and discerns in the simpler formulations of Mk 9:31a and 14:41b, which are without such a reference, the earliest stratum of this Palestinian tradition.[346]   And Jeremias is willing to suggest at least for 9:31a that the *mâshâl* character of this saying may be a clue to its ultimate derivation from Jesus himself, since tradition is in the habit of recording and interpreting enigmatic sayings of Jesus, but not of inventing or gratuitously attributing them to him.[347]   If this is true for 9:31a, it may also be true for 14:41b in its original form, since the latter differs from 9:31a only in the designation of those to whom Jesus is delivered and the additional emphasis gained from the reversal of verb position and the use of articles. There is no convincing argument against Jesus having spoken, if not circumstantially, at least in general terms as here, of his prophetic fate of suffering and rejection.   Indeed, what is altogether improbable is the contrary supposition that his experience would never have led him to express this expectation.   The only question is whether he did in fact express it in terms of the suffering Son of Man.

Here we come up against the more general issue of Jesus' use of "Son of Man" as a self-designation, which critics have not yet satisfactorily resolved.[348]   No a priori case can be made

---

[345] *Ibid.*, pp. 214-219.

[346] Hahn, *op. cit.*, pp. 46-53.

[347] Jeremias, art. cit., pp. 169f.; and further, *idm, New Testament Theology*, I, 30f., 277-286, esp. 281f., and 295.

[348] The opinion that *bar nâsh(â) was used by Jesus as a circumlocution* for "I" has been stoutly defended by T. W. Manson, *The Teaching of Jesus*, 2nd ed. (Cambridge, 1955) and J. Y. Campbell, "The Origin and Meaning of the Term Son of Man," *JTS*, 48 (1947), 145-155, and just as stoutly attacked by Philipp Vielhauer, art. cit. (see above pp. 57-59, n. 339), *ZTK*, 60 (1963), 133-177.   But the attempt to establish Aramaic precedent for the usage continues.   See, for example, R.E.C. Formesyn, "Was there a Pronominal Connection for the 'Bar Nasha' Selfdesignation?" *NT*, 8 (1966), 1-35; and especially Geza Vermes, "The Use of *bar nâsh/bar nâshâ* in Jewish Aramaic," in Matthew Black, *An Aramaic Approach to the Gospels and Acts*, 3rd ed. (Oxford, 1967), Appendix E, pp. 310-328.   But the thesis and examples brought forward by Vermes have met with little acceptance. Cf. the critical remarks of Jeremias, art. cit., p. 165, n. 9; F. H. Borsch, *The Son of Man in Myth and History* (Philadelphia, 1967), p. 23, n. 4; *idem, The Christian and Gnostic Son of Man* (London, 1970), p. 5, n. 19; and in

against the possibility of his having done so, and the gospel evidence is incontestably in favor of tracing the usage back to Jesus, since there it is he, and he alone, who employs this title, and only this title, of himself.[349] Critics like Eduard Schweizer and Carsten Colpe, who recognize as authentic some of the sayings about the Son of Man's earthly activity, would also claim a genuine basis for the passion saying. Schweizer thinks it probable that Jesus alluded in a general way to the rejection of the Son of Man because of the frequency with which the name "Son of Man" and the verb "to hand over" are found together in the tradition.[350] And Colpe argues from the convergence of Jesus as speaker, the notion of propitiatory suffering, and the Son of Man title in the passion announcements for the historical probability of Jesus having spoken of the Son of Man in connection with his own messianic destiny and having reckoned with his own violent suffering and death. Yet he is of the opinion that the passion sayings were originally not Son of Man sayings at all, but "I" sayings.[351] And according to him Mark is responsible for inserting the title in 14:41.[352] This conclusion may receive a measure of confirmation from the results of Jeremias' study, which attempts to prove that the evangelists sometimes insert, but never delete, the title in their source, and that consequently, where there are two "parallel" versions of a saying, the version without the title has the greater claim to originality.[353] Nevertheless, Borsch has made the point that Colpe offers no really satisfactory criteria for determining whether the Son of Man title is a later insertion.[354] Jeremias himself regards Mk 9:31a as very old tradition and considers it an exception to the results he has arrived at with respect to other sayings with "parallel" versions. So it seems to me, then, we must allow the possibility

---

more detail the two review articles of Roger Le Déaut, "Le substrat araméen des évangiles: scolies en marge de l'*Aramaic Approach* de Matthew Black," *B*, 49 (1968), 388-399, and Joseph A. Fitzmyer, *CBQ*, 30 (1968), 417-428.

[349] Only in Acts 7:56 does the title occur in a saying not attributed to Jesus. For Jn 12:34, Apoc 1:13 and 14:14, see Schweizer, "Der Menschensohn," *ZNW*, 50 (1959), 187, n. 6. And for Jesus' use of the title "the Christ," see *loc. cit.* and n. 8. Jeremias has recently taken up this whole question again; see his *New Testament Theology*, I, 257-276.

[350] Schweizer, art. cit., pp. 195-197; *idem*, "The Son of Man," *JBL*, 79 (1960), 120f.; and *idem*, "The Son of Man Again," *NTS*, 9 (1962-63), 258.

[351] Carsten Colpe, art. cit. (see above pp. 57-59, n. 339), p. 446.

[352] *Ibid.*, p. 459.

[353] Jeremias, art. cit., pp. 159-172.

[354] See Borsch, *The Christian and Gnostic Son of Man*, p. 7, n. 25.

that not only the substance of the saying in both verses under consideration, but even its form in 9:31a, can lay serious claims to originality.[355]

Tödt tries to show that Mark used the passion sayings in the two sections of his gospel where they occur to serve his theological purposes. Discerning the obvious role played by the three passion announcements in the composition of Mk 8:27-10:52, Tödt assigns a similar role for the two passion announcements (14:21, 41b) in the analogous section 14:1-42, which is also recognizably a Markan composition. And he claims that Mark has used the passion sayings in his composition to interpret the material he has received from the tradition, and in particular to prepare for the passion itself. At 14:42 there is an observable break in the account. From that point on Mark is relying on a previously fashioned narrative, and there is no further mention of the suffering Son of Man.[356] Hahn does not agree with Tödt that 14:21 and 41b were first worked into his material by Mark,[357] and neither do I. Tödt should recognize at least for v. 41b that he cannot accept Kuhn's analysis and still claim that Mark's principal interest in composing and placing the Gethsemane account lay in an interpretive saying that was to be found in only one of the two sources he was consciously compounding.[358] Moreover, this remark serves to bring out the difference between v. 41b and the other passion announcements in 8:31, 9:31 and 10:33f. This saying is the culmination of a story, the climactic point of an independent piece of tradition, as we shall later attempt to establish,[359] while the other passion announcements are individual logia without a fixed context, which could be used by Mark where and how he chose. In the Gethsemane passage it is the entire scene, not simply the Son of Man saying, that functions for Mark as an interpretation of the passion of Jesus. This is not, however, to deny that the saying serves extremely

---

[355] In addition to Jeremias (see above p. 60, n. 347), cf. Minette de Tillesse, *op. cit.* (see above p. 48, n. 286), pp. 374-380, who concludes to a similar presynoptic formula underlying the gospel passion predictions; and also André Feuillet, "Les trois grandes prophéties de la Passion et de la Résurrection des évangiles synoptiques," *RTh*, 67 (1967), 533-560; 68 (1968), 41-74.

[356] Tödt, *op. cit.*, pp. 144-149; Bultmann, *The History of the Synoptic Tradition*, pp. 277-279; Joachim Jeremias, *The Eucharistic Words of Jesus*, tr. Norman Perrin (London, 1966), pp. 90-96.

[357] Hahn, *op. cit.*, p. 47, n. 1.

[358] Cf. Tödt, *op. cit.*, pp. 147f. and 199f.

[359] See below Chapter 4.

well both to announce the climactic fulfilment of the previous passion predictions and to give a profound theological meaning to the moment of the Arrest, whose arrival is proclaimed in the parallel statement of the following verse.[360]

The verb *paradidômi* which introduces the saying has special force here. Although it cannot strictly be regarded as a "formula," as Jeremias would have it,[361] since it is not self-contained and occurs with a variety of complementary phrases,[362] still it is a technical Jewish legal term and is used as such throughout the Passion account: for Jesus' betrayal by Judas, who is characterized as *ho para(di)dous* (Mk 14:10, 11, 18, etc.), for his handing over by the Sanhedrin to Pilate (Mk 15:1), for his handing over in turn by Pilate to the people (Lk 23:25) and to the soldiers (Mk 15:15).[363] The phrase *paradounai eis cheiras tinos*, on the other hand, has more claim to being regarded as a formula. It is not found in pure Greek, but its origins in the gospels are clear, for it is frequent in the LXX, Josephus and Jewish martyrological literature.[364] The passive voice, here as in Mk 9:31 and 10:33, emphasizes not only that Jesus is delivered up by one of his own disciples (14:21), but also that he is delivered according to God's design, since the "reverential passive" is often used absolutely in place of the active voice with the divine name.[365] Schelkle, Jeremias and Maurer among others see a reference here as well to the Greek of Is 53:6, 12.[366] But Tödt and Hahn are probably right in recognizing the influence of Is 53 only in the cases where *paradidonai* is combined with an interpretive

---

[360] See Colpe, art. cit., pp. 448f., who points to the analogy here of Mk 14:41 and 42 with Lk 22:22 and 21.

[361] W. Zimmerli and J. Jeremias, *op. cit.* (see above p. 59, n. 343), pp. 90, 96.

[362] Tödt, *op. cit.*. pp. 159 f.; Hahn, *op. cit.*, p. 62.

[363] Friedrich Büchsel, "*Didômi ... paradidômi, ktl.*," *TDNT*, II (Grand Rapids, 1964), 169. See also Birger Gerhardsson, "Jésus livré et abandonné d'après la Passion selon Saint Matthieu," *RB*, 76 (1969), 212-215. And for a full study of the term and its New Testament usage, one may consult Wiard Popkes, *Christus Traditus. Eine Untersuchung zum Begriff der Dahingabe im Neuen Testament* (Zürich and Stuttgart, 1967).

[334] *Ibid.*; Karl Hermann Schelkle, *Die Passion Jesu in der Verkündigung des Neuen Testaments* (Heidelberg, 1949), pp. 70-73; A. Schlatter, *Der Evangelist Matthäus*, 6th ed. (Stuttgart, 1963), pp. 537f.; Tödt, *op. cit.*, p. 160; Hahn, *op. cit.*, pp. 62f.

[365] See Zimmerli and Jeremias, *op. cit.*, p. 96; so also Schelkle, p. 71; Tödt, p. 170; Hahn, p. 62; Schmid, p. 277; and E. Schweizer, *Markus*, p. 181.

[366] For Schelkle and Jeremias, see preceding note; Christian Maurer, "Knecht Gottes und Sohn Gottes im Passionsbericht des Markusevangeliums," *ZTK*, 50 (1953), 1-38.

phrase, particularly one expressing the idea of vicarious expiation central to that chapter (e.g., Mk 10:45).[367]

The similarity of the Son of Man sayings in Jn 12:23 and Mk 14:41 is often noted, particularly the common reference to the arrival of "the hour," and they may stem from the same level of tradition.[368] Matthew Black, dealing in particular with Jn 3:14 and 12:32, suggests that what lies at the origin of the tradition reflected in John and Mark may have been a saying about the exaltation/crucifixion (*hypsôthênai*) of the Son of Man in combination with Isaianic allusions to his surrendering up (*paradothênai*) and rejection (*apodokimasthênai*), all intended to express in a general way the triumphant vindication of the rejected Son of Man. *Hypsôthênai* would here be translating an underlying Aramaic verb with the double meaning indicated above.[369] Borsch, on the other hand, has by-passed the notion of direct allusion to Isaiah in the attempt to connect John's *hypsoô* and *doxazô* with Mark's *paradidômi* as divergent renderings of the notion of "offering up" in the underlying tradition.[370] In any case, provided that we keep the tradition-historical question clearly enough in view, it remains legitimate for us within the context of Mark's gospel to seek the meaning of the deliverance of the Son of Man in the soteriological saying of Mk 10:45, where Jesus is for the only time explicitly identified as both the Son of Man and the Servant of God.[371]

Schelkle instances I Macc 2:50 as an illustration that the expression "give one's life" is also a technical term in Jewish mar-

---

[367] See Tödt, *op. cit.*, pp. 159-161, 202-211; Hahn, *op. cit.*, pp. 54-66. Norman Perrin designates the two traditions in the use of *paradidômi* as apologetic and soteriological, with only the latter using phraseology that recalls Is 53. See his "The Creative Use of the Son of Man Traditions by Mark," *USQR*, 23 (1967-68), 359f., and "The Son of Man in the Synoptic Tradition," *BR*, 13 (1968), 19.

[368] Colpe, art. cit., *TWNT*, VIII, 472.

[369] Matthew Black, "The 'Son of Man' Passion Sayings in the Gospel Tradition." *ZNW*, 60 (1969), 7; and see *idem*, "The Son of Man Problem in Recent Research and Debate," *BJRL*, 45 (1962-63), 305-318; and *An Aramaic Approach*, p. 103.

[370] Borsch, *The Son of Man in Myth and History*, pp. 281-291, 305-313, 338f.

[371] For a careful analysis of this saying attempting to establish its originality and priority over the parallel saying in Lk 22:27, see A. Feuillet, "Le logion sur la rançon," *RSPT*, 51 (1967), 365-402. Colpe, art. cit., *TWNT*, VIII, 451, 458, also traces the saying back through the oldest Palestinian tradition to a genuine saying of Jesus, but attributes the Son of Man title to Mark.

tyrologies.[372] But use of the active voice *dounai tên psychên*
reveals still another aspect. It is not only God who acts in the
deliverance of Jesus. It is also Jesus himself who acts, and, as
Tödt points out, he acts in the full sovereignty of the *exousia*
which is his as the Son of Man. In Mk 14:21, "the Son of Man
goes," i.e., he acts as the one who goes of his own accord. Again
in 14:42, it is he who initiates the events that follow when he
says, "Rise, let us be going; see, my betrayer is at hand." Yet
the sovereignty of this Son of Man who "is delivered" is different
from that of the Son of Man who "is to come" as Judge enforc-
ing prompt recognition of his claims by all. It is a sovereignty
subject to opposition and exposed to blasphemy, simply because
it is conditioned by the earthly existence signified in the title
"Son of Man." Nevertheless, this title expresses the real sovereignty of Jesus, even in Gethsemane, where "the one who sub-
ordinates his will to the Father is *in so doing* delivered into the
hands of sinners, [and] the one who is not overwhelmed by the
power of darkness is delivered up by God."[373]

In contrast with Mk 9:31, which speaks in a general way of
the deliverance of the Son of Man *eis cheiras anthrôpôn*, and
10:33, which speaks specifically of his deliverance first to the
chief priests and the scribes, and then to the gentiles, 14:41b
says that he is being delivered *eis tas cheiras tôn hamartôlôn*.
Mk 10:33 is in all likelihoood a redactional expansion of 9:31 on
the basis of the passion account.[374] And it seems probable that
the phrase in 14:41b is also a secondary modification of a formula which must originally have read like 9:31 *eis (tas) cheiras
(tôn) anthrôpôn*.[375] Thus "into the hands of sinners" stands as
a kind of mean between the sweepingly universal statement of
9:31 and the explicitly particular statement of 10:33, and it raises
the problem of exactly who is meant by "sinners." Rengstorf,
followed by Taylor [376] and Nineham,[377] argues that "sinners" is
often synonymous with "the Gentiles" in O. T. thought, and that
here it can hardly mean Jewish sinners, but must refer to the
Roman soldiers, who actually executed the crucifixion (cf. Acts
2:23). The antithesis *physei Ioudaioi* and *ex ethnôn hamartôloi*

---

[372] *Op. cit.*, p. 72.
[373] Tödt, *op. cit.*, pp. 187, 199f.; quotation on p. 200.
[374] Hahn, *op. cit.*, p. 47; but Tödt, *op. cit.*, pp. 172-175, 202, judges otherwise.
[375] So Hahn (see above p. 59, n. 343).
[376] *Op. cit.*, p. 205.
[377] *Op. cit.*, p. 393.

in Gal 2:15, as well as the equivalence of *hamartôloi* and *ethnikoi* between Lk 6:32-34 and Mt 5:47, only reinforces this conclusion.[378] Swete[379] and Lagrange[380] both take this meaning, but feel the need to include the priests and Scribes and Pharisees as well. But a larger number of commentators, while admitting the equivalence of sinners with pagans elsewhere, reject that meaning here.[381] The suggestion of Menzies[382] that it refers to the class of people characterized earlier in the designation "publicans and sinners" (Mk 2:16-17) is not worth considering. E. Klostermann[383] simply leaves the reference general, as do Montefiore,[384] Rawlinson,[385] and Schmid,[386] who apply it unspecifically to all of Jesus' adversaries. Given the closer relation of Mk 14:41 to the saying in 9:31 than to that in 10:33, this more general meaning for *hamartôloi* seems the most appropriate.[387]

According to Tödt, the use of "sinners" here is one more expression of the tension that exists in all three types of Son of Man sayings between the full *authority* of the Son of Man and the *sinfulness* of this generation which opposes his claims. "At first sight," he writes, "this delivering looks as if men had won a victory over Jesus' claim to sovereignty; 'this is your hour, and the power of darkness' (Lk 22:53). God himself seems to admit the legitimacy of this sinful generation's claim. It is fundamentally paradoxical that God delivers the one to whom he has given authority over all men into the hands of sinners."[388]

---

[378] Karl Heinrich Rengstorf, "*Hamartôlos, anamartêtos,*" *TDNT*, I (Grand Rapids, 1964), 325-328.

[379] *Op. cit.*, p. 348.

[380] *Op. cit.*, p. 392.

[381] So Wellhausen, Menzies, Klostermann, Rawlinson, Hauck, Schmid, *ad loc.*

[382] *Op. cit.*, p. 260.

[383] *Op. cit.*, p. 151.

[384] *Op. cit.*, p. 346.

[385] *Op. cit.*, p. 213.

[386] *Op. cit.*, p. 277.

[387] Of course the very use of the word *hamartôloi* is a grave denunciation of the moral responsibility and guilt of those who hand Jesus over to death. They have closed their ears to his words and their eyes to the light. See Uricchio and Stano, op. cit., p. 589.

[388] Tödt, *op. cit.*, pp. 177-180; quotation on p. 177.

Verse 42: *Egeiresthe, agômen; idou ho paradi-dous me êngiken.*

As Jesus faced the approach of this hour in the anguish of prayer, so now he faces its arrival with decisive action. *Egeiresthe, agômen* is the stirring cry with which he rouses his disciples from their torpor, not to flee, but rather to go forward with him and meet the threat.[389]

Again it is he who reveals to them the nature of the threat. What the saying in v. 41 had described in eschatological and universal terms, he now specifies as the historical initiative of a particular person: *idou ho paradidous me êngiken.* Repetition of the same verb used for the expression of divine purpose in v. 41 underlines here that even Judas is the unwitting agent of God's predetermined design.[390] Cranfield[391] finds the force of the phrase in the ignorance of the disciples as to who was coming. But Haenchen[392] believes that Jesus himself was taken by surprise, since otherwise we should have to presuppose his fore-knowledge of all the ensuing events. Nineham[393] feels no dif-ficulty in assuming that Jesus was supernaturally aware of the traitor's approach before his arrival and considers that this is actually suggested by what follows in 14:43. But many other commentators are content to suppose that Jesus simply saw or heard the approaching crowd and recognized Judas in it before his disciples did.[394] On the other hand, if the redactional charac-ter of v. 42 is admitted, then solving such problems becomes superfluous.

What militates against regarding the verse as purely redac-tional, however, is the surprising attestation we find at least for the traditional character of v. 42a: *egeiresthe agômen.* This ex-pression recurs in a somewhat different context, but with a quite similar meaning in Jn 14:31. And although it is possible that John is echoing Mark here, it is just as likely that the words were not limited to any single form of the tradition. The situation

---

[389] So B. and J. Weiss, Swete, Menzies, Plummer, E. Klostermann, La-grange, Cranfield, *ad loc.*

[390] See Barnabas Lindars, *New Testament Apologetic* (Philadelphia, 1961), p. 81.

[391] *Op. cit.*, p. 436.

[392] *Op. cit.*, p. 495.

[393] *Op. cit.*, p. 393.

[394] So B. and J. Weiss, Swete, Plummer, Montefiore, Rawlinson, *ad loc.*

in John, as C. H. Dodd has observed, is essentially the same as that in Mark. Jesus notes the approach of the enemy: *erchetai ho tou kosmou archôn* (Jn 14:30), although here and now the real assailant is the devil rather than his tool Judas, who is to be met with only later (18:1ff.). He expresses his resolve to do the Father's will: *kathôs eneteilato moi ho patêr houtôs poiô* (v. 31). And he bids his disciples to join him in meeting the advancing enemy: *egeiresthe agômen enteuthen.* Although in John this has become a confrontation conceived wholly in terms of obedience to God's will, it is not hard to see how the essentials of the tradition have been preserved in this reshaping.[395] And if, as seems altogether probable from the way John deals with the rest of the details of the Gethsemane tradition, his source is independent of the synoptics, then we have good reason not only to doubt the redactional character of the words *egeiresthe agômen* in Mk 14:42a, but even to regard Mark's placement as their natural setting. No such conclusion, however, can be established for v. 42b.

---

[395] C. H. Dodd, *The Interpretation of the Fourth Gospel* (Cambridge, 1963), pp. 406-409; *idem, Historical Tradition in the Fourth Gospel* (Cambridge, 1963), p. 72; and see R. Bultmann, *Das Evangelium des Johannes* (Göttingen, 1964), pp. 488 and .n1, 489; and M. Dibelius, "Gethsemane," *CQ*, 12 (1935, 262, and *BG*, I, 267f.

CHAPTER TWO

LITERARY ANALYSIS OF MATTHEW 26:36-46

Verse 36: *Tote erchetai met' autôn ho Iêsous eis chôrion legomenon Gethsêmani, kai legei tois mathêtais: kathisate autou heôs hou apelthôn ekei proseuxômai.*

Matthew here as elsewhere substitutes the somewhat more emphatic *tote* for Mark's colorless *kai*, thereby tightening the tie with the previous conversation.[1] He changes *erchontai* to the singular, though retaining Mark's historical present, contrary to custom.[2] Matthew thus makes Jesus the subject of the action from the start and centers the whole narrative on him much more than Mark does.[3] *Met' autôn* here and the addition of *met' emou* in vv. 38 and 40 are features that emphasize for Matthew the need and desire of Jesus for the company of his disciples.[4] Matthew reads *legomenon* for Mark's *hou to onoma*. More likely than not he omits *autou* with *tois mathêtais*.[5] And this may be due to his adverbial use of the same form to replace Mark's *hôde* with the immediately following *kathisate*. This substitution of *autou*, which occurs only here in Matthew and not for *hôde* in v. 38, may well be by design and intended to echo Gen 22:5, where Abraham says, "*Kathisate autou, ktl.*," before leaving his servants

---

[1] Bernhard Weiss, *Das Matthäus-Evangelium*, 3rd ed. (Göttingen, 1898), p. 459.

[2] Willoughby C. Allen, *A Critical and Exegetical Commentary on the Gospel according to S. Matthew*, 3rd ed. (Edinburgh, 1957), p. 278; and on the historical present tense here, see above Chapter 1, pp. 6-8.

[3] Ernst Lohmeyer, *Das Evangelium des Matthäus*, ed. Werner Schmauch, 3rd ed. (Göttingen, 1962), p. 360.

[4] Paul Gaechter, *Das Matthäus Evangelium* (Innsbruck, 1963), p. 864; Julius Daniel Schniewind, *Das Evangelium nach Matthäus* (Göttingen, 1964), p. 259.

[5] So B ƒ L Γ Δ Φ 074 33 157 565 892 *pm*; but p⁵³ (apparently) ℵ A C D W Fam 1 700 1424 *al* latt sy^s ^p sa^pt bo read the same as Mark.

to climb the mount of sacrifice with Isaac,[6] and perhaps also Ex 24:14, where Moses instructs the elders, "*Hêsychazete autou, ktl.*," before ascending the mountain alone.[7] *Kathisate* in any case has the meaning "stay" or "remain," like *meinate* in v. 38, rather than "sit."[8] In Mark's text, as we saw, *heôs* may mean either "while" or "until." But Matthew uses *heôs hou* in five other places with the meaning "until" (1:25; 13:33; 14:22; 17:9; 18:34); so it probably has that meaning here as well.[9] With the word *ekei* Jesus seemingly points away to the place where he will withdraw to pray.[10] Matthew's addition of *apelthôn* and the contrast he draws between *autou* and *ekei* emphasizes Jesus' separation from the disciples more sharply than Mark's text.[11]

Verse 37:   *Kai paralabôn ton Petron kai tous dyo huious Zebedaiou êrxato lypeisthai kai adêmonein.*

Employing the participle *paralabôn* in place of the indicative, Matthew avoids as usual Mark's historical present.[12] Peter, alone of the three disciples whom Jesus takes along, is designated by his proper name. This is in accord with the prominence given him elsewhere by Matthew,[13] although Lohmeyer[14] thinks that the phrasing derives rather from considerations of a rhythmic nature. The indirect *met' autou* of Mk 14:33 drops out to be replaced by the direct *met' emou* in vv. 38, 40. With *êrxato* the passion of Jesus begins in earnest.[15] Matthew evidently

---

[6] A. H. McNeile, *The Gospel according to St. Matthew* (London, 1915), p. 389; A. Schlatter, *Der Evangelist Matthäus*, 2nd ed. (Stuttgart, 1963), p. 750.

[7] B. Weiss, *loc. cit.*

[8] F. S. Stooke-Vaughan, "Sit Ye Here," *ET*, 6 (1894-95), 94f.; Carl Schneider, "*Kathêmai, kathizo, kathezomai*," *TDNT*, III (Grand Rapids, 1965), 444; Pierre Bonnard, *L'Évangile selon Saint Matthieu* (Neuchatel, 1963), p. 383.

[9] Allen, *loc. cit.*; B.-D.-F., 216 (3), 383, 455 (3).

[10] H. A. W. Meyer, *Critical and Exegetical Handbook to the Gospel of Matthew*, tr. Peter Christie from 6th German ed., rev. and ed. William Stewart (Edinburgh, 1879), II, 218.

[11] Bernhard Weiss, *Das Matthäusevangelium und seine Lucas-Parallelen* (Halle, 1876), p. 551.

[12] Allen, *loc. cit.*

[13] McNeile, *loc. cit.*

[14] *Op. cit.*, p. 361.

[15] Meyer, McNeile, *loc. cit.*

formed the rather weak *lypeisthai* from *perilypos* of v. 38.[16]   It is certainly softer than Mark's *ekthambeisthai*,[17] and according to Lohmeyer [18] practically synonymous with *adêmonein*.   Previously it had been the disciples who were saddened: *elypêthêsan sphodra* (Mt 17:23); *lypoumenoi sphodra êrxanto* (Mt 26:22). Now it is Jesus himself.   He who came to bring the joy of the wedding feast (Mt 9:15 par.) now faces the desolation of the cross (Mt 27:46) for the joy that is set before him (Heb 12:2).[19] Jewish tradition certainly knew of joyful martyrs, but the glory of the martyr is a quality very distant from Matthew's account.[20]

> Verse 38:   *Tote legei autois: perilypos estin hê psychê mou heôs thanatou; meinate hôde kai grêgoreite met' emou.*

This verse differs from Mark only in its first and last words. *Tote* — for Mark's *kai* again — according to Lohmeyer [21] here serves to give greater emphasis to Jesus' account of his sorrow.

Met' emou is added to the plea for wakefulness here and in v. 40 probably, as was mentioned above, to emphasize Jesus' need and desire for his disciples' companionship in watching.   Read in the Christian community, it could not but carry an unmistakably parenetic force.

> Verse 39:   *Kai proelthôn mikron epesen epi prosôpon autou proseuchomenos kai legôn: pater mou, ei dynaton estin, parelthatô ap' emou to potêrion touto; plên ouch hôs egô thelô all' hôs sy.*

The reading *proselthôn* 'approaching' is also very well attested here, but it makes little sense and is probably a scribal error arising from the frequent occurrence of this verb in Matthew.[22]

---

[16] B. Weiss, *loc. cit.*

[17] Allen, *loc. cit.*

[18] *Op. cit.*, p. 361, n. 1.

[19] Schniewind, *op. cit.*, pp. 259f.

[20] Schlatter, *op. cit.*, pp. 750f.

[21] *Op. cit.*, p. 361.

[22] McNeile, *op. cit.*, p. 390; Floyd V. Filson, *A Commentary on the Gospel according to St. Matthew* (London, 1960), p. 279.

Matthew loses the vividness of Mark's imperfect tense here by changing to the aorist *epesen*, as often elsewhere. *Epi prosôpon autou*, instead of Mark's *epi tês gês*, recalls the attitude of the fear-stricken disciples at the Transfiguration (Mt 17:6). And, as Lohmeyer remarks, the expression preserves more of a biblical echo than Mark's.[23]

Matthew abbreviates Mark's account of the prayer by omitting the indirect form of the petition for the passing of the hour, and running the two introductory verbs of Mark together into the single participial phrase *proseuchomenos kai legôn*. He omits the Aramaic *abba*, doubtless translating it as *pater mou*, a usage common elsewhere in Matthew,[24] although only here and in v. 42 does it occur as an address, paralleling the address in his version of the Lord's Prayer.[25] We have already mentioned in connection with Mk 14:36 that *abba* was the constant Aramaic address of Jesus to God in prayer. The invocation makes its appearance altogether nineteen times in the gospels in four different Greek forms: *ho patêr* (Mk 14:36; Mt 11:26; Lk 10:21b); *patêr* (Jn 17:21, 24, 25); *pater* (Mt 11:25; Lk 10:21a; 22:42; 23:34, 46; Jn 11:41; 12:27, 28; 17:1, 5, 11); and *pater mou* (Mt 26:39, 42).[26] Why Matthew chose to render *abba* here by *pater mou*, when Mark had already supplied *ho patêr* as the equivalent, is a matter of conjecture.[27] Marchel suggests either that Matthew was reading *abba* as a substitute for the Aramaic *abbi*, which was no longer in use, or else that he was intentionally giving *abba* the meaning of the Hebrew *abbi*, which at that time was still used in Palestinian Judaism at least as an affirmation of divine fatherhood.[28] Since in fourteen of the other forty-two instances in this gospel where the title "Father" is referred to God it is accompanied by the first person possessive pronoun, it is clear

---

[23] *Loc. cit.*; cf. Gen 17:3, 17; Num 14:5; 16:4; Ruth 2:10; 2 Sam 9:6; 1 Kings 18:39, 42.

[24] Mt 7:21; 10:32, 33; 11:27; 12:50; 15:13; 16:17; 18:10; 19:35; 20:23; 25:34; 26:29, 53. Cf. Lk 2:49; 10:22; 22:29; 24:49; Jn 2:16; 5:17. The expression does not occur in Mark.

[25] Mt 6:9. See Lohmeyer-Schmauch, *loc. cit.*

[26] Gottlob Schrenk, "*Patêr, ktl.*," TDNT, V (Grand Rapids, 1968), 985 and n. 251; for details see Witold Marchel, *Abba, Père! La prière du Christ et des chrétiens* (Rome, 1963), pp. 129-145.

[27] C. Spicq, *Dieu et l'homme selon le Nouveau Testament* (Paris, 1961), p. 68, n. 5 (cited by Marchel, *op. cit.*, p. 138, n. 45), arguing that the Greek definite article often has the meaning of a possessive pronoun, holds that *pater mou* is here identical with *ho patêr*.

[28] *Op. cit.*, pp. 137f.

that Matthew is here pursuing a tendency of his own. Moreover, he has observably altered the Markan material elsewhere in the same direction.[29] Schrenk concludes from its use in different contexts that the expression "my Father" serves as a kind of catchword for Matthew's theology of Jesus' unique relationship to the Father as Son and Revealer.[30]

Apart from Mt 27:46, which is a Psalm citation after Mark, there is only one other instance in Matthew's gospel similar to Gethsemane in that Jesus addresses his Father directly: the great Thanksgiving Prayer of Mt 11:25f. The actual form of address there is twofold: *pater* (v. 25) and *ho patêr* (v. 26). But the ex--pression *ho patêr mou* also appears in the same context (v. 27). Marchel is of the opinion that the theological function of this passage is to justify Jesus' constant employment of the term *abba* for God.[31] At once traditional yet original in form and expression, this prayer of Jesus not only exhibits a fulfilment of O. T. promises and expectations of a whole new relationship of God as Father to His people, but goes farther still to bespeak a profound consciousness in Jesus of being uniquely related to the Father in a bond both of nature and of knowledge that equips him to become Revealer of the very depths of God's own life. The term *abba* along with its gospel equivalents functions as the vehicle of this revelation, communicating at a stroke the intimate mystery of God's Fatherhood and Jesus' Sonship, the supreme secret of Jesus' person and mission.[32] It is against the background of this earlier prayer of Jesus in Matthew's gospel that we should understand the profound meaning of *pater mou* in Mt 26:39, 42. In both contexts it is Jesus, in his unique relationship of union with the Father, who affirms the Father's dominion and the limits of his own Sonship by accepting in a prayer of grateful abandon and adoration the solely normative will of the Father in the face of all self-will.[33]

At this point Matthew introduces elements from Mark's indirect form of Jesus' prayer apparently to tone down the force of the report. Thus he carries over the phrase *ei dynaton estin* from Mk 14:35, replacing the blunt *panta dynata soi* and putting

---

[29] Cf. Mt. 12:50 with Mk 3:35; Mt 20:23 with Mk 10:40; Mt 26:29 with Mk 14:25. Schrenk, art. cit., p. 987 and n. 261.

[30] *Ibid.*, pp. 988f.

[31] *Op. cit.*, p. 147.

[32] *Ibid.*, pp. 150-177.

[33] See Schrenk, art. cit., pp. 989, 992; Marchel, *op. cit.*, p. 164.

the whole prayer under this condition from the start. Lk 22:42, similarly but still more simply, reads: *pater, ei boulei*. The verb *parerchesthai* is carried over too, and in the form *parelthatô* considerably softens Mark's *parenengke*. In the final phrase of the prayer Matthew uses *plên* for the initial *alla*, and *hôs* in the place of Mark's more difficult *ti*.[34] *Hôs* may echo the language of the Lord's Prayer.[35] And quite probably even the seemingly insignificant substitution of *plên* for *alla* plays a definitely modifying role. Since Matthew employs this conjunction only five times all told,[36] he must intend it here as something more than a simple equivalent for *alla*. Margaret E. Thrall has suggested that, while it may serve as a balancing adversative particle (= "nevertheless": cf. 18:7), comparison with the second and third prayer in Matthew (vv. 42 and 44) favors assigning it a limiting, conditional function (= "on condition that"), which would have the effect of making all three prayers alike and modifying the conflict in Mark noticeably by representing it as something already resolved.[37]

If, however, instead of following Thrall's lead, we take *plên* adversatively here, then we shall have to recognize a development by stages in the prayer of Jesus. We have already noted in the preceding chapter how Matthew builds the whole scene into a threefold prayer of Jesus, while for Mark the focus is on his threefold return to the sleeping disciples.[38] Zahn suggests that the tripling may be meant to show that the first prayer did not obtain a full hearing. Thus there is a progress from the first to the second prayer. The first prayer contains the petition for the passing of the cup; it is offered under the positive condition *ei dynaton estin*, but remains subject to the Father's will. The second prayer (v. 42) contains no such petition; it is offered under the negative condition *ei ou dynatai, ktl.*, and asks only that the Father's will be done.[39] Plummer even suggests a third stage for

---

[34] See Allen, *op. cit.*, pp. 278f., who sums up the difference he feels between the two accounts thus: "In Mk. the request is conditioned by the last clause, but the whole verse leaves the impression of an ungranted request more strongly than Mt.'s modified rendering" (279).

[35] Lohmeyer-Schmauch, *loc. cit.*

[36] The other four occurrences are at 11:22, 24; 18:7; 26:64.

[37] Margaret E. Thrall, *Greek Particles in the New Testament. Linguistic and Exegetical Studies* (Leiden, 1962), pp. 67-70; and see pp. 20-24. She adduces several examples from the LXX of *plên* as introducing a condition: Josh 1:17; Num 36:6; Judg 10:15; 1 Kings 12:24; 2 Kings 3:13; Jer 10:24.

[38] See, for example, B. Weiss, *loc. cit.* (see above p. 70, n. 11).

[39] Theodor Zahn, *Das Evangelium des Matthäus*, 4th ed. (Leipzig and Erlangen, 1922), pp. 701f.

the unreported prayer of v. 44, where the "if" of the foregoing positive and negative conditions becomes equivalent to "since": "Since this cup cannot pass from Me, Thy will be done." [40]   But such a supposition is unnecessary, since in the first and second prayer everything has already been expressed: Jesus has passed from questioning to certainty of God's will (Schniewind), from petition to humble surrender (Lohmeyer). Moreover, if the first prayer can be said simply to echo the Lord's Prayer, the second ends with a direct citation: *genêthêtô to thelêma sou* (Mt 6:10). Mark knows no such development as this.   And Matthew reveals his own intention of illuminating and resolving Jesus' struggle at prayer in terms of the very prayer he had taught his disciples.[41]

> Verse 40: *Kai erchetai pros tous mathêtas kai heuriskei autous katheudontas, kai legei tô Petrô: houtôs ouk ischysate mian hôran grêgorêsai met' emou?*

This verse is nearly identical with Mk 14:37, even to the unusual preservation of the historical present tense of Mark's verbs. The differences are slight, but worth remarking: the addition of *pros tous mathêtas, houtôs,* and *met' emou,* the omission of *Simôn, katheudeis,* and the changing of *ischysas* to the second person plural.

The addition of *pros tous mathêtas* (cf. Mt 26:45; Lk 22:45) raises the question of whom Matthew means. Why does he not say "the three" instead of "the disciples"? For since Peter is mentioned, it would seem that Jesus returns and speaks to the three, as in Mark, rather than to the eleven. This phrase may well be meant to serve a double purpose: to indicate the disciples on the scene in a general way, but also to include "the disciples" to whom the gospel is addressed. The suspicion that a parenetic motive is operative here is only confirmed by the other differences we have noted. The focus of reproachful admonition is removed from Peter by the omission of Mark's "Simon, are you asleep?" dressed. *Ischysate* in the plural now possesses the same generality as the verbs in the clearly parenetic v. 41 which follows.

---

[40] Alfred Plummer, *An Exegetical Commentary on the Gospel according to St. Matthew* (London, 1910), p. 370.
[41] See especially Lohmeyer, Schiewind, *ad loc.*

And finally, we have already seen how widespread was the theme
of spiritual wakefulness in the preaching of the early Church.
Yet nowhere else in the gospels does Christ speak of watching
with him. It is Matthew, then, who has introduced this community theme in an explicit way, and by so doing resolved the
tension in the shift from the singular to the plural address in
Mk 14:37-38.

Understanding in this way what Matthew has done with the
verse does away with the need for explaining historically why it
is Peter who is addressed,[42] or why the address here is plural,[43]
or for desperate expedients like putting a question mark after
houtôs — Jesus' exclamation of pained surprise — so that we can
have something in Matthew's text addressed specifically to Peter.[44]
That Matthew is sparing the apostles here, and again in v. 43 by
the omission of Mk 14:40c, may be true,[45] but more significantly
Matthew is exhorting the community.

> Verse 41: ·*Grêgoreite kai proseuchesthe, hina mê*
> *eiselthête eis peirasmon; to men pneuma prothy-*
> *mon, hê de sarx asthenês.*

The only difference from Mark in this verse is Matthew's
eiselthête for *elthête*, which he shares in common with Lk 22:40,
46. It is possible that both he and Luke thereby intend simply a
closer echo than Mark of the final petition of the Lord's Prayer:
mê eisenengkês hêmas eis peirasmon (Mt 6:13 / Lk 11:4). And if,
as was noted above,[46] Hebrew or Aramaic would have used but a
single root in both contexts, as in fact the Syriac versions do, then
there is additional reason for approximating *eiserchesthai* to
eispherein through a common prepositional prefix.

---

[42] Thus Meyer, *op. cit.*, II, 200, sees a special appropriateness in addressing to Peter what is meant for all, since he had boasted more than the rest.
[43] Lohmeyer-Schmauch, *loc. cit.*, finds it more suitable that Jesus addresses all, since precisely in *their* sleep he perceives that their help, as
well as God's, is denied him, and *met' emou* only serves to bring this out
more sharply.
[44] Thus, for example, Euthymius Zigabenus, Maldonatus, Beza. See
Meyer, *loc. cit.*; and Paul Schanz, *Commentar über das Evangelium des
heiligen Matthäus* (Freiburg im Breisgau, 1879), p. 521 and n. 2.
[45] Plummer, *op. cit.*, pp. 370f.
[46] See above Chapter 1, p. 36, n. 225.

Verse 42: *Palin ek deuterou apelthôn prosêuxato*
legôn: Pater mou, ei ou dynatai touto parelthein
ean mê auto piô, genêthêtô to thelêma sou.

This second prayer, as we have already noted in commenting on v. 39, is entirely Matthew's construction. It expresses the climax of Jesus' resignation and submission in terms approximating the Lord's Prayer.[47]

Touto (read by p^{37} ℵ B C A W 067 Fam. 1 *al* b ff² q sa) is interesting, and to judge by the textual variants, was early felt to need clarification. Standing by itself, it could doubtless carry a more general reference; but controlled in context by the qualification *ean mê auto piô*, it can refer only to the cup of v. 39, and thereby evidences the superfluity of the secondary readings *to potêrion touto* (D Fam. 13 *al* g¹ 1 syˢ) or *touto to potêrion* (ƙΓΘΦ *pm* lat syᵖ bo).

In speaking of a progress intended by Matthew in Jesus' prayer, we must stress with Bonnard that it is not a question of a passage by stages from refusal of obedience to final acceptance, but rather of the anguish of Jesus in the face of the particular obedience required by his death (*to potêrion touto*): "En d'autres termes, le Christ veut (*thelô*) obéir, mais il voudrait obéir autrement.... Jesus ne passe de la désobéissance à l'obéissance mais d'une obéissance qui aurait pu être glorieuse à l'obéissance de la croix." [48]

Verse 43: *Kai elthôn palin heuren autous katheu-*
dontas, êsan gar autôn hoi ophthalmoi bebarê-
menoi.

Except for the inversion of the phrase *palin elthôn* [49] and the substitution of *bebarêmenoi* (cf. Lk 9:32) for Mark's *katabaryno-*

---

[47] See Meyer, B. Weiss, Allen, *ad loc.*, and Gerhard Barth, "Matthew's Understanding of the Law," in Günther Bornkamm, Gerhard Barth and Heinz Joachim Held, *Tradition and Interpretation in Matthew* (Philadelphia, 1963), p. 144 and n. 3. For the Semitic usage of the exceptive *ean mê* in pplace of the adversative here, see Klaus Beyer, *Semitische Syntax im Neuen Testament*, Vol. I, Satzlehre Teil 1, 2nd ed. (Göttingen, 1962), pp. 139f.

[48] Bonnard, *op. cit.*, p. 384.

[49] B. Weiss, *op. cit.* (see above p. 69, n. 1), p. 461, takes *palin* as belonging with *heuren*.

menoi, this verse is like the first part of Mark 14:40. But Matthew has omitted altogether any equivalent of v. 40c, i.e., Mark's description of the confusion of the disciples, possibly from a motive of sparing them,[50] but more likely because here as elsewhere (e.g., Mk 6:52; 9:6) he regarded such phrases as interpretive additions of Mark bearing the weight of his special theological viewpoint.[51]

> Verse 44: *Kai apheis autous palin apelthôn proséuxato ek tritou, ton auton logon eipôn palin.*

Having shortened the previous verse by the omission of Mk 14:40c, Matthew now enlarges upon Mark, who merely implies a third withdrawal to prayer by his mention of a third return (14:41). He does so by expanding somewhat Mark's description of Jesus' second withdrawal (14:39). McNeile notes the force of the added *apheis autous*: "The Lord left them to their sleep, which was worse than a rebuke." [52]

Ek tritou balances *ek deuterou* of v. 42 and makes explicit Matthew's intention of centering his narrative on Jesus' threefold prayer, even though he can offer no further content. B. Weiss [53] notes that the *palin* at the end of this verse likewise points back to v. 42, and since no deeper surrender to the Father's will is possible, the same prayer is repeated.[54]

Meyer [55] speaks of the "simple pathos" of the polysyndeton (*kai ... kai ... kai*) in v. 40. Still more striking is the fourfold repetition of *palin* between vv. 42 and 44. It "adds a mournful force." [56] There is good authority for omitting the fourth *palin* (C ƙ A D W Γ Δ Fam. 1 and 13 *pm* lat), and, if it is retained, some question about its placement. It is tempting to search for a symmetrical pattern when a word is repeated so frequently within a

---

[50] Plummer, *loc. cit.*
[51] See above Chapter 1, pp. 47ff.
[52] *Op. cit.*, p. 392.
[53] *Op. cit.* (see above p. 70, n. 11), p. 552.
[54] But in addition to Plummer's suggestion reviewed above, see Paul Gaechter, *op. cit.*, p. 866, who, against the notion that the triple prayer here is a literary form and that the third prayer is simply identical with the other two, maintains that v. 45 shows Jesus returning from his last prayer a changed man.
[55] *Op. cit.*, II, 220.
[56] McNeile, *loc. cit.*

brief context. And one almost emerges when the attempt is made
to take each *palin* with a successive coming or going of Jesus.
By analogy with Mark this works for the first three occurrences,
although Matthew's additions and inversions, even apart from
the textual variants, would not leave such a result unchallenged.
A marginal reading in Westcott-Hort regards as equally possible
the placement of the fourth *palin* at the end of v. 44 or the beginning of v. 45. Taken with *erchetai* at the beginning of v. 45,
it would complete the symmetrical pattern. But McNeile [57] makes
the point that Matthew's use of *tote* does not allow of this possibility. So it may be best to see the symmetry as chiasma (*palin
ek deuterou apelthôn ... elthôn palin ... palin apelthôn ... eipôn
palin*), or simple inclusion,[58] which gives literary expression to the
pathos of Christ's increasingly intense prayer to the Father and
disappointment with his disciples.

Verse 45: *Tote erchetai pros tous mathêtas kai
legei autois: katheudete loipon kai anapauesthe;
idou êngiken hê hôra kai ho huios tou anthrôpou
paradidotai eis cheiras hamartôlôn.*

As earlier in vv. 36 and 38, Matthew puts *tote* for Mark's *kai*.
And Lohmeyer [59] feels that here it seems to emphasize the final
clarity achieved in struggle during the hours that have intervened
since that first *tote* standing at the head of the account.
Matthew has added the explicit *pros tous mathêtas* to Mark's
account. Again, as in v. 40, Jesus' words are addressed to the
community of disciples. But he omits *to triton*, not because he
wants to spare the disciples, but because for him it is the threefold prayer of Jesus (v. 44: *prosêuxato ek tritou*) that is significant, not his threefold return.[60]
The change from *to loipon* to the simple *loipon* is incon-
sequential. But the omission of the problematic *apechei* indicates
that perhaps even for Matthew it was already unintelligible.[61] The

---

[57] *Loc. cit.*
[58] For the extensive occurrence of these stylistic devices in Matthew,
see J. C. Fenton, "Inclusio and Chiasmus in Matthew," in *Studia Evangelica*,
I (Berlin, 1959), 174-179.
[59] *Op. cit.*, p. 362.
[60] B. Weiss, *loc. cit.*
[61] B. Weiss, Plummer, *ad loc.*

anticipation of *idou* and the change of *êlthen* to *êngiken* makes
the announcement of v. 45 exactly parallel with that of v. 46. The
theological meaning of Mark's "hour" does not figure in Matthew's
account. All mention of it has dropped out of Jesus' prayer, and
now it is assimilated to the historical hour of his betrayal and
arrest through the simple parallelism of *idou êngiken* between
vv. 45 and 46, through the designation of the hour resulting from
the addition of *kai* 'when,'[62] and finally through the replacement
of Mark's *euthus* with a third *idou* in v. 47.[63]

W. R. Hutton, in a study of the uses of the verb *engizo* in the
N. T., concluded that seventeen of its forty-two occurrences demand a translation like "come," "come to," or "arrive," rather
than the lexical meaning of "approach" or "draw near," while
for at least nine others — among them Mt 26:45 f. — such a translation seems preferable.[64] Martin A. Simpson seconded this conclusion, contending that *êngiken* (Mt 26:45) is simply equivalent
to *êlthen* (Mk 14:41) and is meant to emphasize the correspondence with the following verse in Matthew.[65] But Peter Staples
subsequently objected to this identification of these two verbs
here, and I believe rightly so, though his arguments are feeble.
He relates the "hour" of Mk 14:35, 41 to the act of betrayal by
Judas, because that is the only event in the passion which at this
point can be said to have "come" (*êlthen*). The "cup" of Mt 26:39,
on the other hand, he relates to the arrest or crucifixion, and
explains that Matthew's change to *êngiken* in v. 45 is perfectly
correct, since the "hour" of these events still lies in the future.
Moreover, he notes that in Mark *êlthen* (14:41) and *êngiken* (v. 42)
do not have the same meaning, the latter according to Kümmel
bearing here a futuristic meaning,[66] corroborated by the fact
that only in the following verse is the actual arrival of Judas
mentioned.[67]

There are, however, several things wrong with these arguments. First of all, if *êlthen* and *êngiken* do not have the same

---

[62] B.-D.-F., 442 (4).
[63] See B. Weiss, *op. cit.*, pp. 552f.
[64] W. R. Hutton, "The Kingdom of God has Come," *ET*, 64 (1952-53), 89-91.
[65] Martin A. Simpson, "The Kingdom of God has Come," *ET*, 64 (1952-53), 188.
[66] Werner Georg Kümmel, *Promise and Fulfilment. The Eschatological Message of Jesus*, tr. Dorothea M. Barton, 2nd ed. (London, 1961), says
that *engizein* conveys the meaning that "one has come nearer to a place
than before but has not yet reached it" (p. 19).
[67] Peter Staples, "The Kingdom of God has Come," *ET*, 71 (1959-60), 87f.

meaning in Mark, then the hour that has come (*êlthen*) in 14:41 cannot be simply the hour of betrayal by Judas, since in v. 42 the betrayer is said only to have come near (*êngiken*) but not to have arrived, and the hour of betrayal can hardly be said to begin before the arrival of the betrayer. Matthew's "hour," then, is the hour of betrayal, not Mark's,[68] since only in Matthew does the double use of *êngiken* make the hour and the traitor equally proximate. Secondly, while the connection between the "hour" and the "cup" in Mark's text is tenuous enough, in Matthew's text there is no connection between them at all, with the result that, whatever the "cup" of 26:39 may mean, it in no way controls the meaning of the "hour" in v. 45. Consequently, Matthew's change to *êngiken* has nothing to do with the question of whether the events represented under the image of the cup are present or future. Rather, it simply brings about the parallelism with v. 46 which reveals to us that for Matthew the "hour" means the hour of betrayal. Finally, what should have been noted is that Matthew preserves the distinction between *êngiken* and *êlthen* much more obviously than Mark. For the words of Jesus in 26:45f., which have the character of a final announcement of the imminence of his betrayal and passion, Matthew uses *êngiken*. For his own historical description of the traitor's arrival in v. 47 he uses *êlthen*, where Mark has *paraginetai*.[69] Clearly, the difference between the two verbs as employed by Matthew is the difference between approach and arrival, imminence and presence. And thus *êngiken* retains its usual meaning in his account.[70]

B. Weiss [71] remarks how Matthew's omission of the articles from the phrase *eis cheiras hamartôlôn* brings into even sharper relief the kind of hands into which Jesus is about to be delivered.

---

[68] But see Kümmel, *op. cit.*, pp. 22f., who maintains the contrary.

[69] B. Weiss, *op. cit.*, p. 553, comments that Mt 26:47 repeats the *idea* of vv. 45f., "weil nun eben geschiet, was dort angekündigt."

[70] For the meaning of *êngiken*, see further G. D. Kilpatrick, "Some Notes on Marcan Usage," *The Bible Translator*, 7 (1956), 53; and Jacques Dupont, *Les Béatitudes*, Vol. II: *La Bonne Nouvelle* (Paris, 1969), pp. 109-111.

[71] *Ibid.*, pp. 552f.

Verse 46: *Egeiresthe, agômen; idou êngiken ho paradidous me.*

There is complete verbal correspondence between this verse and Mk 14:42. The only change Matthew has made is to transpose the order of the subject and the verb in the second half of the verse.[72] And our exegesis of v. 45 has already yielded the reason for this change. It renders possible the parallelism of *idou êngiken* in both verses, which is the key to Matthew's interpretation of *hôra* as the historical moment of Jesus' betrayal and arrest.

---

[72] Cf. Mt 3:2; 4:17; 10:7; Walter Grundmann, *Das Evangelium nach Matthäus* (Berlin, 1971), p. 541.

CHAPTER THREE

LITERARY ANALYSIS OF LUKE 22:39-46

Verse 39: *Kai exelthôn eporeuthê kata to ethos eis to oros tôn elaiôn; êkolouthêsan de autô kai hoi mathêtai.*

Luke's account of the Gethsemane scene is considerably different from that of Mark or Matthew. It is both abbreviated and expanded in that it omits and adds to details contained in the other two synoptics. It is closest to them in the introduction (v. 39), the words of Christ's prayer (v. 42), and the conclusion (v. 46), although even in these cases the verbal correspondence is at most partial.[1] Obviously Luke has his own source for vv. 43-44, if they are genuine. But whether he is following this special source throughout,[2] or condensing Mark,[3] or enlarging in his own way the simpler source that underlies the Mark-Matthew expansions,[4] are questions that will have to wait until the chapter on the editorial history of Luke's text to be resolved.

The Gethsemane scene is inserted somewhat differently into Luke's context, too. The singing of the hymn on the way to the Mount of Olives (Mk 14:26 par.) has disappeared, and the subsequent conversation with its prediction of Peter's denial has been assimilated to the expanded supper discourse.[5] As a result, Jesus' passage from the supper to the garden is immediate, and one cannot tell whether *exelthôn* at the beginning of v. 39 refers

---

[1] See Alfred Plummer, *A Critical and Exegetical Commentary on the Gospel According to S. Luke*, 5th ed. (Edinburgh, 1960), pp. 507-511.

[2] So Rengstorf, Grundmann, Taylor.

[3] So Wellhausen, Zahn, Lagrange, Schlatter, Klostermann, Finegan, Hauck, Creed, Schmid.

[4] So Plummer, Loisy, Bussmann, Spitta.

[5] Karl Heinrich Rengstorf, *Das Evangelium nach Lukas*, 8th ed. (Göttingen, 1958), p. 250; W. Grundmann, *Das Evangelium nach Lukas* (Berlin, 1961), p. 410.

to his leaving the house or his leaving the city.[6] But since the following phrase *kata to ethos* is generally taken to refer back to Lk 21:37, and since there it is a question of Jesus' leaving the city, that is most likely to be the meaning here too. *Kata to ethos*, however, raises a problem of its own; for, as Schlatter points out, Luke can hardly be speaking of a "custom" in reference to the few days between the trimphal entry and the passion. So the expression may derive from Luke's source and envision a repeated or a longer stay in Jerusalem than Luke recounts.[7] In any case, the phrase can serve more than one purpose. It points forward as well as back and makes clear, like Jn 18:2, that Jesus withdrew not to delay or escape deliverance to his enemies, but to ready himself for it when they came to find him where he usually passed the night.[8]

All that Luke has to say about the disciples is that they followed Jesus there. None of them is singled out, neither Peter nor the three, and Jesus addresses his two exhortations to prayer and his brief rebuke for sleeping to all of them alike. Nothing of his need and desire for them to be with him in his hour, as expressed by Mark and Matthew, comes through here. In Luke Jesus struggles alone without them. And his exhortations and rebuke show only his concern for their weakness before the trial facing them, not for their failure in facing his with him.[9]

Verse 40: *Genomenos de epi tou topou eipen autois: proseuchesthe mê eiselthein eis peirasmon.*

Luke, once again like Jn 18:2, calls the place where Jesus comes with his disciples *topos* rather than *chôrion* (Mk, Mt), and omits the name "Gethsemane." Since the name is also omitted in John, it may have been omitted in Luke's source and be a piece of evidence for his independence from Mark. But Bailey explains Luke's omission on the grounds of his aversion for Semitic place

---

[6] Erich Klostermann and H. Gressmann, *Handbuch zum Neuen Testament*, ed. Hans Lietzmann (Tübingen, 1919), II, 582.

[7] A. Schlatter, *Das Evangelium des Lukas* (Stuttgart, 1931), p. 432; and cf. Theodor Zahn, *Das Evangelium des Lucas*, 3rd and 4th ed. (Leipzig, 1920), p. 686.

[8] So Schlatter, *loc. cit.*; Rengstorf, p. 250; Grundmann, p. 411; and Josef Schmid, *Das Evangelium nach Lukas*, 4th ed. (Regensburg, 1960), p. 335.

[9] See Schlatter, pp. 432f.; Schmid, pp. 335f.

names and John's on the grounds of its traditional association with a prayer John thought unworthy of Jesus.[10] In any case, the simple identification of the Mount of Olives as the place of Jesus' agony has the effect of bringing the scene into closer relationship with both the Transfiguration and the entry into Jerusalem.[11]

The skeletal indication *epi tou topou* hardly seems enough, and as Wellhausen [12] remarks, we feel the need for some kind of relative clause to flesh it out. Klostermann [13] argues by analogy with Lk 10:32 and Jn 18:2 that it should refer to some place already clearly indicated in the text, but he questions whether it can go all the way back to the Mount of Olives in 21:37. Creed considers that it is not a natural designation for the Mount of Olives (22:39) anyway, and he suggests that it has resulted from Luke's substituting a more general expression of place when he abbreviated Mark.[14] Thus it appears to be somehow an element from the tradition, and this fact needs to be explained. Accordingly, B. Weiss may be closest to correct in explaining it as "die Stätte der Verhaftung, die unter den Lesern der Quelle noch allgemein bekannt war." [15]

An important difference between Luke's account and the synoptic parallels is that he frames his account of Jesus' own prayer with his exhortation to the disciples to pray that they may not fall into temptation. Thus the exhortation comes twice, once at the beginning and once at the end of the account, whereas in Mark and Matthew it comes only once in the middle, in combination with the exhortation to watch, after Jesus returns to find the disciples sleeping. In Luke the exhortation to watch has dropped out altogether, and the exhortation to pray is essentially connected not with the sleep of the disciples, but rather with the perilous situation in which they are about to be caught up. Here as in the supper discourses (22:28-38), Luke focuses on the concern of Jesus for them (v. 31), and now he asks them to pray

---

[10] John Amedee Bailey, *The Traditions Common to the Gospels of Luke and John* (Leiden, 1963), p. 53; and see J. Wellhausen, *Das Evangelium Lucae* (Berlin, 1904), p. 127; E. Klostermann, *loc. cit.*; Schmid, p. 335.

[11] Helmut Flender, *St. Luke: Theologian of Redemptive History*, tr. Reginald H. and Ilse Fuller (London, 1967), pp. 31 and n. 4, 32.

[12] *Loc. cit.*

[13] *Loc. cit.*

[14] John Martin Creed, *The Gospel according to St. Luke* (London, 1930), p. 272.

[15] Bernhard Weiss, *Die Evangelien des Markus und Lukas* (Göttingen, 1901), p. 645.

themselves not to fall victims in the trial, since only those who pray will be able to withstand (cf. Lk 11:4).[16]

The initial and concluding exhortations differ in form. G. L. Hahn has pointed out that the *proseuchesthai* of v. 40, which is ordinarily followed by a *hina*-clause, as in v. 46, occurs only here in the N. T. with the simple infinitive.[17] And we have already seen what Loisy makes of the difference. According to him, the formula from v. 40 originally read *proseuchesthe mê eiselthein [me] eis peirasmon*: i.e., Jesus was asking the disciples to pray for *him* in his trial. And Luke's preservation of v. 40 as a variant of v. 46 only exhibits the hesitation he felt in substituting the apostles under trial for Jesus.[18] But this is reading far too much into a simple turn of style, and we have already reviewed the grounds for opposing Loisy's suggestion.[19]

More significantly, Luke's doubling of the exhortation at the beginning and end of the account, and his dropping of its essential connection with the sleep of the disciples leaves vv. 41-46 vulnerable to the charge of interpolation in the context. Spitta presses home the charge, claiming that v. 47 should follow on v. 40, and that what lies between them forms "kein Teil der synoptischen Grundschrift."[20] But he is simply taking advantage of one weakness in Luke's construction, and when we come to the editorial history of the synoptic material, we may see better reason for recognizing the whole scene, including vv. 39-40, as secondary to the earliest passion account.

Verse 41: *Kai autos apespasthê ap' autôn hôsei lithou bolên, kai theis ta gonata proseucheto.*

As in Mark and Matthew, Jesus' prayer in Luke takes place apart from his disciples. Luke has given no indication of the feelings of Jesus at the beginning of this scene, omitting any equivalent to Mk 14:33b-34 par. But the violent movement implied by *apespasthê* in contrast to *proelthôn* (Mk 14:35 par.) may

---

[16] See Friedrich Spitta, *Die synoptische Grundschrift in ihrer Überlieferung durch das Lukasevangelium* (Leipzig, 1912), p. 388; and Klostermann, Rengstorf, Grundmann, *ad loc.*

[17] G. L. Hahn, *Das Evangelium des Lucas erklärt* (Breslau, 1892-94), II, 614.

[18] Alfred Loisy, *Les Évangiles synoptiques* (Ceffonds, 1907-08), II, 562.

[19] See above Chapter 1 on Mk 14:38.

[20] *Loc. cit.*

be meant to picture the force of the emotions that drove him away from his disciples to seek the solitude of prayer.[21] But, on the other hand, it is possible that nothing more than a simple separation from the disciples is meant (cf. Acts 21:1).[22] At a short distance from them — *hôsei lithou bolên* (cf. Gen 21:16) — probably about thirty meters [23] and so within calling and hearing distance,[24] he falls to his knees to pray. The usual Jewish position at prayer was standing.[25] And the kneeling position of Jesus here is an expression of the urgency and humility of his prayer.[26] Lagrange [27] observes that Luke has employed almost liturgical terminology here — *theis ta gonata* — to describe the movement which in Mark and Matthew threw Jesus prostrate to the ground. And Plummer [28] comments that elsewhere in the N. T. the only Christian position mentioned at prayer is kneeling, perhaps in imitation of Jesus praying here (cf. Acts 7:60; 9:40; 20:36; 21:5; Eph 3:14). The imperfect tense *prosêucheto*, as in Mark 14:35, brings home in its own way the intensity of Jesus' continuing and repeated prayer.

Verse 42:   *Legôn: Pater, ei boulei parenengke touto to potêrion ap' emou; plên mê to thelêma mou alla to son ginesthô.*

This prayer of Jesus is in structure and substance the same as that reported in Mk 14:36 and Mt 26:39b. Its opening preserves the distinctive address of Jesus to his Father; its center section expresses conditionally (cf. Mk 14:35) the petition for the removal of this cup from him; and its conclusion is a surrender of his will to that of the Father (cf. Mt 26:42).

Luke's simple *pater* is the briefest address of the three synoptics and it parallels the address in his own version of the

---

[21] So B. Weiss, Hahn, Plummer, *ad loc.;* Loisy, *loc. cit.;* and M.-J. Lagrange, *Évangile selon Saint Luc*, 8th ed. (Paris, 1948), p. 559.

[22] So Klostermann, Grundmann, *ad loc.*, after B.-A.-G., s. v.

[23] Lagrange, *loc. cit.*

[24] Grundmann, *loc. cit.*

[25] Cf. 1 Sam 1:26; Mk 11:25; Mt 6:5; Lk 18:11; and S.-B., II, 259.

[26] Cf. 1 Kings 8:54; Ezra 9:5; Dan 6:10; S.-B., II, 260f.; and Plummer, Rengstorf, Grundmann, *ad loc.*

[27] *Loc. cit.*

[28] *Op. cit.*, p. 508.

Lord's Prayer (11:2), just as Matthew's *pater mou* (26:39) parallels the address *pater hêmôn* (6:9) in his.

More directly and more personally than Mark's or Matthew's
ei dynaton estin Luke's *ei boulei* places the whole prayer that
follows subject to the Father's decision. And one cannot miss
the juxtaposition thereby effected between *boulei* in the first
part of the verse and *thelêma* in the last. *Boulomai* and *thelô*
as the two verbs for willing had a long history of competition for
predominance in Greek usage, and philologists still dispute the
character of their original difference in meaning. Their frequency
in the LXX is about equal, with *boulomai* having a slight edge.[29]
By N. T. times, however, *thelô* is in possession of the field, and
boulomai evidences but a scant six occurrences in the gospels as
compared to one hundred and eighteen for *thelô*.[30] It was no
doubt this fact that led Blass-Debrunner to suggest that Luke's
use of *boulei* in the present passage stems from literary language,
but the relative frequency of *boulomai* in the papyri lends little
support to this contention.[31] And despite a tendency in Hellenistic
Greek toward indifferently synonymous employment of *boulomai*
and *thelô*,[32] Luke seems to intend a conscious contrast between
their root meanings here in the prayer of Jesus. *Boulomai* occurs in the N. T. with a connotation of mature deliberation and
resolve in willing something, while *thelô* generally expresses a
more spontaneous intention, wish or choice. *Boulomai* represents
the will as resulting from reason and reflection, *thelô* the will
as arising from natural bent or desire.[33] These fundamentally
distinct connotations are not always rigidly maintained. Both
words and their derivatives are used of the will of God, though
boulomai appears to convey the nuance of the divine will as
eternal purpose, counsel or design.[34] This latter feature cor-

---

[29] See Gottlob Schrenk, "*Boulomai, ktl.,*" *TDNT*, I (Grand Rapids,
1964), 629f.

[30] Paul Joüon, "Les verbes *boulomai* et *thelô* dans le Nouveau Testament," *RSR*, 30 (1940), 230.

[31] Cf. B.-D.-F., 27 and J. H. Moulton and G. Milligan, *The Vocabulary of
the Greek Testament* (Grand Rapids, 1960), s. v.

[32] B.-A.-G., s. v. *boulomai;* B.-D.-F., 101, s. v. *thelein.*

[33] Cf. Zorell, B.-A.-G., Moulton and Milligan, s. vv.; Joüon, art. cit., pp.
228f.; and Plummer, *loc. cit.* By contrast the opinion of Lagrange, *op. cit.,*
p. 560, which admits a larger element of understanding in the volition of
boulomai, yet finds *thelêma* somehow more definitive than *boulê,* seems
strange.

[34] See Schrenk, art. cit., pp. 631-637; and *idem,* "*Thelô, ktl.,*" *TDNT*, III
(Grand Rapids, 1967), 47f., 53-59, 61f.

responds closely to Luke's use of *boulê*, especially in Acts, where the foreordaining counsel of God also expressly embraces the deliverance of Jesus over to death.[35]   On the other hand, with but a single exception, Luke is alone among the Synoptics in using *thelêma* unambiguously for human will or preference.[36]   So we are perfectly justified in concluding that the contrast intended by Luke in the two halves of v. 42 is that between the resolute, pre-determined and immutable counsel of God and the natural in-clination of the human will of Jesus.   At the very moment when he is humanly most anxious for deliverance, Jesus makes his appeal and his surrender to God's foreordaining purpose, negating in self-sacrificing struggle any will of his own independent of that purpose.[37]   The deliberate plan of God takes precedence over every human wish.   Thus Luke has made clear by linguistic means what is not so clear in the parallels: namely, that the struggle of Jesus in prayer is not simply to align his will with that of the Father (v. 42b), but rather to grasp whether the drinking of this cup of rejection, suffering and death is genuinely the design (*ei boulei*)[38] of God for him and for his mission.   That the cup is not removed becomes for him the sign of its inclusion in the Father's purposes.

Among the textual variants, *parenengke* is clearly the easiest reading and therefore the most readily suspect.   G. L. Hahn[39] reads the infinitive *parenengkein* (𝔅 A W Γ Δ *pm*) with *boulei* and interprets *ei* as introducing not a direct question or a wish, but a condition with the final clause suppressed (supply, for example, "that is my wish too").   Deissmann, reading *parenengkai* (ℵ K L

---

[35] See Acts 2:23 and Schrenk, *TDNT*, I, 635.   Cf. Luke 7:30; Acts 4:28; 13:36; 20:27.

[36] See Lk 12:47; 22:42; 23:25 and Schrenk, *TDNT*, III, 59.   *To thelêma tou patros* in Mt 21:31 is the sole exception and, like Lk 12:47, perhaps not altogether unequivocal.

[37] See Schrenk, *TDNT*, I, 633; III, 49, 56; Joüon, art. cit., p. 231.   Joüon apparently equates *thelêma so exclusively with* "ce que je veux par ten-dance naturelle" (n. 2) as to suggest that ‚had Luke chosen to give express mention to the Father's will in v. 42b, he would have used *boulêma* (n. 3). The comment is gratuitous, since in fact *to son ginesthô* already has *thelêma* for its antecedent and Luke employs *thelêma* consistently in Acts 13:22, 21:14, and 22:14 for God's will.

[38] We should also recognize something of the nature of a formula in this introduction, since many old Jewish prayers begin in this manner. See S.-B., II, 262.

[39] *Op. cit.*, pp. 614f.

Fam. 13 *al*), takes the same view.[40]   Loisy, reading the same form, finds this aposiopesis strained, and prefers with B. Weiss to understand it as an imperative rather than an infinitive. *Parenengkai* occurs also as a variant in Mk 14:36 (אA C K *al*), and there it can be nothing but an imperative.[41] This interpretation is, in effect, equivalent to the reading *parenengke*. Klostermann and Grundmann both read the infinitive with *boulei*, whether it is *parenengkein* or *parenengkai*. As for interpretation, Klostermann[42] hesitates between the opinion of Deissmann mentioned above and that of Zahn,[43] who regards the phrase as an unclassical direct question introduced by *ei*, which serves here as an interrogative particle after the analogy of Lk 13:23; 22:49; Acts 1:6; 7:1; 19:2. Grundmann[44] opts for the latter view.

The need to resolve such questions, however, disappears if *parenengke* is the original reading. And despite the fact that it remains the *lectio facilior*, it does seem by comparison to possess the best text-critical claims. Of the three readings we have mentioned, *parenengkein* is the most likely to be secondary, resting entirely on the support of Byzantine witnesses. *Parenengkai* has more to be said for it, since it claims Alexandrian witnesses as well, but its attestation apart from Codex Sinaiticus is relatively late. Thus it appears that *parenengke* (p[75] B D Θ Fam 1 157. 1241 *al* Vg and some of the Old Latin versions) presents the strongest case, possessing both the earliest attestation (2nd-3rd c.) and the broadest base in Alexandrian, Western and Caesarean, as well as Byzantine, text types. The presence of this reading in the recently edited (1961) Bodmer Papyrus p[75] adds great weight to an already persuasive body of evidence and leaves little doubt that it is to be preferred.

The word order *touto to potêrion* would ordinarily call for no comment, except that Heinz Schürmann has adduced it as evidence for the disputed originality of the so-called "long text" in Luke's account of the institution of the Eucharist in 22:19-20. Assuming Luke's dependence on Mark and contrasting his order with

---

[40] Adolf Deissmann, *Light from the Ancient East*, tr. Lionel R. M. Strachan from the 4th German ed. (New York and London, [1927]), p. 151, n. 5; and see B.-D.-F., 482.

[41] Loisy, *op. cit.*, II, 565 and n. 6; and see B.-D.-F., 81 (2).

[42] *Op. cit.*, p. 582.

[43] *Op. cit.*, p. 687.

[44] *Op. cit.*, pp. 411f.

to potêrion touto in Mk 14:36,[45] he argues that the reversal cannot be explained on stylistic or literary grounds, but only as a reminiscence of Luke's earlier formula at the supper. Since the difference from Mark stems from the influence of *touto to potê-rion* in 22:20, Schürmann considers it at least a well-founded presumption that Lk 22:42a is our oldest witness to the originality of 22:19-20.[46] Rengstorf [47] has observed that there is no earlier saying in this gospel, as there is in Mark, to which we can refer in interpreting the meaning of the cup for Luke (cf. Lk 12:50 with Mk 10:38). And so he attempts to develop an interpretation from a wider context of sayings in Luke's special material (e.g., 12:50; 13:32-33; 22:28, 37). But he has overlooked altogether the parallelism of the formulas called to our attention by Schürmann, and consequently failed to note the only explicit interpretation of the cup which Luke provides: namely, the inauguration of the new covenant in the shedding of Christ's blood for sinful men.

The textual variants which we noted for *parenengke* led Loisy to suspect that the primitive text of this verse did not contain the resignation clause (v. 42b), but found *ei boulei* sufficient to express the notion.[48] The parallels, not only in Mk 14:36 and Mt 26:39, 42 but also in Jn 12:27f., would seem to speak strongly for the traditional threefold structure of the prayer concluding in a resignation clause. Still, if Mk 14:35 stems from a different source than v. 36, as the editorial history of Mark's scene may suggest, then Loisy's suspicion is not unexampled in the tradition of this passage. If v. 42b is original to Luke's account, it seems to exhibit the influence of Mt 26:39, 42 or even 6:10.[49]

---

[45] *To potêrion touto* is also a secondary variant for Lk 22:42 in ʀ A W Γ Δ Fam 1 and 13 *pm*.

[46] Heinz Schürmann, "Lk 22, 42a das älteste Zeugnis für Lk 22,20?" *MTZ*, 3 (1952), 185-188.

[47] *Op. cit.*, p. 250.

[48] *Op. cit.*, II, 565, n. 3, 574.

[49] *Ibid.*, pp. 565f.; so also Plummer, Lagrange, Creed, Grundmann, *ad loc*. Margaret E. Thrall, *Greek Particles in the New Testament. Linguistic and Exegetical Studies* (Leiden, 1962), pp. 21f., 67f., believes that Luke's use of *plên* here, unlike Matthew's (see above Chapter 2 on Mt 26:39), is probably a simple equivalent for *alla*, as elsewhere in his gospel (e.g., 12:31; 23:28), especially since there can be no question of Luke's intending to tone down the conflict in Mark if the authenticity of the following two verses is granted.

Verse 43: *Ôphthê de autô angelos ap' ouranou
enischyôn auton.*

Verse 44: *Kai genomenos en agônia ektenesteron
prosêucheto; kai egeneto ho hidrôs autou hôsei
thromboi haimatos katabainontes epi tên gên.*

These two verses of Luke, unparalleled in Mark and Matthew,
present the most taxing text-critical problem of the synoptic
Gethsemane account. Scholars to this day remain divided over
the question of their originality,[50] owing to the practically equal
balance of witnesses for and against the passage.[51] In their edition
of the Greek New Testament Westcott and Hort double-bracketed
the verses as a sign of their inclusion among a group of "five
interpolations omitted on authority other than Western, where
the omitted words appeared to be derived from an external written or unwritten source, and had likewise exceptional claims to

---

[50] With no attempt to be exhaustive, we may note that the majority
of modern Protestant and Catholic authors favor retention of the verses,
among them: Tischendorf, Blass, [Westcott-Hort], [Nestle], [von Soden],
in their editions of the N. T. and [Aland] in his synopsis (the latter bracket
the verses); H. Aschermann, W. Bauer, P. Benoit, G. Bertram, I. M. Bover,
W. R. F. Browning. L. Brun, G. B. Caird, M. Dibelius, M. Goguel, W. Grundmann, A. von Harnack, E. Hirsch, H. J. Holtzmann, O. Aoltzmann, E. Klostermann, K. G. Kuhn, M.-J. Lagrande, A. Loisy, A. Merk, E. Meyer, Morgenthaler, A. Schlatter, J. Schmid, B. H. Streeter, H.-W. Surkau, V. Taylor,
Th. Zahn. Opposed to the retention of these verses are, for example: the
Greek New Testament of Erwin Nestle and Kurt Aland, 26th ed., and that
of K. Aland, M. Black, B. M. Metzger, and A. Wikgren; R. Bultmann, B. S.
Easton, J. Finegan, F. Hauck, E. Lohse, A. Merx, A. M. Perry, A. Plummer,
B. Weiss, J. Weiss, J. Wellhausen.

[51] The text is included with minor variations in ℵ *, ᵇ D F G H K L M Q
U X Γ Δ * Θ Λ Π * Ψ 0171 Fam 1 565 700 892 * 1009 1010 1071ᵐᵍ 1230 1241 1242
vg syrᶜ, ᵖ, ʰ, ᵖᵃˡ bo (pt) arm eth Diatessaronᵃ, ᵉarm, i, n Justin Irenaeus
1253 1344 1365 1546 1646 2148 2174 ℓ 1¹⁸⁴, ²¹¹ (pt) itᵃ, aur, b, c, d, e, ff², i, l, q, r¹
Hippolytus Dionysius Arius ᵃᶜᶜ. ᵗᵒ ᴱᵖⁱᵖʰᵃⁿⁱᵘˢ Eusebius Hilary Caesarius-
Nazianzus Gregory-Nazianzus Didymus Pseudo-Dionysius Epiphanius Chry-
sostom Jerome Augustine Theodoret Leontius Cosmos Facundus. It is
read with asterisks or obeli by E S V Γ Δᶜ Πᶜ 892ᶜ ⁱⁿ ᵐᵍ 1079 1195 1216
copᵇᵒ (mss). It is omitted by [p⁶⁹ ᵛⁱᵈ] p⁷⁵ ℓ ᵃ A B R T W 1071* 579 1⁶⁹ (pt),
70 (pt), 211 (pt), 1127 (pt) itᶠ syrˢ copˢᵃ, ᵇᵒ (pt) geo Marcion Clement Origen
mssᵃᶜᶜ. ᵗᵒ ᴴⁱˡᵃʳʸ Athanasius Ambrose mssᵃᶜᶜ. ᵗᵒ ᴱᵖⁱᵖʰᵃⁿⁱᵘˢ mssᵃᶜᶜ. ᵗᵒ ᴶᵉʳᵒᵐᵉ
Cyril John-Damascus. And it is transposed after Mt 26 : 39 by Fam 13
160, 69 (pt), 70 (pt), 1127 (pt).

retention in the body of the text." [52]   Thus while they regarded vv. 43f. as authentic, albeit extra-canonical, evangelical tradition, they argued particularly from the convergence of ℵ * D, the Old Latin, and the Syriac versions — "a frequent Western combination" — for the passage being "an early Western interpolation adopted in eclectic texts," and they could see no validity to the claims that its omission elsewhere was influenced by doctrinal considerations or lectionary practice.[53]   Lagrange [54] objects to the wholesale classification as Western of the witnesses which contain the reading, and he counters that the witnesses which omit it geographically represent hardly any place but Egypt, and not all of Egypt at that (e.g., ℵ *).   Moreover, he stresses that among the Fathers who attest the reading, Justin and Irenaeus may have employed a Western text, but Dionysius of Alexandria certainly did not.   Wellhausen [55] judges that the presence of the verses in the Curetonian Syriac and their absence from the earlier Sinaitic Syriac version is persuasive evidence of the probability of later origin.   But Lagrange [56] finds the Sinaitic Syriac by no means so trustworthy a witness.   And Streeter points out that in the oldest MS. of the Armenian there is a note to the effect that these verses were present in the "first translations" but were left out of the "newly issued translations."   And since the oldest Armenian seems to have been translated from the Syriac, he concludes that these verses were just possibly "revised out" of the Sinaitic Syriac.[57]

What can be said presently is that the Alexandrian witnesses are preponderantly, but not exclusively or decisively, for the omission of vv. 43-44.[58]   Previous to the discovery of Bodmer Papyrus P[75], the strongest textual evidence for and against the verses was evenly divided between the fourth century witness

[52] Brooke Foss Westcott and Fenton John Anthony Hort, *The New Testament in the Original Greek*, 2nd ed., II (London and New York, 1896), Introduction, p. 296.

[53] *Ibid.*, II, Appendix, pp. 64-67; quotations on p. 66; and so also Plummer, *op. cit.*, p. 544.

[54] *Op. cit.*, pp. 562f.

[55] *Op. cit.*, p. 127.

[56] *Loc. cit.*

[57] B. H. Streeter, *The Four Gospels: A Study of Origins* (London, 1927), p. 137.

[58] Thus p[75] ℵ ᵃ B T 579, the largest number and the best of the Bohairic MSS. and some of the Sahidic MSS., Athanasius, Cyril of Alexandria and [Origen] omit the verses, while they are found in ℵ *, ᵇ, ᶜ L Q 892 *, ᶜ ⁱⁿ ᵐᵍ 1241 sa (pt) bo (pt) Dionysius.

of ℵ* and B. Now the evidence against them reaches back to the end of the second or the beginning of the third century, and just possibly affords proof of an even earlier proto-Alexandrian archetype, in which the omission may also well have occurred.[59] The Western witnesses, on the other hand, are stronger for retaining the verses, but again not conclusive.[60] Caesarean[61] and Byzantine witnesses stand on both sides; and although they predominantly favor the retention of the verses, yet the two oldest Byzantine MSS. (A W) omit them altogether, while a number of later ones (E S V Γ Δ^c Π^c) include them marked with asterisks or obeli.[62] External evidence at the present time, then, seems, if anything, to tip the scales against the originality of the disputed verses. But it does not decide the question definitively. And we must look for other proof. Loisy,[63] following B. and J. Weiss, pointed out that the verses are only loosely joined to the context, although their separation leaves the account notably weakened. For one thing, the angel's intervention is unnecessary after the complete resignation of Jesus' prayer in v. 42; and for another, v. 45 seems to ignore the angel and the agony and to refer back only to the prayer of v. 42. The intervening verses are thus not indispensable to the sequence.

What of the intrinsic probability of addition or suppression of the verses? Lagrange argues that, while later interpolation is not absolutely impossible, it remains highly improbable since the author would have to have lived before the middle of the second century and to have composed the verses in Luke's style.

---

[59] See Bruce Metzger, *The Text of the New Testament* (Oxford, 1964), pp. 215f. On the strength of the attestation of P^{75} Nestle/Aland, *Novum Testamentum Graece,* 26th ed., and Aland/Black/Metzger/Wikgren, *The Greek New Testament,* both relegate these verses to the apparatus. The 25th and earlier editions of Nestle Aland had double-bracketed them. For the justification, see Kurt Aland, "Neue Neutestamentliche Papyri II," *NTS,* 12 (1965-66), 199, 203; and *idem, Studien zur Überlieferung des Neuen Testaments und seines Textes* (Berlin, 1967), pp. 160f., 165.

[60] D 0171 $it^{a, aur, b, c, d, e, ff^2, i, l, q, r^1}$ $syr^{c, h}$ Justin, Irenaeus and Augustine retain the verses, while they are missing from R it^f syr^s Marcion and Clement.

[61] The verses are read by Θ Fam 1 565 700 1071^{mg} syr^{pal} Arm Eusebius; omitted by 1071 * Geo; and transposed after Mt 26:39 by Fam 13.

[62] Among the Byzantine witnesses containing the verses are F G H K M U X Δ * Λ Π * Ψ, the Ethiopic version, and in general the majority of Byzantine MSS.

[63] *Op. cit.,* II, 572.

Thus the addition of the verses could really be explained only on the grounds of authentic tradition. Suppression, on the other hand, could be explained on doctrinal grounds. For example, the text was cited against the Docetists in the second century, but its antiquity had to be defended in the fourth century by Epiphanius, who claimed that it was a cause of perplexity among orthodox believers because of the use made of it by the Arians.[65] "Presumably," writes Streeter, pursuing the same argument, "it seemed beneath the dignity of the Uncreated Word Incarnate to evince such a degree of *pathos;* and still more to require a created angel as a comforter. Hence there was every reason, if not for excising it from the text, at least for regarding MSS. in which it had been accidentally omitted as original. We conclude then that B W 579, etc., which omit the words, though they may possibly give the earliest Alexandrian text, do not preserve the original words of Luke." [66] But while this line of explanation may rationalize the discrepancies, it labors under a very serious weakness. For if such is the case, it is without analogies, since, as Westcott and Hort observed, "there is no tangible evidence for the excision of a substantial portion of narrative for doctrinal reasons at any period of textual history." [67]

Having examined the extrinsic evidence and the intrinsic probabilities, we have now to look at the literary characteristics of the text itself. The argument for the Lukan authorship of vv. 43-44 from stylistic considerations had been proposed before Harnack, but it gained great force when he submitted the passage to a detailed analysis of language and style.[68] And his affirmative conclusions found wide acceptance thereafter. In an article published some thirty years later, however, Lyder Brun contended that Harnack's findings were not nearly so unambiguous or decisive as he imagined, and that still further criteria were needed to resolve the issue for good.[69] In particular, he makes the following points:

1. While *ôphthê* is certainly used more frequently by Luke than by Mark (only in 9:4) or Matthew (only in 17:3), it is not

---

[65] Lagrange, *op. cit.,* pp. 562f.

[66] Streeter, *op. cit.,* pp. 137f.

[67] *Op. cit.,* II, Appendix, p. 66.

[68] See Adolph von Harnack, "Probleme im Text der Leidensgeschichte Jesu," *SAB,* (1901), pp. 251-255.

[69] Lyder Brun, "Engel und Blutschweiss, Lc 22, 43-44," *ZNW,* 32 (1933), 265-276.

the case, as Harnack claimed, that *ôphthê de autô* here and in
1:11 are verbal equivalents, since *angelos* is modified here, but
nowhere else in Luke, by *ap' ouranou*; and furthermore, apart
from 22:43 angelophanies in Luke occur only where they occur
in Matthew, i.e., in the infancy and resurrection narratives, and
not even in the Temptation account.

   2. While Lk 22:43 and Acts 9:19 represent the only two
N.T. occurrences of the verb *enischyein*, usage and sense are
not parallel in the two passages: in Acts it is used intransitively
and refers to strengthening through bodily nourishment.

   3. While *ektenesteron proseucheto* (v. 44) finds a genuine
parallel in Acts 12:5 (*proseuchê de ên ektenôs ginomenê*) and
perhaps in 26:7 (*en ekteneia*), such expressions are not specifically Lukan, but already common in the Septuagint (cf. Joel 1:14;
Jon 3:8; Jdt 4:7, 12).

   4. While constructions with *ginesthai* are particularly common in Luke, the use of *ginesthai en* here and in Acts 22:17 is not
exclusively Lukan (cf. Rom 16:7; Phil 2:7; Apoc 1:10).

   5. Finally, while *agônia*, *hidrôs* and *thrombos* are N.T.
hapaxlegomena and do not occur in the Apostolic Fathers, that
does not prove that vv. 43-44 must have been written by Luke,
but only that they might have been. Accordingly Brun claims
that the genuine parallel between 22:44 and Acts 12:5 is out-
weighed by the unexampled *angelos ap' ouranou* and the divergent use of *enischyein* in 22:43 and Acts 9:19, and therefore
that Harnack's linguistic and stylistic evidence remains inconclusive for determining the Lukan authorship of these verses.[70]

   Yet Brun comes to the same conclusion as Harnack by following another route. From literary analysis of the Gethsemane
account in the total context of Luke's passion narrative, he argues
that the shorter text is materially possible, but thoroughly improbable by analogy with the rest of the passion. For nowhere
among the numerous instances in the passion where Luke short-
ens Mark's account do we find him doing so without compensating for the omission by a substitution of his own. The shorter
text of the Gethsemane account, if adopted, would represent the
sole exception to this otherwise general pattern. "Der sonstigen
Art der lukanischen Leidensgeschichte weit mehr entsprechend
ist dagegen der längere Text. Auch er stellt freilich eine Umbear-
beitung und Kurzung des Mc-Berichtes dar, aber so, dass gleich-

---

[70] *Ibid.*, pp. 266f.

zeitig das Bild des Seelenkampfes Jesu durch Einarbeitung neuen Stoffes eine wesentliche Bereicherung und ein durchaus eigentümliches Gepräge bekommen hat." [71]   Obviously Brun's conclusion involves the assumption that Luke's Gethsemane account is a literary reworking of Mark's, and we shall not be able to evaluate this assumption before the chapter on the editorial history of Luke's account.   But it must be clear that if Luke represents another tradition altogether, entirely independent of Mark, Brun's case collapses.   In any event, he claims that his analysis resolves the text-critical question in favor of Luke's longer text, and he explains the omission of vv. 43-44 by their absence from Mark and Matthew and their significance for later Christology.

It has long been recognized that the passion narrative of Luke in particular shares many features in common with late Jewish and early Christian accounts of martyrdom.[72]   From this theological characteristic of Luke's gospel one further argument has been adduced for the originality of vv. 43-44.   The image of the cup over which Christ prays (v. 42) was already common in martyrological literature.[73]   But there are parallels, too, for the materials of vv. 43-44: the appearance of the strengthening angel (Dt 32:43 [LXX]; Dan 3:49, 92, 95 [LXX]; 10:18-19)[74] and the struggle of Christ in prayer.[75]   And Hartmut Aschermann has even introduced a parallel for the themes of sweat and blood in Jesus' agony from the martyrdom of Eleazaros in 4 Maccabees 6:6, 11; 7:8.   He claims that the use of these themes along with that of the strengthening angel, reveals the intention of the author of these verses to depict the prayer-struggle of Jesus in the style of the Maccabean martyrologies.   Since the whole of Luke's passion possesses this martyrological character, vv. 43-44 are thereby shown to be essential to the Gethsemane account as revealing its role in the rest of the narrative and hence original with Luke.[76]   We may conclude our discussion of the Lukan au-

---

[71] *Ibid.*, pp. 267-275; quotation on p. 275.

[72] See, for example, Martin Dibelius, *From Tradition to Gospel*, tr. B. L. Woolf from 2nd rev. ed. (London, 1934), pp. 199-203.

[73] Georg Bertram, *Die Leidensgeschichte Jesu und der Christuskult* (Göttingen, 1922), pp. 44f.; Hans-Werner Surkau, *Martyrien in jüdischer und frühchristlicher Zeit* (Göttingen, 1938), p. 85; Martin Dibelius, "Gethsemane," *CQ*, 12 (1935), 260; *idem*, BG, I, 265.

[74] G. Bertram, *op. cit.*, p. 47 and n. 6; H.-W. Surkau, *op. cit.*, pp. 93f.

[75] M. Dibelius, *From Tradition to Gospel*, pp. 201f.; *idem*, *CQ*, 12 (1935), 264; *idem*, BG, I, 269f.; A. Schlatter, *Lukas*, p. 433; Grundmann, *Lukas*, p. 412; H. Flender, *op. cit.*, p. 54.

[76] Hartmut Aschermann, "Zum Agoniegebet Jesu, Luk. 22, 43-44," *Theo-*

thorship of these verses, then, by stating simply that, while the
textual evidence leaves the issue unresolved, and even seems more
negative than positive, the confluence of other indications suggests a positive decision.[77]

In v. 43 the obvious meaning of *ôphthê* in accordance with
Luke's usage elsewhere (cf. Lk 1:11; 9:31; 24:34; Acts *passim*) is
that the appearance of the angel is visible to the bodily eye,[78] not
that it is an ecstatic vision.[79] The words *ap' ouranou* reinforce
the reality of the vision,[80] and make clear that the angel is sent
by God in answer to Jesus' prayer.[81] Luke's tradition here is
similar to Heb 5:7 in seeing Jesus answered for his *eulabeia*.[82]
According to Rengstorf,[83] the angel stands as God's witness that
in spite of his rejection Jesus remains God's Messiah and the
people's king (cf. Lk 2:9-12; Acts 1:10-11).

Loisy,[84] following J. Weiss, felt that the order of vv. 43-44
should be reversed, since the appearance of the angel would
come better after the agony. But the purpose of the angel, expressed in *enischyôn auton*, is not to comfort or relieve, but
precisely to strengthen Jesus for his agony, although we are not
told in what the strengthening consisted.[85] It is clear enough,
as noted above, that we are meant to see Jesus as a martyr being

---

logia Viatorum, 5 (1953-54), 143-149. According to him, the conclusion of
the Song of Moses (Dt 32:35-43), and especially the LXX addition to v. 43
(*kai enischysatôsan autô pantes angeloi theou*), finds its *Sitz im Leben* in
the situation of martyrdom, as is shown by its inclusion in a collection
of consolation texts for martyrs at the end of 4 Maccabees and its use
elsewhere (e.g., 2 Macc 7:6; 4 Macc 18:10ff.) (p. 146). See also Surkau,
op. cit., p. 94, n. 61; and Harold Smith, "Acts xx. 8 and Luke xxii. 43," *ET*,
16 (1904-05), 478.

[77] This has been the general drift of critical opinion until recently. See
C. S. C. Williams, *Alterations to the Text of the Synoptic Gospels and Acts*
(Oxford, 1951), pp. 6-8; and above p. 92, n. 50, and p. 94, n. 59. For the
relevance of theology and theological history to the solution of the text-
critical question here, see the remarks of Ernest C. Colwell, *Studies in
Methodology in Textual Criticism of the New Testament* (Leiden, 1969),
p. 151.

[78] So Hahn, Plummer, Lagrange, *ad loc.*; and Brun, art. cit., p. 269.

[79] So Bertram, *op. cit.*, p. 47.

[80] Plummer, *loc. cit.*

[81] Hahn, *loc. cit.*

[82] Grundmann, *op. cit.*, p. 412.

[83] *Op. cit.*, p. 251.

[84] *Loc. cit.*

[85] See Hahn, Schanz, Lagrange, Schmid.

strengthened for his struggle.[86]   Grundmann[87] suggests that the meaning may also be that Jesus, like Daniel (10:18-19) strengthened by an angel before a revelation, received here some fresh insight into the necessity of his passion (cf. Lk 9:31). But in no sense is Jesus subordinated to the angel; rather, the angel ministers to him as in Mk 1:13; Heb 1:6 (cf. Dt 32:43 [LXX]).[88] In fact, according to Loisy,[89] Luke, who omitted the ministering angels of Mk/Mt after the Temptation, may have introduced the angel here in line with his emphasis on the passion as the supreme trial of Jesus in his struggle against Satan. And Schuyler Brown observes that "Jesus was more in need of heavenly support before the resumption of Satan's offensive than after Satan's first attack had been successfully repulsed."[90]

In v. 44 is the only N. T. occurrence of *agônia*. Consequently, it is difficult to determine its exact meaning from analogies. Plummer,[91] following Field, understands it as an "agony of fear." But Lagrange[92] feels it is an exaggeration to equate *agônia* with fear, since it is only a matter of association, not of identification, in the examples cited by Field. It is certainly the case that the struggle of Jesus in the grip of strong emotions is even more vividly pictured here than in Mk 14:33-34. Yet he is not struggling merely to overcome his fear in the face of death, or to gain peace and composure in fronting his tragic fate. Rather, his *agônia* is like that mentioned in 2 Macc 3:14-21; 15:19 — " 'the supreme concentration of powers' in the face of imminent decisions or disasters." The word embodies his "concern for victory in the face of the approaching decisive battle on which the fate of the world depends" (cf. Lk 12:49-50).[93] And for Luke's readers it must have carried with it a rich train of martyrological associations from New Testament and early Church usage of its cognates.[94]

---

[86] Schlatter, *op. cit.*, p. 433.

[87] *Loc. cit.*

[88] H. Aschermann, art. cit., p. 146.

[89] *Op. cit.*, II, 573; see also Hans Joachim Korn, *PEIRASMOS. Die Versuchung des Gläubigen in der griechischen Bibel* (Stuttgart, 1937), p. 78.

[90] Schuyler Brown, *Apostasy and Perseverance in the Theology of Luke* (Rome, 1969), p. 8.

[91] *Op. cit.*, p. 510.

[92] *Op. cit.*, p. 560.

[93] Ethelbert Stauffer, "Agôn, agônizomai ... agônia," *TDNT*, I (Grand Rapids, 1964), 140; followed by Rengstorf, Grundmann, *ad loc.*

[94] See Stauffer, art. cit., pp. 138-140. Cf. the single occurrence of *agônizesthe* in Lk 13:24 (Mt 7:13 *eiselthate*), which shows that the struggle of

Ektenesteron proseûcheto (cf. Acts 12:5; 26:7) expresses the renewed intensity and insistence of Jesus' prayer.[95] The repetition of the prayer in Mk 14:39 is anticlimactic. But in Luke it builds to a climax in v. 44, not interrupted as in Mark by a return to the disciples, but rendered more intense by the strengthening intervention of the heavenly messenger in v. 43.[96]

The depth and intensity of his inner struggle is revealed in the external phenomenon which accompanies it: his blood-like sweat. We are not able to determine exactly in what sense Luke meant us to understand that Jesus' sweat became like (*hôsei*) falling drops of blood.[97] Does he mean that blood, perhaps mingled with sweat, actually exuded from Jesus' pores, or does he mean to compare the drops of sweat perspired by Jesus in his anguish with blood, say, in amount or color, density or size? Plummer[98] and Lagrange[99] are ready to grant both possibilities, but favor a real rather than a metaphorical interpretation, since the phenomenon seems to be medically attested.[100] Loisy,[101] Klostermann[102] and Brun[103] reject the metaphorical interpretation altogether in favor of the real. Both Loisy and Brun, however, see a symbolic significance to the blood: either in reference to the blood from Jesus' side in Jn 19:34 (Loisy), or in reference to the baptism of blood to come — cf. Lk 12:49-50 (Brun). If

---

Jesus is a struggle shared by his disciples. See Gerhard Schneider, *Verleugnung, Verspottung und Verhör Jesu nach Lukas 22, 54-71* (Munich, 1969), p. 188 and n. 134.

[95] Hahn, Plummer, *ad loc.*

[96] Brun, art. cit., p. 272.

[97] It makes little difference to the sense of the phrase whether we read the participle in the nominative, as in the text, or in the genitive, as in the critical apparatus for ℵ* X 565 *pc* lat sy^p. See Plummer, *op. cit.*, p. 510.

[98] *Loc. cit.*

[99] *Op. cit.*, p. 561.

[100] W. K. Hobart, *The Medical Language of St. Luke* (Dublin, 1882), pp. 81-83, contains examples from Greek medical literature (possibly familiar to Luke?); W. W. Keen, "The Bloody Sweat of our Lord." *BQR*, 14 (1892), 169-175, and *idem*, "Further Studies on the Bloody Sweat of our Lord," *BS*, 54 (1897), 469-483, both contain examples from nineteenth century medical literature; M. Arthus and V. Chanson, "Les sueurs de sang," *RTh*, 6 (1898), 673-696, reviews cases to establish their natural neuropathological causes; K. Holzmeister, "Exempla sudoris sanguinei (Lc. 22, 44)," *VD*, 18 (1938), 73-81, presents a critical review of the literature from ancient to modern times.

[101] *Op. cit.*, II, 575.

[102] *Op. cit.*, p. 584.

[103] *Loc. cit.*

the long text of Luke's eucharistic words is accepted as original, as it should be,[104] then we must also see at least an oblique reference to the blood of the new covenant in 22:20. Hahn,[105] Zahn,[106] Grundmann,[107] and Jeremias,[108] on the other hand, reject the notion of any sweat of blood, and consider the phrase a simple comparison. But it is certainly not clear in what the comparison consists.[109] For Hahn, Zahn and Jeremias the term of comparison is *katabainontes epi tên gên*: the sweat was like blood in the way it flowed and fell. This at least has the virtue of not introducing considerations extraneous to the text. But the question cannot be altogether decided. In any case, we should not miss the point that the image of flowing blood gives vivid expression once again to the martyr-theme which pervades this scene and the rest of Luke's passion narrative.

Verse 45: *Kai anastas apo tês proseuchês, elthôn pros tous mathêtas heuren koimômenous autous apo tês lypês.*

We have already noted above in commenting on vv. 43f. Loisy's opinion that the *anastas apo tês proseuchês* of this verse seems to pass over in silence the angel and the agony of the two preceding verses to connect with the prayer of v. 42. But if it is true, as we have also noted, that Luke in contrast to Mark has really built Jesus' prayer to a climax in the intervening verses, then there is every reason for seeing the antecedent of *proseuchê* here rather in the *ektenesteron proseucheto* of v. 44, and recognizing a genuine continuity throughout.

As in Mark/Matthew, Jesus returns to find the disciples sleeping. There no reason was given for their sleep on the first occasion, but on the second an explanation was offered: "for their eyes were (very) heavy" (Mk 14:40/Mt 26:43). Luke offers another

---

[104] See Joachim Jeremias, *The Eucharistic Words of Jesus* (London, 1966), pp. 138-159. For the importance of the witness of P[75] in deciding this question, see Kurt Aland, art. cit., *NTS*, 12 (1965-66), 198f., 202f.; and *idem, op. cit.* (see above p. 94, n. 59), pp. 160, 164f.

[105] *Op. cit.*, p. 617.

[106] *Op. cit.*, p. 690.

[107] *Op. cit.*, p. 412.

[108] Joachim Jeremias, *New Testament Theology*, I (London, 1971), 52.

[109] Schmid, *op. cit.*, p. 337.

reason: namely, their "sorrow." Plummer [110] and Streeter,[111] for example, have seen this as an excuse deriving from Luke's tendency always to "spare the Twelve." But if it is a genuine excuse, then Jesus' question in v. 46 becomes superfluous. Grundmann [112] understands the sorrow itself as connected with the hour of Jesus' departure. But if this is so, then what we should see here is not simply an excuse for sleep, but a parallel to the Johannine theme of the sorrow of the disciples awaiting Christ's return (Jn 16:20-22). We have observed before that there is much in common between the passion narratives of Luke and John.[113] In particular, Luke's Jesus, like John's, is depicted as more in command of the situation than he is in Mark or Matthew (cf. Lk 23:28-31, 34, 43).[114] Thus we do not find in the introduction to the scene on the Mount of Olives any reference to the distress or trouble or sorrow of Jesus, as we do in Mk 14:33-34 par. Jesus is depicted throughout in prayer, enduring a martyr's struggle to gain a martyr's victory. It is the disciples in Luke, as in John, who are depicted in sorrow before the prospect of the trial that awaits them.[115]

Verse 46: *Kai eipen autois: ti katheudete? anastantes proseuchesthe, hina mê eiselthête eis peirasmon.*

While Jesus prayed, his disciples slept. His victory is accomplished — *anastas apo tês proseuchês* — whereas their trial lies still before them — *anastantes proseuchesthe.* They cannot but face it with sorrow, but they must not face it in sleep. And so he rouses them with a question full of wonder and indignation: *ti katheudete?* [116] The peril is near; it is no longer time to sleep.

---

[110] *Op. cit.,* p. 511.

[111] *Op. cit.,* p. 178.

[112] *Loc. cit.*

[113] See above Chapter 1, p. 9, n. 36.

[114] H. Aschermann, art. cit., pp. 148f.

[115] In the context of these ideas, which reveal a theological intention on Luke's part, it seems idle to raise the question of whether or not he had a special medical theory on the connection between anxiety and sleep. But see Eiliv Skard, "Kleine Beiträge zum Corpus Hellenisticum Novi Testamenti," *SO,* 30 (1953), 100-103; and J. H. H. A. Indemans, "Das Lukasevangelium XXII, 45," *SO,* 32 (1956), 81-83.

[116] Use of the interrogative particle in this sense is a Semitic idiom. See Matthew Black, *An Aramaic Approach to the Gospels and Acts,* 3rd ed. (Oxford, 1967), pp. 121-123.

Anastantes proseuchesthe: prayer is their only weapon against the trial about to front them.[117]   There is no mention here of the betrayer's approach, as in Mark and Matthew,[118] and it is not to meet him that they are roused.[119]   Neither are the disciples called upon to watch, although Lagrange [120] reads Luke's *anastantes* as a kind of substitution for Mark's *grêgoreite*.   They are not even reproved for sleeping,[121] they are only bidden again to pray, although there is no time left for prayer.   All of these features in Luke's account show how he has generalized the meaning of Jesus' admonition here and in v. 40.   The durative force of the present imperative *proseuchesthe* 'pray constantly' [122] only emphasizes this.   And we cannot fail to recognize the fundamentally parenetic intent of Luke's account in comparison with Mark's and Matthew's.   The community is presented with the example of Jesus, framed by his two admonitions to pray in the face of their trials. The disciples are even told what they should pray for in the clause that follows: *hina mê eiselthête eis peirasmon*.   This expresses not the purpose of their prayer, but its very content.[123]   And it thereby points more strongly still than Mk 14:38 par. to the final petition of the Lord's Prayer (Lk 11:4) — the prayer of the Christian under trial.

---

[117] Hahn, *op. cit.*, p. 618.

[118] Mk 14:41 does not disappear entirely from Luke's account, as is evident from the substitution in Lk 22:48. See Heinz Eduard Tödt, *The Son of Man in the Synoptic Tradition* (London, 1965), p. 152. Note also the Markan ring to *êngisen tô Iêsou* (22:47) and *hymôn hê hôra* (22:53).

[119] C. G. Montefiore, *The Synoptic Gospels* (London, 1927), II, 609; Wellhausen, Klostermann, *ad loc.*

[120] *Op. cit.*, p. 563.

[121] Grundmann, *loc. cit.*

[122] B.-D.-F., 336 (1).

[123] Plummer, *op. cit.*, p. 511; K. G. Kuhn, "Jesus in Gethsemane," *EvT*, 12 (1952-53), 285, n. 41.

PART TWO

REDACTION

CHAPTER FOUR

EDITORIAL HISTORY OF MARK 14:32-42

The editorial history of the Gethesemane pericope in Mark has two main questions to face and answer: first, the question of its connection with the surrounding passion narrative; and secondly, the question of its own intrinsic unity.

I

THE QUESTION OF CONTEXT

We begin with the first question: the question of context. It seems clear that the Gethsemane scene (Mk 14:32-42) did not originally belong to the passion narrative which antedated Mark and probably began with the arrest.[1] The editorial process by which it came to its present place is not difficult to trace if we study its connection with what follows and what precedes. What follows (Mk 14:43ff.) is linked with the Gethsemane account by the transitional phrase *kai euthys* and a genitive absolute (*eti autou lalountos*), both of which are frequent features of editorial linkage elsewhere in Mark's gospel.[2] Moreover, the Gethsemane account itself has two conclusions. In 14:41 Jesus' concluding words give an eschatological, Christological meaning to the scene as culminating in the betrayal of the Son of Man into the hands of sinners, while in 14:42 his words bear a simple historical meaning, leading into what follows, viz., the approach of the

---

[1] This conclusion is widely maintained and solidly supported by critics from different points of view. See Xavier Léon-Dufour, "Passion (Récits de la)," *DBS*, VI (Paris, 1960), col. 1419-92.

[2] For *kai euthys* see, for example, Mk 1:12; 15:1. And for the genitive absolute, especially in the passion account, see Mk 14:3, 17, 18, 22, 66; 15:33, 42. Examples cited by Karl Georg Kuhn, "Jesus in Gethsemane,, *EvT*, 12 (1952-53), 261-262.

traitor Judas and the subsequent arrest.[3] It is clear enough that
the original conclusion of the story is in v. 41, and that v. 42 is
an editorial addition of Mark's to fit this independent story with
its own conclusion into the context of the passion narrative as
he found it.[4] The same inference is to be drawn if we examine
the connection of the Gethsemane scene with what precedes it.
Bultmann points to the opposition between the full number of
disciples in v. 32 and the three chosen ones in v. 33 as forcing a
choice of priority. He argues for the originality of v. 32 on the
grounds that the place-name "Gethsemane" can hardly be due to
Mark's editing. And he concludes that the conflict between the
indications of place given in v. 32 — "a place which was called
Gethsemane" — and in v. 26 — "the Mount of Olives" — shows
that 14: 32-41 was an individual story not originally intended for
its present context in Mark.[5]

Vincent Taylor, too, is prepared to recognize the Gethsemane account, along with the Anointing, the Trial before the
Priests, the Denial, and the Mockery by the Soldiers, for example,
as an intercalation by Mark into an earlier passion narrative.[6]
His main criterion for distinguishing the material added later is
the presence of numerous apparent Semitisms [7] in these passages,
while next to none occur in what he conjectures to be the original
narrative. Applying this linguistic criterion, he is able to isolate
"a non-Semitic and continuous narrative, which is marked by
distinctive historical and theological interests." [8] This material
he designates A. The material which he designates B contrasts
notably with A in that it "had a strong Semitic flavor, and consisted of vivid self-contained narratives and of striking supplementary details derived from the reminiscences of Peter." [9] He

---

[3] *Ibid.*, p. 262.

[4] Rudolf Bultmann, *The History of the Synoptic Tradition* (New York
and Evanston, 1963), p. 268.

[5] *Ibid.*; so also Kuhn, *loc. cit.*; and E. Meyer, *Ursprung und Anfänge des
Christentums* (Stuttgart, 1921-23), I, 148, n. 2, notes that the juxtaposition
of Mk 14:26 and 14:32, while not directly contradictory, would have been
avoided in a unified narrative.

[6] Vincent Taylor, *The Gospel according to St. Mark*, 2nd ed. (London,
1966), p. 653.

[7] In the Gethsemane passage he notes on p. 655 the following: "*erchontai* used first and without a subject (32); the name *Gethsemanei* (32);
êrxato c. infinitive (33); *Abba* (36), *palin* (39f.), *êsan katabarynomenoi* (40);
and possibly *apechei* (41), cf. Black, 161f."

[8] *Op. cit.*, p. 664.

[9] *Ibid.*, p. 658.

contends, then, on these linguistic grounds that the Gethsemane account, which was part of B, was inserted quite naturally by Mark into its present position, temporally preceding the arrest (14:43) and locally following the reference to the Mount of Olives (14:26).[10]

In addition to examining the context of Mark, Joachim Jeremias employs a comparison of the Markan and Johannine passion narratives to establish a similar conclusion.[11] The sequence of events in both narratives, up to and including the Gethsemane account, differs widely in arrangement.[12] But beginning with the arrest, both narratives share common material and parallel arrangement to a degree in striking contrast with what has gone before. Significantly, the special character of John's gospel, exhibited by the discourse material of the first seventeen chapters, undergoes a transformation at 18:1 into a continuous narrative of the synoptic type. The obvious conclusion is that, in an earlier stage of the tradition than our present gospels, there was a passion narrative which began with the arrest of Jesus. This narrative Jeremias styles the "short account." [13] Further evidence for the existence of such an account is provided by the passion summaries of the primitive kerygma, none of which includes any events occurring before the betrayal and arrest.[14] Again, the scene of the arrest in Mark opens with the introduction of Judas as *heis tôn dôdeka*, as if he had not already been identified by the same description at 14:10,[15] and as if we could not therefore be expected to remember from the brief mention of

---

[10] *Ibid.*, p. 663.

[11] Joachim Jeremias, *The Eucharistic Words of Jesus* (London, 1966), pp. 90-96.

[12] Jeremias, *op.cit.*, p. 94, gives the following scheme:

Mark		John	
11:1-10		12:12-16	
15-17		2:13-17	
24		14:13f.; 16:23	
28		2:18	
14:1-2, 3-9		11:47-53; 12:1-8	
10-11	cf.	13:2	
18-21		13:21-30	
26-31		18:1a; 16:32; 13:36-38	
32-42		18:1b; 12:27; 18:11b; 14:31	

[13] *Loc. cit.*

[14] Cf. Mk 8:31; 9:31; 10:33f. and par.; Mt 26:2; Lk 17:25; 24:7, 20; Acts 2:23, 36; 3:13f.; 4:10f.; 5:30; 7:52; 10:39; 13:27-29; Gal 3:1; I Cor 1:17f., 23; 2:2; 15:4; I Pet 2:23f.

[15] Cf. Bultmann, *op. cit.*, p. 277.

his name in 3:19 who he was. If Luke's account is independent of Mark's, as has been argued,[16] then, since this peculiarity is present in both, the evidence is all the stronger that the original passion narrative began with the arrest prefaced by the introduction of the betrayer.[17] Finally, as regards the Gethsemane account itself, Rehkopf observes that only here, but not in the passion narrative from the arrest on, are those with Jesus designated as *mathêtai*.[18] Thus all the material evidence points to a clear break in the continuity here and to the independence of the Gethsemane account from the original passion narrative.

Formal considerations, too, can be adduced to support this conclusion. John, though not unaware of the Gethsemane tradition,[19] could not really have reported it in the synoptic manner or sequence without doing violence to the whole design of his gospel. Contextually, Strauss pointed out the impossibility of the prayer of Gethsemane following upon the discourses in John's Chapters 13 to 16 and particularly upon the prayer in Chapter 17.[20] Theologically, Goguel believed that John could not reconcile the Gethsemane incident with his own Christology,[21] though Dodd may be closer to the truth in discounting theological motives here and attributing the omission of Jesus' inner struggle and the overt declaration of his final acceptance to motives of reverence on John's part.[22] In any case, we may well ask whether the tension between the Gethsemane scene and the preceding gospel context is any less real in the synoptics than it is in John. Kuhn at least does not think so, since he claims that it is precisely the theological point of this scene which is at odds with that of the earlier passion predictions and the words of institution at the Last Supper. On the one hand, there is in these latter instances the clear recognition by Jesus of his death as God's salvific plan for

---

[16] See below Chapter 6.

[17] F. Rehkopf, *Die lukanische Sonderquelle. Ihr Umfang und Sprachgebrauch* (Tübingen, 1959), p. 37, sees the striking *ho legomenos Ioudas* of Lk 22:47 as the vestigial indication of a new beginning, which served to introduce Judas as someone still unknown to the reader.

[18] *Ibid.*, pp. 57-58.

[19] Cf. Jn 12:27-30; 14:31; 18:1, 11.

[20] David Friedrich Strauss, *The Life of Jesus Critically Examined*, tr. from the 4th German ed. by George Eliot (London, 1892), pp. 641-642.

[21] Maurice Goguel, *Jesus and the Origins of Christianity, Vol. II: The Life of Jesus* (New York, 1960), p. 494.

[22] C. H. Dodd, *Historical Tradition in the Fourth Gospel* (Cambridge, 1963), p. 68 and n. 1.

men, while in Gethsemane, on the other hand, there is his anguished struggle to accept the hour which he prays may pass him by. The tension is not to be resolved by facile psychologizing, by imagining, for example, a simple change of mood between the Supper and the garden; for the gospels do not intend to tell us anything about the "moods" of Jesus.[23] The tension remains irresolvably theological, and as such constitutes formal evidence for the original independence of the Gethsemane account from its present context.[24]

This conclusion, of course, says nothing one way or the other about the historical character of the account. And indeed the account must be analyzed in much more detail before any historical judgment can be passed. Even more importantly, we may expect more thorough analysis to provide a fuller grasp of the intentions of the evangelists in transmitting this account and therefore of the theology of the passage as it stands in the synoptic gospels.

II

THE QUESTION OF UNITY

We must now take up the second question facing the editorial history of Mark's Gethsemane account: the question of unity. The literary unity of the passage has not lacked its defenders, although they have had to swim up current against the main stream of critical opinion. Lohmeyer, for example, sees such a clear unity in content, construction, and style that he claims no part of Mark's account can be dropped without damage to the whole. He instances particularly what he sees as the triple rhythm controlling the introduction (vv. 32-34), mid-section (vv. 35-41), and the conclusion (vv. 41-42) as evidence of the carefully planned organic structure and emphasis of the entire passage.[25] But it is the very repetitions, which he points to as exhibiting the unity of the passage, that most other exegetes regard as

---

[23] Martin Dibelius, *From Tradition to Gospel* (London, 1934), pp. 178ff.; "Gethsemane," *CQ*, 12 (1935), 255; the same article in German, *BG*, I (Tübingen, 1953), 259-260.

[24] K. G. Kuhn, art. cit., pp. 262-263.

[25] Ernst Lohmeyer, *Das Evangelium des Markus* (Göttingen, 1963), pp. 313-314, 319.

grounds for recognizing its composite character. The analyses of these other exegetes have been many and varied, and, though often beginning from common presuppositions, have seldom arrived at common conclusions. Perhaps it was this very diversity of opinion, as well as a firm conviction of the unity of the passage, which led Ebeling to disavow the possibility of discerning any earlier strata of tradition or redaction behind the passage, even while he admitted that in its present form it is not original.[26] Nevertheless, we must face the issue, not abandon the attempt. And our procedure will be to study the suggestions of exegetes with a view to determining the literary form of the passage, its editorial history, and the character of the traditions that lie behind it. Such a study should enable us to answer the constellation of specific questions posed by the generic question of unity. For convenience of treatment, we shall consider the various attempts to explain the composite character of the account under the rubric of Single Source or Multiple Source Theories.

A. Single Source Theories

Single Source Theories explain the genesis of our present Gethsemane account in Mark as the result of a simpler underlying account expanded through Mark's editorial activity. And they attempt by critical analysis to disengage the one from the other.

Johannes Weiss

Johannes Weiss, deferring to the witness of Papias, holds for an underlying Petrine source for sections of Mark's gospel.[27] The Gethsemane scene and the betrayal, in particular, convince him that the whole sequence to which they belong stems from this source.[28] But while the very name "Gethsemane" speaks for the authenticity of the scene, the account itself seems modelled on the Transfiguration, and shows Mark's hand at work in features like Jesus' separation from the larger group of disciples, the sleepiness of the disciples depicted after the analogy of Mk 9:6, the stylized triple departure and return of Jesus, the literal

---

[26] Hans Jürgen Ebeling, *Das Messiasgeheimnis und die Botschaft des Marcus-Evangelisten* (Berlin, 1939), p. 177.

[27] Johannes Weiss, *Das älteste Evangelium* (Göttingen, 1903), pp. 120-122.

[28] *Ibid.*, p. 299.

quotation of the prayer which no one heard, and the moral drawn for the community in the saying of 14:38. Yet the Petrine source has not been altogether submerged in the process. It survives in the introductory doublet (vv. 32-33), and can be isolated once we recognize that it is Mark who has given us the picture of Jesus accompanied by the larger group of disciples, of whom there is no further trace in the rest of the story. It survives, too, in the verses recording the painful memory of the disciples' sleep and Jesus' reproach (vv. 37, 41a). On the other hand, the suddenness (*euthys*) of Judas' appearance in v. 43 inclines Weiss to consider vv. 41b-42 as Markan expansions, since they presuppose Jesus' complete foreknowledge of what is about to happen and of the betrayer's approach before his arrival.[29]

Weiss, then, on the hypothesis of a Petrine source, would apparently recognize only v. 32a (with the place-name "Gethsemane"), vv. 33-34, v. 37 and v. 41a as representing original tradition. The rest of the account he attributes to Mark.

Emil Wendling

Emil Wendling claims the editorial hand of Mark as responsible for the indirect form of the doublet of Jesus' prayer in 14:35, while considering the direct form in v. 36 as original. He offers two reasons for this unusual choice. First, he regards v. 35 as expressing Jesus' surrender to a fixed plan of redemption (*ei dynaton estin*) in line with the viewpoint of the passion sayings (8:31, 9:11; 14:21), while v. 36 expresses his surrender to the Father's will, which might conceivably have been different (*panta dynata soi*). Secondly, the image of God offering His Son the cup, which he in his turn prays may pass him by, seems more original than the image of a difficult but inevitable hour which he wishes were behind him. Thus v. 35 is a preparatory note of Mark's meant to forestall the impression that Jesus struggled even for a moment against the divine plan.[30] Yet Wendling considers v. 41a, where the image of the hour recurs, as original because of its parallelism with v. 42:

> katheudete to loipon kai anapauesthe;
>   apechei; êlthen hê hôra ...
> egeiresthe, agômen;
>   idou, ho paradidous me êngisen [sic].

---

[29] *Ibid.*, pp. 300-301.
[30] Emil Wendling, *Die Entstehung des Marcus-Evangeliums* (Tübingen, 1908), p. 172.

Here the alternate lines are parallel, and the fourth line completes the meaning of the "hour" in the second. But v. 41b — an obvious doublet of v. 42b — drops out as a secondary addition in the style of the passion predictions in line with 14:21, 35b.[31]

V. 38 is a construction of Mark's, joined to v. 37 by the repetition of *grêgorein* and expanded by the reminiscence of the Our Father (Mt 6:13) in the prayer about temptation, which points forward to the denial (14:66-72). That the saying about spirit and flesh is secondary is shown not only by its Pauline cast, but also by the *men . . . de* antithesis, used nowhere else by Mark or Jesus, except for the clearly secondary saying in 14:21.[32] Wendling recognizes the dependence of v. 34 on Jon 2:6; 4:9. And he regards v. 40 as serving, like 4:40f.; 9:5f.; 9:19, for an indirect characterization of Jesus.

For Wendling the whole account took its origin on the basis of the report in v. 37a — "he came and found them sleeping" — combined with the motif of the parable of the doorkeeper in 13:33-36. *Proelthôn mikron* in 14:35 sets the two scenes of action. At his departure (v. 34) Jesus issues the same warning to his disciples as the master to his doorkeeper. The four possibilities of the parable (13:35) are condensed into the three returns of Jesus, and the motif of the sleeping disciples is appropriately expanded (14:37, 40, 41). A thread stretches from the parable through the Gethsemane scene to the denial; for Peter, who is addressed in 14:37, does not finally awaken until the second cock-crow (cf. 13:35; 14:72).[33]

Wendling's analysis, then, seems to designate as original to the Gethsemane account what is contained in vv. 36, 37a, 41a, and 42. Mark has reworked and expanded this material in his own manner to produce the account we have today.

Alfred Loisy

Alfred Loisy takes the opposite view from Weiss about the introductory doublet in Mk 14:32-33, mostly because he disputes the evidence that there are any genuine reminiscences of Peter underlying Mark's text. Thus he considers what is said of the three in v. 33 to be merely grafted on by Mark to what was said originally of the eleven in v. 32.[34] Contrary to Wendling, on the

---

[31] *Ibid.*, pp. 122, 170-172.
[32] *Ibid.*, p. 171.
[33] *Ibid.*, p. 186.
[34] Alfred Loisy, *Les Évangiles synoptiques* (Ceffonds, 1907-08), II, 560.

other hand, he judges v. 35 as original against v. 36, which he
sees as the work of his "Pauline editor," paralleling the cup here
with the eucharistic cup of the New Covenant.[35] V. 38 was perhaps
original, but in the peculiar form discussed in Chapter One, i.e.,
as a request of Jesus for the disciples' prayers for him. Its present form of an admonition for the disciples in general is due to
Mark (and Luke).[36] V. 41a up to *anapauesthe* represents underlying tradition, and is to be interpreted as a command, whose
execution was frustrated by the sudden arrival of Judas. *Apechei*
forms a poor transition to the editorial expansions in vv. 41b-42,
which are intended by Mark to show Jesus' complete foreknowledge of the providential necessity of the passion.[37] Finally, the
tripling of Jesus' prayer and of his return to the disciples is an
awkward device of Mark's, perhaps meant to emphasize their
insensitivity to his appeal before their own denial and desertion.

What emerges from Loisy's analysis are the elements of a
primitive account which may well have served as source for both
Mark and Luke: After asking his disciples to stay awake and pray
for him, Jesus leaves them to pray at some length for his possible
escape from the impending hour; as he returns to suggest that
his disciples may now sleep, Judas appears unexpectedly upon
the scene.[38] The elements of this original account appear in
vv. 32, 35, [38], and 41a. Mark is responsible for the rest.

Maurice Goguel

Maurice Goguel's analysis of Mark's Gethsemane account is
much less thorough than Loisy's; but he shares with him the
view that both Mark and Luke (apart from 22:43-44) were reproducing elements of a simpler account underlying our present text
of Mark. He sees an editorial hand behind the doublets of
vv. 32/33 (taking the latter as original) and vv. 35/36, and he
notes something distinctly secondary about the verbal report in
this second doublet of a prayer which no one heard. For him
the primitive account, which may well have stemmed from the
memoirs of Peter, reduces to this: Jesus took his disciples to

---

[35] *Ibid.*, p. 563.
[36] *Ibid.*, p. 568; and see above pp. 37-38, 86.
[37] *Ibid.*, p. 570.
[38] *Ibid.*, p. 571.

Gethsemane, where he left them to go and pray; when he came back, he found them asleep and reproached them.[39]

The substance of this account is presumably reproduced by Mark in vv. 32a, 33, 35a and 37. The rest is his own work.

Rudolf Bultmann

Rudolf Bultmann's judgment of the Gethsemane account as an "individual story of thorough-going legendary character"[40] is well known. This description is a conclusion from his analysis of the story itself and its place in the passion narrative. His analysis is important enough to review in some detail. We have already noted above (p. 108) his reason for accepting Mk 14: 32 as the original beginning of this story and therefore rejecting v. 33 as a later addition. And since the saying in v. 34 goes with v. 33, as v. 32b goes with v. 32a, it too drops out of the earlier account. V. 35 belongs to the pre-Markan story; but v. 36 is secondary, an example of the tendency observable in the history of the material toward transposing into direct discourse earlier indirect reports.[41] V. 38 is probably an addition, parenetic in intent, from the language of Christian edification.[42] As for v. 42, we have already seen reason for regarding it as an editorial addition of Mark's (p. 108 above), a conclusion with which Bultmann concurs. Finally, for similar reasons even v. 41b must be considered secondary, and the original ending of the pre-Markan story thus to have been v. 41a with its climactic *apechei*; *êlthen hê hôra.*[43]

Briefly, although not all of the story has survived intact, vv. 32, 35, 37, 39-41a in Mark represent the underlying tradition of the Gethsemane scene, which had been circulating independently of the passion narrative that lay before him, until he came to compose his gospel. We are indebted to Mark for the story in its present form and context, and consequently for vv. 33-34, 36, 38, and 41b-42.[44]

---

[39] Maurice Goguel, *L'Évangile de Marc* (Paris, 1909), p. 269.

[40] *Op. cit.*, pp. 267-268.

[41] *Ibid.*, pp. 268, 312f.

[42] *Ibid.*, pp. 268, 283.

[43] *Ibid.*, p. 268.

[44] Bultmann recognizes that in the threefold prayer and return of Jesus the account has been influenced by the so-called law of repetition and the frequent numbering of persons, things and events by threes (p. 314), and also that the sleep of the disciples is a pure novelistic motif

In general, according to Bultmann, the way in which the Gethsemane tradition became part of the passion narrative is indicative of how the narrative as a whole took shape: viz., not as an organic unity from the start, but rather as a gradual accumulation of originally independent units, chiefly individual stories like this one. That such individual stories form the major component of the passion narrative is proven both by the existence of numerous doublets [45] and by the freedom with which Matthew and Luke introduce some new items into Mark's account [46] and omit others already there.[47] Further application of literary analysis, like that which has separated the Gethsemane scene in Mark from the passion narrative to which he joined it, yields similar results for other scenes as well,[48] and leads to the conviction that Mark was no less free than Matthew or Luke in expanding the narrative that lay before him. Moreover, such analysis reveals that the remaining narrative is not complete in itself and gives us a notion of how it must have developed into the form we find in Mark. Bultmann summarizes the results of the process as he sees it in the following manner:

> There was a *primitive narrative* which told very briefly of the arrest, the condemnation by the Sanhedrin and Pilate, the journey to the cross, the crucifixion and death. This was developed at various stages, in part by earlier stories that were available and in part by forms that had newly appeared. It was enlarged by the story of Peter and furnished with one introduction preparing the way for both elements: Mk 14:27-31. Further, it was joined (through Mk 14:26) with a complex of stories that gathered around

---

meant to draw the contrast between their dullness and Jesus' anxiety about death in the most concrete fashion possible (p. 283, but the translation here is misleading; cf. German text, 2nd ed., p. 306). But he would apparently attribute these developments to the pre-Markan tradition rather than to Mark.

[45] Bultmann, *op. cit.*, p. 276, instances the following doublets: Mk 14:17-21/Lk 22:21-23; Mk 14:22-25/Lk 22:14-18; Mk 14:27-31/Lk 22:31f.; Mk 15:1 or Lk 22:66/Mk 14:55-64; doubtfully Mk 14:65 or Lk 22:63/Mk 15:16-20a; Mk 15:40f./15:47/16:1.

[46] Bultmann, *loc. cit.*, gives the following examples of material added to Mark: Mt 27:3-10, 62-66; Lk 23:6-16, 27-31.

[47] Luke, for example, omits the anointing (Mk 14:3-9), the hearing of the witnesses (Mk 14:56-61), and the mocking (Mk 15:16-20a).

[48] So Bultmann, *op. cit.*, p. 277, for Mk 14:3-9, 22-25, 55-64; 15:6-15a, 16-20a. Furthermore, he regards the story of Peter's denial as not organically related to the overall design of the passion story.

the Last Supper, and then received a further introduction in Mk 14:1f., 10f. Still later Mk 14:3-9, 32-42 and in all probability vv. 55-64 were inserted. It is no longer possible to say at what stage the account of the crucifixion was fashioned, or the closing section in 15:40f., 42-47 was added[49].

The Gethsemane scene, then, in Bultmann's view emerges as one of the latest elements of the tradition to be incorporated in Mark's passion account. As such, it exhibits the tendency of dogmatic motifs in the early Christian community to take shape in increasingly concrete forms.[50] In the faith and worship of this community the passion came to be celebrated as the victory through suffering and death of Jesus the Messiah and Lord. And Bultmann sees a whole group of legends springing up in the tradition to give expression to this belief. Thus the Gethsemane story for him is such a faith- or cult-legend, probably originating in a Hellenistic Christianity of a Pauline sort, since, at least in its secondary meaning, it is merely giving concrete representation to the moment of the exalted Lord's humiliation formulated by Paul in Phil 2:8.[51]

Martin Dibelius

After Bultmann the most influential analysis among Single Source Theories for the Gethsemane account is that of Martin Dibelius. Complementing the conclusions which Bultmann has arrived at analytically are those which Dibelius attempts to establish synthetically.[52] Facing first the problem of determining the earliest stratum of the passion tradition in Mark, he adopts three criteria to guide him in sorting out earlier from later, historical from non-historical material. We may characterize them as follows:

1. Literary criterion: passages with only artificial links to the context are to be deleted;

2. Historical criterion: passages containing references to eyewitnesses of the event are to be retained;

---

[49] *Ibid.*, p. 279.
[50] *Ibid.*, pp. 283-284.
[51] *Ibid.*, p. 306.
[52] Martin Dibelius, "Das historische Problem der Leidensgeschichte," *ZNW*, 30 (1931), 193-201; also in *BG*, I, 248-257; *idem, Jesus* (Berlin, 1939), pp. 112-115; in addition to the works already cited above in n. 23, p. 111.

3. Theological criterion: events found place in the community passion tradition as they were seen to be God's design from the O. T. scriptures.[53]

The first two criteria are readily recognizable as selective principles, the third as genetic.

The application of his literary criterion leads Dibelius immediately to the deletion from the earliest narrative of the second and third prayers in the Gethsemane scene, which unlike Mk 14:34f. display no content, and perhaps even to the deletion of the entire scene.[54] For when the same conclusion follows for the anointing and the trial before the Sanhedrin, the skeleton of an earlier account begins to emerge to which none of these scenes belonged.[55]

The application of his historical criterion brings Dibelius to single out the arrest, with its mention of the unnamed young man in 14:51, and the way of the cross, with its mention of Simon of Cyrene in 15:21, as most certainly historical because the account shows interest in these figures not for themselves but only as eyewitnesses of the events.[56] The case is otherwise for him with the Gethsemane account, which has only sleeping witnesses, so no witnesses at all, and therefore must have had other origins.[57]

It is the application of his theological criterion which ultimately allows Dibelius to dispense with the historicity of the Gethsemane scene altogether and to determine its actual origins. For the situation is clearly paralleled in those Psalms which were most obviously treated by the community as passion announcements: viz., Ps 22, 31 and 69. All three of these Psalms depict the prayer of a man in deep distress, praying for deliverance (22:20; 31:9, 10, 22; 69:1f.), and the "cries" (cf. Heb 5:7) of an in-

---

[53] Idem, From Tradition to Gospel, pp. 182-185.

[54] Ibid., p. 182. Sufficient reasons have already been reviewed above for adopting the more radical conclusion here.

[55] Idem, BG, I, 249-251. [Correction: the citation in line 8, p. 250, should of course read "14:10,11," not "14:11,12."]

[56] Ibid., pp. 252-253; From Tradition to Gospel, pp. 182-183.

[57] Idem, BG, I, 251-252; From Tradition to Gospel, p. 211. The dismissal of the disciples, particularly Peter, as witnesses here, simply because they slept for part of the scene, seems too summary. Even sleeping disciples, after all, could have reported (1) that they slept, (2) what Christ said to them beforehand, (3) that — even if not what — he prayed while they slept, and (4) what he said after awakening them. They could, therefore, have reported the essentials of the Gethsemane tradition. But the decisive reason for Dibeluis' rejection of this conclusion is theological rather than historical, genetic rather than selective, as will appear below.

nocent man suffering persecution (22:2, 24; 31:22; 69:3). And
Psalm 31 even mentions the flight of companions (v. 11) and the
plotting of enemies (v. 13), motifs of the following arrest and
trial scenes in the passion narrative. This clue, together with
that provided by the traditional saying of Jesus preserved in
Mk 14:38, is enough to disclose for Debelius the genesis of the
Gethsemane account. It is impossible to say whether or not the
earlier passion narrative used by Mark contained elements of
this scene, e.g., a lament and prayer of Jesus like that in Mk
14:34f. What can be said is that, wherever he found them, it
was Mark who built up these traditional materials into a process.
He did this by taking the situation of lament and prayer announced in the passion Psalms and fitting into it the traditional
warning of Jesus about watchfulness and prayer. Taking this saying in its physical rather than its eschatological sense, he created
the scene of the sleeping disciples to give it point.[58] Thus the scene
in Dibelius' judgment is neither an historical tradition (Lietzmann) nor a legend current originally in isolation (Bultmann).[59]

That the scene is not an historical tradition Dibelius establishes not only by the absence of eyewitnesses already mentioned,
but more importantly by a study of the elements underlying the
Gethsemane tradition, especially in the N. T. parallels, i.e., Heb
4:14-5:10 and Jn 12:27-30. In Heb 5:7, for example, we are told:
"In the days of his flesh, Jesus offered up prayers and supplica-
tions, with loud cries and tears, to him who was able to save
him from death, and he was heard for his godly fear." The detail
of "loud cries and tears" goes distinctly beyond anything contained in the Gethsemane account, and is therefore independent
of it. The same can be said for the motif of being "heard for
his godly fear." Moreover, precisely these striking details are
announced in Ps 31:22 and 39:12, although partly in different
words.[60] Dibelius is led accordingly to surmise that what is
preserved in Heb 5:7 is not an historical tradition, but rather a
prior community construct, independent of the Gethsemane scene
and based solely on O. T. passion announcements. Jn 12:27-30

---

[58] *Idem, CQ,* 12 (1935), 259; *BG,* I, 263-264; cf. Georg Bertram, *Die Leidensgeschichte Jesu und der Christuskult* (Göttingen, 1922), p. 45.

[59] *BG,* I, 254-255; *From Tradition to Gospel,* pp. 212-213.

[60] Thus *deêsis, proseuchê* (Ps) = *hiktêria* (Heb); *krazein* (Ps) = *kraugê*
(Heb); *ekstasis* (Ps) = *eulabeia* (Heb); and *eisêkousas* is the same in both
Ps and Heb. Dibelius defends a stronger sense of O. T. fulfilment in a
N. T. narrative when equivalent, rather than identical, expressions are
used. See art. cit., *CQ,* 12 (1935), 256 and n. 1, 257; *BG,* I, 261 and n. 1.

reinforces this conclusion, since John finds it necessary to interpret the scene — v. 27: "for this purpose"; v. 30: "for your sake,
not for mine" — and must therefore be taking it over from a pre-
existing tradition, again independent of the Gethsemane scene
but akin to what underlies Heb 5:7.[61] Thus the tradition of Jesus'
lament and prayer is not historical. But neither is the tradition
that fits his warning words about watchfulness and prayer into
the Gethsemane context. For the warning is clearly eschatological and suffers a dislocation of meaning by its insertion here,
with the result that sleeping disciples must be introduced to
provide the necessary background for it.[62]

That the Gethsemane scene is not a legend current originally
in isolation Dibelius establishes through analysis of the way in
which Mark shaped the elements of tradition into the scene as
we have it. Dibelius reproduces the process as follows:

> As a setting for the lament and prayer of Jesus [Mark]
> has introduced the three intimate friends of Jesus and has
> then told about their sleep in order to provide a reason
> for the warning to watch. Then to the account of the lament
> and prayer in indirect discourse as he received it from tradi-
> tion (Mk 14: 33, 35) he added the direct discourse. In doing
> this he used, or at least echoed, biblical words. ... The choice
> of these biblical words furthermore proves that it is not a
> matter of Jesus' perplexity regarding his mission, for the
> man who utters biblical words in prayer knows himself
> in harmony with God. If in the word *Abba* as employed by
> Paul (Rom. 8:15; Gal 4:6) there is an ech o of an early
> Christian exlamation of prayer, and if in the concluding
> word to this prayer in Gethsemane there is perhaps an allusion
> to the content of the third petition of the Lord's Prayer, this
> points in the same direction: Jesus prays as the Christian is
> to pray. ... Jesus is portrayed here in the pattern of a martyr;
> even the symbol of the cup, already common in the martyr
> literature, is due to this [63].

> Furthermore Mark created the second and third acts
> of praying, obviously without having any support for them in
> tradition. He has not given these repetitions any shape, but
> simply mentions them. He is concerned solely with the going
> and coming of Jesus. ... Accordingly it is not upon what Jesus
> says in repeating his prayer but upon what he says on his

---

[61] Art. cit., *CQ*, 12 (1935), 255-258; *BG*, I, 260-263.
[62] *Ibid.*, *CQ*, 12 (1935), 259; *BG*, I, 263-264.
[63] *Ibid.*, p. 260; for the German text see *BG*, I, 265.

third return to the disciples that all the stress is laid. ... The man from heaven falls into the hands of sinners — that is the superscription which is here given to the passion, and with this Christological conclusion Mark has brought the scene out of the realm of human martyrdom and has directed the thoughts of his readers once more to the real meaning of Jesus' suffering [64].

It is clear, then, that for Dibelius the Gethsemane scene is neither an historical account stemming even partially from eyewitnesses, nor an individual story of legendary character. Rather it is Mark's literary and theological elaboration of a community construct, based on the conviction of Jesus' agony and prayer drawn ultimately from the Psalms. The traditional community material underlying Mark's account, in whatever form it came to him, will be found in the indirect reports of Jesus' lament and prayer in vv. 33b and 35, and in the saying of v. 38. The rest of the story comes from Mark himself: vv. 32, 33a, 34, 36-37, 39-42.

Hans Lietzmann

Hans Lietzmann drew Dibelius' fire for the position he took on the Gethsemane scene in his historical analysis of Mark's passion account.[65] Lietzman claimed the special witness of Peter for the four successive pericopes in Mk 14:26-72, beginning with the prediction and ending with the account of his denial. To each of these scenes, he argues, Peter is quite central, and they abound in vivid detail. In the Gethsemane scene he is among the three disciples expressly singled out (v. 33), and the admonition of v. 37 is addressed in a particular way to him. To be sure, the tripling of Jesus' prayer, as of Peter's later denial, is a literary creation, and so are the words of Jesus' prayer reported in vv. 35f., as the reader is intended to see when the sleeping disciples are pointed out in v. 37. But even granting this and the influence of the community in the formation of the account, Lietzmann sees no ground for disputing, as do Bultmann and Dibelius, its basic historicity, especially since the community cannot be credited with inventing a narrative so obviously at odds with its own

---

[64] *Ibid.*, p. 261; for the German text see *BG*, I, 266; cf. also *From Tradition to Gospel*, pp. 212-213.

[65] Hans Litzmann, "Der Prozess Jesu," *SAB* (Berlin, 1931), pp. 313-322.

theological idealization of the voluntary suffering of the Son of God.[66]

Dibelius' critique of this position rests on two foundations, as we saw: the absence of eyewitnesses and the nature of the account as a community construct from O. T. texts.[67] Lietzmann has replied to each of these criticisms in turn.[68] First, as regards Peter, he can see no less reason for invoking his witness than Dibelius claims for invoking that of the young man in Mk 14:51 or of Simon of Cyrene (and his sons) in 15:21. Their role as narrators is no more indicated than Peter's; and his role has nothing more to do with the central theme of Jesus' passion than theirs. His story, like theirs, is told for its own sake, i.e., his presence is noted as the authority of the narrator for this part of his account.[69] Neither has Lietzmann called sleeping witnesses to the stand: it is the witnesses of v. 34, still wide awake, to whom he appeals, not those of v. 37, who are ignominiously asleep. Nor could the community have invented this black picture of their leader's shame, any more than they could have invented his denial on the basis of a dubious Psalm verse, e.g., Ps 69:9.[70]

Secondly, as regards the nature of the account, Lietzmann has shown himself as ready as Dibelius to recognize the editorial elements in Mark's version. Now in answer to Dibelius' critique, he makes one final precision. Once all of these elements have been precipitated, there remains the simple account contained in 14:32-34, 42: Jesus takes the disciples to Gethsemane, begins to grow sad, bids them watch, and goes apart to pray; they fall asleep and he wakes them with the cry that the traitor is approaching. This is as close as we can come to the primitive form of the account, according to Lietzmann, and it is precisely this which is so contrary to the ideal construct of community theology (e.g., Jn 12:27-30) that it could not be a later invention.[71]

---

[66] *Ibid.*, pp. 314-315. Lietzmann sees the sublimation of this scene in Jn 12:27-30 as a very instructive example of the tendencies of the community theology (p. 315).

[67] Dibelius' polemic against Lietzmann is developed particularly in his article "Das historische Problem der Leidensgeschichte." See above p. 118, n. 52.

[68] Hans Lietzmann, "Bemerkungen zum Prozess Jesu I," *ZNW*, 30 (1931), 211-215.

[69] *Ibid.*, pp. 212-214.

[70] *Ibid.*, p. 213; cf. "Der Prozess Jesu," pp. 314-315.

[71] Art. cit., *ZNW*, 30 (1931), 212.

Thus Lietzmann assigns to the tradition underlying Mark the content of vv. 32-34, 42. The rest of the account, including even v. 37, he seems willing to assign to the evangelist.

Jack Finegan

Jack Finegan conducts an analysis of Mk 14:32-42 which leads to even more radical results than those of either Bultmann or Dibelius. He retains v. 32 as genuine since it contains the basic tradition that Jesus came with his disciples to Gethsemane and prayed there alone. But he considers that vv. 33-36 must be relinquished, since it is clear that Peter, James and John are introduced only to make it possible for us to know through them about the behavior of Jesus and the content of his prayer. Besides, the words of v. 34 prove to be not the words of Jesus but a composition from the O.T. scriptures (Ps 41:6, 12; 42:5; Jon 4:9). V. 37a is genuinely traditional. The sleep of the disciples is anything but edifying and could hardly have been invented. Furthermore, the expansion in vv. 37b, 40f. and the sudden appearance of Judas with the mob are unintelligible without it. Vv. 37b and 38, however, come from Mark, since on the one hand they presuppose v. 34 (*grēgoreite*), which Finegan has already shown to be ungenuine, and on the other hand they introduce a parenetic motif out of later community tradition. The same judgment must be made for vv. 39-41a, whose triple rhythm betrays their literary origins. Finegan agrees with Bultmann in seeing v. 41a as the climax and conclusion of the account, but judges, nevertheless, that the *êlthen hê hôra* comes from a later time when the Passion could be seen as a whole. Moreover, both v. 41b and v. 42 are secondary formulations echoing 14:18-21, presupposing an exact foreknowledge on Jesus' part of the betrayal.

While thus only vv. 32 and 37a survive his analysis as underlying tradition, Finegan considers these elements to be genuinely historical because of the mention of the otherwise unknown place-name "Gethsemane" in tension with 14:26, the sleep of the disciples, and the indispensability of this scene for the scene of the arrest which follows.[72]

---

[72] Jack Finegan, *Die Überlieferung der Leidens- und Auferstehungsgeschichte Jesu* (Giessen, 1934), pp. 70-71. This conclusion is weakened, however, by the fact that John does not find the elements of this scene an indispensable prelude to his account of the arrest. He can drop the scene altogether without damage to his general plan, as Bultmann, *op. cit.*, p. 277, has pointed out.

Eduard Lohse

Eduard Lohse holds that the repetitions in Mk 14:32-42, which have given rise to Multiple Source Theories, result not from the combination of two sources but rather from the expansion of an originally shorter form of the Gethsemane tradition. The place-name itself in v. 32a stems from this earlier tradition, since Mark speaks only of the Mount of Olives at 14:26.[73] But just as Luke's account grew by the later addition of the legendary motif of Lk 22:43f., he argues, so Mark's account, too, shows traces of later supplementary material: the separation of the three chosen disciples, the prayer in direct discourse, the tripling of Jesus' prayer without change of content, the introduction of v. 38 from community parenesis, and the rounding out and tying into context of the narrative through vv. 41b-42. In short, Mark has filled out what was originally a very brief tradition about the prayer of Jesus in the hour of temptation before his passion.[74] As for the historical character of this tradition, Lohse adopts lhe position of Dibelius that it is the co-product of the community's theology and Mark's editorial activity.[75]

Eta Linnemann

Recently Eta Linnemann has championed Bultmann's analysis of the Gethsemane pericope and modified it with some contributions of her own.[76] With him she argues for the originality of Mk 14:41a from the fact that it alone supplies the interpretation we are led to expect for the "hour" of v. 35. And she argues against the originality of v. 36, since the metaphor of the "cup" there does not reappear, and against v. 41b as evidence of a decision, also observable in Mt 26:2b, to append another passion prediction near the beginning of the narrative, once the passion stood in context as a unit.[77] She suggests two modifications of Bultmann's results. First, she eliminates v. 37b, the reproof to Peter, as fitting poorly into the original context, where without vv. 34 and 38 there is no

---

[73] Eduard Lohse, *Die Geschichte des Leidens und Sterbens Jesu Christi* (Gütersloh, 1964). pp. 59-70.

[74] *Ibid.*, pp. 65-66.

[75] *Ibid.*, pp. 67f.

[76] Eta Linnemann, *Studien zur Passionsgeschichte* (Göttingen, 1970), pp. 11-40; reconstructed texts on pp. 178f.

[77] *Ibid.*, p. 24.

command to watch and therefore no reason for reproof. Secondly, she reverses the sequence of vv. 40c and 41a, so that the
inability of the disciples to answer now follows the phrase
katheudete to loipon kai anapauesthe taken as interrogative.
This procedure both clarifies the interpretation of the latter
phrase and relates the former explicitly to a corresponding
question. This in turn requires the addition of *kai legei* or
its equivalent before the concluding words of Jesus. The phrase
ton auton logon eipôn in v. 39 is most likely redactional. Thus
for Linnemann the original form of the Gethsemane scene underlying Mark's text would have run as follows: vv. 32, 35, 37a,
39a, 40ab, 41a, 40c, 41b (= [*kai legei*] *apechei*; *êlthen hê hôra*).[78]

Linnemann takes an ambitious step beyond Bultmann by
attempting to trace the prehistory of Mark's text in four stages
from its original form through two successive drafts to its present
form in his gospel. At the second stage, the first reworking of
the original account added v. 36 in order to highlight the exemplary character of Jesus' prayer, employing material from the
Lord's Prayer along with the familiar image of the cup. V. 34
was probably added at this stage too, possibly to provide the
background for gauging the depth and intensity of Jesus' surrender at prayer. Again the image would have been familiar from
the Passion Psalms. Since the author felt the difficilty of po-
sitioning the lament of Jesus either immediately before or after
his command to the disciples, and since he wanted to retain that
command, he inserted v. 33, and by the separation of the three
disciples from the rest he achieved a fresh start and a proper
introduction for Jesus' words of distress.

At the third stage, a further reworking of the tradition took
place, motivated by the desire to give the disciples in the story
an exemplary role with which Christian hearers might identify.
This led to the insertion of the isolated, traditional saying of
Jesus in v. 38, preceded by *kai legei* or its equivalent, and that
insertion led in turn to the inclusion of the command to watch
in v. 34b. Thus it became clear that Jesus expected this behavior
of his disciples, and their sleep in violation of his command took
on the character of a negative example. Linnemann believes that
the developments of this third stage must be later than those
of the second, since vv. 34b and 38 presuppose vv. 33-34a, but,
if they formed a genuine unity with them, would require that

---

[78] *Ibid.*, pp. 25-27, 178.

Jesus ask the disciples to watch for *his* sake (cf. Mattew's *met' emou*), not for theirs.

The final stage of the development was due to Mark. He inserted the reproof to Peter in v. 37b to show how little able Peter was, as one of the three who fell asleep, to live up to the protestations just reported of him in 14:31. It was also Mark who displaced v. 40c to its present position, creating the impression that there was an exchange between Jesus and the disciples at his second return, as well as at the first and third. He was also responsible for expanding v. 41b in the style of a passion prediction, and for linking the present scene to the arrest through the addition of v. 42. We are not told why he added v. 39b.[79]

At this point we have perhaps considered a sufficient number of Single Source Theories, if not to be exhaustive, at least to appreciate their trend, and to draw some conclusions both about their methods in approaching the problem of the literary unity of Mark 14:32-42 and their success in solving it. The most immediately obvious result of all these analyses is that by far the larger portion of Mark's account must be attributed to his editorial activity rather than to the traditions upon which he drew. A verse by verse inspection of how this result has come about will afford perhaps the best way for us to make a judgment on the value of the Single Source Theories among themselves and as a whole.

The principal shared feature which we may note in these analyses is that the presence of doublets among the verses of this account has generally occasioned the choice of priority. Thus with respect to the introductory doublet in vv. 32-33, Loisy, Bultmann, and Finegan decide for the priority of v. 32 on the basis of the originality of the larger circle of disciples and the place-name "Gethsemane." Weiss and Goguel decide for v. 33 on the assumption of an underlying Petrine source, although with Lohse they also recognize the originality of the place-name in v. 32a. Dibelius discovers a doublet in the indirect and direct report of Jesus' lament between vv. 33b and 34, and judges that the indirect form in v. 33b is earlier, especially since v. 34 appears to be a composition based on O. T. scriptures (Wendling, Finegan). Bultmann, on the other hand, regards v. 34 as a doublet of v. 32b, and for that reason as secondary. All of these doublets seem to

---

[79] *Ibid.*, pp. 25, 29-32, 178f.

have escaped the notice of Lietzmann, who takes vv. 32-34 as
original to the tradition underlying Mark.

With respect to the doublet of Jesus' prayer in vv. 35-36,
Wendling regards v. 35 as secondary, because it echoes the viewpoint of the Markan passion announcements and because the
theme of the hour seems less original than the theme of the cup
in v. 36. But the opposite view has also been taken that v. 36
is secondary, either because the cup theme seems less original than
that of the hour (Loisy), or because the direct report of Jesus'
words at prayer must be later than the indirect (Bultmann,
Dibelius, Lohse). Finally, both of these verses have been dropped
as Mark's work, either because the disciples could not have
reported what happened while they slept (Weiss, Goguel, Lietzmann), or because witnesses were introduced simply as a device
to provide us with this information (Finegan).

With respect to the double admonition in vv. 37-38, originality
has sometimes been claimed for the whole of v. 37, on the grounds
that the disciples' sleep and Jesus' reproach must stem from the
reminiscences of Peter (Weiss, Goguel), or at least for v. 37a,
on the grounds that the sleep of the disciples is too basic to the
origin and intelligibility of the rest of the account to have
stemmed from Mark or the community (Wendling, Finegan). Yet
that the sleep of the disciples in v. 37 is an invention of Mark's
has also been maintained, because it is essential to provide a
context for Mark's use of the saying in v. 38 (Dibelius). V. 38 is
generally regarded as Mark's insertion at this point, because of
its homiletic character (Weiss, Bultmann, Finegan, Lohse), although it may represent an original saying of Jesus in another
context (Dibelius), or in another form (Loisy).

With respect to the concluding doublet in vv. 41-42, v. 41a has
at times been judged original, as forming the necessary conclusion
of the pre-Markan account (Loisy, Bultmann) or as representing
Petrine reminiscences (Weiss). Wendling judges it as original
because it is parallel in structure to v. 42, which both he and
Lietzmann take to be original. But for the most part, both
vv. 41 (or 41b) and 42 on account of their similarity to one another are considered to be editorial expansions of Mark's, either
because their content presupposes Jesus' foreknowledge of the
ensuing events (Weiss, Loisy, Finegan), or because they are meant
to exhibit the passion Christology of Mark (Dibelius), or because
they serve only as redactional linkage with what follows (Bultmann, Lohse).

If, finally, we are willing to recognize in v. 39 a doublet of
v. 35, and in v. 40 a doublet of v. 37, both of them meant simply

to effect the literary tripling of Jesus' departure, prayer and return (Weiss, Wendling, Loisy, Bultmann, Dibelius, Lietzmann, Finegan, Lohse), then we are in a position to see that the crucial key to analysis of the Gethsemane pericope in Mark is the fact that it is entirely made up of doublets. Furthermore, the fundamental methodological assumption of the Single Source Theories we have reviewed is that, where doublets occur between two verses, either both verses are redactional (e.g., vv. 41 and 42), or else one verse is redactional and the other original (e.g., vv. 35 and 36). There is no third choice: both verses cannot be original. It is not difficult to see why on this assumption Mark's Gethsemane account, where every verse is a doublet of some other, must prove largely redactional in the analysis.

But we may ask if this is a necessary conclusion. And the answer is that it is not. It follows only on the hypothesis that all elements of the account may be traced back either to a single underlying source or else to the editorial activity of the evangelist. This hypothesis has the merit of simplicity, but does it not distort the data, and ultimately leave more unexplained than it explains? It is all very well to see the editor's hand at work in the final doublet sewing the story into its context; but where every element of the story exists in duplicate, is it not a strain on credibility to attribute this duplication to the editor, when it cannot be shown to be his normal manner of composing and when the doubling of all the details of a story is generally regarded as the most obvious sign of the editor's having combined more than one source in his composition?

Again, what has emerged from the analyses as original underlying tradition has been but the starting-point or the skeleton of a story, not a story. And it is an axiom of form-criticism that oral traditions were transmitted in set forms, not in outline. Bultmann's claim that the original story has not survived intact in Mark is an evasion. The Semitic and Palestinian character of much of the account is altogether ignored by his ill-founded theory of its origin as a Hellenistic cult-legend.[80] And Dibelius' reconstruction of the whole, while brilliantly suggestive, can only be considered arbitrary. His assumption that the community invented, rather than interpreted, incidents of Christ's passion on the basis of O. T. texts rests without proof.[81]

---

[80] See Vincent Taylor, *The Gospel according to St. Mark*, 2nd ed. (London, 1966), p. 655; and see above pp. 59-60.

[81] See Thorleif Boman, "Der Gebetskampf Jesu," *NTS*, 10 (1964), 263-

Distributing the development over a longer period of time through a larger number of redactors, as Linnemann does, avoids to a degree the implausibility of crediting so much editorial work entirely to Mark, but it only ends up positing two more hypothetical collaborators in the work and it fails to resolve the problem of Mark's doublets. In short, the analytical results of the Single Source Theories must leave us questioning, if only because they leave so much of the data systematically unaccounted for.

B. *Multiple Source Theories*

That is why we must now turn to a second group of theories which explain the composition of Mark's Gethsemane account on other grounds. Multiple Source Theories, as we have chosen to call them, begin with the hypothesis that the evangelist made use of a plurality of sources and direct their analysis to the separation of these sources within the account. Naturally, many of these theories are simply an application to the Gethsemane account of findings developed elsewhere in the source analysis of Mark's gospel as a whole or in the passion narrative.

Otto Procksch

Otto Procksch distinguishes two sources behind the Gethsemane account, of which a common or synoptic source is represented by Luke's account, and a special or Marco-Matthean source by the additional material found in Mark and Matthew. Thus the synoptic source contained the basic story that Jesus came to the Mount of Olives with his disciples, where he bade them pray; after one extended prayer, he returned to find them asleep and renewed his admonition; at that point he was arrested. The special Marco-Matthean source contained the name "Gethsemane," the names of the three disciples who were taken apart from the others, and the second and third prayer. Actually, Procksch believes it can be shown that Mark had originally only two prayers, not three: the first in vv. 35-38 from the synoptic source, and the second in vv. 39-42 from the special source, since *ton auton logon eipôn* (v. 39), *palin* (v. 40), and *to triton* (v. 41) are all demonstrably secondary. The *palin* of v. 39

264; and R. S. Barbour, "Gethsemane in the Tradition of the Passion," *NTS*, 16 (1970), 235.

is the editorial link with which Mark joins the material from the special to the material from the synoptic source. Matthew in an obviously secondary way has made the triple division even more obvious (Mt 26:42, 44), but has perhaps retained in v. 42 the variant of the prayer from the special source, which is lacking in Mark.[82]

Wilhelm Bussmann

Wilhelm Bussmann proposes what is closer to being a theory of redactions than of sources with his attempt to identify two stages underlying our present gospel of Mark (E): the first, the basic *Geschichtsquelle* (G) used by Luke; and the second, the revision of this source by a Galilean editor (B) used by Matthew.[83] Bussmann, then, like Procksch regards Luke's text, even with additions from a special source of his own, as closer to the original source of the Gethsemane account as it occurred in G; and the expansions in Mark and Matthew he sees as additions of B to G, with further changes worked in by E to produce the present text of Mark.[84] He reconstructs his hypothetical source G approximately as follows: Lk 22:39a, Mk 14:32b, 35a, 36, 37a, Lk 22:46 par.[85] That basic account was expanded by B, who, relying on his own special Galilean tradition, added the details of the place-name "Gethsemane," the choice of the three disciples, the description of Jesus' sorrow, the triple prayer, the saying on Spirit and Flesh, the explanation for the sleep of the disciples, the reproach at their being unable to watch one hour, and so on.[86] Matthew made slight editorial additions to this. And Mark reworked the material still further to produce his gospel, adding the changes which differentiate him from Matthew: *erchontai, hou to onoma,* and *autou* in 14:32; the names of the Sons of Zebedee and *ekthambeisthai* in v. 33; the indirect form of the prayer in v. 35; *abba, panta dynata soi* for *ei dynaton estin* (B), which was itself a modification of *ei boulei* (G), and *alla* for *plēn* in v. 36; "Simon" and the singular address in v. 37; the simple for the compound verb in v. 38, the compound for the simple in

---

[82] Otto Procksch, *Petrus und Johannes bei Marcus und Matthäus* (Gütersloh, 1920), pp. 183-184.

[83] Wilhelm Bussmann, *Synoptische Studien* (Halle, 1925-31), I, 116-118.

[84] *Ibid.*, p. 193.

[85] *Ibid.*, p. 222. See below Chapter 6 for the analysis which leads to this reconstruction.

[86] *Ibid.*, p. 194.

v. 40, and the addition of v. 40c; and the change of word order in v. 41.[87]

Thus, according to Bussmann, the text of Mark represents a combination of two sources which have passed through two redactions. Its affinity with Luke's text arises from the fact that ultimately basic to both is the *Geschichtsquelle*; its differences, from the fact that G has reached Mark in the revision of the Galilean editor B, who has added to it from his own special source of traditions. Mark's closer affinity with Matthew is explained by the fact that both employed B as a source; his differences, from the editorial work of one or the other.

Wilfred L. Knox

Wilfred L. Knox follows E. Meyer [88] in developing a two source theory for Mark's gospel and for the Gethsemane pericope in particular: a Disciples' source and a Twelve-source, on the basis of the alternative designation of Jesus' followers as "the disciples" or as "the Twelve." Knox identifies the following passages as from the Twelve-source: Mk 3:7-15, 6:7-13, 30-32; 9:33-35, 38-39; 10:32b-45; 11:11; 14:1-2, 10-11, 17-21. And he holds that the conflation of the two sources is no less probable for the passion account than for the rest of the gospel. Moreover, he claims that the Twelve-source "has a distinctly uniform character; it is a summary of the methods of Jesus' teaching in the form of a continuous 'biographical' narrative, with a few incidents inserted dealing with his relations with the Sons of Zebedee as prominent members of the Twelve." [89]

With regard to the Gethsemane account, Knox distinguishes between incidents from the Twelve-source about particular disciples and incidents where Peter, James and John form the inner circle. The latter incidents stem from the Disciples' source, where the three appear only as silent witnesses. In incidents from the Twelve-source, on the contrary, we find the Sons of Zebedee actually taking the initiative (e.g., Mk 9:38; 10:35).[90] Mark, then, in the Gethsemane account has for the most part followed the Disciples' source, which he left at 14:26, whereas Luke has followed the Twelve-source. Mark breaks with his

---

[87] *Ibid.*, pp. 194-195.

[88] *Ursprung und Anfänge des Christentums*, 3 vols. (Stuttgart, 1921-23).

[89] Wilfred L. Knox, *The Sources of the Synoptic Gospels*, I (Cambridge, 1953), 17-31; quotation on pp. 30-31.

[90] *Ibid.*, p. 29.

source at v. 37b, substituting an insertion of his own with a piece of fine homiletical prose in v. 38 for whatever the source reported of Jesus' words at that point. The whole of v. 39 and the phrases in vv. 40-41 which serve to triple Jesus' departure and return are editorial, since Mark's two sources had only one departure and return each. The rest of vv. 40-41 are from the Twelve-source. They differ from v. 42, which returns to the Disciples' source and seems to contemplate the possibility of Jesus' escape, since vv. 40-41 contain no such suggestion, but rather show Jesus reconciled to his betrayal.[91]

In this way, then, Knox blocks off vv. 32-37a, 42 for the Disciples' source, vv. 40 (mostly), 41 for the Twelve-source, and vv. 38, 39, 40 (partly) for Mark's editorial activity.

Thorleif Boman

Thorleif Boman has attempted to work his way back to the traditions underlying the Gethsemane account by noting what he considers historical anomalies in the account itself and explaining them genetically through a theory of sources.[92] He begins by trying to show, against Bultmann and Dibelius, that both Jesus' prayer-struggle and the disciples' sleep are genuinely historical events preserved in community traditions, but that they are mutually incompatible and could not have occurred together. According to him, the disciples' sleep is rightly placed on this final night, or there would be no point in preserving any special recollection of it, since they slept every night. But they could not have slept through Jesus' prayer-struggle as it is reported in Mark. They would have had to stay awake if they heard it at all, especially after his admonition. Likewise the behavior of Jesus, whose calm assurance during the Supper suddenly deserts him in the Gethsemane scene only to return immediately at the arrest, is incomprehensible. Boman suggests that the solution to the riddle posed by these facts lies in a twofold tradition of Jesus' prayer before his passion, which the community gradually blended into one: a prayer-struggle, such as Jn 12:27 records for sometime earlier in the week, and a peaceful prayer in the garden, such as Jn 17 transfers to the celebration in the house. Moreover, he finds in Heb 5:7 independent confirmation of a tradition depicting Jesus' prayer-struggle at

---

[91] *Ibid.*, pp. 125-129.
[29] Thorleif Boman, art. cit. (above p. 129, n. 81), pp. 261-273.

a time indefinitely anterior (*en tais hêmerais tês sarkos autou*) to his passion.[93] On the basis of this historical hypothesis Boman assigns the material in Mark's account to three layers of underlying tradition. The first layer is the tradition of the last night in Gethsemane, relating a peaceful, night-long prayer of Jesus and the sleep of the disciples, and constituted by Mk 14:32-33a, 35a, 37-38, 41-42. The second layer is the tradition of the prayer-struggle of Jesus contained in Mk 14:33b, 36a (up to: *ap' emou*). This is specifically related to Heb 5:7 by the correspondence between the expressions *abba ho pater, panta dynata soi* and *pros ton dynamenon sôzein*. And Boman believes this was a prayer of Jesus for his disciples (cf. Lk 22:31f), not for himself. The third layer of tradition embraces those elements which resulted from the community's blending of the first two layers. Thus v. 34 is the community's interpretation of Jesus' anguish through O. T. texts. V. 36b does not fit the meaning of Jesus' prayer as given in the first or second layer of the tradition, but only the transformation of meaning which the community effected by the combination of the two layers. V. 35b may belong to the second layer as a weak echo of v. 36a, or else it, too, is part of the third layer of tradition.[94]

Rudolf Thiel

With Rudolf Thiel we return to the issue which was brought to the fore as central by the analyses of the Single Source Theories: namely, the significance of the doublets throughout Mark's Gethsemane account. On the basis of the doublets in vv. 32/34, 35/36/39, 37/40, and 41/42, he separates two complete accounts stemming from different sources.[95] Source A is distinguished by the mention of the three chosen disciples and the address to "Simon" by name, and is made up of the following: 14:33-35a, 36-38.[96] Source C speaks of the disciples in general and is exactly parallel to A: 14:32, 39, 35b, 40, 41a (*kai legei autois*), 42. It is clear that Mark's editorial work is responsible for tripling the two departures, prayers and returns of Jesus which he found in his sources, as *palin, ton auton logon eipôn* (v. 39), and *palin* (v. 40) respectively make plain. Consequently, Thiel drops these phras-

[93] *Ibid.*, p. 262-265.
[94] *Ibid.*, pp. 270-272.
[95] Rudolf Thiel, *Drei Markus-Evangelien* (Berlin, 1938), p. 23.
[96] *Ibid.*, pp. 65-66, 190, 214.

es as redactional. The remaining phrase *kai apelthôn prosêu-xato* he recognizes as the introduction to the prayer in Source C.[97] This prayer would have to be the indirect form in v. 35b, which was displaced by Mark to a position before the prayer in v. 36, since, once Jesus had surrendered himself to the Father's will, Mark could hardly have him pray again for the passing of the hour.[98]

Thiel has been at pains throughout his study to vindicate three underlying sources for the gospel of Mark. And he finds one verse here, too, that belongs to his third source (B): namely, v. 41. The first phrase of this verse (*kai erchetai to triton*) he drops from its present place as in part (*to triton*) editorial tripli-cation by Mark and in part (*kai erchetai*) belonging with the scene of the arrest in B. And the second phrase (*kai legei autois*) he retains for his Source C. The rest of the verse he regards as disconnected, out of context, and too brief to be in any sense a parallel to the Gethsemane account from his third source. But since in the sequence of material he assigns to his Source B it follows on the Supper account, he regards these words of Jesus as belonging there, and he concludes that in Source B the arrest took place at the Supper rather than at Gethsemane.[99] Mark imagined that the words would serve as well in Gethse-mane as at the Supper and so transferred them here.[100]

Emanuel Hirsch

Emanuel Hirsch, too, finds in the doublets of Mark 14:32-42 the key to the discernment of two separate but parallel sources combined by the evangelist into one account. The contradiction between v. 41, where Jesus permits the disciples to sleep, and v. 42, where he rouses them, is striking since the words follow one another in the same discourse. The same is true for the contrast between v. 37, where Jesus reproves Peter without exhortation, and v. 38a, where he exhorts the disciples without reproof. The direct form of his prayer in v. 36 seems to exhibit a clear dogmatic correction in *panta dynata soi* against the *ei dynaton estin* of the indirect form in v. 35. Finally, whereas Jesus speaks of his anguish and distress before bidding his dis-ciples to stay and watch in v. 34, in v. 32 he simply lets them sit

---

[97] *Ibid.*, pp. 66, 188-190, 235.
[98] *Ibid.*, pp. 113-114.
[99] *Ibid.*, pp. 66-68, 191, 223.
[100] *Ibid.*, p. 110.

down while he goes off without any word about his feelings to pray alone.[101]

Accordingly, Hirsch believes it possible out of these oppositions to reconstruct the skeleton of two accounts, each with a distinctive character of its own. Mark I (vv. 34, 35, 37, 42), which depicts Jesus as deeply disturbed in the face of the impending events and seeking the human companionship and understanding of his disciples, even the most trusted of whom fail him in his hour of need, is the oldest and most genuine account. Mark II (vv. 32, 36, 38a, 41), which depicts Jesus as surrendering himself, serene and undisturbed, to God's will and the disciples in general simply as victims of natural drowsiness, is a later account which has stylized the behavior of Jesus and the apostles according to the needs of some believing community.[102]

Hirsch fleshes out these skeletal sources by distributing the rest of Mark's verses between them with some overlapping. V. 40 he places with Mark II, since the excuse for the disciples' sleep seems to anticipate the permissive imperatives of v. 41. Common features, connectives and neutral details from vv. 32, 35, 37, 39, and 41 he divides between the two accounts as he sees fit. V. 38b and *to triton* in v. 41 he rejects as editorial additions, and regards *ton auton logon eipôn* in v. 39 as either a later gloss or an addition of Mark II. Mark's two underlying sources, then, take shape in the following manner: Mark I: vv. 32 (up to: *Gethsêmane*), 33-35, 37, 39 (up to: *prosêuxato*), 41 (only: *kai erchetai kai legei autois*), 42; and Mark II: vv. 32, 35 (up to: *prosêucheto*), 36, 37 (only: *kai erchetai kai legei*), 38 (up to: *peirasmon*), 39-41 (without: *to triton*).[103]

Karl Georg Kuhn

Karl Georg Kuhn brings a new precision of method to his investigation of the sources underlying Mark 14:32-42 on the basis of the clues provided by the doublets in the account.[104] He recognizes that the scene contains two introductions (Jesus first leaves the group of disciples in v. 32, then the chosen three in v. 33); two prayers (the first in indirect discourse in v. 35, the second in direct discourse in v. 36); and two concluding sayings

---

[101] Emanuel Hirsch, *Die Frügeschichte des Evangeliums, I. Das Werden des Markus-Evangeliums* (Tübingen, 1951), pp. 156-157.

[102] *Ibid.*, p. 157.

[103] *Ibid.*, p. 158.

[104] Karl Georg Kuhn, "Jesus in Gethsemane," *EvT*, 12 (1952-53), 260-285.

of Jesus (the reproof and admonition to watchfulness in vv. 37-38, and the saying on the coming of his hour and its meaning in v. 41). From a form-critical viewpoint this third doublet is crucial. For the normal structure is that a story have but a single point expressed in but a single saying of Jesus. Consequently, the point of the Gethsemane story cannot be both vv. 37-38 and v. 41. Moreover, the tripling of Jesus' goings and comings at prayer through the insertion of v. 39 is observably artificial, since Jesus has nothing to say on his second return. The words of Jesus at his first and third return, therefore, are the telltale indication that Mark has combined two sources into one account.[105]

Literary analysis only serves to confirm this hypothesis by separating out the sources. Starting with the two crucial concluding sayings, Kuhn shows that the remaining verses of the passage have a decided literary relationship to one or the other of these verses. Thus v. 34 is linked with the point of v. 37 through the key-word *grêgoreite*, and vv. 33f. with vv. 37f. through the identification of Peter among the chosen three. V. 35, on the other hand, is linked with the point of v. 41 through the key-word *hê hôra*, which in both cases has an eschatological sense, as against the purely temporal *mian hôran* of v. 37. But if the indirect form of the prayer (v. 35) belongs with the second conclusion (v. 41), then the direct form (v. 36) must belong to the first (vv. 37f.) Finally, since the second introduction (vv. 33f.) belongs with the first conclusion (vv. 37f.), it follows that the first introduction (v. 32) belongs with the second conclusion (v. 41).

Thus two sources, independent, consistent and complete in themselves, emerge from the analysis, each with a structure parallel to the other but with its own introduction, prayer and saying of Jesus for its concluding point:

Source A: vv. 32, 35, 40, 41;
Source B: vv. 33-34, 36-38.

Kuhn regards as editorial additions of Mark only v. 39, which triples the prayer to emphasize its intensity,[106] hence also the words *palin* in v. 40 and *kai erchetai to triton* in v. 41, and lastly the whole of v. 42, which is nothing more than a link with the

---

[105] *Ibid.*, pp. 263-265.

[106] That the tripling is a literary stereotype appears from other examples, like 2 Cor 12:8, Num 24:10; I Sam 3:8. See above pp. 49-50.

context to follow.[107] The words *proelthôn mikron* (v. 35) or their
equivalent belong with both sources.

Theodor Lescow

Theodor Lescow takes the results of Kuhn's analysis as
clear and conclusive, and goes on to develop some of their theological implications. But he offers some slight modifications worth
noting in the discernment of what he regards as novelistic features not original to the underlying traditions. Thus in Source B
he regards as novelistic expansions the description of Jesus' inner
feelings in vv. 33b-34 and the words of the prayer in v. 36, for
which this description prepares.[109] And in Source A he considers
the explanation of the disciples' sleep as much an insertion of
Mark's in 14: 40bc as it is in 9: 6.[110] It became necessary only after
Mark had joined his two sources into one account and had to
give a reason for the disciples falling asleep again after Jesus'
first return and admonition.[111]

Pierre Benoit

Like Lescow, Pierre Benoit accepts in the main Kuhn's analysis of the Gethsemane pericope into two underlying accounts,
all the more so since he believes that a similar double tradition
behind other portions of Mark's passion narrative can be demon-
strated, e.g., Peter's denial, the session of the Sanhedrin, and the
mockery of Jesus.[112] But, like Lescow again, he feels the need to
modify Kuhn's results in some details. Kuhn has noted the Johannine ring in his Source A to the themes of Jesus' hour and the
disciples' incomprehension.[113] Benoit notes that the Johannine
characteristics of Mark's account are not limited to these, but
extend also to matters of literary detail: Jesus' expression of his

---

[107] Kuhn, art. cit., pp. 265-267. On v. 42 see above pp. 107-108.
[108] Theodor Lescow, "Jesus in Gethsemane," *EvT*, 26 (1966), 141-159.
[109] *Ibid.*, p. 149.
[110] *Ibid.*, p. 148.
[111] *Ibid.*, p. 152.
[112] Pierre Benoit, "Les outrages à Jésus Prophète (Mc xiv 65 par.),"
Neotestamentica et Patristica (Leiden, 1962), pp. 92-110; *idem, Passion et
Résurrection du Seigneur* (Paris, 1966), pp. 10-32; for the session of the
Sanhedrin, see *idem, Exégèse et Théologie* (Paris, 1961), I, 265-311; and for
Peter's denial, see Ch. Masson, "Le reniement de Pierre. Quelques aspects
de la formation d'une tradition," *RHPR*, 37 (1957), 24-35.
[113] Kuhn, art. cit., p. 274.

soul's distress (Mk 14:34/Jn 12:27) and his summons to departure (Mk 14:42/Jn 14:31).[114]   And therefore he attaches vv. 34b
and 42 as well to Source A. He prefers to consider vv. 39 and 42
not as redactional, but as integral to the sources, and so adds
v. 39 to Kuhn's Source B. Finally, he recognizes that the theme
of the sleeping disciples in vv. 40-41 flows much more naturally
from the theme of watchfulnees in Source B than from that of
the hour of the Son of Man in Source A, to which they are at-
tached. So he brackets vv. 40-41a as a sign that he regards them as
a contamination of A by B. Thus Benoit's revised scheme of the
distribution of verses between Kuhn's two sources runs as
follows: [115]

	Source A	Source B
Introduction:	vv. 32a, 34b, 32b	vv. 33, 34ac
Prayer:	v. 35	vv. 39, 36
Saying:	vv. [40-41a], 41b, 42	vv. 37-38

Once again, at this point we have perhaps reviewed a sufficient sampling of Multiple Source Theories to attempt an evalua-
tion of their contribution to the problem of the literary unity of
Mark 14:32-42. The most obvious general result of these analyses
is that nearly all the material of Mark's narrative is systematically
accounted for as issuing from one or another of the underlying
sources, and a minimum is attributed to the editorial work of
the evangelist. This result will be of value, however, only to the
extent that it can be shown to be methodologically superior to
that of the Single Source Theories, which attributed a maximum
of Mark's text to his own editorial work.

The analyses of Procksch, Bussmann and Knox are all based
on the hypothesis of a common source underlying Mark and
Luke: Procksch's "synoptic source," Bussmann's *Geschichtsquelle*," and Knox's "Twelve-source."   And the differences of
Mark from Luke are then ascribed to a second source employed
similarly, but not identically, in Mark's and Matthew's redactions.
But these assumptions do not lead us anywhere. For in the first
place, the opposite could as easily be true: namely, that it is
Luke who has condensed a common source and then added
material of his own from a special source. In the second place,
these analyses do little more than point out the obvious differ-

---

[114] Benoit, art. cit., *Neotestamentica et Patristica*, p. 103 and n. 7.
[115] *Ibid.*, pp. 103-104, n. 8.

ences between Mark's text and Luke's. And in the third place, they fail to deal with the issue which is really central to the literary unity of the passage, since they pass over Mark's doublets in silence.

Boman's analysis, on the other hand, is singularly arbitrary, since, on the basis of a purely psychological estimate of the behavior of Jesus and his disciples, he determines what he regards as a plausible historical sequence for the events, and then assigns the sources for the text accordingly. This is a critique not of the text, but of the impressions which the text has occasioned in the critic. Consequently, it is not surprising that Boman, too, entirely neglects the crucial problem of the doublets in the account.

The proper question posed by Mark's Gethsemane account itself and methodically to be answered by any successful theory of literary origins is this one: how do we explain the fact that every verse in this account is a doublet of some other? It is because they face this question, basic also to the Single Source Theories, that the theories of Thiel, Hirsch, and Kuhn approach, with observably increasing explanatory power, a solution to the literary problem.

In general, Thiel's criteria for distributing the text of Mark between his two main sources A and C are functional enough, but they are incomplete. Surely, the distinction between the larger group of disciples and the trusted three in duplicate verses of the story is indicative of doubled sources. The same can be said for the repetition of Jesus' prayer on two different themes. And the joining of the verses which mention Peter by name as from a common source is methodologically sound. But beyond that his reasons for assigning the verses of Mark's text to one source or the other remain obscure. The parallelism of the underlying accounts can be a confirmation of the results of analysis, but it obviously cannot be the reason for assigning material to one parallel source rather than the other. Finally, his treatment of v. 41 is fanciful in the extreme. Here he has so completely subordinated the data to the caprice of his three source hypothesis that he makes us question his methodology altogether.

Hirsch, like Thiel, begins well by emphasizing the contrast between the verses forming doublets in Mark and separating the skeleton of two parallel accounts on that basis. But he provides no systematic criteria for determining which of the verses belongs to which account, other than the characterization he offers of each account after his initial distribution of the verses. And

while the unity and coherence of such a characterization could
serve as a subsequent confirmation of an analysis made on other
grounds, it cannot serve as prior ground for the analysis. His
placement of v. 40 with his source Mark II rests on the exegeti-
cally questionable grounds of reading the verbs in v. 41a as imperative, and still more questionably as permissive.[116]. His lack of
criteria leads to confusion and overlapping in the distribution of
the remaining verses, with the result that each of his underlying
accounts still contains two departures, prayers (one without content), and returns of Jesus. Obviously, some doublets have gone
unobserved and unexplained in this analysis of Hirsch.

We are now in a position to appreciate the contribution to
our problem made by Kuhn. His careful application of the principles of form-critical method has enabled him to develop a two
source theory of impressive simplicity, coherence, and explanatory power. He begins with the fundamental law of popular traditions, axiomatic in form-criticism, that a story has but one
point. Observing that the Gethsemane story has two, he separates
the sayings of Jesus that convey each point and proceeds to build
backwards to the story whose setting and action give each saying
its significance. Verses identifying Peter, or verses containing
common key-words expressing the point of a given story are
linked together. And finally, once one of the members of a
contrasting doublet has been identified as belonging to one source
in this way, its opposite member can with confidence be assigned
to the other source, or else to the editor where there is evidence
of redactional activity, as in the case of vv. 39 and 42. All of this
is methodologically irreproachable and produces two parallel
accounts, whose consistency and independence only serve to confirm the analysis.

Questions do remain, however, and we must try to deal
with them now before developing our own conclusions. Let us
begin with v. 40. First of all, Kuhn does not really tell us why
he assigns v. 40 to Source A. We must assume that he regards it as
a doublet of v. 37a and therefore as belonging before v. 41, in the
same way that v. 37a belongs before vv. 37b-38 in the parallel
account.[117] Secondly, we have seen Lescow's objection to the
effect that the reason given for the disciples' sleep in v. 40bc is
an insertion of Mark's. Yet the parallels in Matthew (26:43) and
Luke (22:45) both offer a reason for the disciples' sleep, even if

---

[116] See above pp. 50-52.
[117] In any case, see Kuhn, art. cit., p. 263.

Matthew omits any equivalent of Mark's 14:40c. Moreover, while Lescow favors the deletion of v. 40bc as a novelistic digression in an otherwise methodical construction,[118] Kuhn defends the originality of the verse as being very much in harmony with the almost Johannine character of the context in Source A, dealing as it does with the themes of the hour of the Son of Man (Jn 12:23) and the incomprehension (= sleep) of the disciples.[119] Benoit, for his part, speaks of vv. 40-41a as a contamination of Source A by Source B, since he takes the theme of sleep as properly belonging with the theme of watching. But in this respect he, too, overlooks the Johannine quality of Source A, which he is otherwise anxious to recognize and even reinforce. Sleep bears a further meaning in this context, and v. 40c is the index to that meaning. Lastly, with respect to *palin* in this verse, I believe that dropping it by analogy with v. 39 may be too hasty a procedure. It need not originally have signified any second recurrence of Jesus' return, but, according to Markan usage elsewhere in combination with *erchesthai* (2:1; 11:27), may simply mean "when he came *back*." [120] The strongly attested variant *hypostrepsas heuren autous palin* [121] witnesses at once to the confusion about the sense and placement of *palin* here and to the search for an expression bearing the meaning suggested for *palin elthôn*.

Let us pass now to vv. 33b-34. Lescow considers the description of Jesus' inner feelings in these verses, as well as the quotation of his prayer in v. 36, novelistic expansions. But he has failed to note that v. 36 can be an expansion of v. 35 only in the sense that v. 34 is of v. 33b. Yet he considers v. 35 original; so he really has no argument. At most, he might claim that the direct discourse is later than the indirect, which says nothing more than that one source is older than the other. Benoit's suggestion, on the other hand, that the theme of Jesus' distress find its place among the other Johannine themes by the transfer of v. 34b to Source A is worth considering. Nevertheless, his principle of grouping Johannine themes, as it stands, is much too broad. It lacks proper limits and could be applied indiscriminately. For example, we might easily transfer v. 36 as well, on the grounds

---

[118] Lescow, art. cit., p. 148.

[119] Kuhn, art. cit., pp. 273-274; and see also X. Léon-Dufour, "Passion (Récits de la)," *DBS*, VI (Paris, 1960), col. 1458-59; T. Boman, art. cit., p. 265.

[120] See B.-A.-G., s. v. *palin*, 1. a.

[121] C ℵ Γ A W Δ (Θ) Φ 0116 Fam 1 and 13 *pl*.

that the cup in v. 36b [122] and the prayer of submission in v. 36c,[123] and possibly even the address to the Father in v. 36a, are all Johannine themes. Thus the modification which Benoit introduces into Kuhn's Source A cannot be sustained on this principle alone, without entailing further modifications which would ultimately dissolve distinctions legitimately drawn on other grounds. In spite of that, I do consider that a modification similar to what Benoit suggests is desirable, but for different reasons. Dibelius called attention to the fact, noted by few others, that v. 34 is a doublet of v. 33b. Since the verses have exactly the same relation to one another as the direct and indirect reports of Jesus' prayer in vv. 35 and 36, I suggest that methodologically they should be treated in the same manner and assigned to different sources: v. 33b to Source A along with the indirect report of Jesus' prayer in v. 35, and v. 34 to Source B. In effect, this achieves Benoit's recommendation in another way and with proper limitations, though admittedly without the verbal correspondence of *hê psychê mou*, which seems of lesser importance when we note that John's *tetaraktai* corresponds to none of Mark's verbs anyway.[124] It also introduces a parallel element preparing for Jesus' prayer into the accounts of both sources, an element perhaps echoed by Luke's *kai genomenos en agônia ektenesteron proseucheto* (22:44).

We turn now to v. 39, which Kuhn deletes as wholly redactional. Again, I think he may have been too hasty. Benoit prefers to see v. 39 as integral to Source B, but offers no persuasive reason. I should like to offer one. By his deletion of v. 39, Kuhn finds himself compelled to make the phrase *proelthôn mikron* (v. 35a) do double duty for both his sources. He would have done better to drop the admittedly redactional *palin* and the dubiously attested *ton auton logon eipôn* from v. 39, but to retain the *kai apelthôn proseuxato* as his introduction to v. 36. This procedure has two things to recommend it: first, Mt 26:42 does nearly the same thing, and it result in a natural and unforced reading; sec-

---

[122] Cf. Jn 18:11. See Ivor Buse, "St. John and the Marcan Passion Narrative," *NTS*, 4 (1957-58), 216-217; Sydney Temple, "The Two Traditions of the Last Supper, Betrayal, and Arrest," *NTS*, 7 (1960-61), 84.

[123] Cf. Jn 12:28. See X. Léon-Dufour, *loc. cit.*

[124] But see Raymond E. Brown, "Incidents that Are Units in the Synoptic Gospels but Dispersed in St. John," *CBQ*, 23 (1961), 146, n. 10; and C. H. Dodd, *Historical Tradition in the Fourth Gospel* (Cambridge, 1963), pp. 37f., 69f. Barnabas Lindars, *New Testament Apologetic* (Philadelphia, 1961), p. 99, n. 2, thinks that Ps 6:4 is more likely than Ps 42:7 to lie behind Jn 12:27 as its intended source because of the subsequent *sôson me* in Ps 6:5.

ondly, and more to the point, unless v. 39 is introduced in this
way, Source B, while reporting the content of his prayer, fails to
mention that Jesus prayed.

Finally, we must look at v. 42, which like v. 39 Kuhn considers
wholly redactional. Benoit is for retaining it as original, and with
good reason, at least for the expression *egeiresthe agômen* in
v. 42a. I offered my reasons above (pp. 67-68) in the exegesis of
this verse for regarding v. 42a as part of genuine pre-Markan
tradition. But I also indicated at the beginning of this present
chapter my agreement with the arguments that show v. 42b to be
editorial linkage with the context that follows. Therefore I
adopt a position between Kuhn and Benoit, taking v. 42a as original, and attributing v. 42b to Markan redaction. And I believe
this phrase provides an essential element for the correct understanding of the saying which immediately precedes it in v. 41.
Just as *hypagei* balances the passive *paradidotai* of 14:21, so the
stirring *egeiresthe agômen* balances the *idou paradidotai* in v. 41,
showing that although the Son of Man may be delivered by man
(and God) to the will of sinful men, nevertheless he goes forward
to meet his hour in full freedom and full consciousness of God's
will for him.[125]

Like Lescow and Benoit, then, I adopt Kuhn's overall analysis
and solution to the problem of the literary unity of Mk 14:32-42.
But like them, too, I offer my own slight modifications and see the
sources underlying Mark's account as follows:

> Source A
> vv. 32
>   33b
>   35
>   40 (with: *palin*)
>   41 (without: *kai erchetai to triton*)
>   42a
> Source B
> vv. 33a
>   34
>   39 (without: *palin, ton auton logon eipôn*)
>   36-38
> Redactional
> vv. 39 (only: *palin, ton auton logon eipôn*)
>   41 (only: *kai erchetai to triton*)
>   42b

---

[125] The context in John expresses a similar train of ideas. See above
pp. 67-68.

The simplicity and coherence of this theory should be obvious from a comparison of Mark's complex text with the models of the two parallel sources on which he drew. Its explanatory power lies in its ability to take account of all the data of the problem by finding a place for each duplicated element of Mark's account in one or another of his sources with a minimum of editorial residue. Thus the doublets between vv. 32a/33a, 32b/34b, 33b/34a, 35a/39, 35b/36, 37a/40, 37b/41a, 38/41b-42a can all be distributed systematically between Mark's sources; the doublets between vv. 32a/26 and 42b/41b can be recognized as serving to link the account once composed with its present context in his gospel; and the editorial phrases of Mark in vv. 39, 41 and 42b can be definitely determined.[126]

---

[126] Problems which this theory does not succeed in solving are: (1) giving a meaning to *apechei* in v. 41, which Kuhn, art. cit., p. 267, n. 16, omits as meaningless and I retain without being able to decide its meaning; and (2) explaining the shift from singular to plural address between vv. 37 and 38, although the parenetic intent of Source B may be regarded as sufficient justification for the generality of the plural address in v. 38. See Kuhn, art. cit., p. 284. These seem likely to remain exegetical problems.

CHAPTER FIVE

EDITORIAL HISTORY of MATTHEW 26:36-46

The data with which we begin the editorial history of Matthew's Gethsemane account are gathered from a detailed comparison of Matthew and Mark, which reveals at once the very close similarity of the two accounts and their quite significant differences. The overall result of this comparison is striking. For we observe that, although wording is identical in phrase after phrase, there is not a single verse of Matthew's which is identical in every respect with one of Mark's, be their differences as great as a whole new prayer of Jesus (Mt 26:42/Mk 14:39) or as small as a prepositional prefix (Mt 26:41/Mk 14:38) or a simple reversal of word order (Mt 26:46/Mk 14:42).[1] Apart from the question of priority, which with the practically unanimous opinion of present-day scholars we decide in favor of Mark against Matthew, this result raises the question of the relationship of the two gospels. For if these two Gethsemane accounts are independent of each other, why are there so many identities between them? And if they are mutually dependent, why are there so many differences?

Analyses presently proceed to answer the question of the relationship of aMtthew to Mark with three hypotheses: either (a) complete independence, or (b) immediate literary dependence, or (c) mediate dependence. Let us examine each of these solutions with a view to determining which of them can best account for the identities and differences we find between the Gethsemane texts of Matthew and Mark.

A. MATTHEW'S COMPLETE INDEPENDENCE OF MARK

Ernst Lohmeyer ranks perhaps first in the minority camp of scholars who defend the complete independence of Matthew from

---

[1] See Chapter 2 above, pp. 69-82.

Mark.[2] His arguments are based upon the form and content of the account in the Gethsemane pericope, where he sees a rhythmic pattern sustained throughout in the symmetrical alternation of narrative and discourse. Further, he observes that the narrative units are usually composed of three phrases and the discourse units of two. Even the seeming break in the pattern at Jesus' third prayer has its point, since the report given there (Mt 26:44) only in narrative serves to emphasize the futility of the prayer, which has already received its answer in the silence of God and the sleep of the disciples. While something of this rhythm, of course, survives in Mark, it is nowhere near so pure and unbroken as it is in Matthew.

As regards the content, a variety of touches reveal the distinctly non-Markan character of Matthew's account. The emphasis on the person of Jesus, which makes him the subject of the account in v. 36 and adds *met' emou* in vv. 38 and 40; the biblical echoes arising from *kathisate autou* in v. 36 and *epi prosôpon autou* in v. 39; the approximations to the Lord's Prayer in vv. 39 and 42; the echo of the kerygma of the Kingdom in the phrase *êngiken hê hôra* in v. 45; the expressions favored by Matthew elsewhere in his gospel, like *tote, apelthôn ekei* — all of these characteristic divergencies from Mark are evidence of Matthew's literary independence. For Matthew's account proves not only to be purer in form but more meaningful in content, as these differences show. Given the lack of symmetry and exactness in Mark's account and even its occasional meaninglessness (e.g., *apechei* in v. 41), Lohmeyer cannot but conclude to the originality of Matthew's account against Mark's.[3]

B. MATTHEW'S LITERARY DEPENDENCE ON MARK

For the majority of critics, however, such an explanation seems arbitrary and ill-founded, particularly for the passage we are considering in Mark and Matthew, where the identities far outweigh in number and significance the differences.[4] Be-

---

[2] See Ernst Lohmeyer-Werner Schmauch, *Das Evangelium des Matthäus*, 3rd ed. (Göttingen, 1962); and also M.-J. Lagrange, *Évangile selon Saint Matthieu*, 3rd ed. (Paris, 1927); A. Schlatter, *Der Evangelist Matthäus*, 6th ed. (Stuttgart, 1963), *idem, Markus, der Evangelist für die Griechen* (Stuttgart, 1935).

[3] Lohmeyer-Schmauch, *op. cit.*, pp. 360-362.

[4] See, for example, Pierre Bonnard, *L'Évangile selon Saint Matthieu* (Neuchatel, 1963), p. 382.

sides, are there really any divergencies from Mark which cannot
be explained equally well or better by the habitual differences
of Matthew's language, style, editorial practice and theological
tendency? The proponents of the hypothesis of strict literary
dependence do not think so, and they offer accordingly the
explanation that Matthew's text is simply an editorial reshaping
of Mark's.

In v. 36 *tote* (also in vv. 38, 45) is a familiar formula of Matthew's Greek. And Matthew has made a point throughout his
gospel of refashioning inclusive plurals like Mark's *erchontai*
here, in order to put Jesus into greater relief.[5] Matthew's *heôs
hou* is more precise than Mark's abiguous *heôs*. And he gives
a sharper separation to the scenes of action with his contrast
between *kathisate autou* and *apelthôn ekei*.[6]

In v. 37 the designation "Sons of Zebedee" is a common
equivalent for James and John elsewhere both in Matthew and
in Mark.[7] And *lypeisthai* is clearly a toning down of Mark's violent *ekthambeisthai*, which Matthew must have found too
strong.[8] Matthew drops Mark's *met' autou* here without intending any change of meaning, since he has merely carried it over
into the even more emphatic *met' emou* of vv. 38 and 40.[9]

In this latter addition Dibelius regards Matthew as transposing into a Christological key the eschatological theme of watchfulness in Mark, just as he did for the theme of eschatological
offense in Mark 14:27 by his addition of *en emoi* in 26:31. It is
the disciples consecrated to Jesus the Lord who must watch and
it is Jesus they offend when they fail.[10]

In v. 39 with *epi prosôpon autou* Matthew suceeds in making
Mark's *epi tês gês* both more concrete[11] and less brutal, since his
more traditional expression suggests a prostration in prayer or
adoration.[12] And he tightens up the grammatical construction
considerably by changing Mark's *prosêucheto* and *elegen* into

---

[5] Pierre Benoit, *Passion et Résurrection du Seigneur* (Paris, 1966), p. 22.
[6] Theodor Lescow, "Jesus in Gethsemane," *EvT*, 26 (1966), 153 and n. 63.
[7] Cf. Mt 27:56; and Mt 20:20/Mk 10:35; Mt 10:2/Mk 3:17; Mt 4:21/
Mk 1:19.
Jack Finegan, *Die Überlieferung der Leidens- und Auferstehungsgeschichte
Jesu* (Giessen, 1934), p. 18; Benoit, *op. cit.*, p. 23.
[8] Finegan, Benoit, *loc. cit.*; Lescow, art. cit., p. 154.
[9] Finegan, *loc. cit.*
[10] Martin Dibelius, "Gethsemane," *CQ*, 12 (1935), 263; *BG*, I (Tübingen,
1953), 268-269; and see Lescow, *loc. cit.*
[11] Lescow, art. cit., p. 155.
[12] Benoit, *loc. cit.*

participles subordinate to *epesen*.[13]   Mark's indication of the
content of Jesus' prayer in 14:35 seems superfluous to Matthew
beside the prayer itself quoted in 14:36, and likewise the Aramaic
abba beside its Greek translation; so both of these elements he
drops.[14] Mark's reference to the hour here is thus lost altogether,
and Matthew conceives the prayer of Jesus as preparing for the
hour rather than as struggling through it.[15] But Matthew actually
attempts more of a fusion than a suppression of Mark's double
formulation, for he replaces *parapherein* of 14:36 with *parerchesthai* from the preceding verse, and *panta dynata soi* with
ei dynaton estin.[16] Both these substitutions, like previous ones,
serve to attenuate the force of Mark's account,[17] and the latter
one serves also as a base for Matthew's two-stage prayer (vv.39,
42).[18] Loisy remarked that Matthew's use of *parerchesthai* with
the image of the cup is less natural than Mark's with the image
of the hour,[19] but Lescow defends Matthew's choice here as
meant to express the futurity of the event better than Mark's
parapherein.[20]

In v. 40, Matthew's addition of *pros tous mathêtas* (cf. v. 36)
defines the group to whom Jesus returns, which in Mark remains
vague even after the third return,[21] although Matthew indicates
no better than Mark how the two groups separated at the beginning got together again.[22] This addition, along with Matthew's
omission of *Simon, katheudeis*, also makes the plural address of
Jesus to the disciples through Peter somewhat more natural.
Thereby Matthew reveals his apologetic intention of showing that
Peter is not the only one at fault.[23] The Christological motive
that has led Matthew to the addition of *met' emou* here and in
v. 38 now comes somewhat into conflict with the parenetic motive
of Mark's account, weakening the call to eschatological watchfulness by putting the sleep of the disciples in a kind of literary

---

[13] Lescow, *loc. cit.*
[14] Finegan, Dibelius, *loc. cit.*
[15] Lescow, *loc. cit.*
[16] Benoit, *loc. cit.*
[17] Lescow, *loc. cit.*
[18] Finegan, *loc. cit.*
[19] *Les Évangiles synoptiques* (Ceffonds, 1907-08), II, 564.
[20] *Loc. cit.*
[21] Karl Georg Kuhn, "Jesus in Gethsemane," *EvT*, 12 (1952-53), 267.
[22] Finegan, *loc. cit.*
[23] Benoit, *loc. cit.*

contrast with the more emphatic loneliness of Jesus taking his destiny upon himself.[24]

V. 41 of Matthew is practically identical with Mk 14:38, so much so that aMtthew's dependence on Mark, or else the dependence of both upon a common source, cannot be seriously questioned.[25]

In v. 42 Matthew shows his concern to fill in Mark's account with more information about Jesus' second and third prayer by formulating the scribal variant we find here.[26] Kuhn claims that the editorial process is clear, and decisive for the secondary character of Matthew's account: Matthew found Mark's account with the two prayers from his two sources side by side; he left the prayer in Mk 14:36 where it was, but reformulated the prayer of v. 35 to supply for Jesus' second prayer, where Mark has nothing but his editorial v. 39; in doing so, Matthew put the prayer into direct discourse and assimilated it more closely to the prayer of Mk 14:36 (omitting reference to the hour) and to the third petition of the Lord's Prayer.[27] Finegan and Lescow,[28] on the other hand, prefer to see Matthew's second prayer simply as a development of his first in 26:39. Loisy remarks that the recurrence of the cup theme argues against our supposing any source prior to Mark for this second prayer of Matthew's.[29]

In v. 43 Matthew drops the final phrase of Mark 14:40 expressing the disciples' lack of comprehension,[30] either from an apologetic motive of sparing the disciples somewhat,[31] or from a theological motive of portraying their sleep in a more human, less apocalyptic, fashion than Mark.[32]

In v. 44 Matthew again reveals his intention of making clearly explicit what Mark has only suggested in 14:41, where he speaks of Jesus' third return without mentioning any third departure or prayer preceding it. Matthew fills out the gap with the help of Mk 14:39, and balances the composition nicely, although he actually has no more to say about the third prayer of Jesus than Mark had to say about his second.[33]

---

[24] Lescow, art. cit., p. 156.
[25] Benoit, op. cit., pp. 23-24.
[26] Dibelius, loc. cit.; Benoit, op. cit., p. 24.
[27] Kuhn, art. cit., pp. 267-268.
[28] Loc. cit.
[29] Op. cit., p. 565.
[30] Dibelius, loc. cit.
[31] Finegan, Benoit, loc. cit.
[32] Lescow, art. cit., p. 157.
[33] Finegan, Dibelius, Kuhn, Benoit, Lescow, loc. cit.

In v. 45 Matthew again adds *pro tous mathêtas* to Mark's account, conceivably for the same reason as in v. 40, and he omits *apechei*, perhaps because he found it difficult and ambiguous,[34] or perhaps because he wanted to improve the flow of thought it interrupted.[35] The rest of this verse and the whole of v. 46 are practically identical with Mark.

Thus the proponents of this hypothesis, convinced of the strict literary dependence of Matthew on Mark because of the identities between them, explain the differences by a complex variety of motives which have influenced Matthew in his editorial reshaping of Mark's account and which have resulted in the substitution of linguistic features characteristic of Matthew (vv. 36-37); stylistic improvements clarifying, tightening up, or toning down Mark's account (vv. 36-37, 39-40, 42, 44-45); additions, omissions and transformations from dogmatic (vv. 36, 38, 39) or apologetic (vv. 40, 43) reasons. The net result is a polished, symmetrical, harmonious account from which the seams of Mark's own work in combining his sources have been obliterated.[36]

C. MATTHEW'S MEDIATE DEPENDENCE ON MARK

While the preceding analysis is certainly within the realm of possibility, not everyone is satisfied with its assumptions or conclusions. Opposed are not only those who hold for Matthew's complete independence of Mark, but those who believe that the relations between Matthew and Mark are more complex than the hypothesis of simple literary dependence can account for, and are better explained by supposing the interaction of written and oral tradition. We shall consider two such hypotheses before reaching our own conclusions: the hypothesis of Xavier Léon-Dufour,[37] and that of N. A. Dahl.[38]

Léon-Dufour argues that the identities of content, sequence and vocabulary that exist between the passion accounts of Matthew and Mark do not prove Matthew's literary dependence, even granted the assumption of Mark's priority, but prove at most a

---

[34] Benoit, *loc. cit.*
[35] Finegan, *loc. cit.*
[36] Kuhn, *loc. cit.*
[37] "Passion (Récits de la)," *DBS*, VI (Paris, 1960), col. 1419-92.
[38] "Die Passionsgeschichte bei Matthäus," *NTS*, 2 (1955-56), 17-32.

common source. And a detailed examination of their differences gives positive evidence of Matthew's literary independence, since if he depended on Mark, he could not have modified Mark's account to the extent he has. Their identities, then, result from a common source, probably a written document, and their differences from the interplay of oral and written tradition.[39] The proof of this contention rests principally on the occurrence throughout Matthew's account of omissions, transformations and additions which are against his established tendencies. The evidence offered us by the Gethsemane passage is typical.

Proponents of the hypothesis of literary dependence claim that Matthew in v. 45 has ommitted *apechei* (Mk 14: 41) from a motive of clarifying the text. Yet if that was really the case, why does he add to his own text a few verses later on (Mt 26: 50) the equally difficult expression *eph' ho parei* not found in Mark, unless in fact he is operating from no such motive and is independent of Mark in both cases?[40]

It is claimed that Matthew in v. 39 has retained the Greek translation in preference to Mark's Aramaic *abba*. Yet in the short span of the Gethsemane account Matthew has three examples of Semitic phraseology absent from Mark. Butler points out two of them: *legomenos* as used in v. 36 and *genethêtô 'fiat'* in v. 42, which occurs five times in Matthew and nowhere else in the N. T. except in quotations.[41] And Léon-Dufour calls attention to a third: *hê hôra kai, ktl.* in v. 45, which he regards as an example of the *waw*-apodosis so much admired by critics in Mark (e.g., 14:25), but which is not used here by Mark, who has instead *idou*, an expression favored by Matthew.[42]

There is the further claim that on the whole Matthew tends to improve Mark's Greek. Yet there are three cases in this passage alone where Matthew's Greek is a stylistic worsening by comparison with the text supposed to be his source. In v. 39 Matthew attaches three participles to one subject, where in the parallel Mark has but one.[43] Again in v. 44 he does the same

---

[39] Art. cit., col. 1449-50.

[40] *Ibid.*, p. 1451.

[41] B. C. Butler, *The Originality of St Matthew. A Critique of the Two-Document Hypothesis* (Cambridge, 1951), pp. 152-153.

[42] Art. cit., col. 1452.

[43] *Ibid.;* Lohmeyer-Schmauch, *op. cit.*, p. 361, n. 4.

thing.[44] In v. 45 Matthew's placement of *idou* is inferior to Mark's in the parallel.[45].

Léon-Dufour concedes that the variations of Matthew from Mark, taken singly, could conceivably be attributed to Matthew's reshaping of the text for one motive or another. But he regards the conclusion as cumulatively imposed that this cannot be the explanation of so many cases, here and throughout the passion narrative, of variations at odds with Matthew's own established tendencies. We have already tried to show in the preceding chapter the existence and extent of an earlier passion narrative on which Mark himself depends. Léon-Dufour claims that Matthew, too, depends on this more primitive account, but not on Mark directly. His crucial proof of Matthew's independence of Mark here is the distribution of numerous Semitisms in precisely those parts of Matthew's text which are parallel to Taylor's Roman (= non-Semitic) account A in Mark: viz., Mt 26:4, 15-17, 19, 31, 33-35, 47, 60, 64, 66; 27:17, 22, 47, 54-55, 58-59, 61. And he concludes from this that Matthew and Mark represent two recensions — one Semitic and the other Roman — of a more primitive account. The community of their source accounts for their identities, and their divergencies stem from transformations and accretions due to oral tradition, which are not thereby of any less historical value than the initial account to which they have been joined.[46]

He goes on to make this conclusion still more precise through detailed literary analysis of the four passion narratives. And he expounds at the end a genetic theory quite similar to the four-stage theory of Jeremias. The passion narrative grew (1) from an initial confession of faith such as we find in 1 Cor 15:3-5, (2) through a kerygmatic "short account" — whether oral or written — beginning with Jesus' arrest, (3) through a more theologically developed "long account" including also the preludes to the passion and the material preceding the arrest, (4) into our present gospels, which reproduce the elements of this long account as it seems to have reached them through two major streams of tradition that have added further materials in their turn and are reflected in the related but divergent tendencies of the Matthew/Mark and the Luke/John accounts.[47]

---

[44] Lohmeyer-Schmauch, *op. cit.*, p. 362, n. 2.

[45] Léon-Dufour, *loc. cit.*

[46] *Ibid.*, col. 1453-54.

[47] *Ibid.*, col. 1454, 1472-73; cf. Joachim Jeremias, *The Eucharistic Words of Jesus* (London, 1966), pp. 89-96.

Léon-Dufour's analysis of the Gethsemane scene provides an illustration of this process, but it also reveals the crucial weakness of his hypothesis. In the first place, he grants that this scene most probably did not belong to the stage of the "short account," but claims that it came into existence very early in the tradition as part of what he calls the Garden of Olives sequence, represented by Mk 14:26-52 par. (prediction of denial and desertion, prayer-struggle, arrest, and disciples' desertion). In the second place, he follows Kuhn to the extent of recognizing two separate strains underlying what we find combined in the Matthew/Mark tradition of Gethsemane: a dogmatic Christological interpretation of the event echoing the tradition preserved in Jn 12:27-30, and a parenetic interpretation approximating the tradition represented by Lk 22:39-46. In the third place, he considers that the story probably had an independent existence before being inserted through the obvious linkage of vv. 32 and 42 into its present context in the passion.[48]

Now we have seen all these points already. But the question here is whether they can be reasonably maintained along with Léon-Dufour's hypothesis. I do not think they can. Let us take the issues one by one, since the Gethsemane account seems a particularly crucial testing ground for his whole hypothesis.

First of all, there is the issue of the formation of the Garden of Olives cycle (Mk 14:26-52 par.). Agreeing which Jeremias that the "short account" of the passion began with the arrest, Léon-Dufour also follows him to the extent of recognizing that what precedes the arrest in this sequence (Mk 14:26-42 par.) gained entry into the tradition by the time that the stage of the "long account" had been reached.[49] But the evidence is against any prototype of the Mark/Matthew Gethsemane account having entered the tradition by this time and in this way. Taylor has illustrated the Semitic character of Mark 14:32-42 against its immediately surrounding non-Semitic context (14:26-31, 43-46).[50] Bultmann has indicated how the continuity of Mark 14:27-31, 43-52 is actually broken by vv. 32-42,[51] while granting that vv. 27-31 are an earlier addition in function of a passion account expanded

---

[48] Art. cit., col. 1458-59.

[49] Léon-Dufour, art. cit., 1458, 1473; Jeremias, *loc. cit.*

[50] Vincent Taylor, *The Gospel according to St. Mark*, 2nd ed. (London, 1966), pp. 655-656.

[51] Rudolf Bultmann, *The History of the Synoptic Tradition* (New York and Evanston, 1963), pp. 267-268.

by the story of Peter.[52]   And Léon-Dufour himself admits the likelihood of the independent existence of the account because of the redactional seams at either end.[53] The evidence, then, is that the Mark/Matthew Gethsemane scene is not of a piece with the earlier sequence into which it has been sewn, and suggests that it may not even have belonged to the stage of the "long account."

This brings us to the second issue: the combination of the underlying traditions. Léon-Dufour follows Kuhn in recognizing that the Mark/Matthew Gethsemane account is a compound of two separate simple strains of tradition. Yet he wants to follow Jeremias in giving Gethsemane a place in the development of the tradition at the stage of the "long account." But if this account contained the Gethsemane tradition at all, it would have had to be in a simple, not in a compound form. In Jeremias' opinion "we have ... no reason to assume that this third stage of the tradition ever attained written form." [54] And on Kuhn's grounds the Mark/Matthew account is precisely the type of account that could not have developed in the oral tradition. The form in which such a story would be transmitted in the oral tradition would be simple — with but a single introduction, mid-section and conclusion — not compound. Moreover, Kuhn's whole analysis has been at pains to show that the combination of two underlying accounts into one and the insertion of the whole into its present context have both been precisely *literary* operations, the result not of a development in the oral tradition but of the work of a literary redactor. Léon-Dufour cannot, of course, follow Kuhn in admitting that the literary combination was the work of Mark without at the same time admitting Matthew's dependence on Mark. For it is incredible that both could have arrived at identical combinations independently. This leaves us with only two alternatives. Either the "long account" was a written document containing some compound prototype of the Mark/Matthew tradition, an unacceptable alternative since then we are faced with the equally difficult task of explaining how the simple form of the Luke/John tradition could have developed from this common account; or else, the "long account" — whether written or oral — contained at most a simple form of the tradition and the compound form was the work of a literary redactor, somewhere between the stage of the "long account"

---

[52] *Ibid.*, pp. 278-279.
[53] Art. cit., col. 1459.
[54] *Op. cit.*, p. 96.

and the writing of the gospels, who produced a document common
to Mark and Matthew, an alternative that sounds suspiciously
like the justly abandoned Proto-Mark hypothesis. Now not only
do we have no external evidence for the existence of such a document, but its postulation can be shown in the case of the
Gethsemane account to be particularly fruitless and self-defeating.
For it is the analysis of the text of Mark, after all, that has
allowed Kuhn to discover its two underlying accounts, and precisely because the evidence of redactional work is there still
so plainly to be seen. Moreover, the analysis left no residue by
which the redactional work of Mark could be distinguished from
that of a still earlier redactor whose work he was revising. Matthew's text, on the other hand, has obliterated the clues we find
to hand in Mark. What are we to say: that Mark followed the
common source so closely that his work is indistinguishable from
the previous editor's hand? If so, we have resurrected the ghost
of Proto-Mark. Or else that Matthew departed from this source
to such an extent that his account no longer allows us to trace
its compound origins? If so, this is equivalent to saying that
Matthew departed from this hypothetical source to the same
extent that he would have departed from Mark if Mark had been
his source. And with that, the explanatory value of the postulated
document has altogether vanished, and Matthew's divergencies
are residual only in respect to Mark. The evidence is that Mark,
not oral tradition or some previous redactor, is responsible for
the literary combination of the two pre-existing accounts into
one. And if that is so, then Matthew is dependent on him, and
we must find some other explanation of their divergencies than
the hypothesis of Léon-Dufour.

The third issue is that of insertion into the context, which
we touched on briefly above. Léon-Dufour follows Kuhn and
Bultmann in recognizing that the doublets in Mk 14:26/32 and
41/42 are evidence of the insertion of what probably existed in
the tradition as an independent accout. But this, too, is irrecon-
cilable with his hypothesis. For the story would have had to be
circulating either orally or in writing. But how could an independent story have been circulating in *compound* form in the
oral tradition? Or how could a compound story have been circulating *independent* of context in a written document? The
impossibility of answering these questions satisfactorily leads us
to the conclusion that, whatever may have been the case for
simple forms of the Gethsemane account, the compound version
which we find in Mark and Matthew cannot have existed inde-

pendent of its present context *in its present form*. And since we
have seen no reason for supposing its pre-existence in the context
of a document anterior to Mark, we conclude that, as he was
responsible for the present form of the account, so he was responsible for its present context. But this is equivalent to an
assertion of Matthew's dependence on Mark, as we have seen.
And Léon-Dufour's hypothesis must be revised.

Yet his labor is not without results. For if we have shown
that his hypothesis of a common document is not a viable explanation of the Mark/Matthew identities in the crucial case of the
Gethsemane account, he has also shown that the hypothesis of
pure literary dependence is not an adequate explanation of their
divergencies. In this he is at one with N. A. Dahl, whose hypothesis we shall consider now in transition to our own conclusions.[55] For Dahl the dependence of Matthew on Mark as his
only written prototype in the passion account cannot seriously
be questioned: order and sequence are the same without exception, the traditions special to Matthew are clearly secondary in-
sertions into the framework of Mark, and most decisively, Matthew frequently puts into direct discourse what Mark has narrated
in indirect.[56] The Gethsemane account is particularly illustrative
of this last point, as is readily evident from the comparison of
apelthôn ekei (Mt 26:36) with *proelthôn mikron* (Mk 14:35), *met'
emou* (Mt 26:38, 40) with *met' autou* (Mk 14:33), *ei dynaton estin,
parelthatô* (Mt 26:39) with Mk 14:35, and the prayer in Mt 26:42
with Mk 14:35-36, 39.[57] But the mere recognition of this relationship by no means solves the problems. For one thing, as Léon-
Dufour points out, Matthew is sometimes more Semitic than
Mark.[58] For another, Matthew's agreements with Luke against
Mark show the influence of another tradition, as does the use of
material not of Markan origin like v. 42: *genêthêtô to thelêma
sou* (Mt 6:10).[59] Again, the more extensive use of direct discourse
by Matthew than by Mark and his more frequent repetitions
should be evaluated as signs of an oral narrative style.[60] Further,

[55] See N. A. Dahl, art. cit. (above p. 151, n. 38).
[56] *Ibid.*, pp. 17-19.
[57] *Ibid.*, p. 30.
[58] See above p. 153.
[59] For the Gethsemane account Matthew's agreements with Luke are
to be found in 26:39 (*pater, plên*), 40 (*pros tous mathêtas*), 41 (*eiselthête*),
42 (*genêthêtô to thelêma sou/to thelêma ... to son ginesthô* [Lk], 47
(*idou*), and in the common omission of Mk 14:40c. See Dahl, art. cit., p. 31
and p. 21, n. 4.
[60] *Ibid.*, p. 31.

Matthew contains echoes (e.g., Mt 26:44/Mk 14:39) or omissions that seem to presume a knowledge of Mark's text in his audience.[61] Finally, there is an even closer tie to the O. T. in Matthew than in Mark, so that it is possible to observe an influence of O. T. texts even in the shaping of the accounts.[62] Dahl feels that the significance of these observations is that they all move in the direction of a single explanation: namely, the interaction of written and oral tradition within Matthew's own ecclesial community as the primary influence in his reworking of the text of Mark. His editorial activity was not pursued in isolation from the concrete geographical and historical situation in which he lived, with its own traditions of liturgy, preaching, catechesis, study, religious life, and so on. Rather, he lived in a community of Christians who held Mark in high esteem and read him in their liturgy, who engaged actively in O. T. studies, and who were alive to the oral traditions circulating in the Church.[63]

This hypothesis, however, remains to be tested against the whole of Matthew's passion narrative. Here we can only hope to apply it to the Gethsemane account with a view to seeing if it proves more plausible than the hypothesis of strict literary dependence in dealing with the divergencies of Matthew from Mark, the written source familiar to him in his community. Our presentation will pursue the suggestive lines opened by G. D. Kilpatrick [64] and Gottfried Schille.[65] The basic contention of these authors is that the Eucharistic liturgy was the *Sitz im Leben* of the first passion accounts fixed in the early community.[66] The first century Christians, in developing their liturgy, took over the practice of the reading and exposition of the Scriptures from the Synagogue, adding increasingly materials of their own as time went on. Within this context took place the development that stretches between the earliest passion narrative and the first gospel.[67] Even after the first written gospel the situation of worship and exposition in the liturgy continued to be a prime influence on the development of the gospel tradition, as the later

---

[61] *Ibid.*, p. 20.
[62] *Ibid.*, p. 23.
[63] *Ibid.*, pp. 18, 24.
[64] *The Origins of the Gospel according to St. Matthew* (Oxford, 1946), pp. 59-100.
[65] "Das Leiden des Herrn," *ZTK*, 52 (1955), 161-205.
[66] Kilpatrick, *op. cit.*, p. 67; Schille, art. cit., p. 177.
[67] Kilpatrick, *op. cit.*, pp. 64-68.

passion accounts of Luke and John amply show.[68] But Schille
has traced this influence also on Mark's account. And Kilpatrick
sees it at work throughout the gospel of Matthew, which he regards as a kind of revised gospel book that has combined previous sources of tradition in an arrangement more suitable for
the requirements of liturgical reading and exposition.[69] In what
follows I shall attempt to develop this conception into an explanatory hypothesis for the Gethsemane account as we find it in
Matthew. Dahl claims that it is not always possible to decide in
detail what modifications of Mark are due simply to Matthew's
redaction and what came about in the community beforehand.
But he thinks that this question is less important for Matthew,
who is much more of a scribe passing on what he has received,
than it would be for Luke, who is more of an independent
author.[70] Nevertheless, we must try to be as detailed as we can
without forcing the issues.

Our hypothesis can be simply stated: the modifications of
Mark's text which we would anticipate from its presentation and
exposition in community life and worship are systematically realized in Matthew's text. These anticipations may be specified
as follows: (1) the individualization of pericopes, (2) the symmetrization of account, (3) the simplification of language, style and
ideas, (4) the dramatization of narratives, and (5) the assimilation of the whole to community experience. Let us consider each
of these anticipations in turn.

First of all, we should expect to find a greater *individualization* of pericopes in a text intended for public reading. This

---

[68] Luke adds Jesus' farewell address like a homiletic expansion to the
Supper account in order to reveal the meaning of his service and prayer
for his own in the passion (Lk 22:25-38). The passion itself is much more
centered upon the trial and prayer of Jesus and the communion of his
own with him in trial and prayer (22:28-32, 39-46; 23:34, 42-43). And the
resurrection appearances in Chapter 24 assume a liturgical setting, climax-
ing in a common meal with the risen Christ and accompanied by an explanation of his passion through the O. T. Scriptures. The case is very
similar with John, who seems to have substituted for the synoptic Supper
account his own liturgical service as a preface to the passion in Chapters
13-17. The homiletic expansion is much longer than in Luke, and the
prayer before the arrest with which it concludes becomes a kind of ana-
phora, prayed by Jesus to the Father for his own in anticipation of the
actual sacrificial death, which in John is given a strong sacramental color-
ing. Again, the resurrection appearances possess a liturgical character.

[69] *Op. cit.*, p. 70.

[70] Art. cit., p. 20.

would appear in a reworking of the introductions to individual pericopes with a view to their immediate comprehension by the hearers in oral presentation apart from the context of a single continuous reading. We should not assume that the passion narrative was always read or recited as a whole in the early Christian liturgy, any more than it is today. Jewish Christians particularly would have carried over with them from Judaism the custom of cycles of readings from the sacred books, in which individual passages were read and commented upon in a succession of services until the books were finished. This practice usually necessitated the modification of the opening phrase to clarify the setting, the speaker or actor, and the dramatis personae. Our lectionaries and missals to this day are full of such modifications, sometimes quite stereotyped,[71] and sometimes summarizing or simplifying the gospel setting.[72] In these introductory modifications we observe that the subject of the action — usually Jesus — is invariably supplied and the place indicated where necessary or possible.[73] Now throughout Matthew's passion narrative — to limit ourselves to that portion of his gospel — we discover the introductions to individual sections have almost invariably been clarified in respect to Mark in just the manner we have described as developing from the natural requirements of a oral presentation: cf. Mt 26:3, 6, 14, 17, 26, 31, 36, 55, 57, 69; 27:1, 11, 15, 27 and their Markan parallels. These introductory verses seem not to assume the continuity of a written context, as much as Mark's text does, with its constant *kai*-connectives and the series of understood or unnamed subjects and objects for its verbs. Mark's initial *kai* is frequently replaced in Matthew's text with *tote*, which may be only a minor stylistic improvement but does seem to allow the pericopes to stand more easily apart from context. And where Matthew's text retains Mark's *kai*, it seems to intend a stronger connection with what precedes (e.g., Mt 26:21, 47). The name of Jesus occurs much more frequently in Mat-

---

[71] Perhaps the commonest example in the Roman Missal: "At that time Jesus spoke this parable to his disciples, etc."

[72] Cf. Mt 22:34-35 with the liturgical reading for the 17th Sunday after Pentecost: "At that time the Pharises approached Jesus, and one of them, etc."; or Lk 22:1 with the liturgical reading for the 19th Sunday after Pentecost: "At that time Jesus was speaking to the chief priests and Pharisees in parables, saying, etc."

[73] Cf. Lk 19:41 with the bracketed words in the liturgical reading for the 9th Sunday after Pentecost: "At that time when Jesus drew near [to Jerusalem] and saw the city, etc."

thew's passion narrative than in Mark, but we may well question
the Christological motive usually alleged to explain this fact, when
we note that by far the larger number of occurrences are in these
introductory verses, clarifying the subject or object of the action
that follows, and that there is relatively little variation in the
comparative occurrence of the name *within* the pericopes themselves.[74] The case of the introduction to Matthew's Gethsemane
scene (26:36) is typical. Read apart from context as an individual
pericope, the initial *tote* of the account serves almost the same
vaguely chronological function as our lectionary "At that time . . ."
In Mark the place of the action and the presence of the disciples
is already clear, but Matthew's text goes on to specify from the
start for the hearer that they are accompanying Jesus, who is the
subject of the action in this verse and in the story. Matthew's
clarifications in this verse seem intended for easier understanding
by the hearers in liturgical reading.[75]

A second modification we should expect from repeated oral
presentations of a text is a greater *symmetrization* of its parts.

---

[74] See E. P. Sanders, *The Tendencies of the Synoptic Tradition* (Cambridge, 1969), pp. 152-155, 183-185. There are, of course, exceptions, and they
should be mentioned for a full picture of the evidence. First, there are
two cases where Mark seems to have "Jesus" where Matthew does not,
but in both instances Matthew's text, for its own reasons, has simply
anticipated the placement of the name by a few verses (cf. Mk 14:18 par.
with Mt 26:19; and Mk 15:5 par. with Mt 27:11b). Secondly, there are four
cases in which Matthew's text has "Jesus" *within* a pericope where Mark
does not. (1) Mt 26:49-51 par. At the arrest, "Jesus" occurs four times in
the brief space of these three successive verses, while it does not appear
once in the corresponding verses of Mark (we do not take into account
the occurrences in Matthew's special material like v. 52); and here it seems
justifiable to assume a definite motive at work, perhaps the desire to draw
the strongest possible contrast between Jesus and those around him — the
betrayer, the crowd, the disciples. (2) Mt 26:63 par. (3) Mt 26:71 par. In
the scene of Peter's denial, the additional occurrence of "Jesus" results
from Matthew's text reporting three variants of the allegation of Peter's
discipleship, while Mark has only two. (4) Mt 27:15-23 par. In vv. 17
and 22 of this passage Matthew's text substitutes "Jesus who is called
the Christ" for Mark's "the King of the Jews." This is obviously a special
case; but in v. 20 "Jesus" occurs contrasted to Barabbas in Matthew's
text, though not in Mark's. Taken together, these cases do not provide
much evidence for an all-pervasive "Christological centering" of Matthew's
passion narrative by a comparison of his use of the name of Jesus with
Mark's.

[75] So Emanuel Hirsch, *Die Frühgeschichte des Evangeliums. II. Die
Vorlagen des Lukas und das Sondergut des Matthaeus* (Tübingen, 1941),
p. 237; and cf. Kilpatrick, *op. cit.,* pp. 72, 74.

This would be evident in the levelling out of rough sposts, the balancing and filling in of gaps, and the explicitation of what was only implicit before — all with a view to more immediate comprehension and lasting retention.[76] We are indebted to Lohmeyer for showing how a pattern of this sort carries through Matthew's gospel. It is one of the constants to which he has recourse in supporting his claim of Matthew's independence. And we have already had occasion to see in detail for the Gethsemane account how this anticipation is realized there in the overall form and rhythm of Matthew's text.[77] We should also observe that the explicitation of the threefold prayer of Jesus in vv. 42 and 44, and the assimilation to one another of the parallel phrases in vv. 45b and 46 are symmetrizations of the same sort. If Kuhn's analysis has shown the impossibility of Matthew's independence, and if Lohmeyer, Léon-Dufour and Dahl have shown the inadequacy of a purely literary explanation of his differences from Mark, it seems only reasonable to recognize the symmetrization of the earlier account as due to the influence of oral presentation and homiletic development over a period of time, creating a tradition existing alongside of but ultimately deriving from Mark's gospel in Matthew's community.[78]

A third modification we are led to expect under the influence of oral presentation and exposition follows close upon the last: a *simplification* of language, style and ideas, again with a view to comprehension and retention by both preacher and hearer.[79] We should expect to find the intrusion, perhaps quite unconsciously, of the idiom of the community, the substitution of ordinary and familiar expressions for unusual ones, and even the omission or reinterpretation of what proved difficult or meaningless. Matthew's text is generally hailed as an improvement over Mark's Greek. Yet we have noted above examples in the Gethsemane account where Matthew's Greek is not only inferior to that of Mark, but quite uncharacteristic of Matthew himself.[80] And Matthew is sometimes more Semitic than Mark, though not in any programmatic way.[81] These facts find their explanation quite naturally in the influence of oral formulations through

---

[76] Cf. Kilpatrick, *op. cit.*, p. 75.
[77] See above pp. 146-147.
[78] See Dahl, art. cit., p. 21.
[79] See Kilpatrick, *op. cit.*, pp. 72-74.
[80] See above pp. 152-153.
[81] Dahl, art. cit., p. 22; Léon-Dufour, art. cit., col. 1454.

which Mark's gospel with minor modifications has been mediated to Matthew. The occasional awkwardness of Matthew's Greek, when not due to Mark, may well be due to this factor in transmission. In our present passage certainly, the substitution of *lypeisthai* (v. 36) for Mark's unusual and startling *ekthambeisthai*, of the more familiar *bebarêmenoi* (v. 43) for Mark's *katabarynomenoi*, the intrusion of the Semitic *legomenon* (v. 36) and [*hê hôra*] *kai* (v. 45), and even the omission of *apechei* are transformations minor enough to be attributed to oral transmission rather than to a conscious literary reworking of Mark's text, particularly when we find them side by side with such uncharacteristic features of Matthew as the participial usage in vv. 39 and 44. To this same tendency of simplification through oral presentation two even more significant modifications of Mark's Gethsemane account may also be due: the limiting of Jesus' prayer to the theme of the cup, and the omission of Mark's comment on the incomprehension of the disciples (14:40c). We shall see further reason below for these two shifts.

A fourth element in oral presentation which we should expect to exert a modifying influence in the retelling of accounts is that of *dramatization*. In the context of preaching and catechesis it is the rule rather than the exception that stories be presented with as much vividness as possible and that their application to the present audience be underscored in the telling. The passion account of Luke represents a distinct advance in this direction over that of Mark or Matthew.[82] But Matthew's text, too, is notably more dramatic than that of Mark. First of all, there is its more extensive use of direct discourse throughout the passion, several examples of which we have already noted above in the Gethsemane account alone.[83] Secondly, there is the use of the generalizing plural, already evident in Mk 14:38 par., for example, but extended by Matthew's text to the preceding verse as well (26:40). The community saw itself addressed here from the start and the transformation was inevitable.[84] Thirdly, there is the specification of the community's relationship to Jesus. In Matthew's Gethsemane text "the disciples" are mentioned three times (26:36, 40, 45) as against Mark's "his disciples," mentioned once only in 14:32. We are aware that elsewhere in Matthew's text the expression serves as a technical designation for the Christian

---

[82] Léon-Dufour, art. cit., col. 1476-78.
[83] See above p. 157; and Dahl, art. cit., pp. 19-20, 30-31.
[84] Cf. Schille, art. cit., pp. 178, 188-189; Léon-Dufour, art. cit., col. 1435.

community. The omission of *autou* here leaves it suggestively general, not only as if *his* disciples — on the scene formerly — were involved, but as if *the* disciples — here and now in the community — were equally concerned. The recurrence of *pros tous mathêtas* at vv. 40 and 45 leaves no doubt in the community's mind that it is they who are being addressed in the words of Jesus which follow. It is Jesus who has come "with them" (26: 36) to this hour of vigil and prayer against trial, and it is he who asks them now to sit "here" and watch "with me" (vv. 38, 40).[85] We may ask, too, whether Mk 14:40c has not dropped out of community preaching — and Matthew's text — because the incomprehension (= lack of faith) of "his disciples" is no longer applicable to "the disciples" of the post-Easter community. Finally, there is repetition for the sake of its effect on the hearer. This feature is already present in the very structure of Mark's Gethsemane account, but it is greatly heightened in Matthew's, where the three prayers of Jesus are spelled out explicitly and the first two are directly quoted.[86] These elements of dramatization are the most likely of all to have been developed and preserved in the material of homiletic exposition, which Kilpatrick describes as "the only liturgical refuge for an oral tradition," [87] once the written gospels had appeared.

The fifth and perhaps most important factor we should expect to find operative in oral transformations is that of *assimilation* to the community experience of faith and worship. It is clear that from the beginning the biblical faith of the Christian community was the primary factor in the interpretation of the suffering and death of Jesus. The O. T. psalms and prophecies became the chief illumination of these events as the accomplishment of God's design. We noted previously that Matthew's text tends to more and closer contacts with the O. T. than Mark's, even in the shaping of accounts. And after Matthew the trend only continues to grow.[88] For the community was constantly discovering new parallels and echoes between the doings and sayings of Jesus and the O. T. Scriptures. There are already O. T. echoes in Mark's Gethsemane account, for example, but it accords with our anticipations to find further ones in Matthew's text, e.g., *kathisate autou* (v. 36), *epi prosôpon autou* (v. 39).

---

[85] Cf. Schille, art. cit., pp. 188-189, 193-194; but he has taken into account only the text of Mark.

[86] *Ibid.*, p. 194.

[87] *Op. cit.*, p. 83.

[88] Dahl, art. cit., p. 23.

Still more significant are the transformations to be expected from *assimilation* to community worship. Dahl instances the transition at the Last Supper from Mark's indirect formula *epion ex autou pantes* (14:23) to Matthew's direct *piete ex autou pantes* (26:27) as unquestionably due to liturgical practice.[89] Lohmeyer sees in the addition of *ho Iêsous* and *tois mathêtais* to Mt 26:26 an example of textual assimilation to the liturgical formula current in the Eucharistic celebrations of Matthew's community.[90] And in the Gethsemane account we can trace other transformations of significance that should be attributed to this same influence: namely, the modifications of the prayer formulas we find in Matthew's text. First of all, there is the assimilation to the Lord's Prayer discernible in vv. 39, 41 and 42.[91] Jesus' prayer in Matthew has become much more the prayer of the worshipping community, who pray this prayer above all in their liturgy.[92] In Mt 26:39 Mark's address has been modified to *pater mou*, paralleling the address of Matthew's community, *pater hêmôn* (Mt. 6:9); the conditional prayer for the passing (*parelthatô*) of the cup contrasts strongly with the unconditional petition for the coming (*elthatô*) of the Father's kingdom (6:10); and the surrender clause (*ouch hôs egô thelô all' hôs sy*) echoes the second half of the petition for the accomplishment of the Father's will (*hôs en ouranô kai epi gês*), just as the final clause of the prayer in v. 42 directly cites the first half (*genêthêtô to thelêma sou*). In v. 41 the community is exhorted by Jesus, in words echoing the last petition of the Lord's Prayer, to watch and pray so as not to fall victims to the trial. The verb *eiserchesthai* may be related to *eispherein* in the underlying linguistic tradition, as already noted.[93] But it would have a further resonance for the community of Matthew's gospel, where it is used throughout as a technical term for entrance into the kingdom of heaven.[94] Consequently, in Matthew's gospel the notion of "entering into" temp-

---

[89] *Ibid.*, pp. 19-20.
[90] Cited by Kilpatrick, *op. cit.*, p. 77.
[91] See above pp. 71-75, 76, 77.
[92] See Raymond E. Brown, "The Pater Noster as an Eschatological Prayer," in *New Testament Essays* (London/Dublin, 1965), pp. 220-222; and T. W. Manson, "The Lord's Prayer," *BJRL*, 38 (1956), 99-113, 436-448.
[93] See above pp. 76, 36 and n. 225.
[94] Cf. Mt 5:20; 7:21; 18:3; 19:23f.; 22:12; 23:13; 25:10, 21, 23. See Johannes Schneider, "*Erchomai ... eiserchomai, ktl.*," *TDNT*, II (Grand Rapids, 1964), 676-678; and Karl Ludwig Schmidt, "*Basileia, ktl.*," *TDNT*, I (Grand Rapids, 1964), 587.

tation would carry with it the connotation of falling subject to
the powers of darkness, of becoming a part of Satan's rather
than of God's kingdom. For the prayer of Matthew's community
was not simply for deliverance from day to day temptations, but
from the final, all-decisive, eschatological trial which marks the
triumph of God's kingdom over Satan's.[95] In Matthew's community, then, the petition not to enter into temptation becomes equivalent to a petition for entrance into God's kingdom. And this
development exercises its influence upon the transmission of
Mark's text in the slight but significant transformation from *elthête* to *eiselthête* in the tradition of Matthew's community.

In addition to the influence of the Lord's Prayer in assimilat-
ing features of the Gethsemane account to the Christian liturgy,
we must consider in the second place the influence of the Eucharistic symbolism itself. Matthew's text concentrates Jesus' prayer
entirely upon the theme of the cup, eliminating the prayer about
the hour altogether. If Matthew were merely a literary reworking
of Mark, this would remain inexplicable. For in that case what
was omitted from his report of the first prayer should have been
the very material to which Matthew turned in filling out the
second prayer quoted in v. 42. Instead of that, we find vestiges
of vocabulary and phrasing from Mk 14:35 in Mt 26:39 and 42,
but the theme of the cup has completely replaced the theme of
the hour in both cases. A literary reshaping of the materials
would have no special difficulty in preserving two disparate
prayer-themes side by side, as Mark's text demonstrates. The
influence of oral transmission, on the other hand, could only
move in the opposite direction, simplifying the account to con-
centrate upon a single theme. Homiletic commentary, too, would
doubtless prove selective, choosing for expansion themes of most
significance for the community. And in the case of the Gethsemane passage it is not hard to see which of the prayer-themes
would be more meaningful and why. Despite Mt 26:18 and 45,
Jesus' "hour" apparently plays no part in the theology of Matthew or of his community. And the prayer of Jesus about the
passing of his hour quickly lost whatever meaning it had pos-
sessed in Mark's source, for admittedly Mark has provided no
theological context for this theme either. But the case was otherwise for the theme of the cup, which finds an interpretive con-

---

[95] Similarly, understanding the second half of this petition in Matthew
as a prayer for deliverance from "the evil one" conveys the same idea. See
Brown, *op. cit.*, pp. 248-253.

text in Mk 10:35-40 par. and 14:22-25 par. The controlling image in these two passages, even more clearly in Matthew than in Mark, is that of the disciples sitting with Christ and sharing his cup at the Messianic banquet in the kingdom of his Father.[96] Jesus' answer to the Sons of Zebedee, asking for the seats of honor at this banquet, is to promise them that they will drink his cup but to leave the disposition of the places to his Father (Mt 20:23). As they sit together at the last Supper, he fulfills this promise by taking a cup and giving it to "the disciples" to drink with the words of institution (Mt 26:27f). That this gesture is somehow an anticipation of the cup he will share with them, seated in the kingdom of his Father, the following verse makes clear.[97] Now the recurrence of these same images in the Gethsemane setting and the heightened emphasis given them by Matthew's text cannot be accidental. In this scene, too, as just previously at the Supper, the disciples are seated (v. 36) around Jesus while he prays, putting himself at the disposition of his Father. Here, too, there is a cup *to be drunk*, as v. 42 makes explicit, but now it is Jesus who must drink it, and his prayers make plain that it is no easier for him to drink the cup offered him by his Father, than it is for the disciples to drink the cup offered them by Christ. Gethsemane reveals to the disciples seated at the table of their common worship what it means to watch and pray with Christ, as well as what it means to share his cup. To share his cup with him is to share his destiny of suffering and death. To watch and pray with him is to withstand this trial so as to share his destiny of glory with him in the kingdom of his Father. In the liturgy the prayer of the community is the prayer of Christ, and so we find Matthew's Jesus praying in the garden the words of the very prayer that the disciples learned from him. In the liturgy the prayer *par excellence* of the Christian community, sitting with Christ and sharing his cup, is the Lord's Prayer: the prayer for the coming of the Father's kingdom. In the garden Jesus' prayer is basically the same: the prayer for the coming about of the Father's will.[98] The oblique references to the kingdom which we have already noted in v. 39

---

[96] Mt 20:21 has *basileia* for the *doxa* of Mk 10:37, and *basileia tou patros mou* in 26:29 for Mark's *basileia tou theou* (14:25).

[97] Matthew's text adds *tois mathêtais* in 26:26 and *meth' hymôn* in 3629, as wel las changing Mark's indirect description to Jesus' direct prescriptionG *piete ex autou pantes* in 26:27.

[98] For the identity of meaning between the first three petitions of the Matthean form of the Lord's Prayer, see Brown, *op. cit.*, pp. 237-238.

(*parelthatô*), v. 41 (*eiselthête*), and v. 45 (*êngiken hê hôra*) stem from the same context of associations and complete the pattern.

In each of these three related passages — dialogue, Supper, prayer — there is allusion, more or less explicit in vocabulary and imagery, to the disciples sitting with Christ in the Father's kingdom and drinking his cup.[99] The use of these passages in the liturgy only served to assimilate them more closely to one another, so that the influence of the two earlier passages on the Gethsemane scene in Matthew's text becomes clear, especially for v. 42, which may have had its origins in liturgy as a homiletic expansion making the themes sketched above explicit, and have reached Matthew in its present form as a piece of tradition preserved in the liturgical preaching of his community. Given this closer relationship of the Gethsemane scene in Matthew to the earlier dialogue of Jesus with the Sons of Zebedee (20:20-23), the substitution in v. 37 of *tous dyo huious Zebedaiou* should perhaps be seen as a reference back to that episode.[100] If our hypothesis is correct, then, not only the faith of the community expressed in its liturgical preaching, but also the every experience of its worship in the Eucharist has exercised a recognizable influence in the interpretation of Mark's Gethsemane scene and its reshaping in Matthew's account.

What the foregoing analysis has attempted to show is that the variations observable between the text of Mark and that of Matthew in the Gethsemane account, rather than being a purely literary reworking on Matthew's part, are better understood as transformations to be anticipated from the oral presentation and exposition of Mark's text in the community of Matthew, particularly in the liturgy. From this we are led to formulate the following general conclusions. In the Gethsemane account, Matthew is not independent of Mark, and neither do they both depend upon a common document. Their identities show that Matthew is dependent upon Mark, yet not in the sense of immediate literary dependence; for their differences are best explained by a dependence mediated through the interplay of written and oral tradition within Matthew's community, especially in liturgi-

---

[99] Thus: *kathizô* (20:21, 23/26:36) or *anakeimai* (26:20); *patêr* (20:23/ 26:29/39, 42); *basileia* (20:21/26:29/[39, 41, 45]); *pinô* (20:22, 23/26:27, 29/42); *potêrion* (20:22, 23/26:27/39).

[100] Mark is generally the most detailed of the synoptics in adding proper names, but it is not clear that this is the case for 14:33 as compared to Mt 26:37 according to Sanders, *op. cit.* (see above p. 161, n. 74), pp. 171f., 185.

cal presentation and exposition. Whether or not Matthew had a copy of Mark's text at hand when he wrote cannot be decided, but it does not affect the hypothesis in either case. For if not, he was completely dependent upon its oral transmission in his community; and if so, he compared it with the oral presentation with which he was familiar and revised it in accord with this tradition.

CHAPTER SIX

EDITORIAL HISTORY OF LUKE 22:39-46

The Gethsemane account of Luke poses a different problem from that of Mark or Matthew, as we indicated in the chapter on the literary analysis of Luke. His account is somehow related to theirs, yet it differs surprisingly from them, both in the almost skeletal brevity of its common features and in the striking enrichment of the special details provided by vv. 43-44. Three hypotheses have been developed to account for the similarities and differences between Luke and the other two synoptics: a common synoptic source, the editorial abbreviation of Mark, or a special Lukan source. As in the last two chapters, we shall investigate each of these possibilities in turn to determine which affords the most consistent and complete explanation of the data, with which we have already become familiar in the literary analysis.

A. COMMON SYNOPTIC SOURCE

The hypothesis of a single common synoptic source — whether oral tradition or an earlier written gospel — on the basis of which each evangelist developed his own expansions, is hardly maintained with any seriousness today.[1] And so we should not anticipate its contributing greatly to the solution of the problem we are studying. Nevertheless, the appreciation of a genuine solution rests also on the recognition of the inadequacy of others, and this hypothesis, too, is part of the history of the problem.

According to Loisy, Luke's omissions in respect to Mark are intelligible only on the supposition that he employed a shorter source, on which Mark's own account was ultimately based.[2] It

---

[1] L. Cerfaux and J. Cambier, "Luc (Évangile selon Saint)," DBS, V (Paris, 1957), col. 570.

[2] Alfred Loisy, Les Évangiles synoptiques (Ceffonds, 1907-08), II, 559.

ran roughly as follows: after recommending wakefulness and prayer against [his] falling in the trial, Jesus leaves his disciples to pray by himself; and when he returns to suggest that they take some sleep, he is surprised by Judas and the crowd. That Mark is responsible for the expansion of this tradition as we find it in the first two gospels — the artificial separation of two groups of disciples, the triplication of Jesus' departures, returns and prayers (without additional content) — Loisy regards as practically certain and quite in keeping with Mark's particular tendencies. Consequently, Luke, although he has been influenced by Mark, is no abbreviation of him. On the contrary, he represents a closer approximation to their common source.[3] In addition to material from the source he shared with Mark and to what came from the influence of Mark himself, Luke also contributes to the account some material either of his own or from a special tradition in vv. 43-44. The resultant intensification of Jesus' prayer replaces to advantage the triplication in Mark, but Luke has not been altogether successful in achieving a smooth blend of the three elements behind his account.[4]

Goguel and Procksch postulate a common source for the Gethsemane account similar to Loisy's, without adopting the peculiarity of his prayer *for* Jesus under trial or his permissive reading of Jesus' words at his return. Procksch, rather simplistically and without analysis, retains the account of Luke, including vv. 43-44, as representing the common synoptic source, to which Mark and Matthew have added further materials from their special source.[5] Goguel regards the words of Jesus' prayer as the only addition to the primitive source by Luke, who may be reproducing an earlier form of Mark, as Matthew reproduces a later. If vv. 43-44 are genuine, then they have dropped out of Mark and Matthew in the same way that they dropped out of the greater number of MSS. of Luke.[6]

Spitta, on the other hand, while proposing the hypothesis of a common synoptic source, denies that the Gethsemane account could have belonged to it. And it is Luke who provides the evidence for his conclusion. The telltale clues are in the doublet

---

[3] *Ibid.*, pp. 561, 571-572.

[4] *Ibid.*, p. 574; and see above pp. 91, 94, 98-99, 101 for Loisy's views of the difficulties in Luke's account.

[5] Otto Procksch, *Petrus und Johannes bei Marcus und Matthäus* (Gütersloh, 1920), pp. 183-184.

[6] Maurice Goguel, *L'Évangile de Marc* (Paris, 1909), pp. 268-270.

of vv. 40/46, as we noted previously,[7] and in his interpretation of
Jesus' prayer. First of all, the admonition of Jesus to pray in the
face of imminent trial has a much more intelligible sequel in the
immediate approach of that trial in the person of Judas and the
crowd (v. 47) than it does in the prayer of Jesus for deliverance
from death. And Luke's need to repeat the admonition at v. 46
only points this up. Secondly, the prayer-struggle of Jesus does
not fit the context, since he is praying, not for preservation from
trial, but for deliverance from death when he has already spoken
about its necessity and inevitability. Luke's placement of this
scene, then, is due to the influence of the Mark/Matthew account.
Mark was originally responsible for the combination which sets
Jesus' intention to spend the night in prayer (Mk 14:37) at odds
with his foreknowledge of betrayal and arrest, and the contents
of the prayer to which he urges his disciples (14:38) at odds with
his own (14:35f.). The admonition of Jesus to his disciples is
properly placed by Luke at 22:40. The difficulties are created by
his appending a summary of the Mark/Matthew account, sup-
plemented with other tradition in vv. 43f., none of which belonged
to the underlying synoptic source and all of which required his
repeating Jesus' admonition in v. 46 to pick up the context again
at v. 47[8]

Much more ambitiously than his predecessors in the common
source hypothesis, Bussmann attempts a literal reconstruction
of the underlying synoptic source — his "*Geschichtsquelle*" (G) —
by a thorough analysis of the synoptic materials. We have noted
in Chapter 4 how he regards the present text of the Gethsemane
account in Matthew and Mark as stemming from the expansion
of G by a Galilean editor (B), which was followed in the main
by Matthew and still further expanded by Mark (E).[9] He claims
that the basic form of G is better represented by Luke's account,
but here, too, it has undergone expansions and substitutions from
a special source of Luke's. Thus Lk 22:39a is the original introduction to the Gethsemane account in G, anticipated and through
the addition of *hymnēsantes* made to serve as the conclusion of
the Supper account in Mk 14:26 par. The further specification
of the place-name in Mk 14:32 par. is a substitution for what
was originally in G and is preserved in Luke. Luke's *eporeuthē*

---

[7] See above p. 86.
    [8] Friedrich Spitta, *Die synoptische Grundschrift in ihrer Überlieferung
durch das Lukasevangelium* (Leipzig, 1912), pp. 388-390.
    [9] See above pp. 131-132.

is original against Mark, since in Matthew, too, the verb (*erchetai*) is singular. V. 39, on the other hand, is an expansion from Luke's special source, substituting for the simple *met' autôn* found in G and preserved in Mt 26:36. The same is true for v. 40, which displaces the original *kathisate hôde heôs proseuxômai* of G; likewise for v. 41, replacing the equivalent of Mk 14:35a in G; for vv. 43-44, of course; for the expansions *kai anastas apo tês proseuchês* and *apo tês lypês* in v. 45; and finally, for the substitution of *anastantes* for *grêgoreite* in v. 46, although it is difficult to decide in this last case whether *anastantes* belongs to G and *grêgoreite* has come through B to Mark/Matthew (as in Mk 14:34), or whether *grêgoreite* is original and *anastantes* has come to Luke through his special source. The prayer quoted by Luke in v. 42 is from G, with the possible exception of the surrender clause, which may also be from Luke's special source like the next two verses. The account according to the G-source, which has been altered somewhat by Luke with the additions noted, would have run as follows: Jesus goes to the Mount of Olives with his disciples, bids them wait while he goes apart to pray in the words summarily indicated, returns to find them asleep, reproaches them, and bids them watch and pray for preservation from temptation.[10]

On the basis of his analysis Bussmann argues against Spitta for the presence of the Gethsemane account in the common synoptic source. The doublet in vv. 40/46 he regards as evidence not of the insertion of non-synoptic material into the context, but rather of Luke's use of the two sources which he has combined in his account: v. 40 stemming from his special source and v. 46 from G. If Luke is following Mark/Matthew here, as Spitta claims, then we cannot explain either why he has material they do not have (e.g., vv. 43-44) or why he abbreviates their account so drastically when elsewhere he uses to the full whatever expanded sources lie at hand.[11]

---

[10] Wilhelm Bussmann, *Synoptische Studien* (Halle, 1925-31), I, 192-194. The Greek text of the Gethsemane account in G is hypothetically reconstructed as follows on p. 222.

Kai exelthôn eporeuthê met' autôn kata to ethos eis to oros tôn elaiôn. kai eipen autois: kathisate hôde heôs proseuxômai. kai proelthôn mikron epesen epi tês gês, kai proseucheto, legôn: pater, ei boulei parenengkai to potêrion touto ap' emou; plên ou ti egô thelô alla ti sy. kai erchetai kai heuriskei autous katheudontas, kai legei autois: ti katheudete? grêgoreite kai proseuchesthe, hina mê eiselthête eis peirasmon.

[11] *Ibid.*, p. 193.

With Bussmann we have an example of the furthest development to which the synoptic source hypothesis can hope to reach.
And it is not surprising that subsequently this line of explanation has been abandoned, not only because the priority of Mark
and the dependence of Luke are generally conceded today, but
perhaps even more because of the bankruptcy of the hypothesis
itself in offering any genuine explanation of the data. The synoptic source of Loisy, Goguel, Procksch, and Spitta is an amalgam
postulated on common features among the accounts, but too
vague to be a source at all and incapable of explaining the genuine differences among the accounts, since the assumption of a
common source based on the similarities has already begged the
question of the differences. The detailed and laborious reconstruction of Bussmann is a kind of achievement in its own right,
but one that cannot stand for long above the doubly dubious
foundations upon which it has been erected: a hypothetical common source for Mark and Matthew beyond which one reaches a
hypothetical source for Luke that underlies all three synoptics.
In Chapter 5 we have seen reason for rejecting the supposition
of a common source for Mark and Matthew in the Gethsemane
account, and therefore for rejecting the hypothesis of a common
synoptic source.

B. Editorial Abbreviation of Mark

A much larger body of critics shares the opinion that Mark
is Luke's only continuous source for the passion narrative, and
that Luke's Gethsemane account — apart from vv. 43-44 — is
simply an abbreviation of Mark's.[12] Even those who grant the

---

[12] A chronological listing of the most important of these: Heinrich
Julius Holtzmann, *Die Synoptiker*, 3rd ed. (Tübingen and Leipzig, 1901);
Julius Wellhausen, *Das Evangelium Lucae* (Berlin, 1904); Firmin Nicolardot,
Les procédés de rédaction des trois premiers Évangélistes (Paris, 1908);
Johannes Weiss-Wilhelm Bousset, *Das Lukas-Evangelium* (Göttingen, 1917);
Erich Klostermann, *Lukas* in *Handbuch zum N. T.*, Vol. II: *Die Evangelien*
(Tübingen, 1919); Rudolf Bultmann, *The History of the Synoptic Tradition*
(New York and Evanston, 1963); Theodor Zahn, *Das Evangelium des Lucas*,
3rd and 4th ed. (Leipzig, 1920); M.-J. Lagrange, *Évangile selon Saint Luc*,
8th ed. (Paris, 1948); John Martin Creed, *The Gospel according to St. Luke*
(London, 1930); A. Schlatter, *Das Evangelium des Lukas* (Stuttgart, 1931);
Hans Lietzmann, "Der Prozess Jesu," *SAB* (Berlin, 1931), pp. 313-322; Lyder
Brun, "Engel und Blutschweiss Lc 22:43-44," *ZNW*, 32 (1933), 265-276; Fried-
rich Hauck, *Das Evangelium des Lukas* (Leipzig, 1934); Jack Finegan,

Lukan authorship of the two disputed verses remain divided on the question of whether or not Luke drew this material from a special source. In any event, the Gethsemane account represents a special case within the passion narrative as a whole, since the divergencies from Mark are so much greater here than elsewhere that, while they may originate from a desire on Luke's part to unify and attenuate Mark's account, they may also stem from a different presentation altogether.[13] Only detailed analysis will allow a reasoned judgment.

In the hypothesis of editorial abbreviation, it is the agreements between Luke and Mark that are postulated and their differences that remain to be explained on the grounds of editorial motive or consistent tendency. Thus in v. 39, we must account for the differences from Mk 14:26 par. in the omission of *hymnêsantes* and the addition of *kata to ethos*, and from Mk 14:32 par. in the addition of v. 39b. According to M.-J. Lagrange,[14] Luke's reason for omitting the thanksgiving hymn was his insertion of the lengthy discourse following the Supper. The addition of *kata to ethos* is generally recognized as recalling Lk 21:37,[15] and this very agreement, according to Bailey, shows it to be an editorial addition of Luke's, intended to make his account of Jesus' stay in Jerusalem appear more coherent than Mark's.[16] Dibelius sees Luke's "greater concern for the historical circumstances" at work in the integration of the scene of Jesus' agony with the rest of the passion narrative by this mention of his custom in going to the Mount of Olives, since Judas' plan (22:6)

Die Überlieferung der Leidens- und Auferstehungsgeschichte Jesu (Giessen, 1934); Martin Dibelius, *From Tradition to Gospel*, 2nd ed. (London, 1934); "Gethsemane," *CQ*, 12 (1935), 254-265; *BG*, I (Tübingen, 1953), 258-271; Josef Schmid, *Das Evangelium nach Lukas*, 4th ed. (Regensburg, 1960); Francis Wright Beare, *The Earliest Records of Jesus* (Oxford, 1962); John Amedee Bailey, *The Traditions Common to the Gospels of Luke and John* (Leiden, 1963); E. Earle Ellis, *The Gospel of Luke* (London, 1966).

[13] Hauck, *op. cit.*, p. 268.

[14] *Op. cit.*, p. 559.

[15] H. J. Holtzmann, Wellhausen, Klostermann, Lagrange, Creed, Schmid, *ad loc.* But see Zahn, *op. cit.*, p. 686, who thinks, on the countrary, that the custom here has to do with Jesus' praying for a few hours, not with his passing the night on the Mount of Olives.

[16] Bailey, *op. cit.*, pp. 48 and n. 1, 49. Bailey observes after Conzelmann that Luke, by doing away with Mark's division into days and adding this notice, gives the impression that Jesus' activity in Jerusalem lasted a longer time, like that in Galilee or during the journey (p. 49, n. 1). And see Hans Conzelmann, *The Theology of St Luke*, tr. Geoffrey Buswell (London, 1964), pp. 198f.

is actually contingent upon that custom (21:37).[17]   Thus the effect
of this addition is to clarify any misreading of Jesus' intentions
in coming here.[18]   The addition of v. 39b, which expressly mentions the accompanying disciples, is necessitated by the fact that
in the first half of the verse Luke has mentioned only Jesus as
coming to the Mount of Olives.[19]   Mark could afford to be less
explicit here (*erchontai*), since in his gospel the presence of the
disciples is presumed by the conversation of Jesus with them on
the way, which in Luke is absent.[20]

In v. 40, the differences from Mark to be explained are the
omission of the name "Gethsemane" and the designation of place,
the duplication of Jesus' admonition from v. 46, and the absence
of the replication found in Mark's account.   The omission of
the name "Gethsemane" may be explained on the grounds of
Luke's regularly observable tendency to omit indications of place,[21]
and, like other Greek authors of his time, to avoid barbarous
sounding names.[22]   But Dibelius discerns at work the tendency
of Luke to make the account as historical as possible by omitting
a name which had been applied only relatively recently to the
place.[23]   The omission is supplied only by the rather vague designation *genomenos epi tou topou*.[24]   But this, too, may in Luke's
design be intended merely to indicate the place where they usually
went or the place he has in mind without choosing to name.[25]
More surprising, given Luke's usual avoidance of doublets, is the
replication of Jesus' admonition to prayer in vv. 40 and 46.   The
traditional formula found in v. 46 is like that in Mark, and the
variant in perfectly classical Greek found in v. 40 Lagrange explains as an appropriate substitution for the invitation to watch
in Mark, which Luke omits.[26]   Brun, too, emphasizes the appropriateness of the doubled admonition in Luke's context: the preceding prophecy of Satan sifting the disciples like wheat (vv. 31f.),
the idea central to this passage of the Christian under trial, the

---

[17] Dibelius, *CQ*, 12 (1935), 263; *BG*, I, 269.
[18] See above p. 84.
[19] Klostermann, *op. cit.*, p. 583.
[20] Lagrange, *loc. cit.*
[21] For examples see Lagrange, *op. cit.*, Introduction, p. LXII.
[22] Henry J. Cadbury, *The Making of Luke-Acts*, 2nd ed. (London, 1961),
p. 125; and see above pp. 84-85 and n. 10.
[23] Dibelius, *loc. cit.*
[24] Creed, *op. cit.*, p. 272; Finegan, *op. cit.*, pp. 18-19.
[25] Lagrange, *op. cit.*, p. 559.
[26] *Ibid.*

characteristic emphasis of Luke on prayer, and perhaps even the doubled prayer of Jesus (vv. 42, 44) set between this doubled admonition to the disciples to pray.[27] In any case, the duplication serves Luke's theological purpose in strengthening the parenetic motif of the temptation facing Jesus' disciples.[28] But this purpose is not served by the duplications and triplications of Mark, which consequently go by the board in Luke, where there is only one group of disciples, not two, only one departure, prayer and return of Jesus, not three. To be sure, this abbreviation is accompanied by a corresponding expansion, but that is not its only *raison d'être*. If it agrees with Luke's method of reshaping Mark's text elsewhere,[29] that is because there is an apologetic tendency at work here as well.[30] Thus the omission of the three chosen disciples serves not just to generalize the two admonitions, but actually to soften the reproach against Peter and the leaders of the community.[31] For these three are no longer singled out as sleeping in the immediate vicinity of their struggling Master. And when Jesus returns — but only once, not repeatedly — to find the whole group of disciples asleep, their sleep is excused (v. 45) and his question to them is only slightly reproachful (v. 46).[32] Not only are the disciples spared in this way, but the human weakness of Jesus, too, is played down in Luke's omissions. There is no indication of the turmoil which in Mark drove him back and forth two and three times between his Father and the company of his disciples. Instead, there is only one prayer of calm surrender to the Father, and when it is over he returns to the disciples, not to find comfort or companionship, but to strengthen them by his example and admonition to prayer against trial.[33] It is clear that theological motives over and above the simple editorial condensation of Mark's account are operative here.

In connection with v. 41, the differences in Luke requiring explanation are the omission of any equivalent to Mk 14:33b-34 and the vocabulary and phrasing with which he parallels Mk 14:35. Throughout his gospel Luke tends to omit many of the

---

[27] Brun, art. cit., p. 275.
[28] Schmid, *op. cit.*, p. 336.
[29] Brun, *loc. cit.*
[30] Klostermann, *op. cit.*, p. 582.
[31] Hauck, *op. cit.*, p. 269.
[32] Schmid, *loc. cit.;* Wellhausen, *op. cit.*, p. 127.
[33] Schmid, *loc. cit.*

emotional traits attributed by Mark to Jesus,[34] especially those
which show his human weakness. Thus he passes over Mk 14:33b-
34 because these verses depict Jesus as troubled and afraid.[35]
Luke's only heightening of Mark's otherwise generally abbreviated
Gethsemane scene is in the prayer-struggle itself,[36] which, however, may substitute in its own way for these omitted verses of
Mark's.[37] Brun regards the whole of vv. 41 and 42 as a stylization
by Luke of Mk 14:35-36.[38] Certainly v. 41 is composed in Luke's
style,[39] and not too much should be made of his divergent but
equivalent expressions. The initial *kai autos* is typically Lukan
and meant to emphasize the contrast between vv. 40 and 41.[40]
Apespasthê ap' autôn is simply the equivalent of *proelthôn*; and
Luke defines *mikron* as *hôsei lithou bolên*. [41] *Kai theis ta gonata*
is a less expressive toning down of Mark's *epipten epi tês gês*,[42]
motivated by Luke's desire to avoid whatever might offend Christian sensibilities in his depiction of Christ.[43]

In v. 42, what must be accounted for are the divergencies
from Mark of the words of Jesus' prayer in Luke. Luke has dealt
like Matthew with Mark's two variants of Jesus' prayer, dropping
the indirect form and retaining only one prayer in direct discourse,[44] which is practically identical with Mk 14:36.[45] Like Matthew, too, Luke omits the Aramaic synonym *abba*,[46] following his
own tendency to omit Palestinian or Jewish terms unfamiliar to
his readers.[47] If with *ei boulei* Luke means to give the sense of
Mark's *panta dynata soi*,[48] he is also expressing Jesus' surrender to
the Father right from the start.[49] The center portion of the prayer

---

[34] For examples see Lagrange, *op. cit.*, Introduction, pp. LXI-LXII.
[35] Finegan, *op. cit.*, p. 19; Schmid, *loc. cit.*
[36] Dibelius, *CQ*, 12 (1935), 264; *BG*, I, 269.
[37] Brun, art. cit., pp. 275-276; Klostermann, *op. cit.*, p. 584.
[38] *Loc. cit.*
[39] Lagrange, *op. cit.*, p. 559.
[40] Theodor Lescow, "Jesus in Gethsemane bei Lukas und im Hebräerbrief," *ZNW*, 58 (1967), 220; F. Rehkopf, *Die lukanische Sonderquelle: Ihr
Umfang und Sprachgebrauch* (Tübingen, 1959), p. 22; B.-D.-F., 277 (3).
[41] Finegan, *loc. cit.*
[42] Creed, *op. cit.*, p. 273; Dibelius, *CQ*, 12 (1935), 264; *BG*, I, 270; Schmid,
loc. cit.
[43] Nicolardot, *op. cit.*, p. 143.
[44] Bultmann, *op. cit.*, p. 268; Finegan, *loc. cit.*
[45] Lagrange, *op. cit.*, p. 560; Schlatter, *op. cit.*, p. 138; Brun, *loc. cit.*
[46] Creed, Finegan, *loc. cit.*
[47] For examples see Lagrange, *op. cit.*, Introduction, p. LXIII.
[48] Creed, *loc. cit.*
[49] Finegan, *loc. cit.*

in Luke is exactly like Mark's except for the minor change in word order. The conclusion expresses Jesus' surrender in words recalling the Lord's Prayer (Mt 6:10).[50] Mark has depicted Jesus' prayer as a kind of argument or struggle to accept the Father's will, but Luke by these subtle changes, framing the whole prayer in two explicit restrictions, has enhanced the dignity of Jesus.[51]

Vv. 43 and 44 represent the enlargement in Luke's account which compensates for his curtailment of Mark throughout.[52] And although Brun regards them as stemming from a special source, he still finds in these verses parallels to Mark's account. For one thing, as we have seen already, they seem to act as a substitute for Mark's description of Jesus' anguish of soul in Mk 14:33b-34. Secondly, they may well give Luke's conception of Jesus' second prayer, merely alluded to in Mark and filled in by Matthew in his own way. Thirdly, the appearance of the angel may supply the transition from Jesus' first to his second prayer in Luke, as the return to the disciples did in Mark. Fourthly, *enischyôn auton* of v. 43, echoing *ouk ischysas* of Mk 14:37, still draws the contrast between Jesus strengthened in prayer and his sleeping disciples. And finally, without pressing the point, we may have in v. 44 a vivid illustration of Jesus' saying in Mk 14:38, his willing spirit in agony praying more earnestly and his weak flesh exuding a blood-like sweat.[53] However strong or weak these parallels may be, the theological intention behind the addition of these verses is unmistakable: namely, to picture Jesus praying in the guise of a martyr[54] as the model for all the faithful strengthened in trial by God.[55]

In v. 45, we must again explain the equivalence of Luke to Mark short of identity, and the addition of the first and last phrases. The first phrase — *kai anastas apo tês proseuchês* — is probably an editorial transition required by Luke's passing from his special material in the two preceding verses back to Mark in this verse.[56] It finds an echo in v. 46 (*anastantes proseuchesthe*), for which it also prepares. The addition of *pros tous mathêtas* Luke shares with Matthew, and the rest of the wording

---

[50] See above p. 91 and n. 49.

[51] Nicolardot, *loc. cit.*

[52] Lagrange, *op. cit.*, p. 558; Brun, art. cit., pp. 273-275; Dibelius, *CQ*, 12 (1935), 263-264; *BG*, I, 269-270.

[53] Brun, art. cit., pp. 275-276.

[54] Shlatter, *op. cit.*, p. 433; Dibelius, *loc. cit.*; and see above pp. 98-101.

[55] Schmid, *op. cit.*, p. 337.

[56] Cf. Bussmann, *op. cit.*, I, 194.

is equivalent to Mark. The exception is the final phrase —
apo tês lypês — a sympathetic extenuation of the disciples' behavior and further evidence of the apologetic tendency at work in
Luke's reworking of Mark.[57]

Finally in v. 46, we must note the explanations offered in the
hypothesis of editorial abbreviation for Luke's shortening of the
reproof to the disciples, the omission of *grêgoreite* or its substitution by *anastantes,* and the omission of Mark's final verses with
their reference to the hour of betrayal and the coming of the
traitor. Luke's intention in shortening Jesus' reproof to the
disciples in Mark may be apologetic and parenetic all at once:
apologetic in leaving unnamed the disciples addressed and re-
ducing the reproach to the minimum two-word question *ti katheudete,*[58] and parenetic in generalizing for the whole community of disciples the words addressed to Peter in Mark.[59] Creed[60]
considers that in the remainder of this verse Luke has substituted
a reprise of the injunction in 22:40 for the confused and difficult
expressions in Mk 14:41-42. Finegan[61] sees in Luke's *anastantes*
a vestigial survival of *egeiresthe* from these departed verses of
Mark. But Lagrange[62] regards it instead as a substitution for
grêgoreite, which because of Jesus' single prayer and the imminence of the betrayal would not have been so appropriate in
Luke as in Mark. In any case, these verses of Mark have not
disappeared altogether from Luke. Elements of Mk 14:41 reappear at Lk 22:48 and 53b.[63] Dibelius recognizes Luke's historical
concern at work again in the omission of Mark's *egeiresthe agômen* (14:42), for it is here that Judas is to come and here that
Jesus must await him.[64]

It is in this manner that the hypothesis of literary abbreviation seeks to account for the differences between Luke and Mark
in their versions of the Gethsemane scene. And once again, the
dictum of Lietzmann is justified: we possess only one primary
source for the passion story, the gospel of Mark. Luke may seem

[57] Nicolardot, *op. cit.,* pp. 142-143; J. Weiss-W. Bousset, *op. cit.,* p. 500;
Klostermann, *op. cit.,* p. 582; Schmid ,*op. cit.,* p. 336; and Creed, Brun, Finegan, Dibelius, *loc. cit.*
[58] Brun, Finegan, Schmid, *loc. cit.*
[59] Hauck, *loc. cit.*
[60] *Loc. cit.*
[61] *Loc. cit.*
[62] *Op. cit.,* p. 563.
[63] Brun, *loc. cit.;* and see above p. 103, n. 118.
[64] Dibelius, *CQ,* 12 (1935), 263; *BG,* I, 269.

to be following a special source, but that is not the case, for he is simply composing with greater freedom and skill than Matthew.[65] True, Luke has some material in addition to Mark for a few of the individual accounts in the passion, but this material does not approximate a parallel or continuous source. And Luke's departures from Mark are not all to be explained as material of this sort; many are the result of editorial recasting.[66] In particular, the hypothesis of another source for Luke's Gethsemane scene is untenable, since it proves in the analysis to be no more of a special report compared to Mark's than the arrest. And Bultmann suggests that at most Luke may have employed along with Mark "another — and probably older — edition of Mark's copy of the Passion narrative." [67] Thus in the Gethsemane account the simpler hypothesis is the better: Luke is an editorial abbreviation (and expansion in the case of vv. 43f.) of Mark.[68] For the abbreviation is accomplished solely through the omission of materials present in Mark, not through the addition of new materials by Luke; moreover, his redaction exhibits a systematic tendency in the omissions to delete features which emphasize the human weakness of Jesus or discredit the apostles.[69] Apart from the expansion in vv. 43-44, Beare concludes, "there is nothing that is not most naturally explained as a Lucan abbreviation of Mark, with the usual modifications of phrasing here and there." [70]

C. Special Lukan Source

Yet in spite of the confidence with which it is proposed, the hypothesis of editorial abbreviation is by no means universally accepted. And a substantial number of critics have turned to the hypothesis of a special Lukan source as a sounder explanation of Luke's divergencies from Mark for the passion narrative in general and for the Gethsemane account in particular. It is beyond our present scope to establish this conclusion for the general case.[71]

---

[65] Lietzmann, art. cit., p. 313.

[66] Bailey, op. cit., p. 20.

[67] Bultmann, op. cit., pp. 280, 435; quotation on p. 280.

[68] Creed, op. cit., p. 272.

[69] Finegan, op. cit., p. 18; Schmid, op. cit., pp. 335-336.

[70] Beare, op. cit., p. 230.

[71] For the development of this line of thought for the passion as a whole, one may consult the following: P. Feine, Eine vorkanonische Überlieferung des Lukas (Gotha, 1891); J. C. Hawkins, Horae Synopticae, 2nd ed.

But if we can establish it for the particular case of the Gethsemane account, this in itself is a contribution of value to the overall problem. In the previous section we called attention to the fact that Luke's divergence from Mark is notably greater in the Gethsemane account than elsewhere in the passion narrative. We must now see if it is so great as to require the assumption of a non-Markan source and to displace the two hypotheses we have already considered.[72] A detailed analysis of agreements and divergencies from this third point of view is necessary to decide the case.

Let us begin with the agreements of Luke and Mark. With regard to common vocabulary, Taylor has counted in the Gethsemane passage only thirty of Luke's one hundred and fifteen words which are shared in common with Mark, i.e., 26 per cent agreement. And even leaving out of consideration the special material of vv. 43-44, he finds at most 34 per cent agreement, a significantly low figure for a passage of this nature.[73] For the whole passion account Rehkopf counts only seventeen verses

---

(Oxford, 1909); Julius Schniewind, *Die Parallelperikopen bei Lukas und Johannes*, 2nd ed. (Hildesheim, 1958); Alfred Morris Perry, *The Sources of Luke's Passion-Narrative* (Chicago, 1920); Vincent Taylor, *Behind the Third Gospel: A Study of the Proto-Luke Hypothesis* (Oxford, 1926); B. H. Streeter, *The Four Gospels: A Study of Origins* (London, 1927); Karl Heinrich Rengstorf, *Das Evangelium nach Lukas*, 8th ed. (Göttingen, 1958); L.Cerfaux and J.Cambier, "Luc (Évangile selon Saint)," *DBS*, V (Paris, 1957), col. 545-594; Joachim Jeremias, "Perikopen-Umstellungen bei Lukas," *NTS*, 4 (1957-58), 115-119; *idem, The Eucharistic Words of Jesus* (London, 1966); F.Rehkopf, *Die lukanische Sonderquelle. Ihr Umfang und Sprachgebrauch* (Tübingen, 1959); Xaxier Léon-Dufour, "Passion (Récits de la)," *DBS*, VI (Paris, 1960), col. 1419-92.

[72] So Bernhard Weiss, *Die Evangelien des Markus und Lukas* (Göttingen, 1901), p. 645; *idem, Die Quellen des Lukasevangeliums* (Stuttgart/Berlin, 1907), p. 218; Walter E. Bundy, *Jesus and the First Three Gospels* (Cambridge, U.S.A., 1955), pp. 505, 507f.; W. Grundmann, *Das Evangelium nach Lukas* (Berlin, 1961), pp. 410f.; Francesco M. Uricchio and Gaetano M. Stano, *Vangelo secondo San Marco* (Turin, 1966), p. 582; Wilhelm Ott, *Gebet und Heil. Die Bedeutung der Gebetsparänese in der lukanischen Theologie* (Munich, 1965), pp. 82-90. A special Lukan source besides Mark has been argued also for parts of Lk 22:54-71 by Gerhard Schneider, *Verleugnung, Verspottung und Verhör Jesu nach Lukas 22, 54-71. Studien zur lukanischen Darstellung der Passion* (Munich, 1969), and "Gab es eine vorsynoptische Szene 'Jesus vor dem Synedrium'?", *NT*, 12 (1970), 22-39.

[73] Taylor, *op. cit.*, pp. 43-44. Cf. also the statistics worked out for identical, equivalent and synonymous expressions in Bruno de Solages, *Synopse grecque des évangiles. Méthode nouvelle pour résoudre le problème synoptique* (Leiden, 1959), pp. 443-454.

and seven half-verses in Luke where verbal agreement with Mark reaches 40 per cent or more.[74]   Thus strict literary contacts are quite rare, and even where they occur still more rarely imply dependence.[75]   The agreements of Luke and Matthew against Mark,[76] for example, in no way imply the dependence of Luke on Matthew, and should make us cautious in assessing his dependence on Mark for similar reasons, particularly where the divergencies are so marked.[77]   There is no verse of the Gethsemane account where Luke is in complete agreement with Mark, and only two verses, included among Rehkopf's seventeen, where he is close enough even to raise the question of literary dependence: vv. 42 and 46.   Both verses contain sayings of Jesus, which Perry maintains must have been in wide circulation.[78]   We know from elsewhere that the tradition of Jesus' sayings tends to much greater fidelity than the narrative material of the gospels.   So it is not surprising that these two sayings are similar in Mark and Luke.   What is surprising, especially on the supposition that Luke depends on Mark here, is that they should be different at all. For, as Perry points out, the change in the words of submission in v. 42b "seems rather an independent rendering in translation than a natural editorial improvement." [79]   In v. 46 *ti katheudete* is no Markan reminiscence, according to B. Weiss.[80]   And the only doubtful point in the whole account for Taylor is whether the concluding words in v. 46b are a Markan pendant.   Since they are a doublet of the saying in v. 40, they may be a later addition.[81] Nevertheless v. 46, though closer than v. 40 to Mark's wording in 14:38, is not identical either: *grêgoreite* is omitted and *elthête* has become *eiselthête*.   So much for the agreements.

Consideration of the divergencies of Luke from Mark in the Gethsemane passage builds cumulatively toward the conclusion of a special source for Luke.   It is not because, taken individually, they could not be accounted for on one pretext or another; it is

---

[74] Rehkopf, *op. cit.*, p. 2, n. 4.

[75] Léon-Dufour, art. cit., col. 1447-48.

[76] For the Gethsemane account: the common omission of Mk 14:40c; *pros tous mathêtas* (Lk 22:45/Mt 26:40); *pater (mou)* ... *plên* (Lk 22:42/ Mt 26:39); *mê eiselthête* (Lk 22:46/Mt 26:41); and the approximation of *mê to thelêma mou alla to son ginesthô* (Lk 22:42) with *genêthêtô to thelêma sou* (Mt 26:42).

[77] See further Léon-Dufour, art. cit., col. 1444-47.

[78] Perry, *op. cit.*, p. 42.

[79] *Ibid.*

[80] *Op. cit.*, p. 647.

[81] Taylor, *op. cit.*, pp. 44-45.

because, taken together, the number and variety of differences elude any systematic explanation that is not better supplied by the assumption of a special source. We shall consider the differences of vocabulary, placement, content, purpose, and form.

First, with regard to vocabularly, Taylor's statistics show that by far the greater part of Luke's account is dissimilar in vocabulary from Mark's. Moreover, the significant likenesses all occur within the two sayings of Jesus we have just considered in vv. 42 and 46, with which we may also include the four doubled words in v. 40. Similarities in the rest of the account are marginal and involve only six words, without which the story could hardly be told at all: *hoi mathêtai* (v. 39b), *prosêucheto* (v. 41), *legôn* (v. 42), *heuren, autous* (v. 45). Taylor includes in his count the words i nv. 39a which also occur in Mk 14:26, but not properly, since the latter does not form part of Mark's Gethsemane account.[82]

Secondly, we find two major displacements in Luke's account with respect to Mark's. And it is here, as transpositions, that both vv. 39 and 40 come into consideration.[83] Mark 14:26 signalled the end of the Supper and the departure for Gethsemane, which preceded the prediction of the disciples' desertion and Peter's denial. In Luke we find v. 39 transposed to follow the warning to Peter and Jesus' farewell discourse like the similar indication in Jn 18:1. Moreover, the mention of the accompanying disciples in both these places serves a like purpose of resuming the thread of narrative after the preceding discourse.[84] Thus v. 39 not only has a different place in Luke from the corresponding verse in Mark, but a different purpose. The displacement of v. 40, too, is a sufficiently radical alteration in respect to Mark to prove its origin in another source, whether it is regarded as a genuine transposition or as a doublet of v. 46 from a different source.[85] The purpose of this displacement will appear below.

---

[82] Taylor has come to recognize that v. 39, like the opening verses of a few other pericopes in Luke's passion narrative, may stem from Mark, but he can maintain this without jeopardy to his earlier opinion that "the idea that the Lucan Passion Narrative is merely a re-editing of Mark is out of date." Cf. Vincent Taylor, "Modern Issues in Biblical Studies. Methods of Gospel Criticism," *ET*, 71 (1959-60), 69f., with *idem* and Paul Winter, "Sources of the Lucan Passion Narrative," *ET*, 68 (1956-57), 95; and see Schneider, *Verleugnung, Verspottung und Verhör Jesu nach Lukas 22, 54-71* (Munich, 1969), p. 144, n. 24.

[83] Léon-Dufour, art. cit., col. 1447.

[84] Schniewind, *op. cit.*, p. 33; Perry, *op. cit.*, p. 41.

[85] Perry, *op. cit.*, p. 42.

Thirdly, the content of Luke's account is notably increased over that of Mark's. The two and one-half verses of new material out of eight (vv. 43-44, 40b),[86] and the additional exact details — *hôsei lithou bolên, theis ta gonata, apo tês lypês* — all point to another source than Mark or mere editorial embellishment.[87]

Fourthly, the purpose of Luke's account is different from that of Mark's, as the displacement of v. 40, discussed above, reveals. The framing of Jesus' own prayer by the double admonition to pray against temptation may well show Luke's parenetic intent in proposing Jesus' struggle as a model for the community.[88] But more significantly still, as Rengstorf has stressed, the transposition of Jesus' admonition to the head of the account in v. 40 exhibits the same concern for the disciples under trial as Lk 22:31, which is part of Luke's special material.[89] It is no accident that the same concern is present in both contexts if both come from the same special source of Luke's.

Finally, there is the difference of form. Grundmann has pointed out that the simple form of Luke's account, where Jesus goes apart but once to pray, is surely closer to the older form of the tradition than Mark's, and so comes from another source.[90] But we shall have to leave the development of this point until we come to discuss the source itself in more detail.[91]

Significant agreement between Luke and Mark in this scene, then, is to be found almost exclusively in the words of Jesus in vv. 42 and 46, and even there agreement is only partial. For the rest, the remoteness of vv. 41 and 45 from their Markan parallels,[92] the almost complete divergence of vocabularly here and elsewhere, the displacement of vv. 39 and 40, the additional contents of vv. 40b and 43-44, the difference of purpose and form all lead to but one conclusion: the independence of Luke from Mark in this account. If there was reason for asserting the dependence of Matthew's Gethsemane account on Mark, there is much less for asserting Luke's; and if there was reason for recognizing Matthew's independence of Mark, there is much more for recognizing Luke's. The conclusion of Léon-Dufour seems justified by the

---

[86] Rehkopf, *op. cit.*, p. 2, n. 3; Léon-Dufour, *loc. cit.*

[87] Perry, *op. cit.*, pp. 42, 132-133; and similarly C. H. Dodd, *Historical Tradition in the Fourth Gospel* (Cambridge, 1963), p. 66.

[88] Léon-Dufour, art. cit., col. 1458.

[89] Rengstorf, *op. cit.*, p. 250.

[90] Grundmann, *op. cit.*, p. 411.

[91] See below pp. 189-198.

[92] Perry, *op. cit.*, p. 42.

analysis: "Loin d'être un simple remanieur de Marc, Luc offre une tradition profondément différente de celle de Matthieu-Marc, du moins dans son orientation." [93]

We must now turn our attention to that tradition and to the isolation of the special source lying behind Luke's account of the agony of Jesus on the Mount of Olives. The task before us is that of determining still more precisely how much of the present text of Luke comes from his special source, how much, if any, is due to the influence of the Markan parallel, and how much stems from Luke's own editorial activity.

Alfred Morris Perry attempted to establish a second source for Luke's passion narrative with a fixed form and unity of its own, on the basis of the wide departures here in order, language and new materials from Luke's previous agreement with Mark. Since this source would deal exclusively with scenes that transpire in Jerusalem, he dubs in the Jerusalem (J) source.[94] According to Perry, practically the whole of Lk 22:40-46 must derive from this source. V. 39, which has been transposed, would have stood in J, too, but in connection with the departure from the upper room. And *kata to ethos* simply adds to other evidence of a rather protracted stay in Jerusalem. We have already noted above how Perry takes as evidence of origin in J the transposition of v. 40, the additional exact details in vv. 41-46, the change of wording in v. 42b, and the remoteness of vv. 41 and 45 from their Markan parallels. He drops vv. 43-44 as a later "Western interpolation," and so retains no material peculiar to Luke. The wide circulation of sayings like those of Jesus in vv. 42 and 46 is sufficient to account for the similarity of their wording in Mark and J. Perry concedes that the "cup" of the prayer may be Markan, though on the other hand it is a feature common to the passion story (cf. Jn 18:11). But he recognizes in the repetition of the admonition (v. 46) in the slightly changed phrasing a feature characteristic of J.[95] Thus the influence of Mark or the editorial work of Luke remain out of consideration in Perry's source analysis. The account as a whole stems from J.

Emanuel Hirsch attempts a differentiation of Luke's special source here (Lu II) from the two underlying sources which he discovered for Mark and which we discussed in Chapter 4.[96] The

---

[93] Art. cit., col. 1448.
[94] See Perry, *op. cit.*, pp. 21-30.
[95] *Ibid.*, pp. 41-42.
[96] See above pp. 135-136.

clue that Luke is following Lu II here is provided by the dropping of the conversation on the way, since Lu II consistently presupposes the main features of what Mk I contains, and by Hirsch's previous analysis the conversation with Peter belongs to Mk I. As a result of this omission, the transitional vv. 39-40a assume a different character and must likewise be regarded as stemming from Lu II. Since Hirsch also recognizes the authenticity of vv. 43-44, and this is material quite unknown to either of Mark's sources, these verses, too, must originate in Lu II. Their imaginative quality of style is characteristic of the source. There are, however, obvious affinities between Lu II and Mk II: the mention of the disciples only in general, the quotation of Jesus' prayer in direct discourse, and the admonition to pray against temptation. Such features may point to common oral traditions, but they do not demand a common literary root, especially when the two sources diverge on such a major point as vv. 43-44. Other features that stand out against Mk II and consequently derive from Lu II are the transposed admonition in v. 40b, the vivid *hôsei lithou bolên* and *theis ta gonata* in v. 41, and the *ei boulei* in v. 42. The initial words of Jesus in v. 46 (*ti katheudete? anastantes*) must stem from Lu II, since there is nothing corresponding to them in Mk II, but the rest of the verse Luke has taken over from Mk II. Thus the doublet (vv. 40/46) is explained as originating from the combination of Luke's two sources. In v. 39 *kata to ethos*, as pointing back to 21:37, and in v. 45 *apo tês lypês*, as excusing the disciples' sleep, both seem to be from Luke himself. But apart from that and the concluding words of v. 46, Hirsch considers the whole of Lk 22:39-46 to come from Lu II.[97]

Wilfred L. Knox's theory of Luke's divergence from Mark in the Gethsemane account is that Mark followed for the most part what Knox identifies as the Disciples' source, while Luke is following for the most part what Knox calls the Twelve-source.[98] Thus v. 39 stems from the Twelve-source, because, like previous passages from this source, it regards Jesus as regularly spending his nights on the Mount of Olives. Yet since this source is identifiable precisely in its characteristic way of speaking not of "the disciples" but of "the twelve," the mention of "the disciples" in the second half of this verse must be either a substitution or an

[97] Emanuel Hirsch, *Die Frühgeschichte des Evangeliums. II. Die Vorlagen des Lukas und das Sondergut des Matthaeus* (Tübingen, 1941), pp. 261-262.
[89] See above pp. 132-133.

addition of Luke's. The Twelve-source continues in vv. 40 and
41. Knox regards it as more probable that this source had no
direct report of the words used by Jesus at prayer, and consequently that v. 42 is Luke's revision of Mk 14:36, or of Mark's
source, since Mark himself may have revised the wording in the
final clause. The Twelve-source reappears in the special material of vv. 43-44 and in v. 45, or at least in the first part of v. 45
(up to: *mathêtas*); for it cannot be wholly decided whether the
second half of this verse or perhaps Mk 14:40b represents more
faithfully the original wording of the source, which Knox regards
as continuing in 14:41. Finally, v. 46 of Luke's account does not
come from the Twelve-source, but may conceivably represent the
original saying of Jesus in the Disciples' source, which has been
substituted by Mark's expansion in 14:38.[99] According to Knox's
analysis, then, the whole of Luke's account stems from the Twelve-
source, except for v. 39b, which is due to Luke, v. 42, which is a
Lukan revision of Mk 14:36, and v. 46, which may preserve Jesus'
saying from the Disciples' source.

What is so unsatisfactory about these source theories is that
they exhibit little unity of method or results. Accordingly, they
fail to answer the questions raised by the problem at hand. In
the hypothesis of a special source for Luke's account, after all,
it is the differences from Mark that are postulated and that do
not need to be explained. It is the similarities which are to be
accounted for and which test the explanatory power of any source
theory proposed. But in this latter respect all three theories
reviewed come to no results, because they come to contradictory
results and can offer no criteria for evaluating their conflicting
conclusions beyond the arbitrary reconstructions of their sources.
Specifically, it is in vv. 42 and 46 that Luke's account is most
similar to Mark's, and it is here, therefore, that the most crucial
issues arise. In the theories under review it is also here that the
least satisfactory conclusions are reached. Perry places both
verses in Luke's special source J, despite their close relationship
to Mark, on the grounds that such sayings must have had a broad
independent circulation. Hirsch and Knox, on the other hand,
do not know what to do with v. 46 except to exclude it from Luke's
special source and place it instead in a source used by Mark for
his account (Mk II, Disciples' source). Knox does not think that
v. 42 could have occurred in Luke's special Twelve-source, and

---

[99] Wilfred L. Knox, *The Sources of the Synoptic Gospels*, I (Cambridge,
1953), 125-129.

so regards it as an editorial revision of Mark, whereas Hirsch places it in Lu II without even noting that the agreement with Mark which led him to trace v. 46 to Mk II should have led him to trace v. 42 there also. In a word, these source theories remain contradictory in the crucial point at issue and provide no criteria for resolving the conflict. We must search elsewhere for an effective tool of analysis.

Such a tool is provided by the form-critical approach of Karl Georg Kuhn, whose analysis of Mark's account we have reviewed above and in the main adopted. On the grounds examined in Chapter 3,[100] Kuhn takes a positive position for the originality of vv. 43-44. But on other grounds he regards them as having been introduced by Luke into the traditional material on which he drew. In the first place, these verses fit only loosely into the context and break the continuity of the narrative. Secondly, they are typically legendary in style. Thirdly, they appear Hellenistic rather than Palestinian in language (e.g., *agônia*). Fourthly, by analogy with Acts 2:3a in the Pentecost account they appear to be a legendary interpretation inserted by Luke. Since in the latter context *glôssai* obviously cannot be the subject of *ekathisen*, Kuhn supplies *pnoê* from v. 2, and precipitates as a legendary interpretation of Luke's the intervening phrase: *kai ôphthêsan autois diamerizomenai glôssai hôsei pyros*. This supposedly re-establishes the original relationship between the terms *pnoê/ pneuma* (= Heb. *rûᵃch*) intended by the underlying tradition, which related that a wind (*pnoê*) came down from heaven into the house and came to rest upon each of those present, and they were all filled with the Holy Spirit (*pneuma*). Kuhn's claims is that, just as Luke has inserted the legendary feature of tongues of fire here as an interpretive detail, so he has inserted the equally legendary feature of an angel in Lk 22:43 with the same end in view.[101]

Accordingly, Kuhn strikes vv. 43-44 from Luke's prototype and conducts a stylistic analysis of the remaining verses of the account to isolate any typically Lukan characteristics or stylizing touches. He extracts three: *theis ta gonata* in v. 41,[102] *apo tês*

---

[100] See above pp. 92-98.
[101] Karl Georg Kuhn, "Jesus in Gethsemane." *EvT*, 12 (1952-53), 269f. Kuhn's exclusion of Acts 2:3a as a Lukan gloss in contested by Eduard Lohse, "Die Bedeutung des Pfingsterberichtes im Rahmen des lukanischen Geschichtswerkes," *EvT*, 13 (1953), 424, n. 5; and also by Eduard Schweizer, "*Pnoê*," s. v. "*Pneuma, ktl.*," *TDNT*, VI, 453, n. 1.
[102] Cf. Acts 7:60; 9:40; 20:36; 21:5.

lypês in v. 45,[103] and *anastas apo tês proseuchês* in v. 45. The rest of the account — minus vv. 43-44 and these Lukan phrases — he identifies with Luke's prototype. It is a tradition quite different from our text of Mark, but quite like the two traditions Kuhn has traced behind Mark, inasmuch as it has but a single group of disciples, a single departure, prayer and return of Jesus, and a single concluding point. Since its structure is thus the same as Mark's Sources A and B, and since it shares common features with both, yet is identical with neither, Kuhn recognizes in Luke's prototype a third variant of the Gethsemane tradition, independent of Mark or Mark's two sources. That Luke's text is not simply an abbreviation of Mark's is evident from the fact that, unlike the latter, it lacks all connection with the following scene. Kuhn regards it as inconceivable that Luke, if actually condensing Mark, could have omitted the whole of Mk 14: 39-42 with the concluding saying of Jesus and the transition to the arrest, as well as the place-name "Gethsemane" at the beginning. His delineation of a third source for the Gethsemane account, parallel to the two he discovered behind Mark, but not reducible to either of them, is evidence of the capacity of community traditions to vary the details of a story without losing hold of its basic form.[104] And it is also a confirmation of the correctness of his earlier analysis of Mark.

Pierre Benoit and Theodor Lescow both follow in the main Kuhn's analysis, but introduce important modifications, which we shall now review as an avenue to our own conclusions. Since the chief elements of Mark's Source B are paralleled in Luke's account, their attempt is to determine as exactly as possible Luke's prototype in relation to Source B. Benoit regards Luke as having combined two traditions: Source B, which he abridged and retouched, and material from a parallel tradition (vv. 43-44), which he shares with John.[105] Lescow considers Luke's prototype to have been a variant of Source B already combined with v. 44, to which Luke himself added v. 43 and other editorial touches.[106] Let us look first at how Benoit and Lescow deal with the details before we evaluate their principal conclusions.

---

[103] Cf. *apo tês charas* in Lk 24:41.

[104] Kuhn, art. cit., pp. 270-272.

[105] Pierre Benoit, "Les outrages à Jésus Prophète (Mc xiv 65 par.)," *Neotestamentica et Patristica* (Leiden, 1962), p. 103; *idem, Passion et Résurrection du Seigneur* (Paris, 1966), pp. 24-32.

[106] Theodor Lescow, art. cit., (above p. 178, n. 40), pp. 215-239.

In v. 39f. Luke shows himself further from the primitive tradition than Mark with *topos* instead of the place-name "Gethsemane." [107] Since Mark and Luke differ on the number of disciples accompanying Jesus, it is difficult to decide which of them actually represents the report in B. Benoit thinks that the three disciples are due to Mark's editing, since he shows much more interest elsewhere in the three than do either Matthew or Luke.[108] Lescow, however, while allowing the possibility that the story as told of the three in B may have circulated in another form about the rest, thinks that Luke is responsible for generalizing the story as he found it in his prototype. For one thing, Luke had already used the theme of Peter's temptation in 22:31f., and so could omit it here. And for another, Lescow sees the Gethsemane scene in connection with the immediately preceding context (22:21-38), which builds from the prediction of Judas' betrayal through that of Peter's denial to a final warning to all, which seems to require some scene like Gethsemane dealing expressly with all the disciples together to complete the composition.[109]

The anticipation and repetition of the saying of Jesus in vv. 40 and 46 is unusual, to say the least, and quite unlikely to have been in Luke's prototype, according to Lescow. Nevertheless, it is worth noting that even in B there is an adumbration of this feature in the doubled admonition to watch (Mk 14:34, 38). Yet what has most likely happened is that Luke in dropping the three disciples from his prototype has retained only the general admonition (= Mk 14:38a) in v. 46 and substituted in v. 40 a slight variant of the same phrase for what he has omitted about the three there (= Mk 14:33-34).[110] It is altogether possible that Luke's prototype omitted any equivalent of Mk 14:38b, but much more probable that this omission, as well as that of *grêgoreite*, is due to Luke himself, either because he was loathe to characterize the spirit of the apostles as weak,[111] or because he had a different, more Christian notion of *pneuma* than that evidenced in his source.[112]

---

[107] Benoit, art. cit., p. 103, n. 6.

[108] *Ibid.*, p. 103, n. 5; and cf. Mk 5:37 par.; 9:2 par.; and 1:29; 13:3, which have no parallel.

[109] Lescow, art. cit., pp. 218-220.

[110] *Ibid.*, pp. 216-217, 220.

[111] *Ibid.*, p. 220; and see Hans oCnzelmann, *op. cit.* (see above p. 175, n. 16), p. 81.

[112] Benoit, *loc. cit.* Schuyler Brown, *Apostasy and Perseverance in the*

In v. 41 we should recognize not only *theis ta gonata* as Lukan, but also *autos*, which draws the contrast between vv. 40 and 41.[113] The rest of the verse in Lescow's opinion may well represent the portion of B lost in Mark's version, and substituted for in Kuhn's reconstruction by making Mk 14: 35a do double duty.[114]

In v. 42 Luke certainly seems to have reworked his source. This is obvious enough for v. 42b in the closer approximation to the petition in the Lord's Prayer (Mt 6: 10),[115] and in the occurrence of the Lukan *thelêma tou kyriou*.[116] But it is also the case for the Lukan *pater*[117] and for *ei boulei*[118] in v. 42a.

In v. 45 the Lukan origin of both *anastas apo tês proseuchês*[119] and *apo tês lypês*[120] is recognized with Kuhn.

It is in vv. 43-44 that we encounter the principal differences of opinion in respect to Luke's prototype. We have already seen that the case for or against the authenticity of these verses cannot be definitively decided.[121] Lescow points out, sensibly enough, that their absence as a unit from certain MSS. is no indication whatever that Luke inserted them as a unit into his prototype. And he prefers to regard only v. 43 as a Lukan insertion, because it breaks the continuity between vv. 42 and 44, the latter being a popular expansion of B in legendary style corresponding to Mk 14: 33f. and already present in Luke's prototype. Brun has shown that stylistic considerations cannot prove or disprove Lukan authorship of these verses. And Lescow argues that the presence of a Hellenistic word like *agônia* in

---

Theology of Luke (Rome, 1969), pp. 23f., maintains that Luke's omission is due instead to *sarx asthenês*, which he did not consider to be the source of *peirasmos*. What comes to the fore, in any case, is that for Luke the danger is not from the weakness of the flesh but from the situation of trial itself. See Wilhelm Ott, *Gebet und Heil* (Munich, 1965), p. 83; and Gerhard Schneider, *Verleugnung, Verspottung und Verhör nach Lukas 22, 54-71* (Munich, 1969), p. 190.

[113] See above p. 178, n. 40.
[114] Lescow, *loc. cit.*; and see above pp. 138, 143.
[115] Benoit, *loc. cit.*
[116] Cf. Lk 12:47; Acts 13:22; 21:14; 22:14. Lescow, art. cit., p. 221.
[117] Cf. Lk 11:2 with Mt 6:9; and Lk 10:21-22; 22:9; 23:34, 46; 24:49.
[118] For the special significance of the *boulê* of God in Luke, cf. Lk 7:30; 23:51; Acts 2:23; 4:28; 5:38f.; 13:36; 20:27; and for questions initiated by *ei*, cf. Lk 13:23; 22:49; Acts 1:6; 7:1; 19:2. Lescow, *loc. cit.*
[119] Lescow, *loc. cit.*
[120] *Ibid.*; Benoit, *loc. cit.*
[121] See above p. 189, n. 100.

v. 44 — noted by Kuhn — is no anomaly, since B had its origins in Jewish-Hellenistic circles too. Luke, then, added only v. 43, using the strengthening angel to transform the picture in his prototype of Jesus struggling with death into one of the ideal martyr victorious in bloody combat.[122]

Benoit sees the process differently. Like Brun, he regards Luke as having abbreviated his source in order to add the special material of vv. 43-44. Only his source was not Mark, but the tradition underlying Mark in B. And the added verses were not created by Luke, but taken over from a parallel tradition which he shared with John (12:28f.). For in both these gospels the tradition lays stress upon the anguish of Jesus and the help given him from heaven in answer to his prayer.[123]

The task facing us in the final portion of this chapter is that of determining which of the three solutions offered best suits the case. We must decide whether vv. 43-44 are (1) a creation of Luke's (Kuhn), or (2) a part of Luke's prototype (Lescow for v. 44), or (3) an addition by Luke from a parallel tradition (Benoit). Our procedure will be to review the reasons offered for each of these solutions before reaching our conclusions.

Kuhn offers four arguments for regarding vv. 43-44 as a Lukan creation. First, he argues from context: the verses fit the context only loosely and break the continuity of v. 42 with v. 45.[124] Yet Lescow has argued for the continuity of v. 42 with v. 44,[125] and Brun for the continuity of v. 43 with v. 44.[126] And I would suggest that v. 43 is no less in continuity with v. 42. Naturally, if we judge continuity solely on the basis of the synoptic parallels, then we have no case. But if we turn to the traditions represented by Jn 12:28f. and Heb 5:7, we find ourselves on ground shared by Luke, for in all three of these contexts is preserved the tradition of an answer to Jesus' prayer: an unspecified one in Hebrews, a strengthening angel in Luke, a voice from heaven — perhaps an angel (v. 29) — in John. Moreover, the answer serves a similar function in all three contexts: to prepare Jesus for the passion he is about to undergo in obedience to his Father's will.[127] The answer to Jesus' prayer fits the context

---

[122] Lescow, art. cit., pp. 217-218, 221-222.
[123] See above p. 190, n. 105.
[124] Kuhn, art. cit., p. 269.
[125] Lescow, art. cit., p. 218.
[126] Brun, art. cit. (above pp. 174f., n. 12), p. 272.
[127] Cf. Lk 22:44; Jn 12:30-33; Heb 5:8. For the close relationship of Luke, John and Hebrews here, see, for example, C. Spicq, *L'Epître aux Hébreux*

no less well in Luke than it does in John or Hebrews. The angel from heaven no more breaks the continuity with Jesus' prayer in Luke than does the voice from heaven in John, or the angel who appeared to Zachary in answer to his prayer earlier in Luke's gospel (cf. Lk 1:11-13). The continuity of Lk 22:43 with what precedes (v. 42), then, derives from the tradition of an answer to Jesus' prayer, shared by Luke with John and Hebrews. Its continuity with what follows (v. 44) derives from the purpose of this answer, expressed by Luke in the phrase *enischyôn auton*: to strengthen Jesus for the struggle ahead, pictured in the bloody combat of still intenser prayer in v. 44. And v. 44, too, far from having but a loose connection with the two concluding verses, is the climax of the account, illuminating the meaning of Jesus' admonition to pray against falling victim in the trial.[128] Kuhn's argument from context, then, does not hold up under examination.

Kuhn argues, secondly, for the creation of vv. 43-44 by Luke on the basis of style: the strengthening angel and the blood-like sweat are features typical of legendary style.[129] But Lescow has pointed out that even if the premise is true, the conclusion does not follow. The accretion of legendary or novelistic features merely shows that Luke's prototype is correspondingly later than B, as B is recognizably later than A in the additional novelistic features of Mk 14:34, 36.[130] It does not prove the Lukan origin of vv. 43-44, any more than the presence of such features in B proves Markan origin.

Kuhn argues Lukan origin for vv. 43-44, thirdly, on the grounds of language: the vocabulary (e.g., *agônia*) is Hellenistic, and the expressions (e.g., *enischyôn auton, ektenesteron prosêucheto*) Lukan.[131] But we have seen above (pp. 192-193) how Brun and Lescow dispose of this argument.

Finally Kuhn argues for Luke's creation and insertion of vv. 43-44 into the Gethsemane account from an analogy with Acts 2:3a in the context of the Pentecost account. Upon exami-

---

(Paris, 1953), I, 99-104; C. H. Dodd, *Historical Tradition in the Fourth Gospel* (Cambridge, 1963), pp. 70f.; Otto Michel, *Der Brief an die Hebräer*, 11th ed. (Göttingen, 1960), pp. 134, 135 and n. 1; but see also to the contrary Ernst Haenchen, "Historie und Geschichte in der johanneischen Passionsberichten," in *Zur Bedeutung des Todes Jesu* (Gütersloh, 1967), p. 58, nn. 6 and 7.

[128] See above pp. 99f., 101.
[129] Kuhn, *loc. cit.*
[130] Lescow, art. cit., p. 216; and see above p. 138.
[131] Kuhn, art. cit., pp. 268f.

nation this proves to be his least successful argument. For if
v. 3a is omitted, *êchos* becomes the subject of the verb *ekathisen*
in v. 3b, not *pnoê*, which is merely a term of comparison (*hôsper*).
Furthermore, removal of *pyr* as the true subject here renders the
passage meaningless, since while it may be unnatural to speak, as
Kuhn would have it, of a wind "coming to rest" on someone, it
is quite impossible to speak of a sound as doing so. *Hôsper
pheromenês pnoês biaias* in v. 2, which creates the word play
with v. 4, may be an interpretive insertion of Luke's, but that
cannot be said of v. 3a, which remains essential to the meaning
of the passage and so provides no analogy for Kuhn's argument
that Luke inserted vv. 43-44 as a legendary interpretation into
the Gethsemane tradition.

There is, then, no convincing proof for the Lukan authorship
of these verses. So we must either suppose that Luke found
them in his prototype or choose between the alternatives proposed by Lescow or Benoit. The arguments for discontinuity
are not in themselves persuasive, as we have indicated. Yet it
is generally agreed that *anastas apo tês proseuchês* in v. 45 is a
Lukan addition. The asyndetic doubling of the participles tells
against its having been in Luke's source. The analogies both in
Mark and in Source B show that it would not be needed simply
to connect vv. 42 and 45. And we have argued that it is better
taken as a reference to *ektenesteron prosêucheto* in v. 45 than
to *prosêucheto* in v. 41. But we should point out further that
if *apo tês proseuchês* is related to the first half of v. 44, *anastas*
seems no less related to *katabainontes* in the second half. The sim-
ile there of drops of blood falling down upon the ground evokes
the image of death as vividly as the word *anastas* evokes the image
of resurrection. Grammatically, too, there is a neat chiasma
between *prosêucheto ... katabainontes* and *anastas ... proseuchês*. The close relationship of this transitional formula to the
immediately preceding material suggests that it was inserted
precisely in function of the addition of that material to its present
context. Whence came this material and what was the context?

We argued above (pp. 193f.) for the continuity of vv. 43 and
44 with one another and with the surrounding context. Let us
take a closer look at the first argument. These two verses
exhibit three elements of a shared tradition. First, v. 43 represents the development in the tradition of an *answer* to Jesus'
prayer which we find also in John and Hebrews. Secondly, v. 44
represents the tradition of Jesus' *distress*, which in B (cf. Mk 14:
34) preceded and led into his prayer, but which became increas-

ingly absorbed into the prayer itself as this tradition developed. In John the words that speak of Jesus' distress are directly joined with the words of his prayer to the Father. In Hebrews he is said to have prayed "with loud cries and tears." In Luke's special material he is pictured praying in an anguished, blood-like sweat. Thirdly, v. 44 also represents the tradition of an *intensification* of Jesus' prayer, which probably had its origins in the reaction of Mark's repetitions (14:35-36, 39, [41]) on the subsequent development of the tradition, and which is reflected certainly in the *ektenesteron proseucheto* of Luke's special material, but possibly also in the plural *deêseis te kai hiktêrias* of Heb 5:7 and the doubled *pater* of Jn 12:27, 28.

This community of features is indicative of the existence of a tradition other than Source B which Luke, John and Hebrews have all made use of in their own way.[132] Since the shared features are distributed between both verses of Luke's account, we must conclude that vv. 43f. have been incorporated by him as a unit into his prototype of the scene on the Mount of Olives. If these verses pre-existed in another oral or written context dealing with the prayer of Jesus, then it is easy to see why the discontinuity of v. 43 with v. 42 should be so difficult to demonstrate and why Luke can link them with a simple *de*. Tying the verses in with Jesus' return to the sleeping disciples, on the other hand, required the more elaborate transitional formula at the beginning of v. 45, which manages to achieve a certain continuity with what follows but which more importantly provides us with the clue to Luke's redactional activity. This recognition leads us to opt against the solution of considering vv. 43f. as originally part of Luke's prototype, and therefore against the solution of Lescow, and we come to propose a solution like that of Benoit: Luke added these two verses to his prototype from a parallel tradition shared with John and Hebrews.

If we inquire now about the prototype into which these verses were inserted, I would suggest that it was a form of Source

---

[132] I am indebted to Donatien Mollat, S. J., for a conversation pointing out the difference in order, scope and context between John's use of the tradition and Luke's: in John Jesus' anguish precedes his prayer and the heavenly answer, while in Luke the angel from heaven appears before Jesus' agony and prayer; in John the voice was for the sake of the crowd rather than Jesus (12:30), while in Luke the angel is to strengthen Jesus for his struggle; and finally, in John the answer is connected with a prayer about the "hour," while in Luke it is connected with a prayer about the "cup."

B still more developed than the one behind Mark. First of all, that B existed in a form different from that underlying Mark is indicated by the absence of the three chosen disciples from Luke's account (vv. 39, 45). *Pace* Benoit, Mark was not responsible for introducing this detail into B; otherwise he would have introduced it into A as well, obliterating all trace of a larger group of disciples and any possibility of discernment of sources on this point. But neither is Luke responsible for generalizing the report Mark found in B. Lescow's argument from the structure of the Lukan context is inconclusive, since it really gives us no certainty of Luke's intentions and points only to a possibility that would be equally well satisfied if Luke found the general form of the account in his source. His argument from Luke's use of the theme of Peter's temptation at 22:31f. is better, but still inconclusive. For this anticipation does not lead Luke to omit or generalize the incident of Peter's denial, and it might just as well have led him to particularize the scene on the Mount of Olives, so as to draw the connection between 22:31 and 22:61, where he adds a detail to make explicit the influence of Jesus on Peter's conversion. But instead of that, Luke leaves the scene general, as he found it in his source. Given the parenetic character of B, it would have been the form most likely to survive and develop in homiletic practice, and its generalization as a result of this practice seems a foregone conclusion. Luke's prototype simply mirrors this development, which was already observable in Matthew.

A second indication that Luke's prototype was a form of B different from what we find in Mark is provided by the doubled admonition in vv. 40 and 46. Lescow has observed acutely that there were already grounds for this development in the doubled *grêgoreite* of B (cf. Mk 14:34, 38). And it seems quite likely that an assimilation of the two admonitions took place well before Luke in the tradition, and, given the importance of this theme in community parenesis, probably as a result of homiletic practice. The lapidary character of the phrase in Luke is due to its honing in oral tradition rather than to Luke's literary cutting. Homiletic concentration on the theme of prayer in trial would have understandably sheared away the adjacent material. True, Luke himself places more emphasis in his gospel on prayer than either Mark or Matthew, but he also makes a point of joining the themes of watchfulness and prayer elsewhere (e.g., 21:36). His theology would have caused him no more difficulty in using the saying about Spirit and Flesh, if it were in his source, than John experienced in using a similar saying in his gospel (6:63).   In neither case is it the Spirit that is characterized as weak.[133]

The third indication that Luke's prototype differed from B is in 22:41, which supplies what Kuhn felt lacking in the form of B he isolated behind Mark. Lescow thinks that Luke's prototype may have preserved here what was originally in B. But it seems more likely to me that this verse is an expansion which developed in the tradition from the influence of Mark's account in 14:35, and I have already given my reasons for regarding Mk 14:39a as what was originally in B.[134]

The fourth indication of development in B before it reached Luke is in the wording of v. 42. We have even less reason for claiming that the assimilation to the Lord's Prayer here is due to Luke than we have for claiming that it is due to Matthew in Mt 26:39, since the petition in question does not even occur in Luke's version of the Lord's Prayer. The modification of Jesus' words in Luke, as in Matthew, is a transformation in the community tradition due rather to the influence of liturgy and preaching than to literary recasting.[135]

What I conclude from all of this is that Luke's account of Jesus' agony on the Mount of Olives is neither his own elaboration of a common synoptic source, nor an abbreviation of Mark or Mark's source. It is a literary presentation, characteristically Lukan, of a prototype which underwent sufficient development in the tradition to be regarded as a special source, distinct from Mark or the source of Mark to which it is related, and to which Luke added in turn vv. 43f. from a parallel tradition shared with John and Hebrews. Thus Luke's account represents a third independent tradition of the prayer-struggle of Jesus before his passion.

---

[133] But cf. Schuyler Brown, *loc. cit.* (see above p. 191f., n. 112).
[134] See above p. 143f.
[125] See above pp. 164-166.

PART THREE

THEOLOGY

CHAPTER SEVEN

THEOLOGY OF THE GETHSEMANE ACCOUNTS

In the first two sections of this work we have laid the foundations for understanding the theological intent animating the synoptic accounts of the Gethsemane tradition. It remains for us in this concluding section to construct on this basis an integral interpretation for each of the five accounts we have discussed: namely, Source A, Source B, Mark, Matthew, and Luke.

1. SOURCE A (Mk 14:32, 33b, 35, 40-42a)

32. Kai erchontai eis chôrion hou to onome Gethsêmani, kai legei tois mathêtais autou: kathisate hôde heôs proseuxômai.

33b. kai êrxato ekthambeisthai kai adêmonein.

35. kai proelthôn mikron epipten epi tês gês, kai proseucheto hina ei dynaton estin parelthê ap' autou hê hôra.

40. kai palin elthôn heuren autous katheudontas, êsan gar autôn hoi ophthalmoi katabarynomenoi, kai ouk êdeisan ti apokrithôsin autô.

41. ... kai legei autois: katheudete to loipon kai anapauesthe; apechei; êlthen hê hôra, idou paradidotai ho huios tou anthrôpou eis tas cheiras tôn hamartôlôn.

42a. egeiresthe, agômen.

This account brings Jesus together with his disciples (*erchontai*) to the farmstead of the Oil Press, where his passion effectively begins (*êrxato ekthambeisthai, ktl.*). There it immediately separates them: Jesus turning in his distress to prayer, and the disciples in their lack of understanding falling into sleep. Finally, it has Jesus awaken them to reveal the meaning of the situation

and to invite them to face it with him.   The basic structure, the
concluding point, and the individual details of this account all
disclose its theological intent.

First, the basic structure is indicative of the Christological
character of the account. Jesus comes with his disciples to the
critical hour of his passion. He faces it alone in deep distress
and prayer, because they are unable to grasp the meaning of
what is about to happen. Jesus must reveal its meaning to them
and invite them to accompany him.

Seconly, the concluding saying of the story in vv. 41-42a
discloses its Christological point: namely, that only Jesus grasps
the meaning of this hour, the hour of his deliverance to sinful
men, which he has prayed might pass him by, that only Jesus
can reveal its meaning to his disciples, and that only Jesus can
empower them to meet it with him.

Thirdly, the individual details of the account, too, exhibit its
Christological character and significance. In v. 32 Jesus asks
nothing of his disciples but that they stay where he leaves them;
it is he who will pray. In v. 33b his distress is described in the
strongest possible terms (*ekthambeisthai kai adêmonein*), not to
give us any insight into his emotional reactions, but rather to
provide a context for the prayer which precedes and underlies
the whole of his passion: the prayer for the passing of the hour.
This prayer in v. 35 he prays apart from his disciples, and they
are thereby shown incapable of sharing in his prayer with him,
as in the sequel they prove incapable of sharing in his passion.
His prayer is enigmatic, open-ended, incomplete. He asks for
the passing, if possible, of what he designates mysteriously as
"the hour."   There is no resolution to his prayer, no answer, no
surrender.   In v. 40 the disciples are at once blameless and
profoundly guilty before him, when he comes and finds them
sleeping. He had not bidden them to stay awake or pray with
him, but only to stay where they were while he prayed, and since
their eyes were very heavy, they fell blamelessly asleep. And
yet when he awakens them, they are dumb with guilt for never
having understood and for not understanding now. They have
no notion of what they should say to excuse a failure they have
not even begun to grasp. It is Jesus who reveals to them the
meaning of their sleep (v. 41): they have left him alone before
the hour, which in their sleep has dawned for him and them. It
is to these very men and for these very men that he is now abandoned; for these sleeping disciples are one with the sinners into
whose hands he is delivered. Betraying, deserting, denying him,

faithless and fleeing for their lives, they will prove no different from those who will condemn him to death, and mock him, and spit upon him, and scourge him, and kill him. Later in Mark, it will be in his very abandonment by men — the men he dies to ransom and to serve — that Jesus is to experience his abandonment by God (cf. Mk 14:50 and 15:34). That is why their sleep alone, their dull, uncomprehending sleep, has been enough (*apechei*) to disclose to him the answer to his prayer and the onslaught of the hour. Yet still he calls to them (v. 42a), across the ever widening void between them. He can rouse them from their sleep, he can take them forward with him even now. He does not despair of them even though they have abandoned him and will abandon him again. Such is the meaning of this account, wholly centered in Jesus, as he faces alone the hour of his passion and prays to God for deliverance from his abandonment by God into the hands of sinful men. Before this mystery of the Son of Man's deliverance to sinners, all other men stand in bewilderment, impotent to understand or share.

In depicting thus the lonely abandonment of Jesus before his hour, this account has no interest in laying bare his psychology or emotions in themselves, however much our modern sensibilities may be affected or respond. The point is entirely theological and meant to convey in the simplest and most economical fashion the notion of what Wolfgang Schrage calls "das soteriologische solus Christus."[1] From the moment that Jesus and his disciples arrive together at the place where his passion will begin, the disciples play no more than a passive role. They sit inactive, while Jesus in deep distress moves forward to prostrate himself again and again (*epipten, proseucheto*) upon the ground in prayer. They fall obliviously asleep, until Jesus comes and wakes them. They remain speechless, while he reveals to them the frightful secret of his destiny. Actively (*katheudete, anapauesthe*) they are men who sleep and take their rest, while passively (*paradidotai*) Jesus is the one delivered. But paradoxically it is Jesus alone who is active here: they would not stir from their sleep but that he summons them to rise and go with him (*egeiresthe, agômen*). So the account is a theology of the passion: a vivid parable of the sufficiency of Jesus alone and the helplessness of all men — even his disciples — before this hour of

---

[1] Wolfgang Schrage, "Bibelarbeit über Markus 14, 32-42," in *Bibelarbeiten, gehalten auf der rheinischen Landessynode 1967 in Bad Godesberg* (n. p., n. d.), p. 37.

his.   By their sinfulness, by their unbelief, by the very passivity
of their condition, from which they cannot free themselves, they
have brought him here.   But he is not only delivered *to* them; he
also delivers himself *for* them.[2]   And once he has suffered through
in prayer what must be suffered through, he will return to wake
the sleepers and give them power to tread where his feet have
trod: *Egeire, ho katheudôn, kai anasta ek tôn nekrôn, kai epi-
phausei soi ho Christos* (Eph 5:14).

2. SOURCE B (Mk 14:33a, 34, 39, 36-38)

33a.   Kai paralambanei ton Petron kai ton Iakôbon kai ton
Iôannên met' autou.

34.   kai legei autois: perilypos estin hê psychê mou heôs
thanatou; meinate hôde kai grêgoreite.

39.   kai apelthôn prosêuxato,

36.   kai elegen: abba ho patêr, panta dynata soi; parenengke
to potêrion touto ap' emou; all' ou ti egô thelô alla ti sy.

37.   kai erchetai kai heuriskei autous katheudontas, kai legei
tô Petrô: Simôn, katheudeis? ouk ischysas mian hôran
grêgorêsai?

38.   grêgoreite kai proseuchesthe hina mê elthête eis peirasmon; to men pneuma prothymon, hê de sarx asthenês.

In this account Jesus takes aside the three chief disciples,
though where he takes them is left unspecified.   He speaks to
them of his distress in words echoing the Old Testament, and bids
them wait and watch.   Going apart from them, he prays to his
Father for the removal of this cup, but surrenders himself to the
Father's will.   Returning, he finds them sleeping, reproaches
Peter, and admonishes all to watchfulness and prayer against
temptation, given the willingness of the spirit but the weakness
of the flesh.

Again the structure, point and details of this account reveal
its theological intention.   First of all, the structure of the account
builds from the demand (*grêgoreite*) and example (*prosêuxato*)
of Jesus through the failure and reproach of Peter to the general
admonition to the disciples (*grêgoreite kai proseuchesthe*).   This

---

[2] See Theodor Lescow, "Jesus in Gethsemane," *EvT*, 26 (1966), 147-148.

shows that what is of principal importance here is the behavior of the disciples in response to the demand and example of Jesus, and it reveals the basically parenetic character of the account.

Secondly, the point of the account is to be found not in any unveiling of the mystery of Jesus or his destiny, but rather in the exhortation to the disciples occasioned by their leader's failure to stay awake. This saying is no dogmatic revelation, but a call to moral action.

Thirdly, the details of this account serve only to reinforce its parenetic character. The notice in v. 33a that Jesus takes the three chief disciples aside with him already sets the stage for a special teaching of some kind meant just for them. The words that he addresses to them in v. 34 immediately call up the Old Testament picture of the just man under persecution and provide a scriptural interpretation of his distress. His prayer in v. 36 is clearly meant as a model prayer, addressing the Father in a familiar Christian formula (Rom 8:15; Gal 4:6), asking for the removal of the cup which his disciples too must drink (cf. Mk 10:38f.), but placing the Father's will before his own as Christians have been taught to pray (cf. Mt 6:10). The whole of his prayer could be seen as expressing in a traditional Jewish pattern his acceptance of his death from God with love.[3] His prayer is a living exemplification of the meaning of his command to watch. And the disciples are inexcusably guilty in v. 37 for having failed to carry out this single demand he has made of them. There is no hint of their having failed to understand; they have failed to obey. And somehow implicit in this failure is their future, far more terrible failure in the passion. Peter is specifically reproached in the account. But v. 38 reveals that the moral of the story is meant for all of the disciples. This wholly parenetic verse, taking the story as its base, makes clear that if the disciples are going to persevere under persecution such as Jesus sufferend (v. 34), the conditions are constant vigilance and prayer, which alone allow the willing spirit of Jesus to conquer, where the weak flesh of his disciples fails.

Clearly Source B is centered much more in the disciples and directed much more explicitly to their needs than Source A. Jesus is not named, but his three disciples are. And the chief interest of the story is in their behavior rather than in his. If Jesus speaks of his distress, it is already in interpretive O. T.

---

[3] See above pp. 31-32.

terms, through which the community came only later to satisfy its need for understanding the passion of its Lord. If he gives his prayer explicit formulation, it is to provide the disciples with a model for their own. If the theme of the hour has disappeared, that is because this hour, which Jesus goes to meet alone, cannot be shared by his disciples. And if it is replaced by the theme of the cup, that in turn is because the disciples are conscious of sharing in his cup each time they re-enact his Eucharist (cf. Mk 10:38f.), aware that in taking it to themselves they pray, as Jesus prayed, for the final removal of all that it implies, even as they accept with Jesus the will of the Father for the passion of his church. If Jesus addresses his sleeping disciples, it is to manifest his concern for their weakness (*hê de sarx asthenês*), a weakness that is not absent even from the strongest of their leaders, and to exhort them to the only means of sharing in his own strength. For they must suffer through their trial, as he will suffer through his, in the constancy of vigilance and prayer. His cup, his trial, his weak flesh, his troubled soul, his death are also theirs. But his Father, for whom all things are possible, is their Father as well, and if in watchfulness and prayer their will is one with His, He will give them in their turn Christ's willing spirit as their own (*to men pneuma prothymon*).

In this second account, then, we have a theology not so much of Christ's passion as of the passion of his members. Source A has made it clear that the passion of Jesus was uniquely his, unshared even by those he called to be his own. Source B makes it equally clear that these disciples, even if excluded from his passion, have nonetheless a passion of their own to bear, a cup to drink, a trial to endure, wich only following the precept and example of their Master will enable them to sustain.

3. MARK 14:32-42

Since our critical analysis has shown that Mark's account is a combination of Sources A and B with but a minimum of redactional elements, we should expect it simply to exhibit the meanings that A and B bore separately. But such is not the case. Instead, it becomes a third account with a direction, life and meaning of its own,[4] deriving from the context of Mark's gospel, the new

---

[4] So Lescow, art. cit., pp. 151-153.

structure, and the relationship to one another of the elements now in combination.

First of all, by the juxtaposition of vv. 32 and 33 Mark produces the separation of the three chosen disciples from the rest, without ever resolving it within the compass of the account (cf. 14:50). In accord with Mark's tendency elsewhere (5:37; 9:2; 13:3), they seem to be set off in this way as the intended recipients of some special revelation.[5] And indeed it is they who are thereby privy to Jesus' admission of distress (v. 34), to his prayer (vv. 35-36, 39) — if Mark understood them to have heard it, to his exhortation to watch and his rebuke and admonition for failing to do so (vv. 34, 37-38), and apparently also to his final disclosure of the meaning of his hour and the approach of the traitor (vv. 41-42). It may be questionable whether Mark had only the three in mind through all of this, but that is certainly the impression his account gives and there is nothing to relieve it. The anguished prayer of Jesus in Gethsemane becomes as much a special revelation to the three as was his glory on the mountain of the Transfiguration.

Secondly, the juxtaposition of vv. 33b and 34 in Mark effects an immediate Christian interpretation of Jesus' distress through O.T. texts. Jesus casts himself from the start in the role of the just man suffering persecution and sustained by God. That he should take these texts upon his lips even before his prayer is a sign that the very assurance to be won through prayer is somehow already his. This interpretation only succeeds in blunting the edge of urgency and distress in Source A, which led to his bewildered plea in v. 35.

Thirdly, by the juxtaposition of vv. 35 and 36 Mark effects an exegesis of the prayer about the hour through the prayer about the cup. God's eschatological hour of judgment and salvation is thereby defined as the passion of Jesus accepted in obediance to his Father's will.[6] And just as the "hour" in this way loses its enigmatic character, so the prayer as a whole is nicely resolved, thanks to the confident assurance with which *panta dynata soi* interprets *ei dynaton estin*, and the added surrender clause rounds out the conclusion. In Mark the prayer of Source A suffers a

---

[5] *Ibid.*, p. 151.

[6] So Schrage, art. cit., pp. 32-33; but see Lescow, art. cit., pp. 147, 150, 152, who holds just the opposite: viz., that the "hour" first becomes eschatological in Mark by his exegesis of it through the apocalyptic image of the "cup."

loss of meaning through this apparent clarification in the light
of Source B.

Fourthly, by the displacement of v. 39 and the editorial
additions there and in v. 41, Mark builds the scene into a triple
process. When the prayer of Jesus has become as final as Mark
has made it through his interpretation of v. 35 by v. 36, it is hard
to see why Jesus should return to prayer at all. Of course, he
does not do so in Mark's prototypes; but he does in Mark — twice
more. Matthew's text felt the difficulty and dealt with it by
showing a progress in the prayer itself. But we must try to
grasp Mark's intention in doing what he does. Whereas it is
true that by the tripling of prayer elsewhere the Scriptures apparently mean to indicate a special intensity or fervor, that does
not seem to be Mark's intention here, since he gives less attention
to the prayer of Jesus — quoted only once, mentioned only
twice — than to the sleep of the disciples — three times mentioned, twice reproached. It is possible, too, as Schrage suggests,
that Mark meant us to see the temptation of Jesus as something
recurrent, not to be put behind him at a stroke, or indeed at
all, until the passion itself was over and done: "Jesus bleibt der
Angefochtene."[7] But though Mark may have thought of the
passion of Jesus as a temptation, he does not speak of it that
way and his text mentions temptation only in respect to the
disciples (v. 38). So it is better to see the triplication as connected with the sleep of the disciples and meant by Mark to emphasize
their failure. Lescow has remarked how the point of Source B
has been blunted by its placement in the middle of Mark's
account, where it tends to become but one more novelistic trait
in the portrayal of the sleep of the disciples.[8] Perhaps Mark
is compensating for this loss of emphasis upon a major theme
by tripling the reference to the disciples' sleep and using Jesus'
first reproach and admonition in vv. 37f. as an anticipation of
the meaning of his second in vv. 41f.

Fifthly, the new triple structure of the account in Mark
affects also the meaning of v. 40, even though it reads as it read
in Source A. There it functioned as an expression of the disciples'
lack of faith and understanding before the mystery of Jesus' hour.
Here between vv. 37f. and 41f., it becomes simply the second
member of a three-stage indictment of the disciples' failure to
carry out Jesus' command to watch. Its separation from what

---

[7] Schrage, art. cit., p. 34.
[8] Lescow, art. cit., p. 152.

follows by the addition of *kai erchetai to triton* at the beginning of v. 41 makes it natural to interpret its meaning from what has gone before rather than from what comes after, and, since Jesus' rebuke in v. 37 has been framed as a question, to interpret v. 40c as the inability of the sleepy disciples to answer an implied second reproachful question. This constriction of meaning in Mark's context led Lescow to conclude that Mark himself had introduced v. 40bc to provide a reason for the disciples' falling asleep again after Jesus' first warning, a reason which would not have been needed before the two accounts were joined in one.[9] But no excuse is being offered. Rather the discipls are depicted as men whose second failure in temptation has left them simply at a loss for words.[10] And Kuhn is right to note that v. 40 has suffered a constriction of the meaning it bore in Source A when it was combined by Mark with the elements of Source B.[11]

Sixthly, v. 41a likewise feels the influence of vv. 37f., since the editorial triplication effected by the initial phrase makes these verses parallels and places the disciples' sleep in the same light here as there. *Katheudete to loipon kai anapauesthe* was probably indicative in Source A. Mark's context almost requires it to be interrogative.[12] And it takes on a much more reproachful tone than in Source A, both because now it can only echo v. 37 and because its very placement in Mark's triple structure makes in the climactic saying of Jesus to his disciples on the occasion of their third failure. If we ask at this point why Mark has chosen to make so much of the theme of the sleeping disciples, our answer may well lie in the direction of Daube's theory about the Passover *ḥabhura*, of which we spoke in Chapter 1.[13] No reference to the *ḥabhura* was present in Mark's sources. For Source A, which has Jesus' prayer take place in Gethsemane in apparent proximity to the arrest, does not mention the theme of watchfulness and means something else by the theme of the sleeping disciples. And Source B, to which the theme of watchfulness is central, has no place or time indication. These facts suggest that Mark came to construe the behavior of the disciples in terms of the Passover Vigil only when he combined his

---

[9] *Ibid.*

[10] Schrage, art. cit., pp. 36-37.

[11] See Karl Georg Kuhn, "Jesus in Gethsemane," *EvT*, 12 (1952-53), 272-273.

[12] See above pp. 50-52.

[13] See above pp. 17-18, 34, 48-49.

sources. For it was not until Mark's fusion of A and B in his
gospel that the scene in Gethsemane became a vigil at all. And
its placement between the Supper and the arrest could suggest
to Mark only that it was a Passover Vigil. This in turn led conceivably to his reinterpreting the somewhat ambiguous v. 40 in its
new context by association with *habhura* regulations. Once he
had decided in this way to make the rupture of the Paschal
communion by the sleep of the disciples his central theme, the
building of their failure into a three-stage process became both
natural and necessary. It was natural because his sources had
already supplied him with the first two stages. It was necessary
because the second stage in v. 40, according to *habhura* regulations, showed the disciples only dozing and thus still preserving
the Paschal communion to a degree. Thus Mark's addition of
kai erchetai to triton in v. 41 became necessary to give point to
the now climactic words of Jesus: *katheudete to loipon kai
anapauesthe*. For it is these words that express the complete
rupture of the Paschal communion on the part of the disciples
and the ultimate aloneness of Jesus before the hour of the Passover deliverance, which God is about to achieve through the deliverance of Jesus to the hands of sinful men.

Lastly, Mark's addition of v. 42b serves not only as an editorial link with what follows but as an exegetical comment on
what precedes. The juxtaposition of v. 42b with v. 41b functions
like that of v. 36 with v. 35. It approximates the eschatological
hour of the Son of Man's deliverance to sinners to the historical
moment of Jesus' deliverance by Judas. From here it is only a
short step to the complete identification between them which we
find in Matthew's text. *Egeiresthe, agômen*, too, in v. 42a loses
force in Mark's context. It is no longer the summons of the Son
of Man, rousing his disciples to face with him the hour decreed
by God. Now in combination with v. 42b, it seems rather a
prudent call to readiness in the face of the betrayer's imminent
arrival.

Thus, although the theological tendency of Source A seems to
remain predominant in Mark's account, if only because the elements of this source form his climax and conclusion,[14] nonetheless
its original meaning has been largely weakened or transformed by
its combination with Source B and Mark's editorial additions.
V. 33b is now interpreted by v. 34, v. 35 by v. 36, vv. 40 and 41a in

---

[14] So Theodor Lescow, "Jesus in Gethsemane bei Lukas und im Hebräerbrief," *ZNW*, 58 (1967), 273.

the line of vv. 37f., and v. 41b by v. 42.   In the process the meaning
of Source B has, of course, been correspondingly enriched.   And
on the basis of the combination Mark has developed two themes
of his own: that of a special revelation to the three and that
of the Paschal Vigil.   The soteriology of Mark is the same as that
of source A here, but it is now the rupture of communion in the
Paschal Vigil that serves to isolate Jesus in his passion from the
sleeping disciples, rather than their lack of comprehension before
the hour.   On the whole, the result of Mark's combination of
sources has been a kind of historicization of the account, giving
a concrete interpretation of the Christologically oriented Source
A and providing a specific place-time setting for the parenetic and
general Source B.   This tendency becomes still more pronounced
in Matthew.

4. MATTHEW 26:36-46

Critical analysis of Matthew's text has prepared us to recognize the significance of its divergencies from Mark in even the
smallest details.   We must now try to appreciate the theological
meaning of these differences.   For convenience we shall sche-
matize them under three headings: details which serve to contrast
Jesus and the disciples, those which emphasize the role of Jesus,
and those which de-emphasize the role of the disciples.

First of all, let us examine the details of Matthew's account
which contrast Jesus with the disciples.   From the outset of the
account in v. 36 Jesus is the leader who comes *with* his disciples
(*erchetai met' autôn ho Iêsous*) to Gethsemane and directs them
to stay where they are (*autou*) until he has gone apart from them
(*apelthôn ekei*) and prayed.   That they are meant to be with him
in his prayer, even though he prays apart from them, the addition
of *met' emou* to *grêgorein* in vv. 38 and 40 leaves unmistakably
clear.   And their watchfulness is thus construed not as a value in
itself but as a condition and consequence of following in the
company of Jesus.[15]   Yet Matthew's *apelthôn ekei* remains in
irreducible tension with his *met' autôn* and *met' emou*, as the
rest of the account reveals.   For at each return Jesus finds the
disciples not "with him," but as far from him as the unconscious-
ness of sleep can put them.   And at each departure Jesus seems

---

[15] See Schrage, art. cit., p. 22.

to be moving only farther away from them into the loneliness of his hour. Lescow notes two steps of Jesus into the solitude of prayer: the first, when he leaves the larger group of disciples and reveals his distress only to the three; and the second, when he leaves the three behind as well to fall upon his face in solitary abandonment to God.[16] But we should note as well the progressive distancing of Jesus from the disciples at each of his three departures for prayer. On the first occasion, Matthew's text, like Mark, speaks of him as "going a little farther" — *proelthôn mikron*; on the second occasion, it says that "again, for the second time, he went away" — with the stronger *apelthôn* in place of *proelthôn* and an added emphasis (*ek deuterou*) over Mark upon the repetition; and on the third occasion, wich is merely implied in Mark, it describes him as relinquishing them altogether — *apheis autous palin apelthôn.* If Mathew's text shows between the first two prayers of Jesus a progressive abandonment to his Father, it also shows at each of his three departures a progressive distancing from his disciples — *proelthôn, apelthôn, apheis* — until at the climax of the account his hour is imminent in the approach of that disciple from whom Jesus stands at the farthest possible remove. In this way Matthew's text draws the contrast between Jesus and the disciples: first by his separation from the eight, then by his growing separation from the three, and finally by his imminent expectation of the one (*heis tôn dôdeka*), who delivers the Son of Man into sinners' hands.

Secondly, let us consider the details in Matthew's text which serve to emphasize the role of Jesus. We have already noted that attention is centered on Jesus from the start as the one who leads the group to Gethsemane. But more significantly, Matthew's account shows greater interest in Jesus' prayer than Mark's, quoting his words twice and mentioning his third prayer, which remains implicit in Mark. Matthew is not uninterested in the sleeping disciples, as we just saw, but it is Jesus' reaction to their sleep in leaving them ever farther behind him that receives the emphasis. Consequently, their sleep is more of a contrast motif in Matthew than in Mark, and Jesus' prayer comes center-stage. That the primary interest of Matthew's text is in this prayer of Jesus is evident likewise from the fact that the prayer is divided into two stages to show a progress in Jesus' surrender to the Father. The triple prayer in Mark was an accident of literary combination, which Mark made use of for another purpose. Mat-

---

[16] Lescow, art. cit., *EvT*, 26 (1966), 154-155.

thew's text is exegeting Mark here by regarding the triplication as a development in itself: the deeper Jesus enters into his prayer, the farther he moves away from his disciples and the closer he approaches to the threshold of his hour. The petition for the passing of the hour has disappeared altogether, so that Jesus' prayer is now understood as preparing for the hour rather than as struggling through it; and the difficulty of the hour is brought out by the fact that Jesus can enter upon it only step by step in prayer.[17] The formulation of the prayer, too, is less bold in Matthew than in Mark. Conditioned from the start, it portrays Jesus' recognition first of the possibility (v. 39), then of the fact (v. 42) that his petition cannot receive a positive reply. Yet there is a shade of difference introduced by the substitution of *hôs* (v. 39) for Mark's *ti* and *parerchesthai* (vv. 39, 42) for Mark's *parapherein*, which leaves Jesus' prayer open to the meaning that the cup can still pass him by (*parerchesthai*) in a way willed by the Father (*hôs sy* [*theleis*]), even though it is not taken away (*parapherein*) beforehand, as Jesus might wish, and can pass only through his drinking it. In other words, the formulation of Jesus' prayer in Matthew's text is open to an answer that lies beyond — though only through — his passion. Finally, we observe that in the concluding verses of the account (vv. 45-46), Matthew's text is more explicit than Mark in identifying the hour of the Son of Man's deliverance to sinners with the betrayal of Jesus by one of his own,[18] so that the historicization of the apocalyptic "hour" and "Son of Man" adumbrated in Mark is completely carried through in Matthew.[19] And the account ends as it began, wholly centered in Jesus.

Lastly, we should note how Matthew's account in centering on Jesus tends to place less emphasis than Mark upon the role of the disciples. The emphasis on the separation of Jesus from the disciples plays down the importance of Mark's separation of the two groups of disciples from one another. The generalization of Jesus reproach (v. 40) in line with the admonition (v. 41) shows less concern for the individual failure of the disciples on the scene and a broader parenetic intent.[20] Yet the parenetic motive itself is weakened on the whole by the concentration of the account on the loneliness of Jesus in taking to himself his destiny.[21]

---

[17] *Ibid.*, p. 155.
[18] See above pp. 79-82.
[19] See Lescow, art. cit., pp. 157-159.
[20] See above pp. 75-76.
[21] Lescow, art. cit., p. 156.

And if Matthew's generalization of the reproach in v. 40 tends to excuse Peter as no more to blame than the rest of the disciples, the omission of Mk 14:40c gives a similar drift to Mt 26:43 by making this verse now an excuse for the disciples' sleep. With this latter omission the basis for recognizing the sleep of the disciples as a gradual rupture of the Paschal *ḥabhura* disappears. And the increasing solitude of Jesus before his hour, which Mark illustrates by the ever deeper sleep of the disciples, Matthew's text exemplifies through Jesus' growing separation from them in his prayer. Once again, the behavior of the sleeping disciples toward Jesus is less important in Matthew than Jesus' behavior toward them.

So the theological intent of Matthew's account emerges clearly as centered on Jesus, moving in prayer toward the hour of his deliverance to sinners through progressive surrender to his of Father and separation from his disciples. The introduction, prayer and conclusion all reveal this centering of the account on Jesus. The disciples at sleep serve more in the capacity of a contrast to Jesus at prayer, and play a correspondingly less central role than in Mark. Matthew's account thus provides us with a fine example of early Christian theological exegesis of Mark.

5. LUKE 22:39-46

The form and content of Luke's account differ conspicuously from those of any of the four accounts we have reviewed so far. We must now see in what way this is also indicative of a theological intention distinctly different from that which animates the rest.

In Luke's account the disciples follow Jesus to the Mount of Olives, where he admonishes them to pray against temptation. He leaves them and falls upon his knees in submissive prayer to the Father for the removal of this cup. An angel strengthens him for a still deeper agony of prayer in which sweat flows from him like blood. When he returns from prayer to find the disciples asleep, he rouses them with a renewed call to prayer against failure under trial.

The form of the account reveals that it is centered on the theme of prayer under trial. The introduction (vv. 39-40) contains an exhortation to such prayer; the center section (vv. 41-44) presents a vividly detailed description of Jesus' prayer in his own agony; and the conclusion (vv. 45-46) repeats the initial exhortation to prayer under trial as the point of the account. Thus the tendency of this account is clearly parenetic like that of Source B, and understandably so, since, as we saw in the preceding chapter, the tradition of B is at the base of Luke.

Its content, too, reveals this same tendency. Luke's is the only account to say that the disciples "followed" Jesus. As a technical N. T. term for discipleship, *akolouthein* (v. 39) cannot mean for Luke simply that they accompanied him to the Mount of Olives. And more even than a following of the teaching and example of Jesus, it implies on the par tof the disciples a participation in his destiny.[22] Luke's account links all of these notions together to give a complete picture of what it means to "follow" Jesus. Thus the disciples who follow Jesus certainly come with him physically to the mountain where he goes to pray (v. 39). But they are likewise to follow his admonition to pray under trial (v. 40). And they are to follow his example, as he himself prays and is strengthened in the agony prefiguring his passion (vv. 41-44). Finally, they are to follow him by sharing also in his trial in the spirit in which he has already fronted it at prayer (v. 46). This is what it means for the disciples to "follow" Jesus: they are the ones who have continued with him in his trials (Lk 22:28).[23]

In the light of this scheme the details of the account take on their meaning. And we discover that it is not the closed structure that is seems, viz., a revelatory action framed by two exhortations. Rather it proves to be an open structure, where each of the two exhortations in turn is followed by a revelatory action: the first by the agony of Jesus' prayer, and the second by his passion.

The prayer of Jesus which follows upon his first admonition has the nature of a prophetic action revealing the significance of his saying. The exemplary character of his action is clear from

---

[22] See Gerhard Kittel, *"Akoloutheô, ktl.," TDNT*, I (Grand Rapids, 1965), 213-215; K. H. Rengstorf, *"Manthanô, ktl.," TDNT*, IV (Grand Rapids, 1967), 444-445; Anselm Schulz, *Nachfolgen und Nachahmen. Studien über das Verhältnis der neutestamentlichen Jüngerschaft zur urchristlichen Vorbildethik* (Munich, 1962); idem, *Suivre et imiter le Christ d'après le nouveau testament*, tr. Jean-Louis Klein (Paris, 1966); Martin Hengel, *Nachfolge und Charisma. Eine exegetischreligionsgeschichtliche Studie zu Mt 8, 21f. und Jesu Ruf in die Nachfolge* (Berlin, 1968).

[23] See Hans Conzelmann, *The Theology of St Luke*, tr. Geoffrey Buswell (London, 1961), pp. 80-81, 83, 199-200.

the Christian terminology in which it is couched. In v. 41 Luke himself has added *theis ta gonata* to his source to show Jesus praying in a typically Christian — not Jewish — position.[24] And in v. 42 no reader or hearer could fail to note the echo of the Lord's Prayer recited in the community.[25] Vv. 43-44 are evidently meant as an anticipation of Jesus' passion, which, unless he had found strength from God in the total surrender of his prayer, he could not have undergone. And the answer to Jesus' prayer, fortifying him for his agony, is assurance to the disciples, who follow him in his trials, of the strength needed to undergo their agony in turn. Luke's Jesus is not only the model of praying Christians, but also through his very prayer the ideal of Christian martyrs facing a trial like his.[26]

Yet there is a gulf that separates the prayer and the passion of Jesus from that of his disciples. And v. 41 calls attention to it. First, by Luke's use of *autos*, Jesus is contrasted with the disciples, whom he has just exhorted to prayer, as the one who goes to carry out his word, while they sink into sleep (v. 45). Secondly, the physical distance of Jesus from them — *apespasthê ap' autôn hôsei lithou bolên* — is symbolic of the spiritual separation between him and them here at prayer and later in the passion (cf. 22:54; 23:49). In this context Luke's addition of *apo tês lypês* in v. 45 becomes something more than an excuse for the sleeping disciples. It is a sign of their incomprehension, just as the depression of the disciples on the road to Emmaus — *kai estathêsan skythrôpoi* (Lk 24:17) — is a sign that they are "foolish men, and slow of heart to believe" (24:25). And it shows that the disciples' sleep during Jesus' prayer has the same roots as their failure to grasp the meaning and necessity of his passion.[27] The phrase *apo tês lypês* in 22:45 is rightly paralleled with *apo tês charas* in 24:41, but usually for the wrong reason. Luke is not making excuses for the disciples in either case. Rather he is

---

[24] See above pp. 86-87.
[25] See above pp. 87-88, 91.
[26] See above pp. 97-101.
[27] Cf. Gen 40:7, where the faces of Pharoah's officers are *skythrôpa* because they can no more grasp the meaning of their dreams without Joseph's interpretation than the disciples can grasp the meaning of the passion without that of Jesus. And see also Werner Bieder, "Skythrôpos," *TWNT*, VII (Stuttgart, [1964], 451f. Schuyler Brown ,*Apostasy and Perseverance in the Theology of Luke* (Rome, 1969), pp. 75-77, believes that Luke is contrasting the loss of faith of the two Emmaus disciples with the faith — albeit without understanding — of the Jerusalem apostles.

witness to a tradition, developed further by John, which contrasts the present *lypê* of the disciples before Jesus' passion — and their own — with their future *chara* at his resurrection.[28] The passion plunges the disciples into a sleep of uncomprehending dejection (Lk 22:45; 24:17); the resurrection leaves them astounded and incredulous with joy (24:41, 52).

The Lukan addition of *anastas apo tês proseuchês* in v. 45 offers further confirmation of this theme. Jesus rises from his prayer (22:45), as he will rise from his passion (24:7, 46), to question his disciples on their sleep (22:46), as they will be questioned at the resurrection on their lack of faith or understanding (24:5, 17, 26, 38). In the same line, it seems thoroughly probable that Luke is thus responsible for the addition or substitution of *anastantes* in 22:46. The disciples are to rise from their sleep and depression (cf. 24:33) to face the trial that awaits them with courage and joy. Thus this second exhortation to prayer does not function like the first, after which Jesus knelt to pray. Now he has risen, and they are to rise with him to face in the constant spirit of his prayer all that lies before them.[29] There is no question of lingering on here for further prayer, but rather, as Lescow has phrased it, "mit *proseuchesthai* ist jener freudige Mut zum Martyrium gemeint, der allem verzagten Trauern entgegensteht." [30]

The abruptness with which Luke concludes the scene with this second exhortation and the absence of any transition like Mark's to what follows has often been noted. But the reason is now clear: for Luke, what follows is the supreme trial of Jesus — his passion.[31] His last words to his disciples — *mê eiselthête*

---

[28] Cf. Jn 16:20-22; 20-20. See above pp. 101-102; and Rudolf Bultmann, "*Lypê, ktl.*," *TDNT*, IV (Grand Rapids, 1967), 319-322; *idem, Das Evangelium des Johannes* (Göttingen, 1964), pp. 444-451, 536.

[29] See above pp. 102f.

[30] Lescow, art. cit., *ZNW*, 58 (1967), 222.

[31] See Conzelmann, *op. cit.*, pp. 28, 80-82, 156, 199-202; and *idem*, "*Historie und Theologie in den synoptischen Passionsberichten*," in *Zur Bedeutung des Todes Jesu* (Gütersloh, 1967), p. 52. Against Conzelmann, Schuyler Brown has argued that Luke does not regard the passion of Jesus as a renewed *peirasmos* either for him or for his disciples. On the contrary, for Luke *peirasmos* is a strictly negative experience associated with apostasy which ne genuinely faithful Christian can fall victim to, however much he may suffer from tribulation or persecution. What Jesus' prayer achieves for his disciples, and what their prayer will achieve in its own turn, is precisely to prevent their *entering into* temptation. Only if they disregard the injunction of Jesus, will their *siniasai* (22:31) in the passion

eis peirasmon — are still upon his lips — *eti autou lalountos* —
when his passion breaks over him full-tide in the approach of
the crowd led out by Judas to the arrest (22:47). Jesus' victory
in the struggle of his prayer has been the sign that he will also
triumph in the combat of his passion. The sleep of the disciples,
on the other hand, has been the sign of their failure in the face
of trial. But now in his second admonition he invites them not
merely to follow his teaching and example by sharing in his
prayer, but to follow his destiny by sharing in his trial. Thus
Jesus' second exhortation does not simply round out the account
and close it in upon itself. Rather it opens out to a second
prophetic action — the passion itself — which follows immediately and which reveals the point of his saying.

Luke is peculiarly ambiguous about the failure of the disciples
in the passion. That they do fail is clear enough from the betrayal of Judas and the denial of Peter in Chapter 22, as well as
from the reproaches of the risen Christ in Chapter 24. Yet, as
Conzelmann has observed, in accordance with Jesus' saying in
22:28 about the continuance of the disciples with him in his trials,
Luke omits any mention of the disciples' flight.[32] And Schuyler
Brown calls attention to a number of other editorial indications
of how the disciples are "standing by" Jesus in Luke's passion
account.[33] We should note particularly that the significance of the

---

become instead a *peirasmos* to which they have succumbed. Otherwise,
they are assured of remaining faithful to him in his — and ultimately their
— *peirasmoi*. Brown stresses that the plural in Lk 22:28 must have a more
general meaning than the singular *peirasmos* 'temptation.' It signifies
'dangers, afflictions, troubles' and refers rather to human snares or per-
secutions than to diabolical harassments. See Brown, *op. cit.*, pp. 5-19; and
also Rudolf Schnackenburg, "Der Sinn der Versuchung Jesu bei den Synoptikern," *Theologische Quartalschrift*, 132 (1952), 324 (cited by Brown);
and Heinrich Seesemann, "*Peira ... peirasmos, ktl.*," *TDNT*, VI (Grand
Rapids, 1968), p. 29 and n. 35, and p. 35. I have adopted the neutral English
word 'trial(s)' as capable of conveying without prejudice either of the
meanings discussed. Cf. Joachim Jeremias, *New Testament Theology*,
I (London, 1971), 74.

[32] Conzelmann, *The Theology of St Luke*, pp. 81, 200.

[33] Thus, for example: *hoi apostoloi syn autô* (22:14); *êkolouthêsan de
autô kai hoi mathêtai* (22:39); *hoi peri auton* (22:49); *ho de Petros êkolou-
thei makrothen* (22:54); *kai strapheis ho kyrios eneblepsen tô Petrô*
(22:61); *heistêkeisan de pantes hoi gnôstoi autô apo makrothen* (23:49).
According to Brown, the apostles' failure for Luke cannot be one of faith in
Jesus as Messiah, but only of understanding the modality of his Messiahship
as one of suffering. Even Peter's denial is taken for cowardice, not for
loss of faith. And so the constancy of apostolic faith throughout the

disciples' failure has been anticipated (22:31-34), so that Peter's conversion (22:61f.) can become a sign of how they, too, are sharing in the passion, and that Luke's addition of *pantes hoi gnôstoi autô* to the body of witnesses in 23:49 produces a similar effect. Luke actually leaves us with the impression, then, that all the disciples, with the sole exception of Judas, have stood by Jesus as witnesses of his passion. While they may be at a distance from him (22:54; 23:49), as they were during his prayer, still for Luke they are there — continuing with him, as he said, faithful though uncomprehending. The passion can be for them only an immense sorrow, as it is so clearly for Peter, because it is a revelation to them of their weakness and cowardice and incomprehension. It is a nightmare from which sleep itself cannot deliver them. But the prayer of Jesus can and does: *egô de edeêthen peri sou hina mê eklipê hê pistis sou.* And their sorrow can thereby be turned into joy; for to the extent that they share his prayer, they shall be able to share his passion: *anastantes proseuchesthe, hina mê eiselthête eis peirasmon.*

Luke's account, then, moves in a direction different from that of the four others we have considered. Although the sovereignty of Jesus in his prayer as in his passion is no less evident in Luke than in the rest, Jesus is no longer depicted as altogether alone, forsaken by his Father and abandoned by his disciples. Rather the angel sent from heaven shows that his Father is with him, strengthening him for his martyrdom.[34] And his disciples are shown not taking flight, but continuing with him in his trials. The parenetic character of this account as a development of Source B is obvious. But it is also obvious that the account has gone considerably beyond B, achieving in its own way a kind of synthesis of the separate viewpoints stressed in Sources A and B by identifying so closely the passion of Jesus with the passion of his church. There before the eyes of his disciples Jesus carries out his own admonition to prayer under trial. Because they are his followers, his prayer becomes their prayer too, as also his heavenly strengthening for his agony, and his rising victorious from the struggle. By his prayer he has won for them the grace of continuing with him in his trials. And when he returns to rouse them from their slumber, it is to invite them now to share in the supreme trial of all — his passion and theirs.

---

passion can assure the continuity of the Age of Jesus with the subsequent Age of the Church. See Brown, *op. cit.*, pp. 62-74.

[34] See Lescow, *art. cit.*, p. 223.

In this way Luke has not merely maintained but even sharpened the parenetic thrust of the account from Source B as it reached him in his prototype, integrating it into the overall conception of his passion narrative.[35] For throughout this narrative Léon-Dufour has observed: "Jésus est non pas simplement un exemple, il est le type du Juste persécuté, recueillant en sa personne la persécution de tous les temps et révélant par son triomphe la victoire de ses disciples." [36] In this sense Luke's agony of Jesus on the Mount of Olives is a paradigm of the passion of Jesus and his church.

---

[35] See Lescow, loc. cit.
[36] Xaxier Léon-Dufour, "Passion (Récits de la)," DBS, VI (Paris, 1960), col. 1477-78.

EPILOGUE

Our investigation has reached its end. Its principal aim was a theological understanding of the synoptic Gethsemane accounts and their sources. But in the very achievement of that aim we cannot but see how such an understanding is an indispensable presupposition for any historical judgment. We must leave the historical questions to historians to ask, to argue and to answer. Nevertheless, it seems important in conclusion to sketch a perspective in which to view the issues.

The study we have conducted should at least have made clear how arbitrary and unwarranted a procedure it is to dismiss the Gethsemane accounts as legends or community constructs lacking all historical foundation. For the tradition of a prayer of Jesus before his passion proves to be one of the most strongly attested elements in the gospel literature, transmitted in a variety of forms in the synoptics and their sources, and attested to in parallel traditions represented by the gospel of John and the letter to Hebrews.[1]

Basic to this historical tradition, which each of our sources has interpreted in its own way, is the distress of Jesus, his prayer before his death, and the sleep of the disciples.

We have seen that the distress of Jesus is witnessed to in all the strains of the tradition. It remains a constant, despite the variety of independent interpretations: the powerfully direct statement in Source A, the allusion to Ps 42:6 and Jon 4:9 in Source B, the combination of these interpretations in Mark/Matthew, the vivid description of Jesus' agony in Luke, and the interpretations through still further Psalm texts offered by John and Hebrews.

The prayer of Jesus, too, which is the central theme of every account, is not twice identically reported or interpreted. And

---

[1] For what follows see C. H. Dodd, *Historical Tradition in the Fourth Gospel* (Cambridge, 1963), pp. 65-72; and also R. S. Barbour, "Gethsemane in the Tradition of the Passion," *NTS*, 16 (1970), 234-235, 248-251.

yet constant to every form of the tradition is the portrayal of Jesus achieving his obedience to God in a prayer of deep distress.

And the same must be said for the tradition of the sleeping disciples who bore Jesus company at his prayer. Far from being merely a novelistic contrast or an ad hoc setting for the saying of Jesus on vigilance and prayer, this detail is present in every strain of the synoptic accounts we have been able to isolate, and has been subject to the same variety of interpretations as the distress and prayer of Jesus. The disciples' sleep is the basic fact; it is the context of meaning which shifts.

Whatever judgments on detail our investigations have imposed, the basically historical character of the Gethsemane tradition must remain unquestioned. For the faith of the community which has passed on this tradition with the rest is essentially historical. And if the widely differentiated witness of all our sources can be discounted for the Gethsemane tradition, then these sources can hardly be relied upon for any of the traditions they transmit. For the very variety of the forms in which this tradition has come down to us serves to confirm rather than weaken the substantial historicity of the event.[2]

Moreover, fidelity to the data of our sources demands that we eschew any form of reductionism, whether historical of theological. The Gethsemane "event" is neither a basic historical core nor a pure theological meaning to be extracted from the complexus of the accounts. There is a sense in which every event is identical with and inseparable from its meaning. And this is no less true for Gethsemane. More than a happening of nature, it is an event in world history because it is imbued with human intentionality. Further still, it is an event in sacred history because it is a revelation of the designs of God. The "event" of Gethsemane can be grasped only when the fullness of its historical meaning is grasped. But this meaning in all its rich plurality has been preserved and transmitted only in the tradition of the community of Christ's disciples, and is accessible only to those who share their faith, or at least to those who find in that faith a call to believe in what God has done for us and asked of us in the passion of Jesus Christ, his Son.

––––––––––

[2] Xavier Léon-Dufour, "Passion (Récits de la)," DBS, VI (Paris, 1960), col. 1480.